PROBLEMS OF
INDUSTRIAL SOCIETY

PROBLEMS OF INDUSTRIAL SOCIETY

Edited by
WILLIAM J. CHAMBLISS
University of California, Santa Barbara

ADDISON-WESLEY PUBLISHING COMPANY
Reading, Massachusetts
Menlo Park, California · London · Don Mills, Ontario

ISBN 0-201-00958-7
BCDEFGHIJ-CO-79876543

For Jeana

Last night
Did you see the sunset?
A glory of old gold and rose,
A shimmer of silver,
A skein of blue,
And clouds as white as down;
Tapestry-like in the blending.

All Beauty!
The river, grey and shining,
Reflecting the colors above,
And the lights,
On the shore of the city,
Green, yellow, crystal and red.
The buildings in soft silhouette,
The tall trees
With leaves gently swaying.
One star's clear beacon on high,
And the birds swiftly winging to nest.

This night
There was no sunset!
Just ominous shadows of fear.
Smoke, bellowing up from the ruins,
Where the school and the Altar had been,
And now and then in the distance
The rumbling of terrible guns.

All terror!
The river, red with the blood
Of those who have gone on too soon,
And the lights,
Blackened, to darken the city.
The buildings crumpled to ruins;
The tall trees
With roots pointing skyward,
Like spectres of life now departed.
No star that the eye can discern,
And the birds oddly quiet, afraid!

By Jean Chambliss

PREFACE

This book was not written because there are no other books concerned with problems of industrial societies. It was written because most of the available books fail to tie the study of problems into a more general sociological perspective and because even if the link between social problems and sociological theory is made, the perspective within which the problems are analyzed is generally inadequate to the task. The inadequacy reflects the cultural and social conditions of the 1950's and early 1960's, when most social problems texts and readers were published. From the vantage point of the late 1960's and early 1970's the theoretical perspectives underlying these earlier texts are at the very least wanting and at times ludicrous. The change in viable perspectives is neatly summarized (but of course oversimplified) by depicting the change as a shift from a structural-functional view to a conflict view of society. What this shift represents is defined in my introductory reader, *Sociological Readings in the Conflict Perspective* (Addison-Wesley, 1973), as well as elsewhere in the social science literature. For the study of social problems we need not be overly concerned about the theoretical issues that underlie the social science enterprise. What we need instead is a set of concepts and a world view from which problems of society can be described and explained. Such a view cuts through and integrates the readings in this volume and thereby introduces the student to the systematic study of problems of industrial societies.

Santa Barbara, California   W.J.C.
August 1972

CONTENTS

INTRODUCTION

Every age has in common with others the fact that it faces what appear to be insurmountable social problems. Some societies are completely transformed by problems that are unsolved within the context of the prevailing social structure. Other societies bend and change but fall short of a complete transformation. The one constant in the social process is change. And change inevitably means that the society will be fraught with conflicts and problems. The more rapid the changes the more intense are the problems likely to be.

Industrial societies change more rapidly and more drastically than was ever the case in man's past history. As a consequence they face what appear to be more serious and potentially more devastating social problems. In his search for solutions to these problems man is accustomed to call on his instincts rather than his reason. The choice of instinct over reason is especially appealing when the extant perspectives, insights, and policy implications of reason do not seem to come to grips with the roots of the current social problems. When those who represent the institutions of reason, such as the universities, concern themselves with "a breakdown in communication" as a social problem while there is revolution in the ghettoes; when the social scientists are looking at the conflict that inheres in "three person groups" in a small group laboratory while students are raging against the bureaucracy; when the psychologists are devoting incredible personal and institutional effort to teaching chimpanzees to recognize color while the society is expressing massive psychological breakdown in suicides, homicides, and drug addiction — then it is small wonder that people turn away from reason and seek solutions to their problems in gut feelings. It is no wonder that the youth develop a

1

decidedly antiintellectual attitude. If the intellectuals have neither solutions nor reasoned guesses about the causes of critical problems, then those who seek answers can scarcely be expected to stand and wait.[1]

Traditionally sociology has been more concerned with social problems than any of the other social sciences. It is not surprising that it should be expected to come up with a point of view that will, at the very minimum, aid in understanding the current issues. All too often, unfortunately, in the guise of "science," sociology has turned its back on the key problems of the day and in so doing has contributed to a basically conservative stance. That is, it has contributed to a point of view that advocates no action and therefore implicitly supports the status quo.

But there has always been a strong counterforce to the conservative tendencies of social inquiry. From the days of Iban Khaldoun through Rousseau, Marx, Simmel, and more contemporary writers such as G.D.H. Cole, Ralf Dahrendorf, and C. Wright Mills, there has developed a body of sociological thought generally referred to as the conflict perspective. From this perspective it has been possible to anticipate many of today's social problems. More important, the conflict perspective, with its emphasis on studying societies holistically rather than in their particular parts, provides useful insight with which to interpret and understand the problems of industrialized societies.

THE CONFLICT PERSPECTIVE

The advance of a field of study depends as much on the questions it raises as on the answers that are forthcoming.[2] Man's situation is such that there is an almost infinite number of problems that might be selected for investigation. The conflict perspective directs us toward some issues and steers us away from others. Our principal concern in the study of social problems is with those apparently ubiquitous social events which impinge upon man's happiness. The particular problems that fulfill this requirement vary somewhat from one generation to another. For example, during the Victorian era the problem of sexual mores was uppermost in most peoples' minds, whereas it has receded in importance in present-day society.[3] In today's world, wars, economic crises, the role of the state in governing men's lives, the potential for fascism to arise within capitalist states, the distribution of wealth (poverty), race and racism, deviant behavior and the law, estrangement of the individual, and man's ability to work out a harmonious relationship with his physical environment must be seen as the major issues of the day. It is these issues that the conflict perspective directs us to confront. It is these issues that the perspective also suggests ways of understanding.[4]

As the term "conflict perspective" suggests, the starting point for understanding the issues is the realization that contemporary, complex societies are best understood as composed of different groups of people whose interests, values, and behavior patterns conflict with one another. The older view that society was best understood as formed of groups that shared a core of agreed-upon ideas, interests, values, and behavior patterns has proved to be sterile. It is not so much that it was wrong (in fact there is always some agreement in even the most heterogeneous societies) but that it has proved incapable of producing much understanding of how societies work generally and how social problems arise specifically.

The conflict perspective places primary emphasis on the conflicts inherent between (a) social classes – the wealthy and the poor, (b) those who have political power and those who do not, (c) those who work for and manage the bureaucracies and those who must live with them, and (d) those who create technology and the people whose lives are shaped and determined by what has been created. The conflict perspective leads us to see that these problems are all a manifestation of the characteristics of the society in which they occur. They must therefore be understood by looking at the whole society and not simply at the individuals who comprise it. The individuals perform the acts but the acts are determined by the fabric of the society. The emphasis in conflict models is thus holistic rather than individualistic.

From the conflict perspective the problems selected are not necessarily limited to those aspects of life perceived as problems by the members of the society.[5] They are instead those features of society that interfere with the happiness of all men. Thus war and military organizations may not be perceived by the state as social problems; they may in fact be perceived as a solution to social problems. But any responsible sociological analysis of social problems must consider war and militarism as problem areas for men in the 20th century. Similarly imperialism may not be perceived as a social problem, and yet it is at the root of considerable misery for the bulk of the world's population and must, therefore, be considered in an analysis of social problems.

To accept as social problems only those things that are generally perceived as such is to acquiesce to whatever view is convenient to the established authority of the society. For it is axiomatic that the influence over mass opinion exerted by those who control the media of communication determines the general view of what is and what is not problematic. If we accepted the general view of social problems, then, as the criterion of what should be studied as part of the sociology of social problems, we would suppose that in the United States a few years ago Communism was the primary social problem. Today, crime, the hippies, youthful rebellion, and radical professors would be problems of major importance. Marijuana smoking and offensive styles of dress (e.g., long hair) would also rank high. Economic depressions, the military establishment, problems of capitalist economics, infringement of personal liberties, and even poverty would not be considered problems from such a point of view. And in the Soviet Union the freedom of intellectuals to express their views would not be a problem if one accepted "society's own" definition.

For social scientists to accept the prevailing view, culturally and politically determined, of what constitutes a social problem, is at best to be relegated to the role of intellectual gadflies. At worst it is to be completely co-opted by the world view of the society which they seek to understand. For if we limit ourselves to a consideration of those problems that are generally agreed to be "important" then we end either by criticizing piecemeal the legitimacy of defining those things as problems (e.g., marijuana is *not* a problem, just laws against it are), in which case we are gadflies, or we accept a role as an auxiliary to the state and attempt to aid in the repression of anything that is not in its interests.

Neither alternative is acceptable. If we are to make a contribution to mankind (rather than to the state) then we must select a problem on theoretical grounds. That is to say, we must have a general perspective which leads us to analyze those aspects of society that interfere with man's attainment of happiness.

To present the analysis of social problems from the point of view of a conflict model of society is by implication to argue that this perspective is superior to some other. Whenever a discipline advocates one point of view, it is always arguing against some alternative. What then is the alternative view that the readings in this volume are denying? We hinted at the answer when we pointed out that the conflict model denies the ability of a consensus model to produce valid and useful theories concerning contemporary society. The perspective that emphasizes consensus in contemporary social science is most often referred to as the functional approach. Particular differences between the functional and conflict approach will become increasingly clear in the chapters of this book. By way of introduction, however, let us consider an example of the difference between the conflict and functional views. For this purpose we choose to consider deviant behavior, a problem acknowledged by both points of view.[6]

THE STUDY OF DEVIANT BEHAVIOR

When thinking about deviance, social scientists traditionally asked: "Why is it that some people deviate and others do not?" This is an intrinsically reasonable question, and yet like all questions, it focuses our attention in ways that are not immediately apparent. It forces us to look at those people who commit deviant acts and to compare them with people who do not. It assumes that we can reasonably differentiate between the two groups. It leads us to look at persons who are in jail or prison and to compare them with persons who are not. By so focusing our attention, our data-gathering techniques, and our point of view, the question assumes that it is the difference in the acts of the deviants and the acts of the nondeviants that puts them in the different social categories.

From the point of view of conflict theory, such a question begs the key issue. From the conflict perspective we begin with the hypothesis that the difference between those who are defined as deviant and those who are not probably resides in the nature of the conflicts which exist in the society. The central question to be asked is, "How does it happen that some members of the society are labeled as deviant whereas others are not?" And the complement of this question is, "Whose interests are served by labeling some types of acts and some actors as deviant while not so labeling others."

Many possibilities are left open by so phrasing the issue. For one, it is possible that there is as much deviance among the unlabeled members as there is among the labeled. The assumption is not made that we will learn about deviance from studying persons in prison, mental institutions, or juvenile homes. Rather, the implicit assumption is that those persons do not differ profoundly from persons who are "free," except that they are members of classes or groups who best serve the interests of other groups by being incarcerated, labeled, and stigmatized.

The conflict perspective when applied to the study of deviance leads us to pay as much (if not more) attention to the institutions that decide who is deviant as to the deviants themselves. Conflict theory then leads us to study the law as an essential ingredient in the understanding of deviance.

From other perspectives the study of the law by sociologists has been largely ignored. When the law has been the subject of study the inquiry has usually begun with the assumption that the law serves certain useful purposes. This viewpoint sees the law emerging and persisting because of the functions it serves. These analyses inevitably end by arguing that the law exists and has its shape because it contributes to the maintenance of society, because it serves certain perceived needs of society.

But very little is explained simply by saying that a social institution — the law or any other — serves certain needs. It is inconceivable that any institution in a large, pluralistic, complex society would not serve some needs. It is equally inconceivable that any institution would serve the needs of every group or social class simultaneously. The question that must follow from the observation that the law serves certain needs is: Whose needs? Or, slightly varied, the question may be: If the law emerges and persists because it is functional, then for whom does it function?

The conflict perspective on deviance then leads one to look to the social groups in the society that influence and control the legal systems and thereby the processes by which persons are defined as deviant. Given what we have said before about the conflict perspective, it is to be expected that the question of how the law operates would be pursued with considerable emphasis on its historical development as well as its current shape in contemporary society. As the studies in Part VI of this book show, the conflict perspective produces a different set of questions and different answers to the study of deviant behavior than would otherwise be forthcoming. In the end the conflict perspective produces greater insight and understanding of deviance than can be obtained from more traditional approaches.

THE PLAN OF THE BOOK

The first four articles propose a perspective from which to study social problems. These are necessarily brief introductions to what is in fact a philosophically and sociologically complicated theory. There is a companion volume of readings, *Sociological Readings in the Conflict Perspective*, which provides a more adequate introduction to the theoretical model. Nonetheless the four short statements presented here should give some feeling for the perspective which underlies the analysis of social problems contained in the remainder of the book.

One of the intriguing features of social problems in modern industrial societies is their tendency to surface time and again. Although the words change – a depression of one era becomes a recession or a deflation of another – the economic and political crises associated with social change reoccur with surprising regularity. In Part VIII of the book we look at two of the more important recurring issues in industrial societies: a tendency towards fascism as a solution to economic crises and political crises involving student participation in demonstrations and rebellions.

Part II consists of inquiries into poverty. From poverty we move to a discussion of militarism and war. Colonialism and imperialism follow from militarism and war. Next we take up the issue of racism in the industrialized nations and follow it with a discussion of crime, deviance, and the law. Parts VII and IX deal respectively with the quality of life and the relationship between sociology and social policy.

These issues comprise the major problems of industrial societies.

NOTES

1. Robert S. Lynd, *Knowledge for What,* Princeton, N.J.: Princeton University Press, 1969.

2. Suzanne Langer, *Philosophy in a New Key,* 3d ed., Cambridge: Harvard University Press, 1957.

3. John Fowles, *The French Lieutenant's Woman,* Boston: Little, Brown, 1969.

4. Alvin Gouldner, *The Coming Crisis in Western Sociology,* New York, Basic Books, 1970; Robert Frederichs, *A Sociology of Sociology,* N.Y.: Basic Books, 1970.

5. Jerome Skolnick and Elliott Currie, *Crisis in American Institutions,* Boston: Little, Brown and Company, 1970, 1-19.

6. For a more detailed discussion of difference between conflict and other sociological theories, see William J. Chambliss, *Sociological Readings in the Conflict Perspective,* Reading, Mass.: Addison-Wesley, 1972.

Part I
THE CONFLICT PERSPECTIVE

THE SOCIOLOGICAL IMAGINATION

C. Wright Mills

Nowadays men often feel that their private lives are a series of traps. They sense that within their everyday worlds, they cannot overcome their troubles, and in this feeling, they are often quite correct: What ordinary men are directly aware of and what they try to do are bounded by the private orbits in which they live; their visions and their powers are limited to the close-up scenes of job, family, neighborhood; in other milieux, they move vicariously and remain spectators. And the more aware they become, however vaguely, of ambitions and of threats which transcend their immediate locales, the more trapped they seem to feel.

Underlying this sense of being trapped are seemingly impersonal changes in the very structure of continent-wide societies. The facts of contemporary history are also facts about the success and the failure of individual men and women. When a society is industrialized, a peasant becomes a worker; a feudal lord is liquidated or becomes a businessman. When classes rise or fall, a man is employed or unemployed; when the rate of investment goes up or down, a man takes new heart or goes broke. When wars happen, an insurance salesman becomes a rocket launcher; a store clerk, a radar man; a wife lives alone; a child grows up without a father. Neither the life of an individual nor the history of a society can be understood without understanding both.

Yet men do not usually define the troubles they endure in terms of historical change and institutional contradiction. The well-being they enjoy, they do not usually impute to the big ups and downs of the societies in which they live. Seldom aware of the intricate connection between the patterns of their own lives and the course of world history, ordinary men do not usually know what this connection means for the kinds of men they are becoming and for the kinds of history-making in which they might take part. They do not possess the quality of mind essential to grasp the interplay of man and society, of biography and history, of self and world. They cannot cope with their personal troubles in such ways as to control the structural transformations that usually lie behind them.

Surely it is no wonder. In what period have so many men been so totally exposed at so fast a pace to such earthquakes of change? That Americans have not known such catastrophic changes as have the men and women of other societies is due to historical facts that are now quickly becoming "merely history." The history that now affects every man is world history. Within this scene and this period, in the course of a single generation, one sixth of mankind is transformed from all that is feudal and backward into all that is modern, advanced, and fearful. Political colonies are freed; new and less visible forms of imperialism installed. Revolutions occur; men feel the intimate grip of new kinds of authority. Totalitarian societies rise, and are smashed to bits — or succeed fabulously. After two centuries of ascendancy, capitalism is shown up as only one way to make society into an industrial apparatus. After two centuries of hope, even formal democracy is restricted to a quite small portion of mankind. Everywhere in the underdeveloped world, ancient ways of life are broken up and vague expectations become urgent demands. Everywhere in the overdeveloped world, the means of authority and of violence become total in scope and bureaucratic in form. Humanity itself now lies before us, the super-nation at either pole concentrating its most coordinated and massive efforts upon the preparation of World War Three.

The very shaping of history now outpaces the ability of men to orient themselves in accordance with cherished values. And which values? Even when they do not panic, men often sense that older ways of feeling and thinking have collapsed and that newer beginnings are ambiguous to the point of moral stasis. Is it any wonder that ordinary men feel they cannot cope with the larger worlds with which they are so suddenly confronted? That they cannot understand the meaning of their epoch for their own lives? That — in defense of selfhood — they become morally insensible, trying to remain altogether private men? Is it any wonder that they come to be possessed by a sense of the trap?

It is not only information that they need – in this Age of Fact, information often dominates their attention and overwhelms their capacities to assimilate it. It is not only the skills of reason that they need – although their struggles to acquire these often exhaust their limited moral energy.

What they need, and what they feel they need, is a quality of mind that will help them to use information and to develop reason in order to achieve lucid summations of what is going on in the world and of what may be happening within themselves. It is this quality, I am going to contend, that journalists and scholars, artists and publics, scientists and editors are coming to expect of what may be called the sociological imagination.

1

The sociological imagination enables its possessor to understand the larger historical scene in terms of its meaning for the inner life and the external career of a variety of individuals. It enables him to take into account how individuals, in the welter of their daily experience, often become falsely conscious of their social positions. Within that welter, the framework of modern society is sought, and within that framework the psychologies of a variety of men and women are formulated. By such means the personal uneasiness of individuals is focused upon explicit troubles and the indifference of publics is transformed into involvement with public issues.

The first fruit of this imagination – and the first lesson of the social science that embodies it – is the idea that the individual can understand his own experience and gauge his own fate only by locating himself within his period, that he can know his own chances in life only by becoming aware of those of all individuals in his circumstances. In many ways it is a terrible lesson; in many ways a magnificent one. We do not know the limits of man's capacities for supreme effort or willing degradation, for agony or glee, for pleasurable brutality or the sweetness of reason. But in our time we have come to know that the limits of "human nature" are frighteningly broad. We have come to know that every individual lives, from one generation to the next, in some society; that he lives out a biography, and that he lives it out within some historical sequence. By the fact of his living he contributes, however minutely, to the shaping of this society and to the course of its history, even as he is made by society and by its historical push and shove.

The sociological imagination enables us to grasp history and biography and the relations between the two within society. That is its task and its promise. To recognize this task and this promise is the mark of the classic social analyst. It is characteristic of Herbert Spencer – turgid, polysyllabic, comprehensive; of E.A. Ross – graceful, muckraking, upright; of Auguste Comte and Emile Durkheim; of the intricate and subtle Karl Mannheim. It is the quality of all that is intellectually excellent in Karl Marx; it is the clue to Thorstein Veblen's brilliant and ironic insight, to Joseph Schumpeter's many-sided constructions of reality; it is the basis of the psychological sweep of W.E.H. Lecky no less than of the profundity and clarity of Max Weber. And it is the signal of what is best in contemporary studies of man and society.

No social study that does not come back to the problems of biography, of history and of their intersections within a society has completed its intellectual journey. Whatever the specific problems of the classic social analysts, however limited or however broad the features of social reality they have examined, those who have been imaginatively aware of the promise of their work have consistently asked three sorts of questions:

1. What is the structure of this particular society as a whole? What are its essential components, and how are they related to one another? How does it differ from other varieties of social order? Within it, what is the meaning of any particular feature for its continuance and for its change?

2. Where does this society stand in human history? What are the mechanics by which it is changing? What is its place within and its meaning for the development of humanity as a whole? How does any particular feature we are examining affect, and how is it affected by, the historical period in which it moves? And this period – what are its essential features? How does it differ from other periods? What are its characteristic ways of history-making?

3. What varieties of men and women now prevail in this society and in this period? And what varieties are coming to prevail? In what ways are they selected and formed, liberated and repressed, made sensitive and blunted? What kinds of "human nature" are revealed in the conduct and character we observe in this society in this period? And

what is the meaning for "human nature" of each and every feature of the society we are examining?

Whether the point of interest is a great power state or a minor literary mood, a family, a prison, a creed — these are the kinds of questions the best social analysts have asked. They are the intellectual pivots of classic studies of man in society — and they are the questions inevitably raised by any mind possessing the sociological imagination. For that imagination is the capacity to shift from one perspective to another — from the political to the psychological; from examination of a single family to comparative assessment of the national budgets of the world; from the theological school to the military establishment; from considerations of an oil industry to studies of contemporary poetry. It is the capacity to range from the most impersonal and remote transformations to the most intimate features of the human self — and to see the relations between the two. Back of its use there is always the urge to know the social and historical meaning of the individual in the society and in the period in which he has his quality and his being.

That, in brief, is why it is by means of the sociological imagination that men now hope to grasp what is going on in the world, and to understand what is happening in themselves as minute points of the intersections of biography and history within society. In large part, contemporary man's self-conscious view of himself as at least an outsider, if not a permanent stranger, rests upon an absorbed realization of social relativity and of the transformative power of history. The sociological imagination is the most fruitful form of this self-consciousness. By its use men whose mentalities have swept only a series of limited orbits often come to feel as if suddenly awakened in a house with which they had only supposed themselves to be familiar. Correctly or incorrectly, they often come to feel that they can now provide themselves with adequate summations, cohesive assessments, comprehensive orientations. Older decisions that once appeared sound now seem to them products of a mind unaccountably dense. Their capacity for astonishment is made lively again. They acquire a new way of thinking, they experience a transvaluation of values: in a word, by their reflection and by their sensibility, they realize the cultural meaning of the social sciences.

2

Perhaps the most fruitful distinction with which the sociological imagination works is between "the personal troubles of milieu" and "the public issues of social structure." This distinction is an essential tool of the sociological imagination and a feature of all classic work in social science.

Troubles occur within the character of the individual and within the range of his immediate relations with others; they have to do with his self and with those limited areas of social life of which he is directly and personally aware. Accordingly, the statement and the resolution of troubles properly lie within the individual as a biographical entity and within the scope of his immediate milieu – the social setting that is directly open to his personal experience and to some extent his willful activity. A trouble is a private matter: values cherished by an individual are felt by him to be threatened.

Issues have to do with matters that transcend these local environments of the individual and the range of his inner life. They have to do with the organization of many such milieux into the institutions of an historical society as a whole, with the ways in which various milieux overlap and interpenetrate to form the larger structure of social and historical life. An issue is a public matter: some value cherished by publics is felt to be threatened. Often there is a debate about what that value really is and about what it is that really threatens it. This debate is often without focus if only because it is the very nature of an issue, unlike even widespread trouble, that it cannot very well be defined in terms of the immediate and everyday environments of ordinary men. An issue, in fact, often involves a crisis in institutional arrangements, and often too it involves what Marxists call "contradictions" or "antagonisms."

In these terms, consider unemployment. When, in a city of 100,000, only one man is unemployed, that is his personal trouble, and for its relief we properly look to the character of the man, his skills, and his immediate opportunities. But when in a nation of 50 million employees, 15 million men are unemployed, that is an issue, and we may not hope to find its solution within the range of opportunities open to any one individual. The very structure of opportunities has collapsed. Both the correct statement of the problem and the range of possible solutions require us to consider the economic and political institutions of the society, and not merely the personal situation and character of a scatter of individuals.

Consider war. The personal problem of war, when it occurs, may be how to survive it or how to die in it with honor; how to make money out of it; how to climb into the higher safety of the military apparatus; or how to contribute to the war's termination. In short, according to one's values, to find a set of milieux and within it to survive the war or make one's death in it meaningful. But the structural issues of war have to do with its causes; with what types of men it throws up into command; with its effects upon economic and political, family and religious institutions, with the unorganized irresponsibility of a world of nation-states.

Consider marriage. Inside a marriage a man and a woman may experience personal troubles, but when the divorce rate during the first four years of marriage is 250 out of every 1,000 attempts, this is an indication of a structural issue having to do with the institutions of marriage and the family and other institutions that bear upon them.

Or consider the metropolis — the horrible, beautiful, ugly, magnificent sprawl of the great city. For many upper-class people, the personal solution to "the problem of the city" is to have an apartment with private garage under it in the heart of the city, and forty miles out, a house by Henry Hill, garden by Garrett Eckbo, on a hundred acres of private land. In these two controlled environments — with a small staff at each end and a private helicopter connection — most people could solve many of the problems of personal milieux caused by the facts of the city. But all this, however splendid, does not solve the public issues that the structural fact of the city poses. What should be done with this wonderful monstrosity? Break it all up into scattered units, combining residence and work? Refurbish it as it stands? Or, after evacuation, dynamite it and build new cities according to new plans in new places? What should those plans be? And who is to decide and to accomplish whatever choice is made? These are structural issues; to confront them and to solve them requires us to consider political and economic issues that affect innumerable milieux.

In so far as an economy is so arranged that slumps occur, the problem of unemployment becomes incapable of personal solution. In so far as war is inherent in the nation-state system and in the uneven industrialization of the world, the ordinary individual in his restricted milieu will be powerless — with or without psychiatric aid — to solve the troubles this system or lack of system imposes upon him. In so far as the family as an institution turns women into darling little slaves and men into their chief providers and unweaned dependents, the problem of a satisfactory marriage remains incapable of purely private solution. In so far as the overdeveloped megalopolis and the overdeveloped automobile are built-in features of the overdeveloped society, the issues of urban living will not be solved by personal ingenuity and private wealth.

What we experience in various and specific milieux, I have noted, is often caused by structural changes. Accordingly, to understand the changes of many personal milieux we are required to look beyond them. And the number and variety of such structural changes increase as the institutions within which we live become more embracing and more intricately connected with one another. To be aware of the idea of social structure and to use it with sensibility is to be capable of tracing such linkages among a great variety of milieux. To be able to do that is to possess the sociological imagination.

3

What are the major issues for publics and the key troubles of private individuals in our time? To formulate issues and troubles, we must ask what values are cherished yet threatened, and what values are cherished and supported, by the characterizing trends of our period. In the case both of threat and of support we must ask what salient contradictions of structure may be involved.

When people cherish some set of values and do not feel any threat to them, they experience *well-being*. When they cherish values but *do* feel them to be threatened, they experience a crisis — either as a personal trouble or as a public issue. And if all their values seem involved, they feel the total threat of panic.

But suppose people are neither aware of any cherished values nor experience any threat? That is the experience of *indifference*, which, if it seems to involve all their values, becomes apathy. Suppose, finally, they are unaware of any cherished values, but still are very much aware of a threat? That is the experience of *uneasiness*, of anxiety, which, if it is total enough, becomes a deadly unspecified malaise.

Ours is a time of uneasiness and indifference — not yet formulated in such ways as to permit the work of reason and the play of sensibility. Instead of troubles — defined in terms of values and threats — there is often the misery of vague uneasiness; instead of explicit issues there is often merely the beat feeling that all is somehow not right. Neither the values threatened nor whatever threatens them has been stated; in short, they have not been carried to the point of decision. Much less have they been formulated as problems of social science.

In the 'thirties there was little doubt — except among certain deluded business circles that there was an economic issue which was also a pack of personal troubles. In these arguments about "the crisis of capitalism," the formulations of Marx and the many unacknowledged re-formulations of his work probably set the leading terms of the issue, and some men came to understand their personal troubles in these terms. The values threatened were plain to see and cherished by all; the structural contradictions that threatened them also seemed plain. Both were widely and deeply experienced. It was a political age.

But the values threatened in the era after World War Two are often neither widely acknowledged as values nor widely felt to be threatened. Much private uneasiness goes unformulated; much public malaise and many decisions of enormous structural relevance never become public issues. For those who accept such inherited values as reason and freedom, it is the uneasiness iteslf that is the trouble; it is the indifference itself that is the issue. And it is this condition, of uneasiness and indifference, that is the signal feature of our period.

All this is so striking that it is often interpreted by observers as a shift in the very kinds of problems that need now to be formulated. We are frequently told that the problems of our decade, or even the crises of our period, have shifted from the external realm of economics and now have to do with the quality of individual life – in fact with the question of whether there is soon going to be anything that can properly be called individual life. Not child labor but comic books, not poverty but mass leisure, are at the center of concern. Many great public issues as well as many private troubles are described in terms of "the psychiatric" – often, it seems, in a pathetic attempt to avoid the large issues and problems of modern society. Often this statement seems to rest upon a provincial narrowing of interest to the Western societies, or even to the United States – thus ignoring two-thirds of mankind; often, too, it arbitrarily divorces the individual life from the larger institutions within which that life is enacted, and which on occasion bear upon it more grievously than do the intimate environments of childhood.

Problems of leisure, for example, cannot even be stated without considering problems of work. Family troubles over comic books cannot be formulated as problems without considering the plight of the contemporary family in its new relations with the newer institutions of the social structure. Neither leisure nor its debilitating uses can be understood as problems without recognition of the extent to which malaise and indifference now form the social and personal climate of contemporary American society. In this climate, no problems of "the private life" can be stated and solved without recognition of the crisis of ambition that is part of the very career of men at work in the incorporated economy.

It is true, as psychoanalysts continually point out, that people do often have "the increasing sense of being moved by obscure forces within themselves which they are unable to define." But it is *not* true, as Ernest Jones asserted, that "man's chief enemy and danger is his own unruly nature and the dark forces pent up within him." On the contrary: "Man's chief danger" today lies in the unruly forces of contemporary society itself, with its alienating methods of production, its enveloping techniques of political domination, its international anarchy — in a word, its pervasive transformations of the very "nature" of man and the conditions and aims of his life.

It is now the social scientist's foremost political and intellectual task — for here the two coincide — to make clear the elements of contemporary uneasiness and indifference. It is the central demand made upon him by other cultural workmen — by physical scientists and artists, by the intellectual community in general. It is because of this task and these demands, I believe, that the social sciences are becoming the common denominator of our cultural period, and the sociological imagination our most needed quality of mind.

4

In every intellectual age some one style of reflection tends to become a common denominator of cultural life. Nowadays, it is true, many intellectual fads are widely taken up before they are dropped for new ones in the course of a year or two. Such enthusiasms may add spice to cultural play, but leave little or no intellectual trace. That is not true of such ways of thinking as "Newtonian physics" or "Darwinian biology." Each of these intellectual universes became an influence that reached far beyond any special sphere of idea and imagery. In terms of them, or in terms derived from them, unknown scholars as well as fashionable commentators came to re-focus their observations and re-formulate their concerns.

During the modern era, physical and biological science has been the major common denominator of serious reflection and popular metaphysics in Western societies. "The technique of the laboratory" has been the accepted mode of procedure and the source of intellectual security. That is one meaning of the idea of an intellectual common denominator: men can state their strongest convictions in its terms; other terms and other styles of reflection seem mere vehicles of escape and obscurity.

That a common denominator prevails does not of course mean that no other styles of thought or modes of sensibility exist. But it does mean that more general intellectual interests tend to slide into this area, to be formulated there most sharply, and when so formulated, to be thought somehow to have reached, if not a solution, at least a profitable way of being carried along.

The sociological imagination is becoming, I believe, the major common denominator of our cultural life and its signal feature. This quality of mind is found in the social and psychological sciences, but it goes far beyond these studies as we now know them. Its acquisition by individuals and by the cultural community at large is slow and often fumbling; many social scientists are themselves quite unaware of it. They do not seem to know that the use of this imagination is central to the best work that they might do, that by failing to develop and to use it they are failing to meet the cultural expectations that are coming to be demanded of them and that the classic traditions of their several disciplines make available to them.

Yet in factual and moral concerns, in literary work and in political analysis, the qualities of this imagination are regularly demanded. In a great variety of expressions, they have become central features of intellectual endeavor and cultural sensibility. Leading critics exemplify these qualities as do serious journalists — in fact the work of both is often judged in these terms. Popular categories of criticism — high, middle, and low-brow, for example — are now at least as much sociological as aesthetic. Novelists — whose serious work embodies the most widespread definitions of human reality — frequently possess this imagination, and do much to meet the demand for it. By means of it, orientation to the present as history is sought. As images of "human nature" become more problematic, an increasing need is felt to pay closer yet more imaginative attention to the social routines and catastrophes which reveal (and which shape) man's nature in this time of civil unrest and ideological conflict. Although fashion is often revealed by attempts to use it, the sociological imagination is not merely a fashion. It is a quality of mind that seems most dramatically to promise an understanding of the intimate realities of ourselves in connection with larger social realities. It is not merely one quality of mind among the contemporary range of cultural sensibilities — it is *the* quality whose wider and more adroit use offers the promise that all such sensibilities — and in fact, human reason itself — will come to play a greater role in human affairs.

The cultural meaning of physical science — the major older common denominator — is becoming doubtful. As an intellectual style, physical science is coming to be thought by many as somehow inadequate. The adequacy of scientific styles of thought and feeling, imagination and sensibility, has of course from their beginnings been subject to religious doubt and theological controversy, but our scientific grandfathers and fathers beat down such religious doubts. The current doubts are secular, humanistic — and often quite confused. Recent developments in physical science — with its technological climax in the H-bomb and the means of carrying it about the earth — have not been experienced as a solution to any problems widely known and deeply pondered by larger intellectual communities and cultural publics. These developments have been correctly seen as a result of highly specialized inquiry, and improperly felt to be wonderfully mysterious. They have raised more problems — both intellectual and moral — than they have solved, and the problems they have raised lie almost entirely in the area of social not physical affairs. The obvious conquest of nature, the overcoming of scarcity, is felt by men of the overdeveloped societies to be virtually complete. And now in these societies, science — the chief instrument of this conquest — is felt to be footloose, aimless, and in need of re-appraisal.

The modern esteem for science has long been merely assumed, but now the technological ethos and the kind of engineering imagination associated with science are more likely to be frightening and ambiguous than hopeful and progressive. Of course this is not all there is to "science," but it is feared that this could become all that there is to it. The felt need to reappraise physical science reflects the need for a new common denominator. It is the human meaning and the social role of science, its military and commercial issue, its political significance that are undergoing confused re-appraisal. Scientific developments of weaponry may lead to the "necessity" for world political rearrangements — but such "necessity" is not felt to be solvable by physical science itself.

Much that has passed for "science" is now felt to be dubious philosophy; much that is held to be "real science" is often felt to provide only confused fragments of the realities among which men live. Men of science, it is widely felt, no longer try to picture reality as a whole or to present a true outline of human destiny. Moreover, "science" seems to many less a creative ethos and a manner of orientation than a set of Science Machines, operated by technicians and controlled by economic and military men who neither embody nor understand science as ethos and orientation. In the meantime, philosophers who speak in the name of science often transform it into "scientism," making out its experience to be identical with human experience, and claiming that only by its method can the problems of life be solved. With all this, many cultural workmen have come to feel that "science" is a false and pretentious Messiah, or at the very least a highly ambiguous element in modern civilization.

But there are, in C.P. Snow's phrase, "two cultures": the scientific and the humanistic. Whether as history or drama, as biography, poetry or fiction, the essence of the humanistic culture has been literature. Yet it is now frequently suggested that serious literature has in many ways become a minor art. If this is so, it is not merely because of the development of mass publics and mass media of communication, and all that these mean for serious literary production. It is also owing to the very quality of the history of our times and the kinds of need men of sensibility feel to grasp that quality.

What fiction, what journalism, what artistic endeavor can compete with the historical reality and political facts of our time? What dramatic vision of hell can compete with the events of twentieth-century war? What moral denunciations can measure up to the moral insensibility of men in the agonies of primary accumulation? It is social and historical reality that men want to know, and often they do not find contemporary literature an adequate means for knowing it. They yearn for facts, they search for their meanings, they want "a big picture" in which they can believe and within which they can come to understand themselves. They want orienting values too, and suitable ways of feeling and styles of emotion and vocabularies of motive. And they do not readily find these in the literature of today. It does not matter whether or not these qualities *are* to be found there; what matters is that men do not often find them there.

In the past, literary men as critics and historians made notes on England and on journeys to America. They tried to characterize societies as wholes, and to discern their moral meanings. Were Tocqueville or Taine alive today, would they not be sociologists? Asking this question about Taine, a reviewer in *The Times* (London) suggests:

> Taine always saw man primarily as a social animal and society as a collection of groups: he could observe minutely, was a tireless field worker and possessed a quality . . . particularly valuable for perceiving relationships between social phenomena — the quality of springliness. He was too interested in the present to be a good historian, too much of a theorist to try his hand as a novelist, and he thought of

literature too much as documents in the culture of an age or country to achieve first-class status as a critic . . . His work on English literature is less about English literature than a commentary on the morality of English society and a vehicle for his positivism. He is a social theorist before all else.[1]

That he remained a "literary man" rather than a "social scientist" testifies perhaps to the domination of much nineteenth-century social science by the zealous search for "laws" presumably comparable to those imagined to be found by natural scientists. In the absence of an adequate social science, critics and novelists, dramatists and poets have been the major, and often the only, formulators of private troubles and even of public issues. Art does express such feelings and often focuses them — at its best with dramatic sharpness — but still not with the intellectual clarity required for their understanding or relief today. Art does not and cannot formulate these feelings as problems containing the troubles and issues men must now confront if they are to overcome their uneasiness and indifference and the intractable miseries to which these lead. The artist, indeed, does not often try to do this. Moreover, the serious artist is himself in much trouble, and could well do with some intellectual and cultural aid from a social science made sprightly by the sociological imagination.

5

It is my aim . . . to define the meaning of the social sciences for the cultural tasks of our time. I want to specify the kinds of effort that lie behind the development of the sociological imagination; to indicate its implications for political as well as for cultural life; and perhaps to suggest something of what is required to possess it. In these ways, I want to make clear the nature and the uses of the social sciences today, and to give a limited account of their contemporary condition in the United States.[2]

At any given moment, of course, "social science" consists of what duly recognized social scientists are doing — but all of them are by no means doing the same thing, in fact not even the same sort of thing. Social science is also what social scientists of the past have done — but different students choose to construct and to recall different traditions in their discipline. When I speak of "the promise of social science," I hope it is clear that I mean the promise as I see it.

Just now, among social scientists, there is widespread uneasiness, both intellectual and moral, about the direction their chosen studies seem to be taking. This uneasiness, as well as the unfortunate tendencies that contribute to it, are, I suppose, part of a general malaise of contemporary intellectual life. Yet perhaps the uneasiness is more acute among social scientists, if only because of the larger promise that has guided much earlier work in their fields, the nature of the subjects with which they deal, and the urgent need for significant work today.

Not everyone shares this uneasiness, but the fact that many do not is itself a cause for further uneasiness among those who are alert to the promise and honest enough to admit the pretentious mediocrity of much current effort. It is, quite frankly, my hope to increase this uneasiness, to define some of its sources, to help transform it into a specific urge to realize the promise of social science, to clear the ground for new beginnings: in short, to indicate some of the tasks at hand and the means available for doing the work that must now be done.

Of late the conception of social science I hold has not been ascendant. My conception stands opposed to social science as a set of bureaucratic techniques which inhibit social inquiry by "methodological" pretensions, which congest such work by obscurantist conceptions, or which trivialize it by concern with minor problems unconnected with publicly revelant issues. These inhibitions, obscurities, and trivialities have created a crisis in the social studies today without suggesting, in the least, a way out of that crisis.

Some social scientists stress the need for "research teams of technicians," others for the primacy of the individual scholar. Some expend great energy upon refinements of methods and techniques of investigation; others think the scholarly ways of the intellectual craftsman are being abandoned and ought now to be rehabilitated. Some go about their work in accordance with a rigid set of mechanical procedures; others seek to develop, to invite, and to use the sociological imagination. Some — being addicts of the high formalism of "theory" — associate and disassociate concepts in what seems to others a curious manner; these others urge the elaboration of terms only when it is clear that it enlarges the scope of sensibility and furthers the reach of reasoning. Some narrowly study only small-scale milieux, in the hope of "building up" to conceptions of larger structures; others examine social structures in which they try "to locate" many smaller milieux. Some, neglecting comparative studies altogether, study only one small community in one society at a time; others in a fully comparative way work directly on the national social structures of the world. Some confine their exact research to very short-run sequences of human affairs; others are concerned with issues which are only apparent in long historical perspective. Some specialize their work according to academic departments; others, drawing upon all departments, specialize according to topic or problem, regardless of where these lie academically. Some confront the variety of history, biography, society; others do not.

Such contrasts, and many others of similar kind, are not necessarily true alternatives, although in the heat of statesman-like controversy or the lazy safety of specialization they are often taken to be. At this point I merely state them in inchoate form . . . I am hopeful of course that all my own biases will show, for I think judgments should be explicit. But I am also trying, regardless of my own judgments, to state the cultural and political meanings of social science. My biases are of course no more or no less biases than those I am going to examine. Let those who do not care for mine use their rejections of them to make their own as explicit and as acknowledged as I am going to try to make mine! Then the moral problems of social study — the problem of social science as a public issue — will be recognized, and discussion will become possible. Then there will be greater self-awareness all around — which is of course a pre-condition for objectivity in the enterprise of social science as a whole.

In brief, I believe that what may be called classic social analysis is a definable and usable set of traditions; that its essential feature is the concern with historical social structures; and that its problems are of direct relevance to urgent public issues and insistent human troubles. I also believe that there are now great obstacles in the way of this tradition's continuing — both within the social sciences and in their academic and political settings — but that nevertheless the qualities of mind that constitute it are becoming a common denominator of our general cultural life and that, however vaguely and in however a confusing variety of disguises, they are coming to be felt as a need.

Many practitioners of social science, especially in America, seem to me curiously reluctant to take up the challenge that now confronts them. Many in fact abdicate the intellectual and the political tasks of social analysis; others no doubt are simply not up to the role for which they are nevertheless being cast. At times they seem almost deliberately to have brought forth old ruses and developed new timidities. Yet despite this reluctance, intellectual as well as public attention is now so obviously upon the social worlds which they presumably study that it must be agreed that they are uniquely confronted with an opportunity. In this opportunity there is revealed the intellectual promise of the social sciences, the cultural uses of the sociological imagination, and the political meaning of studies of man and society.

6

Embarrassingly enough for an avowed sociologist, all the unfortunate tendencies (except possibly one) . . . fall into what is generally thought to be "the field of sociology," although the cultural and political abdication implicit in them no doubt characterizes much of the daily work in other social sciences. Whatever may be true in such disciplines as political science and economics, history and anthropology, it is evident that in the United States today what is known as sociology has become the center of reflection about social science. It has become the center for interest in methods; and in it one also finds the most extreme interest in "general theory." A truly remarkable variety of intellectual work has entered into the development of the sociological tradition. To interpret this variety as A Tradition is in itself audacious. Yet perhaps it will be generally agreed that what is now recognized as sociological work has tended to move in one or more of three general directions, each of which is subject to distortion, to being run into the ground.

Tendency I: Toward a theory of history. For example, in the hands of Comte, as in those of Marx, Spencer, and Weber, sociology is an encyclopedic endeavor, concerned with the whole of man's social life. It is at once historical and systematic — historical, because it deals with and uses the materials of the past; systematic, because it does so in order to discern "the stages" of the course of history and the regularities of social life.

The theory of man's history can all too readily become distorted into a trans-historical strait-jacket into which the materials of human history are forced and out of which issue prophetic views (usually gloomy ones) of the future. The works of Arnold Toynbee and of Oswald Spengler are well-known examples.

Tendency II: Toward a systematic theory of "the nature of man and society." For example, in the works of the formalists, notably Simmel and Von Weise, sociology comes to deal in conceptions intended to be of use in classifying all social relations and providing insight into their supposedly invariant features. It is, in short, concerned with a rather static and abstract view of the components of social structure on a quite high level of generality.

Perhaps in reaction to the distortion of Tendency I, history can be altogether abandoned: the systematic theory of the nature of man and of society all too readily becomes an elaborate and arid formalism in which the splitting of Concepts and their endless rearrangement becomes the central endeavor. Among what I shall call Grand Theorists, conceptions have indeed become Concepts. The work of Talcott Parsons is the leading contemporary example in American sociology.

Tendency III: Toward empirical studies of contemporary social facts and problems. Although Comte and Spencer were mainstays of American social science until 1914 or thereabout, and German theoretical influence was heavy, the empirical survey became central in the United States at an early time. In part this resulted from the prior academic establishment of economics and political science. Given this, in so far as sociology is defined as a study of some special area of society, it readily becomes a sort of odd job man among the social sciences, consisting of miscellaneous studies of academic leftovers. There are studies of cities and families, racial and ethnic relations, and of course "small groups." As we shall see, the resulting miscellany was transformed into a style of thought, which I shall examine under the term "liberal practicality."

Studies of contemporary fact can easily become a series of rather unrelated and often insignificant facts of milieu. Many course offerings in American sociology illustrate this; perhaps textbooks in the field of social disorganization reveal it best. On the other hand, sociologists have tended to become specialists in the technique of research into almost anything; among them methods have become Methodology. Much of the work — and more of the ethos — of George Lundberg, Samuel Stouffer, Stuart Dodd, Paul F. Lazarsfeld are present-day examples. These tendencies — to scatter one's attention and to cultivate method for its own sake — are fit companions, although they do not necessarily occur together.

The peculiarities of sociology may be understood as distortions of one or more of its traditional tendencies. But its promises may also be understood in terms of these tendencies. In the United States today there has come about a sort of Hellenistic amalgamation, embodying various elements and aims from the sociologies of the several Western societies. The danger is that amidst such sociological abundance, other social scientists will become so impatient, and sociologists be in such a hurry for "research," that they will lose hold of a truly valuable legacy. But there is also an opportunity in our condition: the sociological tradition contains the best statements of the full promise of the social sciences as a whole, as well as some partial fulfillments of it. The nuance and suggestion that students of sociology can find in their traditions are not to be briefly summarized, but any social scientist who takes them in hand will be richly rewarded. His mastery of them may readily be turned into new orientations for his own work in social science.

NOTES

1. *Times Literary Supplement*, 15 November 1957.

2. I feel the need to say that I much prefer the phrase, "the social studies" to "the social sciences" – not because I do not like physical scientists (on the contrary, I do, very much), but because the word "science" has acquired great prestige and rather imprecise meaning. I do not feel any need to kidnap the prestige or to make the meaning even less precise by using it as a philosophical metaphor. Yet I suspect that if I wrote about "the social studies," readers would think only of high school civics, which of all fields of human learning is the one with which I most wish to avoid association. "The Behavioral Sciences" is simply impossible; it was thought up, I suppose, as a propaganda device to get money for social research from Foundations and Congressmen who confuse "social science" with "socialism." The best term would include history (and psychology, so far as it is concerned with human beings), and should be as non-controversial as possible, for we should argue *with* terms, not fight *over* them. Perhaps "the human disciplines" would do. But never mind. With the hope of not being too widely misunderstood, I bow to convention and use the more standard "social sciences."

   One other point: I hope my colleagues will accept the term "sociological imagination." Political scientists who have read my manuscript suggest "the political imagination"; anthropologists, "the anthropological imagination" – and so on. The term matters less than the idea. . . . By use of it, I do not of course want to suggest merely the academic discipline of "sociology." Much of what the phrase means to me is not at all expressed by sociologists. In England, for example, sociology as an academic discipline is still somewhat marginal, yet in much English journalism, fiction, and above all history, the sociological imagination is very well developed indeed.

The case is similar for France: both the confusion and the audacity of French reflection since World War Two rest upon its feeling for the sociological features of man's fate in our time, yet these trends are carried by men of letters rather than by professional sociologists. Nevertheless, I use "sociological imagination" because: (1) every cobbler thinks leather is the only thing, and for better or worse, I am a sociologist; (2) I do believe that historically the quality of mind has been more frequently and more vividly displayed by classic sociologists than by other social scientists; (3) since I am going to examine critically a number of curious sociological schools, I need a counter term on which to stand.

THE CONTEMPORARY RELEVANCE OF KARL MARX

William A. Williams

Once upon a time, even as recently as a century ago, Americans talked about America in positive terms. True enough, their conception of Utopia was cramped and confined within existing axioms and ideals, but their attitude was at least creative within those limits. Even in their negative moments, as when Thomas Jefferson could say no more for America than that it was the "last best hope" of the world, or when they admitted their shortcomings and criticized their mistakes, they were guided by a vision of a significantly better society.

In our time, by contrast, a debate on national purpose is a forced and labored exercise in journalistic commerce, political sophistry, and ideological casuistry. Even the participants acknowledge their boredom and embarrassment, and the enterprise slides unnoticed into bankruptcy. The supposedly great dialogue becomes just another statistic of business failure in a business society. The causes: insufficient capital and enterprise, and an unwillingness to innovate and take risks. Nobody involved has a concept of national purpose, let alone a program calculated to realize that vision, capable of exciting and engaging the population at large.

Consider another illustration. The era's most celebrated essay in political economy, John Kenneth Galbraith's imaginative report on his meanderings in a mythical land called *The Affluent Society*, is a complacent, inaccurate, misleading, and dangerously stultifying exercise in self-congratulation. The root meaning of *affluent* involves a free flow of plenty and abundance, and hence of wealth. Yet the sputtering, fluctuating performance of the American economy can hardly be characterized as an unfettered coursing, or as a free and easy operation — even during those periods when it has been assisted by the stimulus of war and cold war.

As for plenty and abundance, Galbraith simply discounts somewhere between 35 and 50 million human beings who exist under conditions of severe deprivation or outright poverty. These are people to whom the morning paper is "a luxury"; or who remember buying "my wife a pint of sherbet" as a rare and memorable event; or unemployed men aged thirty-seven who talk of themselves in stories like this: "I'll tell you something very funny. I hate wine. I almost puke every time I drink it. But if I didn't stay drunk, the chances are I'd kill myself." These people are not affluent. But Galbraith's term *society*, whatever its limitations as an ideal of human relationships, is an inclusive concept and does refer to everyone in the system.

As for wealth, Galbraith clearly and arbitrarily re-defines it to mean nothing more than the possession of a certain quantity of material goods and automatic or personal services. Yet the essential meaning of *wealth* has to do with an individual's effective, participating influence within his society. The great majority of Americans do not possess or exercise that kind of share or stake in contemporary society. From time to time, and in political as well as in economic affairs, a significant number of Americans register approval or disapproval of ideas or policies proposed — or already acted upon — by other people. But this does not constitute wealth in any meaningful sense.

Along with other examples of the same idiom (as, for example, Frederick Lewis Allen's *The Big Change* and Daniel Bell's *The End of Ideology*), Galbraith's rhetoric of triumphant achievement suggests — and sometimes indicates explicitly — that America has proved Karl Marx wrong in theory and in prophecy, and wrong everlastingly. In one form or another, this article of faith is accepted by men of all religions, races, creeds, functions, classes, incomes, statuses, I.Q.'s, and ideologies. For that matter, those who avow their radicalism seem at times to be shouting it a bit louder than anyone else.

This contemporary consensus on having proved Marx wrong does not involve any fundamentally new idea or attitude on the part of Americans. The formulation of the proposition in terms of Marx is clearly a product of the survival and progress of the Soviet Union, and of the appearance of other socialist and communist revolutions since the end of World War II. The central argument itself, however, is nothing more than a reassertion of the traditional doctrine of America's immaculate uniqueness. (It is worth noting that a people calling themselves unique thereby define themselves, perhaps only implicitly but nevertheless irrevocably, as either non-human, sub-human, or superhuman. Outsiders often perceive this corollary of the assertion of uniqueness, even if Americans overlook it, and it underpins a good deal of their antagonism and resentment toward individual Americans and toward the United States.) In and of itself, the psychology of this almost obsessive assertion of uniqueness suggests that it may not be true. One has more than a hunch that we do insist too much.

For all these reasons, therefore, it seems the greater part of prudence to test the dogma by comparing the reality of Marx with the reality of America, instead of merely asserting that America has made Marx irrelevant. It is possible, for example, that Marx could be wrong and still offer insights relevant to contemporary problems. And it is conceivable that he was correct in defining the problems themselves, even though his prophecies may have been wrong.

Such an examination should direct itself to, and center itself upon, the broad nature and the principal themes of Marx's analysis of capitalism. *First*, the record of American diplomacy in the light of his analysis of the assumptions and dynamic nature of capitalist foreign relations. *Second*, the performance of the United States measured against his famous argument about the propensity of capitalism to produce increasing proletarianization and increasing misery. And *third*, the degree of American achievement in constructing society as an ethical and equitable and creative community. These issues lie at the heart of Marx's critique, and the claim to have proved him wrong can be sustained only if the facts reveal that the United States has transcended his description, analysis, and predictions.

Several general considerations should be kept in mind throughout such an evaluation, however, so as to counteract the habit of confusing the issues and faulting Marx on points not germane to the central line of his argument. Perhaps the most important of these involves his fidelity to the facts and his commitment to open-ended inquiry. Marx did discount, in his time, certain logical implications in his analysis of capitalism that later emerged as actual characteristics of the system. He also underestimated the impact or strength of some tendencies that were appearing at the end of his life. These are errors of judgment that can properly be criticized. But these mistakes do not necessarily destroy the broad lines of his argument.

Marx's work flowed from the methodological axiom that reality and change could be explained, and prognostications offered, by reference to the tension, conflict, and contradictions between the methods of production and the relations of production. By this he meant, fundamentally, the interaction between the way work could be done in any given circumstance and the way men organized themselves to do the work. Sticks and rocks demanded a certain kind of organization for cultivating fields, for example, and that organization begot new ideas about how men ought to be organized, as well as about how the ground might be tilled in different ways. Men acted on these ideas, either in favor of them or against them; that caused changes, and the new conditions generated more ideas.

Men therefore made their own history, but they did so within the limits of existing reality (which of course included old as well as new ideas). It should be clear, though it is often overlooked, that Marx understood and acknowledged the influence of ideas. He did argue, however, that basic ideas changed only very slowly. Hence he insisted that the economic rules, practices, habits, and relationships created by one such set of ideas became and remained the predominant — and even an almost independent — factor in a given situation until new ideas changed the system.

This is often misunderstood as saying that all human action can be, or even must be, explained as flowing from individual, personal economic motives. Marx was no such fool as that. He was quite aware that men could and did act from economic motives, but he also realized that they could and did act on the much broader basis of thinking that the whole network of political and social relationships depended upon maintaining certain economic patterns. They could act, that is, to sustain the marketplace per se as well as an entrepreneur within the marketplace. And Marx explicitly acknowledged the role of passion and chance in affecting the *short-run* development of the system.

Given this basic approach, Marx was intellectually incorruptible. As he put it time and time again, it was the facts — not the conclusions already demonstrated or the wishes of the student — that determined the analysis in each specific case. "I am not a Marxist!" he once cried in disgust and anguish over self-appointed followers who applied a schematic version of his complex analytic approach to the facts and produced brittle explanations and stereotyped predictions. "One will never succeed," Marx flatly asserted, "with the open sesame of an historico-philosophical theory, of which the supreme virtue consists in its being *supra-historical*." Marx's assumptions, axioms, and methods, and his broad analysis, rather than any particular or detailed prognostication he offered, are the crucial elements of his contribution.

It is worth re-emphasizing that Marx did not neglect or discount ideas. This is one of the most common criticisms of him. Its proponents claim he made man into a machine guided by a kind of economic radar. This is simply wrong. He was unequivocal on the point that men could entertain ideas that were broader than those derived from their specific economic role or position. A radical, revolutionary "class consciousness," he pointed out, "can of course also rise in other classes from the observation of the situation of [the proletarian] class."

Marx could not discount ideas for the simple reason that he was principally concerned with the central axioms and dynamic propensities of capitalist development. Indeed, one might argue with considerable effect that it was his very overemphasis on the power of ideas that led him repeatedly, and in a way that contradicted another part of his analysis of ideas, to underestimate the time required for the full evolution of the dynamic features he defined as being the causal engines of the capitalist process. He was very prone to assume that men would perceive the true nature of their condition, and proceed to improve it, much more quickly than they actually did — or have.

Marx's foreshortened sense of time did have the effect of distorting some of his specific projections and predictions. But it seems fair to point out that the problem of understanding and being right about time is a difficulty that plagues all historians and social scientists. Even economists have trouble with time. Those who dismiss Marx have not met this challenge any more effectively than he did. If anything, they have foreshortened time even more drastically. Marx talked about capitalism over a period of at least five centuries, whereas his critics dismiss him as hopelessly wrong on the evidence of less than one. For that matter, most Americans who dispense with him as being irrelevant base their argument on the events of an infinitesimal period between 1941 and 1955.

Finally, it is pertinent to recall Marx's uninhibited praise of capitalist performance. He never intimated, let alone asserted, that capitalism was an unmitigated failure or an unrelieved agony. This seems particularly relevant in connection with America, where the achievement has been great – even if the resources and the favorable circumstances have been grandiose.

The bourgeoisie, Marx commented quite without niggardliness, "has played a most revolutionary part . . . It has been the first to show what man's activity can bring about. It has accomplished wonders far surpassing Egyptian pyramids, Roman aqueducts, and Gothic cathedrals; it has conducted expeditions that put in the shade all former Exoduses of nations and crusades . . . [It] has created more massive and more colossal productive forces than have all preceding generations together . . . What earlier century had even a presentiment that such productive forces slumbered in the lap of social labor?" And, furthermore, the bourgeoisie "has given a cosmopolitian character to production and consumption in every country . . . National one-sidedness and narrow-mindedness become more and more impossible, and from the numerous national and local literatures, there arises a world literature . . ."

THE MEANING OF MARXISM

G. D. H. Cole

MARX AND HEGEL

Marx, of course, did not accept the Hegelian Dialectic; but he did accept Hegel's notion of conflict as the essential form of progress, and on the basis of this notion he built his own very different Dialectic upon Hegel's

From G.D.H. Cole, *The Meaning of Marxism*, Ann Arbor, The University of of Michigan Press, pp. 272-275, 135-149. Copyright © 1948 by The University of Michigan Press.

method. In Marx's conception, as in Hegel's, thesis, antithesis and synthesis replace and transcend the categories of Formal Logic, and reality is conceived in dynamic instead of static terms. What is, is becoming: nothing ever stands still in the real world.

Marx's real world, however, is very different from Hegel's; for it is nothing other than the phenomenal world of everyday experience. The things we experience in ordinary life are not; Marx holds, abstractions or derivative and imperfect expressions of a superior reality existing outside space and time, but ultimates beyond which we cannot and need not go — for beyond them there is nothing. They *are* reality — the one and only reality on which all thought, all ideas, all purely mental or spiritual constructions are built. Men can seek to understand this reality, and, what is more, to make themselves increasingly masters of the laws which govern its development. But men cannot go outside or beyond it; for it and nothing else is the universe in which they are. Being precedes thought; for thought can be only thought of being, and about being. There can be no perception without something to perceive; no conception without a mind reflecting upon its experience of things. The external world is the external world, and is not either an idea in our minds or a reflection of some ideal substance outside and beyond our experience. The description "phenomenal" is thus, in Marx's use of it, applicable not to things but to ideas about things. Things are real, and are not mere appearances, but they often appear to men distorted by the notions men entertain about them. Reality and phenomenon, in Marx's usage as compared with Hegel's, change places.

But the real world of experience is not static. Nothing is static save the abstractions which men make in their own minds in their attempts to rationalise their experience. Everything changes: human history is the process of human change writ large in the common experience of mankind. In that Hegel was abundantly right; but Marx held that, as things are real and are not mere reflections of the Idea, the dynamic Logic which Hegel applied to the Idea must be applied directly to the things themselves, and used directly in explaining the course of historical movements. Things change. Things, in the ordinary temporal process of human development, are continually becoming that which were not. But by what law do they change? Marx answered "By the dialectical law of human conflict." What, then, are the nature and the method of this historic law?

THE POWERS OF PRODUCTION

Since things, and not ideas, are the ultimate realities, things and not ideas must, it seems, be the ultimate motive forces of human history. But what things? Marx, as we have seen in earlier chapters, made answer that the underlying forces of history are the changing 'powers of production.' As these expand with the increase in men's knowledge and opportunities, human history passes through corresponding phases of development. To each broad phase of development of the powers of production corresponds a phase of human evolution.

Marx, then, regards the 'powers of production' as things, and not as ideas about things. The 'powers of production,' however, are not and cannot be merely material things as such, in the ordinary sense of the word "material." A machine is no doubt a "thing"; but it becomes a 'power of production' only in the hands of someone who knows how to make it work. It is, moreover, a thing in which is embodied someone's knowledge of the means of constructing it. These forms of knowledge — how to make instruments of production and how to work them — both became social forms of knowledge, as possessions of the society in which they exist and are handed on from man to man and from generation to generation. Most "inventions" are really improvements on what was previously known: most inventors use the work of many men's minds in devising their improvements: most skill is taught by men to men, even if there is in it a factor of natural aptitude. Thus, the powers of production embody in a social form not only the natural materials of which they are made but also immaterial factors of human mental achievement. Nor are all the powers of production embodied in material things: a chemical formula may be as much a 'power of production' as a machine. Of course, such a formula has to be in someone's mind, and that mind has to be in a body. But this can be said also of ideas of the most abstract sort. The 'powers of production,' then, though they include many material objects and cannot be exercised except in connection with material objects, cannot be defined exclusively in terms of "matter" in any sense in which "matter" excludes "mind." They exist in fact as the outcome of a relation between mind and matter, and are made up of both material and mental elements.

We have, then, a picture of the 'powers of production' developing, as a result of the advance of men's practical knowledge, and of each major advance involving a change in men's social organisation, and also, therewith, in men's ideas and beliefs. . . .

THE BASIS OF THE MARXIAN DIALECTIC

Each stage reached by the powers of production, Marx holds, gives rise among men to a set of economic relationships designed to further their use; and to these economic relationships correspond appropriate political and social relationships which arise out of, and react upon, the economic conditions. Marx's point was that throughout human history these relationships have hitherto necessarily ranged men in economic classes, and that it is between these classes that the struggles which make human history have been waged. The theses and antitheses, according to Marx, are these classes; and the syntheses are the new classes which arise out of the struggle of class against class at each turning point of history, up to the conflict which succeeds at length in establishing a classless society, and therewith brings the dialectical process of class-conflict to an end.

This process, as Marx describes it, cannot truly be regarded as "materialist," in the most familiar sense of that term, because the forces upon which the entire movement rests – the 'powers of production' – are not forces of matter as opposed to mind, but embody the result of mind's action upon matter – man's command over nature, for short. Still more clearly, the struggle by which the process of historical evolution is carried on is not one of matter with matter, in any sense in which matter can be contrasted with mind, but of men with men. According to Marx, it is a class-struggle, or rather a series of class-struggles which continues to its end in the total obliteration of class-distinctions and in the establishment of a classless society.

What then becomes of the dialectical process? Clearly it cannot continue to obey the formula of class-struggle; for no classes remain in being. For the new phase of human history which then begins, and for the further phases that are to follow, a new formula is needed. "Pre-history ends," Marx writes, "and history begins." But what is to be the law of this new history of a classless world?

The Marxists' answer is that they do not know. For Marx held that each age sets itself only the problems which it needs to solve, and is in a position to solve; and mankind is neither able nor in need to solve as yet the problems of the Socialist future. Clearly this need not mean that the Dialectic will no longer apply; for the law of the Dialectic admits of many different formulae besides that of the class-struggle, and the formula may be changed without changing the dialectical character of the historical process. Struggle can proceed upon other planes than that of class, and in higher and less brutal forms. But what these forms will be the Marxist neither pretends nor even wishes to know in advance of the event. All he does pretend to know is that, whatever is to come after the winning of a classless society, it is not in the nature of reality ever to become static and unchanging. As long as mankind exists, mankind will have a history, and that history will proceed dialectically, in some form.

A CONFLICT MODEL OF SOCIETY

John Rex

The main lines of our conflict model for the analysis of social systems are now fairly clear. They may be summarized as follows:

1. Instead of being organized around a consensus of values, social systems may be thought of as involving conflict situations at central points. Such conflict situations may lie anywhere between the extremes of peaceful bargaining in the market place and open violence.

2. The existence of such a situation tends to produce not a unitary but a plural society, in which there are two or more classes, each of which provides a relatively self-contained social system for its members. The activities of the members take on sociological meaning and must be explained by reference to the group's interests in the conflict situation. Relations between groups are defined at first solely in terms of the conflict situation.

3. In most cases the conflict situation will be marked by an unequal balance of power so that one of the classes emerges as the ruling class. Such a class will continually seek to gain recognition of the legitimacy of its position among the members of the subject class and the leaders of the subject class will seek to deny this claim and to

From John Rex, *Key Problems of Sociological Theory*, London: Routledge and Kegan Paul, Ltd.; New York: Humanities Press, Inc. Reprinted by permission.

organize activities which demonstrate that it is denied (e.g., passive resistance).

4. The power situation as between the ruling and subject classes may change as a result of changes in a number of variable factors which increase the possibility of successful resistance or actual revolution by the subject class. Amongst these variable factors are leadership, the strength of the members' aspirations, their capacity for organization, their possession of the means of violence, their numbers and their role in the social system proposed by the ruling class.

5. In the case of a dramatic change in the balance of power the subject class may suddenly find itself in a situation in which it cannot merely impose its will on the former ruling class, but can actually destroy the basis of that class's existence. New divisions within the revolutionary class may open up, but these may be of an entirely different kind from those which existed in the previous conflict situation.

6. The social institutions and culture of the subject class are geared to, and explicable in, terms of the class's interest in the conflict situation. So far as its long-term aims are concerned, these tend to be expressed in vague and Utopian forms. When the subject class comes to power its actual practices will still have to be worked out. But it is likely that they will be justified and even affected by the morality of conflict and by pre-revolutionary charters and Utopias.

7. A change in the balance of power might lead not to complete revolution, but to compromise and reform. In this case new institutions might arise which are not related simply to the prosecution of the conflict, but are recognized as legitimate by both sides. Such a truce situation might in favourable circumstances give rise to a new unitary social order over a long period, in which limited property rights and limited political power are regarded as legitimately held by particular individuals. But such situations are inherently unstable because any weakening of the countervailing power of the formerly subject class would lead the former ruling class to resume its old ways and the maintenance of this power could easily encourage the subject class to push right on to the revolutionary alternative.

These points would appear to provide a useful framework in terms of which many important contemporary social situations might be analysed.

The classification of basic conflict situations, the study of the emergence and structure of conflict groups, the problem of the legitimation of power, the study of the agencies of indoctrination and socialization, the problem of the ideological conflicts in post-revolutionary situations and in situations of compromise and truce, the study of the relations between norms and systems of power — all these have their place within it.

The model has been developed, of course, in relation to the study of total social systems and with special emphasis upon their overtly political aspects. But it is by no means without relevance to the design of research into problems of particular institutions and social segments. There are, as Dahrendorf[1] was right to point out, always conflicts or potential conflicts between those exercising authority and those over whom it is exercised whatever the institutional context, and wherever such conflicts occur the model suggested is relevant for at least a partial analysis of the problems of the institutions concerned. Sometimes it may serve to supplement the model of a stable system. On other occasions when the conflict is central to the life of the institution it may actually displace it entirely. . . .

NOTE

1. Ralf Dahrendorf, "Out of Utopia: Towards a Re-orientation of Sociological Analysis," *American Journal of Sociology,* 1958, Vol. 64, pp. 115-127.

Part II
POVERTY

At the beginning of the twentieth century sociologists were writing essays and books on "the social problem." At that time "the social problem" was poverty. All else – crime, divorce, family strife, war – were seen as a consequence of the fact that there was poverty. Although the fact of a large proportion of the population being impoverished did not change, the sociological perspective did. By the middle of the twentieth century (1950-1960) "poverty" was virtually ignored by social scientists and politicians. Then in the sixties it broke through again and we are, once more, looking systematically at poverty and building theories about it.

The studies of poverty in this section of the book are mainly descriptive; that is, they do not attempt to explain why there is poverty but rather they describe what poverty is like. Engels's article, which is the first in this section, deals in a way with the root causes of poverty, which he sees as residing in the economic structure of capitalist societies; in his view, it is to the benefit of those who control the means of production to have an impoverished class of cheap labor available.

The description by Elliott Liebow of life in a black ghetto provides an excellent description of an urban slum neighborhood. It also shows very nicely the important sociological point that one's day-to-day existence is determined by the structured opportunities for finding pleasure, employment, and companionship. The description of rural poverty in the Cumberland Plateau also gives us insight into the culture of poverty and points to the exploitation of land and people by coal, lumber, and political interests who for generations have combined to create a devastatingly and permanently poor population. The American Indians share many

41

similarities with the residents of the Cumberland Plateau, but their unique history and politically powerless role in contemporary America also create unique features in their poverty, and these features are captured well in the article by Stan Steiner on "Ghettos in the Desert."

THE CONDITION OF THE WORKING-CLASS

Frederick Engels

A town, such as London, where a man may wander for hours together without reaching the beginning of the end, without meeting the slightest hint which could lead to the inference that there is open country within reach, is a strange thing. This colossal centralisation, this heaping together of two and a half millions of human beings at one point, has multiplied the power of this two and a half millions a hundredfold; has raised London to the commercial capital of the world, created the giant docks and assembled the thousand vessels that continually cover the Thames. I know nothing more imposing than the view which the Thames offers during the ascent from the sea to London Bridge. The masses of buildings, the wharves on both sides, especially from Woolwich upwards, the countless ships along both shores, crowding ever closer and closer together, until, at last, only a narrow passage remains in the middle of the river, a passage through which hundreds of steamers shoot by one another; all this is so vast, so impressive, that a man cannot collect himself, but is lost in the marvel of England's greatness before he sets foot upon English soil.

But the sacrifices which all this has cost become apparent later. After roaming the streets of the capital a day or two, making headway with difficulty through the human turmoil and the endless lines of vehicles, after visiting the slums of the metropolis, one realises for the first time that these Londoners have been forced to sacrifice the best qualities of

Reprinted from "The Condition of the Working-Class in England," in *Karl Marx and Frederick Engels on Britain*, Chap. 5, Moscow: Foreign Languages Publishing House (1953).

their human nature, to bring to pass all the marvels of civilisation which crowd their city; that a hundred powers which slumbered within them have remained inactive, have been suppressed in order that a few might be developed more fully and multiply through union with those of others. The very turmoil of the streets has something repulsive, something against which human nature rebels. The hundreds of thousands of all classes and ranks crowding past each other, are they not all human beings with the same qualities and powers, and with the same interest in being happy? And have they not, in the end, to seek happiness in the same way, by the same means? And still they crowd by one another as though they had nothing in common, nothing to do with one another, and their only agreement is the tacit one, that each keep to his own side of the pavement, so as not to delay the opposing streams of the crowd, while it occurs to no man to honour another with so much as a glance. The brutal indifference, the unfeeling isolation of each in his private interest becomes the more repellant and offensive, the more these individuals are crowded together, within a limited space. And, however much one may be aware that this isolation of the individual, this narrow self-seeking is the fundamental principle of our society everywhere, it is nowhere so shamelessly bare-faced, so self-conscious as just here in the crowding of the great city. The dissolution of mankind into monads, of which each one has a separate principle and a separate purpose, the world of atoms, is here carried out to its utmost extreme.

Hence it comes, too, that the social war, the war of each against all, is here openly declared. Just as in Stirner's recent book, people regard each other only as useful objects; each exploits the other, and the end of it all is, that the stronger treads the weaker under foot, and that the powerful few, the capitalists, seize everything for themselves, while to the weak many, the poor, scarcely a bare existence remains.

What is true of London, is true of Manchester, Birmingham, Leeds, is true of all great towns. Everywhere barbarous indifference, hard egotism on one hand, and nameless misery on the other, everywhere social warfare, every man's house in a state of siege, everywhere reciprocal plundering under the protection of the law, and all so shameless, so openly avowed that one shrinks before the consequences of our social state as they manifest themselves here undisguised, and can only wonder that the whole crazy fabric still hangs together.

Since capital, the direct or indirect control of the means of subsistence and production, is the weapon with which this social warfare is carried on, it is clear that all the disadvantages of such a state must fall upon the poor. For him no man has the slightest concern. Cast into the whirlpool, he must struggle through as well as he can. If he is so happy as to find work *i.e.,* if the bourgeoisie does him the favour to enrich itself by means of him, wages await him which scarcely suffice to keep body and soul together; if he can get no work he may steal, if he is not afraid of the police, or starve, in which case the police will take care that he does so in a quiet and inoffensive manner. During my residence in England, at least twenty or thirty persons have died of simple starvation under the most revolting circumstances, and a jury has rarely been found possessed of the courage to speak the plain truth in the matter. Let the testimony of the witnesses be never so clear and unequivocal, the bourgeoisie, from which the jury is selected, always finds some backdoor through which to escape the frightful verdict, death from starvation. The bourgeoisie dare not speak the truth in these cases, for it would speak its own condemnation. But indirectly, far more than directly, many have died of starvation, where long continued want of proper nourishment has called forth fatal illness, when it has produced such debility that causes which might otherwise have remained inoperative, brought on severe illness and death. The English working-men call this "social murder," and accuse our whole society of perpetrating this crime perpetually. Are they wrong?

The manner in which the great multitude of the poor is treated by society to-day is revolting. They are drawn into the large cities where they breathe a poorer atmosphere than in the country; they are relegated to districts which, by reason of the method of construction, are worse ventilated than any others; they are deprived of all means of cleanliness, of water itself, since pipes are laid only when paid for, and the rivers so polluted that they are useless for such purposes; they are obliged to throw all offal and garbage, all dirty water, often all disgusting drainage and excrement into the streets, being without other means of disposing of them; they are thus compelled to infect the region of their own dwellings. Nor is this enough. All conceivable evils are heaped upon the heads of the poor. If the population of great cities is too dense in general, it is they in particular who are packed into the least space. As though the vitiated atmosphere of the streets were not enough, they are penned in dozens into single rooms, so that the air which they breathe at night is enough in itself to stifle them. They are given damp dwellings, cellar dens that are not waterproof from below, or garrets that leak from above. Their houses are so built that the clammy air cannot escape. They are supplied bad, tattered, or rotten clothing, adulterated and indigestible food. They are exposed to the most exciting changes of mental condition, the most violent vibrations between hope and fear; they are hunted like game, and not permitted to attain peace of mind and quiet enjoyment of life. They are deprived of all enjoyments except that of sexual indulgence and drunkenness, are worked every day to the point of complete exhaustion of their mental and physical energies, and are thus constantly spurred on to the maddest excess in the only two enjoyments at their command. And if they surmount all this, they fall victims to want of work in a crisis when all the little is taken from them that had hitherto been vouchsafed them.

Thus are the workers cast out and ignored by the class in power, morally as well as physically and mentally. The only provision made for them is the law, which fastens upon them when they become obnoxious to the bourgeoisie. Like the dullest of the brutes, they are treated to but one form of education, the whip, in the shape of force, not convincing but intimidating. There is, therefore, no cause for surprise if the workers, treated as brutes, actually become such; or if they can maintain their consciousness of manhood only by cherishing the most glowing hatred, the most unbroken inward rebellion against the bourgeoisie in power. They are men so long only as they burn with wrath against the reigning class. They become brutes the moment they bend in patience under the yoke, and merely strive to make life endurable while abandoning the effort to break the yoke.

And when all these conditions have engendered vast demoralisation among the workers, a new influence is added to the old, to spread this degradation more widely and carry it to the extremest point. This influence is the centralisation of the population. The writers of the English bourgeoisie are crying murder at the demoralising tendency of the great cities; like perverted Jeremiahs, they sing dirges, not over the destruction, but the growth of the cities. Sheriff Alison attributes almost everything, and Dr. Vaughan, author of "The Age of Great Cities," still more to this influence. And this is natural, for the propertied class has too direct an interest in the other conditions which tend to destroy the worker body and soul. If they should admit that "poverty, insecurity, overwork, forced work, are the chief ruinous influences," they would have to draw the conclusion, "then let us give the poor property, guarantee their subsistence, make laws against overwork," and this the bourgeoisie dare not formulate. But the great cities have grown up so spontaneously, the population has moved into them so wholly of its own motion, and the inference that manufacture and the middle-class which profits from it alone have created the cities is so remote, that it is extremely convenient for the ruling class to ascribe all the evil to this apparently unavoidable source; whereas the great cities really only secure a more rapid and certain development for evils already existing in the germ.

In view of all this, it is not surprising that the working-class has gradually become a race wholly apart from the English bourgeoisie. The bourgeoisie has more in common with every other nation of the earth than with the workers in whose midst it lives. The workers speak other dialects, have other thoughts and ideals, other customs and moral principles, a different religion and other politics than those of the bourgeoisie. Thus they are two radically dissimilar nations, as unlike as difference of race could make them. . . .

MEN AND JOBS
Elliott Liebow

A pickup truck drives slowly down the street. The truck stops as it comes abreast of a man sitting on a cast-iron porch and the white driver calls out, asking if the man wants a day's work. The man shakes his head and the truck moves on up the block, stopping again whenever idling men come within calling distance of the driver. At the Carry-out corner, five men debate the question briefly and shake their heads no to the truck. The truck turns the corner and repeats the same performance up the next street. In the distance, one can see one man, then another, climb into the back of the truck and sit down. In starts and stops, the truck finally disappears.

What is it we have witnessed here? A labor scavenger rebuffed by his would-be prey? Lazy, irresponsible men turning down an honest day's pay for an honest day's work? Or a more complex phenomenon marking the intersection of economic forces, social values and individual states of mind and body?

Let us look again at the driver of the truck. He has been able to recruit only two or three men from each twenty or fifty he contacts. To him, it is clear that the others simply do not choose to work. Singly or in groups, belly-empty or belly-full, sullen or gregarious, drunk or sober, they confirm what he has read, heard and knows from his own experience: these men wouldn't take a job if it were handed to them on a platter.[1]

Quite apart from the question of whether or not this is true of some of the men he sees on the street, it is clearly not true of all of them. If it were, he would not have come here in the first place; or having come, he would have left with an empty truck. It is not even true of most of them, for most of the men he sees on the street this weekday morning do, in fact, have jobs. But since, at the moment, they are neither working nor sleeping, and since they hate the depressing room or apartment they live in, or because there is nothing to do there,[2] or because they want to get away from their wives or anyone else living there, they are out on the street, indistinguishable from those who do not have jobs or do not want them. Some, like Boley, a member of a trash-collection crew in a suburban housing development, work Saturdays and are off on this weekday. Some, like Sweets, work nights cleaning up middle-class trash, dirt, dishes and garbage, and mopping the floors of the office buildings, hotels, restaurants, toilets and other public places dirtied during the day. Some men work for retail businesses such as liquor stores which do not begin the day until ten o'clock. Some laborers, like Tally, have already come back from the job because the ground was too wet for pick and shovel or because the weather was too cold for pouring concrete. Other employed men stayed off the job today for personal reasons: Clarence to go to a funeral at eleven this morning and Sea Cat to answer a subpoena as a witness in a criminal proceeding.

Also on the street, unwitting contributors to the impression taken away by the truck driver, are the halt and the lame. The man on the cast-iron steps strokes one gnarled arthritic hand with the other and says he doesn't know whether or not he'll live long enough to be eligible for Social Security. He pauses, then adds matter-of-factly, "Most times, I don't care whether I do or don't." Stoopy's left leg was polio-withered in childhood. Raymond, who looks as if he could tear out a fire hydrant, coughs up blood if he bends or moves suddenly. The quiet man who hangs out in front of the Saratoga apartments has a steel hook strapped onto his left elbow. And had the man in the truck been able to look into the wine-clouded eyes of the man in the green cap, he would have realized that the man did not even understand he was being offered a day's work.

Others, having had jobs and been laid off, are drawing unemployment compensation (up to $44 per week) and have nothing to gain by accepting work which pays little more than this and frequently less.

Still others, like Bumdoodle the numbers man, are working hard at illegal ways of making money, hustlers who are on the street to turn a dollar any way they can: buying and selling sex, liquor, narcotics, stolen goods, or anything else that turns up.

Only a handful remains unaccounted for. There is Tonk, who cannot bring himself to take a job away from the corner, because, according to the other men, he suspects his wife will be unfaithful if given the opportunity. There is Stanton, who has not reported to work for four days now, not since Bernice disappeared. He bought a brand new knife against her return. She had done this twice before, he said, but not for so long and not without warning, and he had forgiven her. But this time, "I ain't got it in me to forgive her again." His rage and shame are there for all to see as he paces the Carry-out and the corner, day and night, hoping to catch a glimpse of her.

And finally, there are those like Arthur, able-bodied men who have no visible means of support, legal or illegal, who neither have jobs nor want them. The truck driver, among others, believes the Arthurs to be representative of all the men he sees idling on the street during his own working hours. They are not, but they cannot be dismissed simply because they are a small minority. It is not enough to explain them away as being lazy or irresponsible or both because an able-bodied man with responsibilities who refuses work is, by the truck driver's definition, lazy and irresponsible. Such an answer begs the question. It is descriptive of the facts; it does not explain them.

Moreover, despite their small numbers, the don't-work-and-don't-want-to-work minority is especially significant because they represent the strongest and clearest expression of those values and attitudes associated with making a living which, to varying degrees, are found throughout the streetcorner world. These men differ from the others in degree rather than in kind, the principal difference being that they are carrying out the implications of their values and experiences to their logical, inevitable conclusions. In this sense, the others have yet to come to terms with themselves and the world they live in.

Putting aside, for the moment, what the men say and feel, and looking at what they actually do and the choices they make, getting a job, keeping a job, and doing well at it is clearly of low priority. Arthur will not take a job at all. Leroy is supposed to be on his job at 4:00 P.M. but it is already 4:10 and he still cannot bring himself to leave the free games he has accumulated on the pinball machine in the Carry-out. Tonk started a construction job on Wednesday, worked Thursday and Friday, then didn't go back again. On the same kind of job, Sea Cat quit in the second week. Sweets had been working three months as a busboy in a restaurant, then quit without notice, not sure himself why he did so. A real estate agent, saying he was more interested in getting the job done than in the cost, asked Richard to give him an estimate on repairing and painting the inside of a house, but Richard, after looking over the job, somehow never got around to submitting an estimate. During one period, Tonk would not leave the corner to take a job because his wife might prove unfaithful; Stanton would not take a job because his woman had been unfaithful.

Thus, the man-job relationship is a tenuous one. At any given moment, a job may occupy a relatively low position on the streetcorner scale of real values. Getting a job may be subordinated to relations with women or to other non-job considerations; the commitment to a job one already has is frequently shallow and tentative.

The reasons are many. Some are objective and reside principally in the job; some are subjective and reside principally in the man. The line between them, however, is not a clear one. Behind the man's refusal to take a job or his decision to quit one is not a simple impulse or value choice but a complex combination of assessments of objective reality on the one hand, and values, attitudes and beliefs drawn from different levels of his experience on the other.

Objective economic considerations are frequently a controlling factor in a man's refusal to take a job. How much the job pays is a crucial question but seldom asked. He knows how much it pays. Working as a stock clerk, a delivery boy, or even behind the counter of liquor stores, drug stores and other retail businesses pays one dollar an hour. So, too, do most busboy, car-wash, janitorial and other jobs available to him. Some jobs, such as dishwasher, may dip as low as eighty cents an hour and others, such as elevator operator or work in a junk yard, may offer $1.15 or $1.25. Take-home pay for jobs such as these ranges from $35 to $50 a week, but a take-home pay of over $45 for a five-day week is the exception rather than the rule.

One of the principal advantages of these kinds of jobs is that they offer fairly regular work. Most of them involve essential services and are therefore somewhat less responsive to business conditions than are some higher paying, less menial jobs. Most of them are also inside jobs not dependent on the weather, as are construction jobs and other higher-paying outside work.

Another seemingly important advantage of working in hotels, restaurants, office and apartment buildings and retail establishments is that they frequently offer an opportunity for stealing on the job. But stealing can be a two-edged sword. Apart from increasing the cost of goods or services to the general public, a less obvious result is that the practice usually acts as a depressant on the employee's own wage level. Owners of small retail establishments and other employers frequently anticipate employee stealing and adjust the wage rate accordingly. Tonk's employer explained why he was paying Tonk $35 for a 55-60 hour workweek. These men will all steal, he said. Although he keeps close watch on Tonk, he estimates that Tonk steals from $35 to $40 a week.[3] What he steals, when added to his regular earnings, brings his take-home pay to $70 or $75 per week. The employer said he did not mind this because Tonk is worth that much to the business. But if he were to pay Tonk outright the full value of his labor, Tonk would still be stealing $35-$40 per week and this, he said, the business simply would not support.

This wage arrangement, with stealing built-in, was satisfactory to both parties, with each one independently expressing his satisfaction. Such a wage-theft system, however, is not as balanced and equitable as it appears. Since the wage level rests on the premise that the employee will steal the unpaid value of his labor, the man who does not steal on the job is penalized. And furthermore, even if he does not steal, no one would believe him; the employer and others believe he steals because the system presumes it.

Nor is the man who steals, as he is expected to, as well off as he believes himself to be. The employer may occasionally close his eyes to the worker's stealing but not often and not for long. He is, after all, a businessman and cannot always find it within himself to let a man steal from him, even if the man is stealing his own wages. Moreover, it is only by keeping close watch on the worker that the employer can control how much is stolen and thereby protect himself against the employee's stealing more than he is worth. From this viewpoint, then, the employer is not in wage-theft collusion with the employee. In the case of Tonk, for instance, the employer was not actively abetting the theft. His estimate of how much Tonk was stealing was based on what he thought Tonk was able to steal despite his own best efforts to prevent him from stealing anything at all. Were he to have caught Tonk in the act of stealing, he would, of course, have fired him from the job and perhaps called the police as well. Thus, in an actual if not in a legal sense, all the elements of entrapment are present. The employer knowingly provides the conditions which entice (force) the employee to steal the unpaid value of his labor, but at the same time he punishes him for theft if he catches him doing so.

Other consequences of the wage-theft system are even more damaging to the employee. Let us, for argument's sake, say that Tonk is in no danger of entrapment; that his employer is willing to wink at the stealing and that Tonk, for his part, is perfectly willing to earn a little, steal a little. Let us say, too, that he is paid $35 a week and allowed to steal $35. His money income — as measured by the goods and services he can purchase with it — is, of course, $70. But not all of his income is available to him for all purposes. He cannot draw on what he steals to build his self-respect or to measure his self-worth. For this, he can draw only on his earnings — the amount given him publicly and voluntarily in exchange for his labor. His "respect" and "self-worth" income remains at $35 — only half that of the man who also receives $70 but all of it in the form of wages. His earnings publicly measure the worth of his labor to his employer, and they are important to others and to himself in taking the measure of his worth as a man.[4]

With or without stealing, and quite apart from any interior processes going on in the man who refuses such a job or quits it casually and without apparent reason, the objective fact is that menial jobs in retailing or in the service trades simply do not pay enough to support a man and his family. This is not to say that the worker is underpaid; this may or may not be true. Whether he is or not, the plain fact is that, in such a job, he cannot make a living. Nor can he take much comfort in the fact that these jobs tend to offer more regular, steadier work. If he cannot live on the $45 or $50 he makes in one week, the longer he works, the longer he cannot live on what he makes.[5]

Construction work, even for unskilled laborers, usually pays better, with the hourly rate ranging from $1.50 to $2.60 an hour.[6] Importantly, too, good references, a good driving record, a tenth grade (or any high school) education, previous experience, the ability to "bring police clearance with you" are not normally required of laborers as they frequently are for some of the jobs in retailing or in the service trades.

Construction work, however, has its own objective disadvantages. It is, first of all, seasonal work for the great bulk of the laborers, beginning early in the spring and tapering off as winter weather sets in.[7] And even during the season the work is frequently irregular. Early or late in the season, snow or temperatures too low for concrete frequently sends the laborers back home, and during late spring or summer, a heavy rain on Tuesday or Wednesday, leaving a lot of water and mud behind it, can mean a two or three day workweek for the pick-and-shovel men and other unskilled laborers.[8]

The elements are not the only hazard. As the project moves from one construction stage to another, laborers – usually without warning – are laid off, sometimes permanently or sometimes for weeks at a time. The more fortunate or the better workers are told periodically to "take a walk for two, three days."

Both getting the construction job and getting to it are also relatively more difficult than is the case for the menial jobs in retailing and the service trades. Job competition is always fierce. In the city, the large construction projects are unionized. One has to have ready cash to get into the union to become eligible to work on these projects and, being eligible, one has to find an opening. Unless one "knows somebody," say a foreman or a laborer who knows the day before that they are going to take on new men in the morning, this can be a difficult and disheartening search.

Many of the nonunion jobs are in suburban Maryland or Virginia. The newspaper ads say, "Report ready to work to the trailer at the intersection of Rte. II and Old Bridge Rd., Bunston, Virginia (or Maryland)," but this location may be ten, fifteen, or even twenty-five miles from the Carry-out. Public transportation would require two or more hours to get there, if it services the area at all. Without access to a car or to a car-pool arrangement, it is not worthwhile reading the ad. So the men do not. Jobs such as these are usually filled by word of mouth information, beginning with someone who knows someone or who is himself working there and looking for a paying rider. Furthermore, nonunion jobs in outlying areas tend to be smaller projects of relatively short duration and to pay somewhat less than scale.

Still another objective factor is the work itself. For some men, whether the job be digging, mixing mortar, pushing a wheelbarrow, unloading materials, carrying and placing steel rods for reinforcing concrete, or building or laying concrete forms, the work is simply too hard. Men such as Tally and Wee Tom can make such work look like child's play; some of the older work-hardened men, such as Budder and Stanton, can do it too, although not without showing unmistakable signs of strain and weariness at the end of the workday. But those who lack the robustness of a Tally or the time-inured immunity of a Budder must either forego jobs such as these or pay a heavy toll to keep them. For Leroy, in his early twenties, almost six feet tall but weighing under 140 pounds, it would be as difficult to push a loaded wheelbarrow, or to unload and stack 96-pound bags of cement all day long, as it would be for Stoopy with his withered leg.

Heavy, backbreaking labor of the kind that used to be regularly associated with bull gangs or concrete gangs is no longer characteristic of laboring jobs, especially those with the larger, well-equipped construction companies. Brute strength is still required from time to time, as on smaller jobs where it is not economical to bring in heavy equipment or where the small, undercapitalized contractor has none to bring in. In many cases, however, the conveyor belt has replaced the wheelbarrow or the Georgia buggy, mechanized forklifts have eliminated heavy, manual lifting, and a variety of digging machines have replaced the pick and shovel. The result is fewer jobs for unskilled laborers and, in many cases, a work speed-up for those who do have jobs. Machines now set the pace formerly set by men. Formerly, a laborer pushed a wheelbarrow of wet cement to a particular spot, dumped it, and returned for another load. Another laborer, in hip boots, pushed the wet concrete around with a shovel or a hoe, getting it roughly level in preparation for the skilled finishers. He had relatively small loads to contend with and had only to keep up with the men pushing the wheelbarrows. Now, the job for the man pushing the wheelbarrow is gone and the wet concrete comes rushing down a chute at the man in the hip boots who must "spread it quick or drown."

Men who have been running an elevator, washing dishes, or "pulling trash" cannot easily move into laboring jobs. They lack the basic skills for "unskilled" construction labor, familiarity with tools and materials, and tricks of the trade without which hard jobs are made harder. Previously unused or untrained muscles rebel in pain against the new and insistent demands made upon them, seriously compromising the man's performance and testing his willingness to see the job through.

A healthy, sturdy, active man of good intelligence requires from two to four weeks to break in on a construction job.[9] Even if he is willing somehow to bull his way through the first few weeks, it frequently happens that his foreman or the craftsman he services with materials and general assistance is not willing to wait that long for him to get into condition or to learn at a glance the difference in size between a rough

$2'' \times 8''$ and a finished $2'' \times 10''$. The foreman and the craftsman are themselves "under the gun" and cannot "carry" the man when other men, who are already used to the work and who know the tools and materials, are lined up to take the job.

Sea Cat was "healthy, sturdy, active and of good intelligence." When a judge gave him six weeks in which to pay his wife $200 in back child-support payments, he left his grocery-store job in order to take a higher-paying job as a laborer, arranged for him by a foreman friend. During the first week the weather was bad and he worked only Wednesday and Friday, cursing the elements all the while for cheating him out of the money he could have made. The second week, the weather was fair but he quit at the end of the fourth day, saying frankly that the work was too hard for him. He went back to his job at the grocery store and took a second job working nights as a dishwasher in a restaurant,[10] earning little if any more at the two jobs than he would have earned as a laborer, and keeping at both of them until he had paid off his debts.

Tonk did not last as long as Sea Cat. No one made any predictions when he got a job in a parking lot, but when the men on the corner learned he was to start on a road construction job, estimates of how long he would last ranged from one to three weeks. Wednesday was his first day. He spent that evening and night at home. He did the same on Thursday. He worked Friday and spent Friday evening and part of Saturday draped over the mailbox on the corner. Sunday afternoon, Tonk decided he was not going to report on the job the next morning. He explained that after working three days, he knew enough about the job to know that it was too hard for him. He knew he wouldn't be able to keep up and he'd just as soon quit now as get fired later.

Logan was a tall, two-hundred-pound man in his late twenties. His back used to hurt him only on the job, he said, but now he can't straighten up for increasingly longer periods of time. He said he had traced this to the awkward walk he was forced to adopt by the loaded wheelbarrows which pull him down into a half-stoop. He's going to quit, he said, as soon as he can find another job. If he can't find one real soon, he gusses he'll quit anyway. It's not worth it, having to walk bent over and leaning to one side.

Sometimes, the strain and effort is greater than the man is willing to admit, even to himself. In the early summer of 1963, Richard was rooming at Nancy's place. His wife and children were "in the country" (his grandmother's home in Carolina), waiting for him to save up enough money so that he could bring them back to Washington and start over again after a disastrous attempt to "make it" in Philadelphia. Richard had gotten a job with a fence company in Virginia. It paid $1.60 an hour. The first few evenings, when he came home from work, he looked ill from exhaustion and the heat. Stanton said Richard would have to quit, "he's too small [thin] for that kind of work." Richard said he was doing O.K. and would stick with the job.

At Nancy's one night, when Richard had been working about two weeks, Nancy and three or four others were sitting around talking, drinking, and listening to music. Someone asked Nancy when was Richard going to bring his wife and children up from the country. Nancy said she didn't know, but it probably depended on how long it would take him to save up enough money. She said she didn't think he could stay with the fence job much longer. This morning, she said, the man Richard rode to work with knocked on the door and Richard didn't answer. She looked in his room. Richard was still asleep. Nancy tried to shake him awake. "No more digging!" Richard cried out. "No more digging! I can't do no more God-damn digging!" When Nancy finally managed to wake him, he dressed quickly and went to work.

Richard stayed on the job two more weeks, then suddenly quit, ostensibly because his pay check was three dollars less than what he thought it should have been.

In summary of objective job considerations, then, the most important fact is that a man who is able and willing to work cannot earn enough money to support himself, his wife, and one or more children. A man's chances for working regularly are good only if he is willing to work for less than he can live on, and sometimes not even then. On some jobs, the wage rate is deceptively higher than on others, but the higher the wage rate, the more difficult it is to get the job, and the less the job security. Higher-paying construction work tends to be seasonal and, during the season, the amount of work available is highly sensitive to business and weather conditions and to the changing requirements of individual projects.[11] Moreover, high-paying construction jobs are frequently beyond the physical capacity of some of the men, and some of the low-paying jobs are scaled down even lower in accordance with the self-fulfilling assumption that the man will steal part of his wages on the job.[12]

Bernard assesses the objective job situation dispassionately over a cup of coffee, sometimes poking at the coffee with his spoon, sometimes staring at it as if, like a crystal ball, it holds tomorrow's secrets. He is twenty-seven years old. He and the woman with whom he lives have a baby son, and she has another child by another man. Bernard does odd jobs – mostly painting – but here it is the end of January, and his last job was with the Post Office during the Christmas mail rush. He would like postal work as a steady job, he says. It pays well (about $2.00 an hour) but he has twice failed the Post Office examination (he graduated from a Washington high school) and has given up the idea as an impractical one. He is supposed to see a man tonight about a job as a parking attendant for a large apartment house. The man told him to bring his birth certificate and driver's license, but his license was suspended because of a backlog of unpaid traffic fines. A friend promised to lend him some money this evening. If he gets it, he will pay the fines tomorrow morning and have his license reinstated. He hopes the man with the job will wait till tomorrow night.

A "security job" is what he really wants, he said. He would like to save up money for a taxicab. (But having twice failed the postal examination and having a bad driving record as well, it is highly doubtful that he could meet the qualifications or pass the written test.) That would be "a good life." He can always get a job in a restaurant or as a clerk in a drugstore but they don't pay enough, he said. He needs to take home at least $50 to $55 a week. He thinks he can get that much driving a truck somewhere . . . Sometimes he wishes he had stayed in the army . . . A security job, that's what he wants most of all, a real security job. . . .

When we look at what the men bring to the job rather than at what the job offers the men, it is essential to keep in mind that we are not looking at men who come to the job fresh, just out of school perhaps, and newly prepared to undertake the task of making a living, or from another job where they earned a living and are prepared to do the same on this job. Each man comes to the job with a long job history characterized by his not being able to support himself and his family. Each man carries this knowledge, born of his experience, with him. He comes to the job flat and stale, wearied by the sameness of it all, convinced of his own incompetence, terrified of responsibility – of being tested still again and found wanting. Possible exceptions are the younger men not yet, or just, married. They suspect all this but have yet to have it confirmed by repeated personal experience over time. But those who are or have been married know it well. It is the experience of the individual and the group; of their fathers and probably their sons. Convinced of their inadequacies, not only do they not seek out those few better-paying jobs which test their resources, but they actively avoid them, gravitating in a mass to the menial, routine jobs which offer no challenge — and therefore pose no threat — to the already diminished images they have of themselves.

Thus Richard does not follow through on the real estate agent's offer. He is afraid to do on his own — minor plastering, replacing broken windows, other minor repairs and painting — exactly what he had been doing for months on a piecework basis under someone else (and which provided him with a solid base from which to derive a cost estimate).

Richard once offered an important clue to what may have gone on in his mind when the job offer was made. We were in the Carry-out, at a time when he was looking for work. He was talking about the kind of jobs available to him.

> I graduated from high school [Baltimore] but I don't know anything. I'm dumb. Most of the time I don't even say I graduated, 'cause then somebody asks me a question and I can't answer it, and they think I was lying about graduating. . . . They graduated me but I didn't know anything. I had lousy grades but I guess they wanted to get rid of me.
>
> I was at Margaret's house the other night and her little sister asked me to help her with her homework. She showed me some fractions and I knew right away I couldn't do them. I was ashamed so I told her I had to go to the bathroom.

And so it must have been, surely, with the real estate agent's offer. Convinced that "I'm dumb . . . I don't know anything," he "knew right away" he couldn't do it, despite the fact that he had been doing just this sort of work all along.

Thus, the man's low self-esteem generates a fear of being tested and prevents him from accepting a job with responsibilities or, once on a job, from staying with it if responsibilities are thrust on him, even if the wages are commensurately higher. Richard refuses such a job, Leroy leaves one, and another man, given more responsibility and more pay, knows he will fail and proceeds to do so, proving he was right about himself all along. The self-fulfilling prophecy is everywhere at work. In a hallway, Stanton, Tonk and Boley are passing a bottle around. Stanton recalls the time he was in the service. Everything was fine until he attained the rank of corporal. He worried about everything he did then. Was he doing the right thing? Was he doing it well? When would they discover their mistake and take his stripes (and extra pay) away? When he finally lost his stripes, everything was all right again.

Lethargy, disinterest and general apathy on the job, so often reported by employers, has its street-corner counterpart. The men do not ordinarily talk about their jobs or ask one another about them.[13] Although most of the men know who is or is not working at any given time, they may or may not know what particular job an individual man has. There is no overt interest in job specifics as they relate to this or that person, in large part perhaps because the specifics are not especially relevant. To know that a man is working is to know approximately how much he makes and to know as much as one needs or wants to know about how he makes it. After all, how much difference does it make to know whether a man is pushing a mop and pulling trash in an apartment house, a restaurant, or an office building, or delivering groceries, drugs, or liquor, or, if he's a laborer, whether he's pushing a wheelbarrow, mixing mortar, or digging a hole. So much does one job look like every other that there is little to choose between them. In large part, the job market consists of a narrow range of nondescript chores calling for nondistinctive, undifferentiated, unskilled labor. "A job is a job."

A crucial factor in the streetcorner man's lack of job commitment is the overall value he places on the job. *For his part, the streetcorner man puts no lower value on the job than does the larger society around him.* He knows the social value of the job by the amount of money the employer is willing to pay him for doing it. In a real sense, every pay day, he counts in dollars and cents the value placed on the job by society at large. He is no more (and frequently less) ready to quit and look for another job than his employer is ready to fire him and look for another man. Neither the streetcorner man who performs these jobs nor the society which requires him to perform them assesses the job as one "worth doing and worth doing well." Both employee and employer are contemptuous of the job. The employee shows his contempt by his reluctance to accept it or keep it, the employer by paying less than is required to support a family.[14] Nor does the low-wage job offer prestige, respect, interesting work, opportunity for learning or advancement, or any other compensation. With few exceptions, jobs filled by the streetcorner men are at the bottom of the employment ladder in every respect, from wage level to prestige. Typically, they are hard, dirty, uninteresting and underpaid. The rest of society (whatever its ideal values regarding the dignity of labor) holds the job of the dishwasher or janitor or unskilled laborer in low esteem if not outright contempt.[15] So does the streetcorner man. He cannot do otherwise. He cannot draw from a job those social values which other people do not put into it.[16]

Only occasionally does spontaneous conversation touch on these matters directly. Talk about jobs is usually limited to isolated statements of intention, such as "I think I'll get me another gig [job]," "I'm going to look for a construction job when the weather breaks," or "I'm going to quit. I can't take no more of his shit." Job assessments typically consist of nothing more than a noncommittal shrug and "It's O.K." or "It's a job."

One reason for the relative absence of talk about one's job is, as suggested earlier, that the sameness of job experiences does not bear reiteration. Another and more important reason is the emptiness of the job experience itself. The man sees middle-class occupations as a primary source of prestige, pride and self-respect; his own job affords him none of these. To think about his job is to see himself as others see him, to remind him of just where he stands in this society.[17] And because society's criteria for placement are generally the same as his own, to talk about his job can trigger a flush of shame and a deep, almost physical ache to change places with someone, almost anyone, else.[18] The desire to be a person in his own right, to be noticed by the world he lives in, is shared by each of the men on the streetcorner. Whether they articulate this desire (as Tally does below) or not, one can see them position themselves to catch the attention of their fellows in much the same way as plants bend or stretch to catch the sunlight.[19]

Tally and I were in the Carry-out. It was summer, Tally's peak earning season as a cement finisher, a semiskilled job a cut or so above that of the unskilled laborer. His take-home pay during these weeks was well over a hundred dollars — "a lot of bread." But for Tally, who no longer had a family to support, bread was not enough.

"You know that boy came in last night? That Black Moozlem? That's what I ought to be doing. I ought to be in his place."

"What do you mean?"

"Dressed nice, going to [night] school, got a good job."

"He's no better off than you, Tally. You make more than he does."

"It's not the money. [Pause] It's position, I guess. He's got position. When he finish school he gonna be a supervisor. People respect him . . . Thinking about people with position and education gives me a feeling right here [pressing his fingers into the pit of his stomach]."

"You're educated, too. You have a skill, a trade. You're a cement finisher. You can make a building, pour a sidewalk."

"That's different. Look, can anybody do what you're doing? Can anybody just come up and do your job? Well, in one week I can teach you cement finishing. You won't be as good as me 'cause you won't have the experience but you'll be a cement finisher. That's what I mean. Anybody can do what I'm doing and that's what gives me this feeling. [Long pause] Suppose I like this girl. I go over to her house and I meet her father. He starts talking about what he done today. He talks about operating on somebody and sewing them up and about surgery. I know he's a doctor 'cause of the way he talks. Then she starts talking about what she did. Maybe she's a boss or a supervisor. Maybe she's a lawyer and her father says to me, 'And what do you do, Mr. Jackson?' [Pause] You remember at the courthouse, Lonny's trial? You and the lawyer was talking in the hall? You remember? I just stood there listening. I didn't say a word. You know why? 'Cause I didn't even know what you was talking about. That's happened to me a lot."

"Hell, you're nothing special. That happens to everybody. Nobody knows everything. One man is a doctor, so he talks about surgery. Another man is a teacher, so he talks about books. But doctors and teachers don't know anything about concrete. You're a cement finisher and that's your specialty."

"Maybe so, but when was the last time you saw anybody standing around talking about concrete?"

The streetcorner man wants to be a person in his own right, to be noticed, to be taken account of, but in this respect, as well as in meeting his money needs, his job fails him. The job and the man are even. The job fails the man and the man fails the job.

Furthermore, the man does not have any reasonable expectation that, however bad it is, his job will lead to better things. Menial jobs are not, by and large, the starting point of a track system which leads to even better jobs for those who are able and willing to do them. The busboy or dishwasher in a restaurant is not on a job track which, if negotiated skillfully, leads to chef or manager of the restaurant. The busboy or dishwasher who works hard becomes, simply, a hard-working busboy or dishwasher. Neither hard work nor perseverance can conceivably carry the janitor to a sit-down job in the office building he cleans up. And it is the apprentice who becomes the journeyman electrician, plumber, steam fitter or bricklayer, not the common unskilled Negro laborer.

Thus, the job is not a stepping stone to something better. It is a dead end. It promises to deliver no more tomorrow, next month or next year than it does today.

Delivering little, and promising no more, the job is "no big thing." The man appears to treat the job in a cavalier fashion, working and not working as the spirit moves him, as if all that matters is the immediate satisfaction of his present appetites, the surrender to present moods, and the indulgence of whims with no thought for the cost, the consequences, the future. To the middle-class observer, this behavior reflects a "present-time orientation" – an "inability to defer gratification." It is this "present-time" orientation – as against the "future orientation" of the middle-class person – that "explains" to the outsider why Leroy chooses to spend the day at the Carry-out rather than report to work; why Richard, who was paid Friday, was drunk Saturday and Sunday and penniless Monday; why Sweets quit his job today because the boss looked at him "funny" yesterday.

But from the inside looking out, what appears as a "present-time" orientation to the outside observer is, to the man experiencing it, as much a future orientation as that of his middle-class counterpart.[20] The difference between the two men lies not so much in their different orientations to time as in their different orientations to future time or, more specifically, to their different futures.[21]

The future orientation of the middle-class person presumes, among other things, a surplus of resources to be invested in the future and a belief that the future will be sufficiently stable both to justify his investment (money in a bank, time and effort in a job, investment of himself in marriage and family, etc.) and to permit the consumption of his investment at a time, place and manner of his own choosing and to his greater satisfaction. But the streetcorner man lives in a sea of want. He does not, as a rule, have a surplus of resources, either economic or psychological. Gratification of hunger and the desire for simple creature comforts cannot be long deferred. Neither can support for one's flagging self-esteem. Living on the edge of both economic and psychological subsistence, the streetcorner man is obliged to expend all his resources on maintaining himself from moment to moment.[22]

As for the future, the young streetcorner man has a fairly good picture of it. In Richard or Sea Cat or Arthur he can see himself in his middle twenties; he can look at Tally to see himself at thirty, at Wee Tom to see himself in his middle thirties, and at Budder and Stanton to see himself in his forties. It is a future in which everything is uncertain except the ultimate destruction of his hopes and the eventual realization of his fears. The most he can reasonably look forward to is that these things do not come too soon. Thus, when Richard squanders a week's pay in two days it is not because, like an animal or a child, he is "present-time oriented," unaware of or unconcerned with his future. He does so precisely because he is aware of the future and the hopelessness of it all.

Sometimes this kind of response appears as a conscious, explicit choice. Richard had had a violent argument with his wife. He said he was going to leave her and the children, that he had had enough of everything and could not take any more, and he chased her out of the house. His chest still heaving, he leaned back against the wall in the hallway of his basement apartment.

"I've been scuffling for five years," he said. "I've been scuffling for five years from morning till night. And my kids still don't have anything, my wife don't have anything, and I don't have anything.

"There," he said, gesturing down the hall to a bed, a sofa, a couple of chairs and a television set, all shabby, some broken. "There's everything I have and I'm having trouble holding onto that."

Leroy came in, presumably to petition Richard on behalf of Richard's wife, who was sitting outside on the steps, afraid to come in. Leroy started to say something but Richard cut him short.

"Look, Leroy, don't give me any of that action. You and me are entirely different people. Maybe I look like a boy and maybe I act like a boy sometimes but I got a man's mind. You and me don't want the same things out of life. Maybe some of the same, but you don't care how long you have to wait for yours and *I — want — mine — right — now.*"[23]

Thus, apparent present-time concerns with consumption and indulgences — material and emotional — reflect a future-time orientation. "I want mine right now" is ultimately a cry of despair, a direct response to the future as he sees it.[24]

In many instances, it is precisely the streetcorner man's orientation to the future — but to a future loaded with "trouble" — which not only leads to a greater emphasis on present concerns ("I want mine right now") but also contributes importantly to the instability of employment, family and friend relationships, and to the general transient quality of daily life.

Let me give some concrete examples. One day, after Tally had gotten paid, he gave me four twenty-dollar bills and asked me to keep them for him. Three days later he asked me for the money. I returned it and asked why he did not put his money in a bank. He said that the banks close at two o'clock. I argued that there were four or more banks within a two-block radius of where he was working at the time and that he could easily get to any one of them on his lunch hour." "No, man," he said, "you don't understand. They close at two o'clock and they closed Saturday and Sunday. Suppose I get into trouble and I got to make it [leave]. Me get out of town, and everything I got in the world layin' up in that bank? No good! No good!"

In another instance, Leroy and his girl friend were discussing "trouble." Leroy was trying to decide how best to go about getting his hands on some "long green" (a lot of money), and his girl friend cautioned him about "trouble." Leroy sneered at this, saying he had had "trouble" all his life and wasn't afraid of a little more. "Anyway," he said, "I'm famous for leaving town."[25]

Thus, the constant awareness of a future loaded with "trouble" results in a constant readiness to leave, to "make it," to "get out of town," and discourages the man from sinking roots into the world he lives in.[26] Just as it discourages him from putting money in the bank, so it discourages him from committing himself to a job, especially one whose payoff lies in the promise of future rewards rather than in the present. In the same way, it discourages him from deep and lasting commitments to family and friends or to any other persons, places or things, since such commitments could hold him hostage, limiting his freedom of movement and thereby compromising his security which lies in that freedom.

What lies behind the response to the driver of the pickup truck, then, is a complex combination of attitudes and assessments. The streetcorner man is under continuous assault by his job experiences and job fears. His experiences and fears feed on one another. The kind of job he can get — and frequently only after fighting for it, if then — steadily confirms his fears, depresses his self-confidence and self-esteem until finally, terrified of an opportunity even if one presents itself, he stands defeated by his experiences, his belief in his own self-worth destroyed and his fears a confirmed reality.

NOTES

1. By different methods, perhaps, some social scientists have also located the problem in the men themselves, in their unwillingness or

lack of desire to work: "To improve the underprivileged worker's
performance, one must help him to learn *to want* . . . higher social
goals for himself and his children . . . . The problem of changing the
work habits and motivation of [lower class] people . . . is a problem
of changing the goals, the ambitions, and the level of cultural and
occupational aspiration of the underprivileged worker." (Emphasis in
original.) Allison Davis, "The Motivation of the Underpriviliged
Worker," p. 90.

2. The comparison of sitting at home alone with being in jail is
commonplace.

3. Exactly the same estimate as the one made by Tonk himself. On the
basis of personal knowledge of the stealing routine employed by
Tonk, however, I suspect the actual amount is considerably smaller.

4. Some public credit may accrue to the clever thief but not respect.

5. It might be profitable to compare, as Howard S. Becker suggests,
gross aspects of income and housing costs in this particular area with
those reported by Herbert Gans for the low-income working class in
Boston's West End. In 1958, Gans reports, median income for the
West Enders was just under $70 a week, a level considerably higher
than that enjoyed by the people in the Carry-out neighborhood five
years later. Gans himself rented a six-room apartment in the West
End for $46 a month, about $10 more than the going rate for
long-time residents. In the Carry-out neighborhood, rooms that could
accommodate more than a cot and a miniature dresser – that is,
rooms that qualified for family living – rented for $12 to $22 a
week. Ignoring differences that really can't be ignored – the privacy
and self-contained efficiency of the multi-room apartment as against
the fragmented, public living of the rooming-house "apartment,"
with a public toilet on a floor always different from the one your
room is on (no matter, it probably doesn't work, anyway) – and
assuming comparable states of disrepair, the West Enders were paying
$6 or $7 a month for a room that cost the Carry-outers at least $50 a
month, and frequently more. Looking at housing costs as a
percentage of income – and again ignoring what cannot be ignored:
that what goes by the name of "housing" in the two areas is not at all
the same thing – the median income West Ender could get a six-room
apartment for about 12 percent of his income, while his 1963
Carry-out counterpart, with a weekly income of $60 (to choose a
figure from the upper end of the income range), often paid 20-33
percent of his income for one room. See Herbert J. Gans, *The Urban
Villagers*, pp. 10-13.

6. The higher amount is 1962 union scale for building laborers. According to the Wage Agreement Contract for Heavy Construction Laborers (Washington, D.C., and vicinity) covering the period from May 1, 1963 to April 30, 1966, minimum hourly wage for heavy construction laborers was to go from $2.75 (May 1963) by annual increments to $2.92, effective November 1, 1965.

7. "Open-sky" work, such as building overpasses, highways, etc., in which the workers and materials are directly exposed to the elements, traditionally begins in March and ends around Thanksgiving. The same is true for much of the street repair work and the laying of sewer, electric, gas, and telephone lines by the city and public utilities, all important employers of laborers. Between Thanksgiving and March, they retain only skeleton crews selected from their best, most reliable men.

8. In a recent year, the crime rate in Washington for the month of August jumped 18 percent over the preceding month. A veteran police officer explained the increase to David L. Bazelon, Chief Judge, U.S. Court of Appeals for the District of Columbia. "It's quite simple. . . . You see, August was a very wet month. . . . These people wait on the street corner each morning around 6:00 or 6:30 for a truck to pick them up and take them to a construction site. If it's raining, that truck doesn't come, and the men are going to be idle that day. If the bad weather keeps up for three days . . . we know we are going to have trouble on our hands – and sure enough, there invariably follows a rash of purse-snatchings, house-breakings and the like. . . . These people have to eat like the rest of us, you know." David L. Bazelon, Address to the Federal Bar Association, p. 3.

9. Estimate of Mr. Francis Greenfield, President of the International Hod Carriers, Building and Common Laborers' District Council of Washington, D.C., and Vicinity. I am indebted to Mr. Greenfield for several points in these paragraphs dealing with construction laborers.

10. Not a sinecure, even by streetcorner standards.

11. The overall result is that, in the long run, a Negro laborer's earnings are not substantially greater – and may be less – than those of the busboy, janitor, or stock clerk. Herman P. Miller, for example, reports that in 1960, 40 percent of all jobs held by Negro men were as laborer's or in the service trades. The average annual wage for nonwhite nonfarm laborers was $2,400. The average earning of nonwhite service workers was $2,500 (*Rich Man, Poor Man*, p. 90). Francis Greenfield estimates that in the Washington vicinity, the

1965 earnings of the union laborer who works whenever work is available will be about $3,200. Even this figure is high for the man on the streetcorner. Union men in heavy construction are the aristocrats of the laborers. Casual day labor and jobs with small firms in the building and construction trades, or with firms in other industries, pay considerably less.

12. For an excellent discussion of the self-fulfilling assumption (or prophecy) as a social force, see "The Self-Fulfilling Prophecy," Ch. XI, in Robert K. Merton's *Social Theory and Social Structure*.

13. This stands in dramatic contrast to the leisure-time conversation of stable, working-class men. For the coal miners (of Ashton, England), for example, "the topic [of conversation] which surpasses all others in frequency is work — the difficulties which have been encountered in the day's shift, the way in which a particular task was accomplished, and so on." Josephine Klein, *Samples from English Cultures*, Vol. I, p. 88.

14. It is important to remember that the employer is not entirely a free agent. Subject to the constraints of the larger society, he acts for the larger society as well as for himself. Child labor laws, safety and sanitation regulations, minimum wage scales in some employment areas, and other constraints, are already on the books; other control mechanisms, such as a guaranteed annual wage, are to be had for the voting.

15. See, for example, the U.S. Bureau of the Census, *Methodology and Scores of Socioeconomic Status*. The assignment of the lowest SES ratings to men who hold such jobs is not peculiar to our own society. A low SES rating for "the shoeshine boy or garbage man . . . seems to be true for all [industrial] countries." Alex Inkeles, "Industrial Man," p. 8.

16. That the streetcorner man downgrades manual labor should occasion no surprise. Merton points out that "the American stigmatization of manual labor . . . *has been found to hold rather uniformly in all social classes*" (emphasis in original; *Social Theory and Social Structure* p. 145). That he finds no satisfaction in such work should also occasion no surprise: "[There is] a clear positive correlation between the over-all status of occupations and the experience of satisfaction in them." Inkeles, "Industrial Man," p. 12.

17. "[In our society] a man's work is one of the things by which he is judged, and certainly one of the more significant things by which he judges himself. . . . A man's work is one of the more important parts

of his social identity, of his self; indeed, of his fate in the one life he has to live." Everett C. Hughes, *Men and Their Work*, pp. 42-43.

18. Noting that lower-class persons "are constantly exposed to evidence of their own irrelevance," Lee Rainwater spells out still another way in which the poor are poor: "The identity problems of lower class persons make the soul-searching of middle class adolescents and adults seem rather like a kind of conspicuous consumption of psychic riches" ("Work and Identity in the Lower Class," p. 3).

19. Sea Cat cuts his pants legs off at the calf and puts a fringe on the raggedy edges. Tonk breaks his "shades" and continues to wear the horn-rimmed frames minus the lenses. Richard cultivates a distinctive manner of speech. Lonny gives himself a birthday party. And so on.

20. Taking a somewhat different point of view, S.M. Miller and Frank Riessman suggest that "the entire concept of deferred gratification may be inappropriate to understanding the essence of workers' lives" ("The Working Class Subculture: A New View," p. 87).

21. This sentence is a paraphrase of a statement made by Marvin Cline at a 1965 colloquium at the Mental Health Study Center, National Institute of Mental Health.

22. And if, for the moment, he does sometimes have more money than he chooses to spend or more food than he wants to eat, he is pressed to spend the money and eat the food anyway since his friends, neighbors, kinsmen, or acquaintances will beg or borrow whatever surplus he has or, failing this, they may steal it. In one extreme case, one of the men admitted taking the last of a woman's surplus food allotment after she had explained that, with four children, she could not spare any food. The prospect that consumer soft goods not consumed by oneself will be consumed by someone else may be related to the way in which portable consumer durable goods, such as watches, radios, television sets or phonographs, are sometimes looked at as a form of savings. When Shirley was on welfare, she regularly took her television set out of pawn when she got her monthly check. Not so much to watch it, she explained, as to have something to fall back on when her money runs out toward the end of the month. For her and others, the television set or the phonograph is her savings, the pawnshop is where she banks her savings, and the pawn ticket is her bankbook.

23. This was no simple rationalization for irresponsibility. Richard had indeed "been scuffling for five years" trying to keep his family going. Until shortly after this episode, Richard was known and respected as

one of the hardest-working men on the street. Richard had said, only a couple of months earlier, "I figure you got to get out there and try. You got to try before you can get anything." His wife Shirley confirmed that he had always tried. "If things get tough, with me I'll get all worried. But Richard get worried, he don't want me to see him worried. . . . He *will* get out there. He's shoveled snow, picked beans, and he's done some of everything. . . . He's not ashamed to get out there and get us something to eat." At the time of the episode reported above, Leroy was just starting marriage and raising a family. He and Richard were not, as Richard thought, "entirely different people." Leroy had just not learned, by personal experience over time, what Richard had learned. But within two years Leroy's marriage had broken up and he was talking and acting like Richard. "He just let go completely," said one of the men on the street.

24. There is no mystically intrinsic connection between "present-time" orientation and lower-class persons. Whenever people of whatever class have been uncertain, skeptical or downright pessimistic about the future, "I want mine right now" has been one of the characteristic responses, although it is usually couched in more delicate terms: e.g., Omar Khayyam's "Take the cash and let the credit go," or Horace's *"Carpe diem."* In wartime, especially, all classes tend to slough off conventional restraints on sexual and other behavior (i.e., become less able or less willing to defer gratification). And when inflation threatens, darkening the fiscal future, persons who formerly husbanded their resources with commendable restraint almost stampede one another rushing to spend their money. Similarly, it seems that future-time orientation tends to collapse toward the present when persons are in pain or under stress. The point here is that, the label notwithstanding, (what passes for) present-time orientation appears to be a situation-specific phenomenon rather than a part of the standard psychic equipment of Cognitive Lower Class Man.

25. And proceeded to do just that the following year when "trouble" — in this case, a grand jury indictment, a pile of debts, and a violent separation from his wife and children — appeared again.

26. For a discussion of "trouble" as a focal concern of lower-class culture, see Walter Miller, "Lower Class Culture as a Generating Milieu of Gang Delinquency," pp. 7, 8.

EASTERN KENTUCKY: THE PERMANENT POOR

Harry M. Caudill

The Cumberland Plateau of Kentucky is one of the great natural resource regions of the American continent. Industrialists bought up its great wealth three quarters of a century ago and soon after 1900 commenced the large-scale extraction of its timber and minerals. When the development of the eastern Kentucky coalfields began, mining was largely a manual pursuit. Mining machines were displacing mules and ponies, and electricity was making it possible to do an increasing number of tasks with electric power rather than muscle power. Nevertheless, some of the undercutting of coal, much of the drilling, and practically all of the loading into cars were done by armies of grit-blackened miners. Industrial wages enticed thousands of mountaineers to turn from the plow and hoe to the pick and shovel. Hordes of Negroes were induced away from the cotton rows of Georgia, the Carolinas, Tennessee, Mississippi, and Alabama and forsook plantation life for the mines. Shiploads of Europeans were brought to the southern coalfield. The extraction of the region's mineral wealth was undertaken in the atmosphere of a tremendous industrial boom.

The Depression destroyed the coalfield's prosperity, but the Second World War revived it, and for a few years the boom returned and the miner was again a useful and honored citizen. The coal industry depended upon his skill and courage, and steel production, electric-power generation, and other basic industries were dependent upon coal. The collapse of the war and of the post-war boom is now history, and we have an opportunity to reflect upon the social, political, and economic consequences that result when a modernized industry is able to cast aside three quarters of its workmen within the span of a decade.

In the post-war years technologists were able to design and manufacture machines of remarkable power and efficiency. Their genius was nowhere better demonstrated than in the coal industry. Devices were developed for boring directly back into the face of the coal seam, and chewing out immense quantities of the mineral, thus eliminating the need

Reprinted by permission of the author and publisher from *The Atlantic Monthly*, June 1964, pp. 49-53. Copyright © 1964 by The Atlantic Monthly Company (Boston, Massachusetts).

to undercut or blast the seam. Simultaneously, the conveyor belt displaced the tracks, mining locomotives, and strings of cars in many mines. Roof bolting made its appearance. This method of supporting the roof eliminated the need for wooden props and proved most effective. A single mechanical loading machine could load more coal than two dozen hardworking shovelers.

Machines were costly, but investment capital was plentiful. The mine operators borrowed from the banks and mechanized and automated the mines and tipples to a remarkable degree. Big, amply financed operations bought up their small competitors. Many inefficient and nearly worked-out pits suspended operations altogether. Thus in a few years the fragmented and archaic coal industry became surprisingly modern and technologically advanced. The operators were delighted. Corporations that were bankrupt only a few years before now basked in a sustained new prosperity. For example, Consolidation Coal Company, which had been in receivership, paid off all its obligations and acquired a controlling interest in Chrysler Corporation.

While a new optimism pervaded the offices of the automated and mechanized companies, disaster befell thousands of the men who had depended for so long upon the old industry. By the thousands they found the scrip offices and payroll windows closed in their faces. Mining companies for which they and their fathers had worked, in some instances for two generations, simply vanished altogether. Some three fourths of eastern Kentucky's miners found themselves without work. They had become the victims of a materialistic social order which venerates efficiency and wealth above all other things and largely disregards social and human consequences. When they were no longer needed, their employers dropped them as a coal miner might have thrown away the scrip coins of a bankrupt company.

The legions of industrial outcasts were left with three choices. They could leave the area and find work elsewhere if employment of any kind could be found. Many thousands followed this course, and the population of the mining counties subsided dramatically. A third of the people fled from the shadow of starvation.

They could remain within the region and attempt to live by mining coal from the thin seams not monopolized by the big and highly efficient operations. These men could operate small "doghole" mines with little equipment and trifling capital, pitting their arms and backs against the tireless machines of their big competitors. They were goaded to desperation by the fact that in a camp house or a creek shanty a wife and five to ten children depended upon them for clothes and bread. They had been educated for the mines at a time when little formal education was required for that calling. Thus, in the contest with the big coal corporations they could contribute little except their muscles and their will. Thousands entered these small mines, often "gang-working" as partners and sharing the meager profits at paydays.

In the third situation was the miner who for one reason or another could not or would not leave the area, and found that however hard he toiled in the small mines his income was too meager to provide for the needs of his household. He and his family became charges of the government. Federal and state agencies came to his relief with a wide variety of cash and commodity doles. He was confined to a kind of dull, bleak reservation-existence reminiscent of that imposed by military fiat on the reservation Indians of the Western plains.

Living by welfare, without work and without purpose save existence, these numerous mountaineers settled down to while away the years and await developments.

The men who left the region for the great cities of the North and Middle West did not always find smooth sailing. The rapid process of industrial modernization which had first, and so dramatically, waved its wand across the eastern Kentucky coalfield had penetrated into the immense industrial complexes of the nation's cities. Assembly lines which had traditionally required hundreds of swarming workmen were reorganized, and wonderfully efficient machines were introduced into the automobile and other great manufacturing industries. In many instances, these machines were guided by sensitive electronic masters which, with belts of punched plastic and electric current, could impose unerring and immediate obedience.

In some respects, to be sure, eastern Kentucky is unique. Its people were dependent for fifty years on but a single industry, and, remarkably, they were an industrial people living in a rural rather than an urban setting. The coal industry, like extractive industries generally, invested little of its profits back in the region and allowed its communities to maintain schools of only the most rudimentary sort. It created an environment which left its workmen almost totally dependent upon their employers for bread and leadership, then provided only a small measure of the former and practically none of the latter. Nevertheless, the collapse of coal as a mass hirer of men left in the Kentucky mountains a splendid case study of the social and political implications arising from the displacement of men by machines.

Government at all levels was wholly unprepared for the dramatic developments that ensued. To be sure, these developments were a logical outgrowth of the continuing industrial revolution, which, once set in motion, appears to be destined to carry us inevitably toward a day when a few people and many machines will do the work for a leisurely population of consumers. But between the first spinning jenny and the distant utopia lie many pitfalls, some of which yawn before us today.

In short, government in our democratic society proved practically bankrupt of ideas when confronted with this new challenge. Hoping against hope that expansion in other industries would eventually absorb the displaced miners, government agencies waited. When the stranded miner had exhausted his unemployment insurance benefits and his savings, when he had come to the ragged edge of starvation and was cloaked in bewilderment and frustration, government came to his rescue with the dole. It arranged to give him a bag of cheese, rice, cornmeal, beef, butter, and dried milk solids at intervals, and in most instances to send him a small check. Having thus contrived to keep the miner and his family alive, the government lost interest in him. Appropriations were made from time to time for his sustenance, but little thought was given to his spirit, his character, his manhood. He was left to dry-rot in the vast paleface reservation created for his perpetuation in his native hills.

And, inevitably, he fell prey to the politicians who dispense the bread and money by which he lives. Coal mining and thirty years of subservience to the scrip window had already done much to impair the mountaineer's ability to adapt well to rapidly changing circumstances. He had dwelt too long as a kind of industrial serf in company-owned houses, on company-owned streets, in company-owned towns. For too long the company had buffered him from the swift-flowing social and economic tides swirling in the world outside his narrow valleys. When his employers cast him aside, he still possessed only a single valuable remnant of his birthright – the ballot. He was essential to the politicians because he could vote, so he was placed in a sort of suspended animation in which he came fully to life only at election time. He became increasingly dependent upon the political machines that ran his counties. He accepted the food doles and the welfare checks and ratified the arrangement by voting for the men and women who thus sustained him. The politicians expanded their operations into other fields where public funds could make the difference between life and death. In all too many counties they captured the school systems, thereby acquiring large new sums to be dispensed as patronage. The positions of schoolteacher, bus driver, lunchroom director, truant officer, and a multitude of others were treated as so many plums to be dispensed to the acquiescent, the obedient, and the meek. The union of school politics and welfare politics resulted in a formidable prodigy indeed. Its power was quickly recognized at Frankfort and Washington. New political pacts were made, and a wide range of state jobs were placed at the disposal of the local overloads. Thus their power became virtually complete.

Today in many eastern Kentucky counties political machines of remarkable efficiency are to be found. Their effectiveness surpasses Tammany Hall at its best. In a typical county the school board and state agencies control the biggest payrolls. The politicians who run them can also reach and influence the many small merchants, automobile dealers, and service-station operators with whom they do business. Thus they are masters of the majority of those who still work for a living.

The state and federal governments act as tax-collecting enterprises, which funnel vast sums into the hands of merciless and amoral local political dynasties. The county machines dispense the funds so as to perpetuate themselves and their allies at Frankfort and Washington. Increasingly, these omniscient organizations manage to gather into their hands funds and gifts from private charities, including even the American Red Cross. Taxpayers in fifty states, oblivious to what their dollars buy, pay little heed to this ominous course of events.

These developments raise a disquieting question which Americans have never confronted before:

How fares the American concept of government of the people, by the people, and for the people when a clear majority become permanently dependent upon and subservient to their elected leaders?

Indeed, can democratic government survive at all in such a setting?

The situation in eastern Kentucky is new to the American scene, but much of the pattern is as old as Rome.

In ancient Italy the social order was remarkably healthy so long as the populace consisted, in the main, of freeholding farmers and self-employed artisans and artificers. The scene darkened when Roman armies conquered distant territories and sent home multitudes of captives. The rich bought up the small plots of farmers and cultivated the resultant plantations with the labor of slaves. Other slaves were set to work in mass manufactories. Because of their great numbers, their carefully planned organization, and their specialization, they were able to produce far more cheaply than their self-employed, free competitors. The corporations that ran these huge enterprises provided grain, leather goods, cloth, and weapons for the empire. The free men and women flocked to the towns and cities to cluster in slums. To keep them orderly the government fed them, clothed them, and entertained them with games. An astoundingly complex system of doles and subsidies was perfected to sustain the idled millions of Roman citizens. In idleness the Roman decayed. He became bitter, vengeful, irresponsible, and bloodthirsty. The mutterings of Roman mobs came to speak more loudly than the voice of Caesar. Rome withered within, long before alien armies crashed through her walls.

These ancient events cast shadows of portent for us today. The machine is a far more profitable servant than any slave. It is untiring, wears out slowly, and requires no food or medication. Technological progress is inexorable and moves toward perfection. What will be the final consequences of it all for the American ideals of equality, liberty, and justice?

We are in the throes of a rapidly quickening new technological revolution. Fifty years ago 700,000 American coal miners were able to mine less coal than 140,000 dig today. Experts tell us that coal production may double by 1980 without any increase in the number of miners. Automobile production increases year by year, but the number of workmen declines. In every field of manufacturing, sensitive, accurate, unfailing steel monsters crowd men and women from workbench and turning lathe, from well and mine. On the land the number of farmers decreases as farms are consolidated into giant tracts. Tractors and mechanical cotton pickers and threshers have rendered the farm laborer as obsolete as the coal miner of 1945.

New turns of the technological wheel are in sight. In twenty years nuclear power may render all fossil fuels obsolete, valued only for their chemical derivatives. If this occurs, new legions of workmen will follow the coal miner into abrupt obsolescence.

On the material side, this revolution undoubtedly represents only progress. It brings us more and more goods for less and less work, thus bringing to fruition one of mankind's ancient dreams.

But what of man's social, spiritual, and political aspects? Is it possible we are moving rapidly forward on the one hand and going backward to barbarism on the other?

What is to become of the jobless miner who takes his family to a Chicago housing development, there to press in upon a onetime automobile assembler from Detroit and a discarded tool and die maker from Pittsburgh? What results when these men and their wives and children are joined by a Negro from Mississippi whose job as a cotton picker was taken over by a machine, or by a white hill-farmer from Tennessee whose ninety acres could not produce corn in competition with the splendidly mechanized farms of Iowa? Are the mushrooming housing developments of the great cities to become the habitations of millions of permanently idled people, supported by a welfare program as ruinous as the one devised by the Caesars? Are whole segements of American citizenry to be consigned to lifetimes of vexatious idleness, resentment, and bitterness? Are these centers to become vast new slums out of which will issue the ominous rumblings of titanic new mobs?

And what torrents of new bitterness will be added to the nation's bloodstream when computers send multitudes of white-collar workers into abrupt idleness in the mortgaged houses of suburbia?

In my opinion these questions pose the foremost issue of our time.

It strikes me that our scientists may develop the explosive power to send a few Americans to Mars while, simultaneously, our society prepares a vastly greater explosive power among disillusioned millions of Americans who remain behind on our own battered planet.

The industrialists who run the eastern Kentucky coalfield laid careful plans for the creation and use of mining machines but cast aside their mining men as lightheartedly as one might discard a banana peel. Most of the victims of this callous treatment accepted their fate resignedly. Some did not, however, and in the winter of 1962–1963 the hills in four eastern Kentucky counties resounded with gunfire and nocturnal explosions. For several months a situation bordering on anarchy prevailed across a wide region. Tipples and mines were blasted. Automobiles, power lines, and mining machines were destroyed. Such acts were committed by desperate men seeking to strike at a social and economic order which had rejected them.

Today the challenge of eastern Kentucky is a great national challenge. If we can triumph over it, the solutions we find will offer hope to the entire nation. Increasingly, the agony of eastern Kentucky is but a part of the misery that afflicts great cities, mill towns, and mining regions everwhere. The pain grows out of the evil paradox of mass idleness in the midst of booming production.

Liberty, like a chain, is no stronger than its weakest part. If the freedom and well-being of a part of the people are lost, the freedom and well-being of all are mortally imperiled. If the nation writes off our southern highlands as unworthy of rescue and rehabilitation, then the nation as a whole is unworthy of survival. As an optimist and a liberal I believe that the nation will rise to the challenge of the depressed and backward Appalachian region, and that in so doing, it will find many of the answers that democracy requires for survival throughout the nation.

A population equivalent to the present population of New York State is being added to the nation every four or five years. Technology eliminates some 40,000 jobs each week. These facts tell us that we must successfully master new frontiers of social justice, and do so in a hurry, or become another nation of regimented serfs.

A social and political crisis of the first magnitude will confront America before the end of another decade. Substitutes for such presently accepted goals as full employment will have to be found. Fresh definitions of the concepts of work, leisure, abundance, and scarcity are imperatively needed. Economic theories adequate to an infant industrial revolution are wholly unsatisfactory when applied to a full-fledged scientific revolution such as that which now engulfs us. The complexity and interdependence of the scientific-industrial nation call for national planning and action. Government must and will intervene more and more in the nation's industrial life. The destiny toward which we move is a national economy under the law. A radical change in public attitude toward law and government is necessary if the general welfare is to be achieved without the total sacrifice of individual liberty. Having bargained for the benefits of technology on all fronts, law is our only means of assuring that it serves the common good.

In 1963 the American economy brought unprecedented prosperity to some 80 percent of the people. Simultaneously, a segment of the population as numerous as the inhabitants of Poland consisted of paupers, and 5.5 percent of the nation's bread-winners were without jobs. Clearly a new tack must be taken soon unless America the Beautiful is to become a crazy quilt of bustle and sloth, brilliance and ignorance, magnificence and squalor.

For more than a dozen years the prevailing political ideology has implemented a *de facto* return to the Articles of Confederation. This doctrine holds that action at the state or local level is admirable while any direct effort by Washington to deal with social or economic malaise is un-American and dangerous. The result is a growing paralysis of the national government as an instrumentality of the public will. This reasoning has brought tremendous outpouring of federal grants-in-aid to states and communities, under circumstances which entail much waste and, often, minimal benefits.

In eastern Kentucky, and in many other depressed areas, the state government will not act effectively to combat poverty and economic decline because it is allied to or controlled by the interests that produced the problems. Thus, state officials talk piously about reform but strenuously oppose any real effort to attack the status quo. They respond to the politcal machines nurtured by welfare grants and founded on impoverished and dependent citizens. It is not too much to expect that, as matters now stand, federal funds trickling through state treasuries will finance the rebuilding of new political machines in practically every state — machines more odious than those once bossed by Crump, Pendergast, and Hague.

Common sense and past experience argue strongly for a system of federally administered public works. Only in America are able-bodied men permitted to loaf in idleness amid a profusion of unperformed tasks. Should not the thousands of jobless Kentucky coal miners be set to work reforesting the wasted hills, building decent consolidated schoolhouses and roads, and providing decent housing in lieu of the dreadful shacks that now dot every creek and hollow? And why not a modernized version of TVA — a Southern Mountain Authority — to develop the immense hydro- and thermal-power potential of the Appalachian South for the benefit of the entire nation, and to stop the hideous waste of the land now being wrought by the strip- and auger-mining industries? What of the possibility of an educational Peace Corps to break the old cycle of poor schools, poor job preparation, poor pay, and poor people?

Unless the nation can profit from the terrible lesson eastern Kentucky so poignantly teaches, new multitudes of once prosperous Americans may find themselves slipping inexorably into an economic mire that breeds poverty, despair, dependency, and, eventually, revolution.

GHETTOS IN THE DESERT: THE AMERICAN INDIAN
Stan Steiner

Where the old U.S. 66 winds and unwinds through the lava beds, west of Albuquerque, N.M., a hitch-hiker flagged my car. He was a young man from the Pueblo de Acoma: "The City in the Sky." And as we drove through the black-rock country that spreads out from the highway we got to talking about how little work there was thereabouts and how hard it was to farm such land.

"How do you earn a living?" I asked.

"Living?" he smiled. "I just live."

He got out a crossroads to nowhere, laughingly waved goodby, and walked off toward the Pueblo de Acoma, some twenty miles away.

Surveying unemployment figures among Indians in the winter of 1962-63, the House Committee on Interior and Insular Affairs found that at the Pueblo de Acoma, of 1,380 adults between the ages of eighteen and fifty-five years, 197 were then working. The unemployment rate: 89.6%. Cash income of these Pueblo Indians for the previous year was estimated at $500 to $1,000 *per family*. In answer to the question, how many of residents had "completed an apprenticeship or other training program" during that past year, the reply was a terse "None." Jerry P. Garcia, Governor of Pueblo de Acoma, when asked "How is the morale of the Indian people?" said merely, "They want employment."

Similarly, the United Pueblo Agency of the Bureau of Indian Affairs found that of 13,711 adults on eighteen New Mexican pueblos, 3,212 were employed; half of these temporarily. Unemployment rate: 77%. Income of these tranquil and ancient people, believed to be among the oldest inhabitants of the country, was said to average from $750 to $1,000 yearly per family. The Hopis, too, whose idyllic reputation as the "Peaceful People" has won for their legends the status of a perennial Christmas Book, reported a somewhat less than idyllic unemployment rate of 71.7%.

To the north, on the Blackfeet reservation of Montana, the House committee uncovered a "permanent unemployment" rate of 72.5% with approximately 1,500 of the 2,000 Blackfeet jobless. The yearly income: "less than $500 per family."

From *The Nation*, June 22, 1964, pp. 624-627. Reprinted by permission.

On the plains of the Dakotas, the Sioux reservations reported: the Pine Ridge Sioux had 1,225 of 3,400 tribal adults employed (yearly income per family: $105), the Sisseton Sioux had 543 of 835 employed (income, $600), the Rosebud Sioux had 1,276 of 2,996 employed (income: $1,000) and the Standing Rock reservation listed 380 of 880 "heads of households" as employed (income: $190). Down in Mississippi, on the Choctaw reservation, 170 of the 1,225 adults had jobs. Unemployment rate: 86.1%.

The Navajos, the most populous of American Indian tribes, numbering upward of 96,000, fared not much better. Of 33,734 Navajos in the labor force of Arizona, 23,331 were listed, in August, 1963, as unemployed. The Indian Bureau was reluctant even to estimate the "median annual cash income," fearing it was too low to be "meaningful." If this economic quagmire had engulfed the Dinch, "The People," as the Navajos proudly call themselves, it had no less bogged down their linguistic cousins, the Apaches. The San Carlos and Fort Apache reservations reported that 2,170 of 3,390 Apaches — 61% — were out of work.

The "oil millionaires" offered statistics as dismal. In the mythology of the oil-rich Indians, so credulously celebrated in after-dinner jokes and romantic tales, none are supposedly wealthier than the Creek, Cherokee, Chickasaw, Choctaw and Seminole. But when the House Indian Unemployment Survey investigated some 19,000 adults in these Five Civilized Tribes, approximately 10,000 were listed as jobless. The annual income per family — including the fabled oil lease and royalty disbursements — came to $1,200.

Each year in Washington there is a ceremonial wringing of hands over "The Indian Problem." It took place this year in the East Room of the White House, where tribal leaders presented President Johnson with an appeal from the National Congress of Indians that stated: "Unemployment is our major concern. Almost one-half of the employable American Indians are without jobs. On some reservations three-fourths are unemployed. Indian reservations are indeed pockets of poverty."

Unemployment among the Indians is thus *ten times* the national average. Their family incomes, though reports are frequently inconclusive and difficult to verify, are generally estimated to be from one-third to one-fifth of the national average. Indian poverty is so widepread and so intense that it tends to fall outside national calculations on the problem. Perhaps this partially explains why studies such as the Conference on Economic Progress report, *"Poverty and Deprivation in the U.S.,"* do not as a rule delve into it. Chronic unemployment of the majority of a people that is not due to technological change, nor to depressed areas in the economy, appear to be beyond measure, or remedy, by methods that are applied elsewhere. Especially is this so on the reservations, where poverty, as the Sioux Chief, Standing Bear, had said, is but one of the conditions that have "dehumanized" his people.

"Statistics permit us to walk untouched through the world of extremely low-income groups, uneducated children, substandard housing, disease and hopelessness," wrote Congressman George F. Senner, Jr., (D., Ariz.) in *The Navajo Times* this winter. But the conditions of the nearly 400,000 Indians – of an estimated 600,000 – who live on the neglected reservations cannot be ignored. "We cannot avoid the truth," Senner wrote, "no matter how impersonally it may be presented."

It has been calculated, for example, that 90% of the Indians live in substandard housing. But substandard, when applied to the reservation Indian, is actually a euphemism for a rural slum of shacks and one-room huts. The wikiups of grass, logs and canvas of the Apaches, the earth and log hogans of the Navajos, the sod igloos of the Eskimos and the adobes of the Pueblo Indians may house legends of enchantment, but the living conditions of the occupants are less than enchanting to Public Health Service doctors.

Dr. Carruth J. Wagner, Chief of the Division of Indian Health, of the PHS, has testified that "The burden of disease is heavy [among Indians] and much of it is associated with the hazards and rigors of the environment in which these Indian beneficiaries live. . . . The one-room structure is occupied by an average of four or five people. This serious overcrowding promotes the transmission of disease."

He reported that the average "death age" of an Indian is forty-two years (thirty years for the Alaskan native and about thirty-one years for the Arizona Indians), compared to an average of sixty-two years for the general population.

The death rate of Indian babies is three times higher (for Alaskan natives six times higher) than the national average. Of 1,000 Indian babies born alive, forty-three die before their first birthday, Dr. Wagner said, and "many [of these deaths are] associated with the home environment." Moreover, infant mortality accounts for 21% of all Indian deaths, compared to 6% for the general population.

Speaking of specific disease rates, Dr. Wagner estimated the incidence of tuberculosis to be seven times higher among Indians (fifteen times higher among Alaskan natives). Tuberculosis death rates are four times higher among Indians (seven times higher among Alaskan natives). And the death rate from infectious diseases such as dysentery, gastroenteritis, influenza and pneumonia averages from two to five times higher than those of the rest of the population.

These disease and death rates continue despite the expanded Public Health Service care and treatment of the past few years. Dr. Wagner indicated his dismay, as have others in the field, that unalleviated poverty, subsistence diets and chronic unemployment frustrate the efforts of government and tribal health officials. "Nutritional deficiencies are associated with many of the illnesses and diseases," the Indian Health chief said; "Malnutrition of babies results in long periods of hospitalization and premature, unnecessary death."

Approaching another aspect of the problem, the Public Health Service studied sanitation conditions among 42,506 Indians in eleven states. "The unsafe water supply is a very common cause of many of the diseases," the survey found. More than 81.6% of the Indians haul their drinking water, many from "distances of a mile or more," and from "irrigation ditches and ponds." "Potentially contaminated water" sources supplied more than 77% of this water. On several reservations the entire water supply was condemned. "Many families have to get along on one to three gallons of water a day, when the poorest non-Indian rural family has double and triple this amount." And of the Indians surveyed, 78.1% were found to "use unsatisfactory excreta disposal facilities."

Confronted with this appalling bill of particulars, the late Congressman Iljalmar C. Nygaard (R., N.D.) blandly said: "I hope some day these problems can be solved."

Indian education is the one field where government officials and tribal councils have reached some agreement. Educators in the Bureau of Indian Affairs point with pride to figures showing that, in 1963, 88.4% of all Indian children between the ages of six and eighteen years were enrolled in schools. More than half of these were in local public schools. Even allowing for the discrepancy between statistics and facts in reservation school enrollments, it does seem that the educational situation has been substantially improved since World War II, and especially in the past few years.

Within this aura of rising hopes, however, it should be noted that 3.7% of Indian children are dismissed as "unknown." In Oklahoma these "unknown" children total 20.7% and on the Montana reservations they total 14.1%.

Even more serious, as it reflects the relationship between Indian poverty and education, is the discrepancy between elementary-school enrollment and that of the vocational and high schools, where job training is to be had. In these later years the dropout rate is estimated to be 60%!

The chairman of the Navajo Tribe, Raymond Nakai, has emphasized the concern of the Indian leaders, not only because of the rudimentary education offered Indian children, but because training in job skills is so often aborted by the dead-end economics of reservation life. "However high the quality of vocational training," Nakai has said, "it will only aggravate the worker's frustration if the vocation for which he has been trained is barred to him because of his present economic and reservation condition." Or, he added, because "racial discrimination stands in his path."

Still others, like Martin Vigil of Tesuque Pueblo, head of the All Pueblo Council of New Mexico, are skeptical of the congratulations the Indian educators award themselves. "There are thousands of Indian children who have no school." Vigil has said: "The level of Indian education is the fifth grade, while that of the white man's is the tenth grade. It that right? Is this getting the Indian ready for the space age?"

In a comprehensive study of "the Indian problem," Ralph Nader, editor of *The Harvard Law Record*, offered this rather bleak view: "Notwithstanding the improvements in Indian education, the school day is often extraordinarily short, the quality of teaching is inferior and there are still many children not enrolled." In spite of the "gradual improvements," to which it paid judicious tribute, *The Harvard Law Record*, in 1956, editorially commented that the "American Indians are by far the worst-fed, worst-clad and worst-housed group in the United States. These people, recipients of the poorest educational and medical services in the country, are in a state of social and psychological maladjustment. This is a situation of which the American public is only dimly aware."

The American Indian "may be technically free," Attorney General Robert F. Kennedy told the convention of the National Congress of American Indians at Bismarck, N.D., last summer, "but he is the victim of social and economic oppressions that hold him in bondage. He is all too likely to become the victim of his own proud anger, his own frustrations, and – most humiliating of all – the victim of racial discrimination in his own land."

"Will the injustice go on?" the Attorney General rhetorically asked his Indian audience.

Kennedy's reply was hopeful. "I believe there are signs of a change," he said, "clear signs of a turning of the tide." There had been in fact "signs" of something new in the approach to Indian needs ever since the late President Kennedy established a Special Task Force early in his administration. The Task Force, in 1961, set forth three major goals for the Indians: maximum economic self-sufficiency, full participation in American life and equal privileges and responsibilities of citizenship. The then newly appointed Commissioner of Indian Affairs, Philleo Nash, hailed these goals as "an important shift in program emphasis."

Somewhat reserved Oliver La Farge endorsed this hopeful prognosis, but suggested that "major changes must be taken *now*." Last year, just before his death, La Farge returned to this theme and – feeling that "On the positive side there is little that is striking" by way of "major changes" – said that the situation called for "the vigor and determination of Paul Bunyan, and his ox Babe, yes, and Bunyan's goad and his axe."

The impatience here voiced, and expressed with still greater force by tribal leadership, none the less recognized a change of approach. La Farge himself wrote of the possibility of "bold new advances." What buoyed these hopes was not merely the Task Force's report. It was also the reaction to Commissioner Nash's stated belief that henceforth the economic development of the reservation Indian "of course is a job which will have to be accomplished by the Indians themselves. If the plans are worth the paper they are written on they must be basically *Indian* plans, reflecting Indian thinking." Similar was the statement of Attorney General Kennedy that the new Administration's "firm policy has been to consult with tribal groups and work with them in determining every phase of federal action in their behalf – in marked contrast to the long-standing custom of the past, when the wishes of the tribal organizations were all too often ignored."

Traditionally the non-Indian, whether in government or business, has sought to make the Indian over in the white man's image. When this could not be done through the "policy of extermination" of "the War Camp" (*The New York Times*, July 7, 1876), it has been attempted through the humane persuasions of paternalism. But since that too provided ineffective, legal means have been found – as for example, the reservation "Termination Acts" of the Eisenhower administration.

Equally traditionally, the Indian has viewed these policies with little enthusiasm. Reluctant to give up his beliefs, or his way of life, in spite of the "fight, coax or run" programs of the nineteenth-century Bureau of Indian Affairs, he has been treated as incorrigible, and relegated to social oblivion.

The Indian's poverty was not a social accident, nor a historical aberration. It was the inevitable result of policy. The friend of the Indian, or the dedicated public servant, discovered that whatever he accomplished to improve the condition of the Indians in one field was too often nullified by a decline in another. The plight of the Indian was endemic to his economic and social status.

"We cannot expect good health and the desire for education if there is poor housing, unemployment and dire poverty," said Robert Burnette, a Rosebud Sioux and director of the National Congress of American Indians. "So we believe all of these things go hand in hand." Walter Wetzel, Chief of the Blackfeet, has said: "We must seek a new policy." And this new policy, if it is to succeed must, in the opinion of many tribal councils, deal with fundamental problems in a comprehensive way and from an Indian point of view. The Kiowa, Amos Hopkins-Dukes, who heads the Tribal Indian Land Rights Association, speaks for the younger leaders when he says: "If the U.S. is to grow and improve its Indian policy, the U.S. will have to be willing to let the American Indians grow also – as Indian people."

Another Indian leader recently startled officials by suggesting that if Indian poverty was really in the forefront of the "War on Poverty," then a government loan of at least $200 million to the tribes, for industrial and resource development – by the tribes – might be a "good start." But, he added, the tribes would have to be free to use such funds "as they see fit." This was a practical application of Robert Burnette's sardonic comment: "The government must allow the Indians to make a few of their own mistakes."

The variety of present-day approaches to "the Indian problem" is in itself encouraging. The Tribal Indian Land Rights Association has evolved a plan to apply the original provisions of the Allotment Act of 1887, not to break up the reservations, but to enable non-reservation Indians to claim federal lands which, it contends, are theirs by legal right. Suits based on treaty rights have long concerned the Indian Rights Association and similar groups. "Indian Health Year" has been proclaimed by the Association on American Indian Affairs, in cooperation with the Public

Health Service. And the Bureau of Indian Affairs is concentrating on the Area Redevelopment Act, the "Youth Job Training Corps," educational expansion and the Public Housing Act.

The most immediately pertinent programs, however, are those aimed at expanding industries that might employ Indians. The Association of American Indian Affairs has been singularly, if modestly, successful in its campaign to relocate small industries on or near reservations. The Bureua of Indian Affairs, for its part, has brought nineteen new plants into Indian population areas since 1961; they are said to provide more than 1,000 jobs.

Federal work projects, as urged by the National Congress of American Indians, have proved to be another job source. Under an accelerated program, projects begun on some eighty-eight reservations employ a fluctuating Indian labor force of 2,700 to 5,700. However, these APW projects are of a service character: improvements of roads, soil conservation, reforestry, building of community centers, etc. They are more likely to offer temporary and emergency employment than to assure long-term economic opportunity.

Unfortunately, between the many programs and their fulfillment, there is what might be called a "capital gap." Commissioner Nash had noted: "A common characteristic of underdeveloped communities, on reservations and off, at home and abroad, is lack of capital." In the Indian communities the "gap" is increased by the reluctance of private industry to invest plants and equipment in areas often far from markets and where available labor is poorly trained and untested. Furthermore, non-Indian interests have a historic itch for Indian lands and resources, which even now are mostly leased to non-Indians. Hoping for direct ownership, such interests have ever been willing to drive the reservation Indians to the economic wall. Private and public capital has thus been doled out sparingly. "And the reservations are starved for both kinds," Nash has said.

In the face of this economic and industrial backwardness, a development program that might have meaningful results would appear to require goals substantially larger than any we have yet projected. A few years ago, Oliver La Farge suggested that a program of federal loans and aid for reservation self-help might take the form of an American Indian Point Four Program — with a budget at least as large as those extended to underdeveloped countries overseas. More recently, a somewhat scaled-down version — "Operation Bootstrap" — has been proposed.

Since the government has from 1787 on, and before the present Administration came into office, appropriated more than $2.25 billion for its less than successful Indian programs, an investment of Point Four dimensions is not wholly unreasonable.

A moral obligation to the Indians is implicit in all these considerations. But leaving morality quite aside, there is the consideration of the relentless cost to the nation incurred by failure to lift the bondage of perpetual poverty from these proud, intensely patriotic and undefeatable people.

Part III
MILITARISM AND WAR

Organized military conflict between nations has become so much a part of the present-day world that one can scarcely count the instances of such violent confrontations. As this is being written the Vietnam War is entering its eleventh year, and despite official optimism that America will soon withdraw from groundfighting, there is no indication whatsoever that the war will soon end. We are certainly close to the situation described by George Orwell in his classic novel *1984*, in which there is a permanent war in some obscure part of the world that seems to have gone on forever with no beginning and no end. Portugal, with military and economic aid principally from the United States and West Germany through NATO, has had over 100,000 men fighting in Angola since 1961, in Guinea since 1963, and in Mozambique since 1964 in an effort to retain the last of the Western world's colonies in Africa. Only a short time ago Bangladesh fought a short and violent war against Pakistan before achieving independence. Northern Ireland is in one of its periodic violent conflicts that bring forth the use of military and police force from England. Uganda was the scene of considerable violence in the wake of a recent military coup. In Chad and Ethiopia civil war is raging as well. The Middle East, with the sporadic but continual conflict between Israel and the Arab countries, is at this hour peaceful, but no one has any hope that it will remain so for long.

War is a part of the ideological and economic fabric of Western societies and is therefore not seen as a social problem by those who control the decision-making institutions. William Appleman Williams's analysis of America's entry into World War II points up the interrelationship between the economic structure of capitalism and the role of war in solving the periodic crises experienced by capitalist economies. Noam Chomsky analyzes the tone and tenor of international conflicts since World War II and points out how the prevailing perspective on communism was an essential ingredient in the involvement of the United States in Vietnam. In these two articles can be seen, then, the importance of both economic and ideological forces working to create a constant state of war in the modern world.

AMERICA'S ENTRANCE INTO WORLD WAR II

William A. Williams

America's increasing opposition to Germany and Italy [prior to World War II] began not with the attacks on Czechoslovakia or Poland, but in connection with basic Axis economic policy (such as barter agreements in place of open marketplace transactions) as early as 1933, and in response to German penetration of Latin-American economic affairs during that decade. Germany's increasing resort to force to extend the sway of such ideas and policies, and others including racial persecution, carried the economic and ideological conflict into the military arena before Japan's attack on Pearl Harbor. From the very beginning, moreover, American leaders openly acknowledged that the tension with Japan was created by the decision to uphold and enforce the principles of the Open Door Policy in China and southeastern Asia in the face of Japanese expansion.

Antagonism toward the Soviet Union involved the same issues in an even more central and unqualified manner. This struggle, which had begun in 1917 and 1918, involved an outright rejection by the Soviets of the cardinal principles of the capitalist marketplace. The United States never fully reconciled itself to this withdrawal by Russia from the capitalist world. In the more narrow and explicit sense, this opposition manifested itself at the end of World War II in an openly proclaimed American determination to preserve and institutionalize the principles of the Open Door Policy in northeastern Asia and in eastern Europe. The Soviet

Union's avowed willingness to negotiate particular and more limited rights for the capitalist world in those regions was never explored in any serious, sustained manner. The United States defined the choice as lying between an acceptance of the principles of the Open Door Policy or a condition of opposition and antagonism.

None of this means (in any of the three instances) that the United States entered upon war simply to make money. Certain freedoms and liberties are essential to capitalists and capitalism, even though capitalists and capitalism are not essential to freedom and liberty. There is no discrepancy, therefore, in going to war for a free marketplace and going to war to defend, secure, and even extend the particular freedoms and liberties associated with such a marketplace political economy. But if either war had been fought solely for those freedoms and liberties, then the condition of the underdeveloped part of the world would have been quite different as early as 1920. And its circumstances would have changed much more rapidly, and with considerably less violence against the advanced Metropolitan countries, after the victory in 1945.

Hence none of these actions involved either a series of terrible conspiracies or a kind of narrow, crude economic motivation or determinism on the part of American leaders or their constituency. All parties had a sincere and practical commitment to the kind of freedom inherent in the Open Door Policy per se, and in the informal empire constructed by the United States between 1898 and 1950. The issue is not how bad or evil Americans were, but rather the far more profound and human theme of their tragic inability to realize their desire for peace and freedom so long as they declined to modify seriously the principles of possessive individualism that lie at the heart of capitalism.

As far as America's informal empire itself is concerned, the case of Cuba serves perfectly – if horribly – to illustrate the validity of Marx's analysis. Or, for that matter, the accuracy of Adam Smith's argument. To Marx's axiom about who takes more labor from whom, add his principle that "violent eruptions are naturally more likely to occur in the extremities of the bourgeois organism than in its heart," and top it off with his conclusion that the ideals of the capitalist fight a generally losing battle with the economic axioms of the system. The result is a definition of, and a set of major insights into, the principal features of Cuban-American relations from 1895 to the present. Marx was not primarily concerned to predict when the convulsion would occur, or who would ride its first wave. He was engaged in explaining what would happen, and why it would occur, if the Metropolis continued to act on the principles of the marketplace in its relationships with a colonial or otherwise dependent society. The origins and evolution of the Cuban Revolution, and the nature and course of its confrontation with the United States, verify the central themes of his analysis.

The Cuban missile crisis of 1962 offers an international example of Marx's fundamental argument that a change in the forces of production ultimately causes a change in the relations of production. In the confrontations of war and cold war, of course, the means of production are ultimately defined in military terms. During the years that the United States enjoyed a monopoly or a significant advantage in nuclear weapons, from 1945 to 1955, it unilaterally established and in large measure maintained the ground rules for international relations in the atomic age.

There were exceptions, particularly in China, that provided clear warnings that this vast preponderance of productive power did not provide the United States with an ability to control every situation. The policy was based on a far too narrow, and even typically marketplace, definition of power. It provided an excellent illustration of the way in which the mind concerned with commodities discounts the significance of people. The instruments of power were confused with the sources of power.

The signs indicating the dangers in this outlook were largely ignored until the Russians developed the same productive forces and the same instruments of power. Even then, however, the evidence continued to be generally discounted for a considerable period. Americans continued to make a fetish of producing the commodity of the atom and hydrogen bombs, arguing quite irrationally that the power to kill everybody twice or thrice gave them more security than only being able to do so once. The situation took on the characteristics of a macabre extension of the national attitude toward buying multiple automobiles. Thorstein Veblen might have discussed the phenomenon under the heading of the urge to conspicuous annihilation.

Then came the Cuban Revolution. It was an example of the impotence of nuclear supremacy that could not be evaded or rationalized away. American control of the island had been too obvious for too long a time, and the absurdity of vaporizing the revolution in order to save trade and investments was so evident as to be humorous despite the frustration. Americans sensed, when they did not realize it more explicitly, that the revolution was the product of their own administrative colonialism and informal empire. Even the Pavlovian exercises in explaining it as the work of a communist conspiracy were feeble and generally unimpressive examples of casuistry.

The first direct attempt to destroy the revolution employed the strategy of using conventional weapons inside what was thought to be the womb of safety provided by nuclear predominance. But the strength of the revolution foiled that American effort to combine superficial morality and rhetorical righteousness with secret malice. The subsequent nuclear showdown with the Russians was a direct consequence of that unsuccessful effort to square the circle. Cuban leaders became convinced that the United States would try again with vastly greater forces. This may not have been true, but they declined to risk their revolution on the word of an American administration that had already acted differently than it had talked.

On the surface, it is true, the productive forces of the United States emerged triumphant in the resulting confrontation with the Soviet Union. "The other fellow blinked," as the story goes. But as Secretary of State Dean Rusk later acknowledged, the United States for the first time caught a glimpse of the true nature of nuclear reality. The Soviets withdrew their missiles, but the United States gradually realized that it, the world's greatest Metropolis, had become a colony. A colony, that is to say, of the vast forces of production that it had created and put on the marketplace.

For in a profound sense, the increasing recognition of the necessity of co-existence that dates from the Cuban missile crisis stands as proof of Marx's central thesis that the productive forces will ultimately determine the relations of production. No single entrepreneur can impose his will on the economic marketplace if he is blocked by an element of comparable strength, save at a price so dear as to be self-destructive. Neither can one superpower impose its will upon the international nuclear marketplace if it is matched by another superpower, save at the cost of the very influence it is seeking to enlarge. There is considerable evidence, moreover, that one of the main reasons Soviet leaders placed their weapons in Cuba was to dramatize this truth to the United States.

It is conceivable that, despite that encounter, the United States will continue trying to prove Marx wrong by sustaining the essential structure and attitudes of the Cold War. That approach reveals a powerful inherent propensity to devolve into nuclear war. It is a dynamism that is not effectively checked, let alone redirected, by mere changes in the rhetoric or the means employed in connection with the existing policy. Even if the policy somehow avoided nuclear war, America would not really have proved that Marx was wrong. Another decade of cold war, even more sophisticated and more gentlemanly cold war, would destroy capitalism in any meaningful — let alone American — sense. The result would be a form of non-violent, totalitarian state managerialism that would make C. Wright Mills's power elite look like the founding fathers of Jacksonian Democracy.

AT WAR WITH ASIA
Noam Chomsky

I

The overriding goal of American policy has been to construct a system of societies that are open to free economic intervention by private enterprise (which in many ways is publicly subsidized). The goal was formulated clearly by George Ball, who "urged a greater unification of the world economy to give full play to the benefits of multinational corporations," which are "a distinctly American development." "Through such corporations," he observed, "it has become possible for the first time to use the world's resources with maximum efficiency" — for the benefit of whom, he does not reveal.[1] It is hardly surprising that the world-dominant power should oppose the resort to state controls by its weaker neighbors or that it should speak of "economic liberalism" and the benefits of unifying the world economy. Nor is it surprising that others see the matter rather differently. Thus a Tanzanian planner comments:

> A country whose industrial development depends on foreign invest-ments cannot adequately control its own destiny. It might succeed in attaining a successful take-off, but its economy might be likened to an unmanned aircraft whose course and safety are maintained by remote controls. It is a flying economy with no pilot aboard. The foreign investors who control it from a distance might decide to do anything with it.[2]

Words that might be spoken as well in South Korea, Canada, even England, and many other countries today.

That such subservience creates and perpetuates unbalanced development and severe underdevelopment has been demonstrated in many studies.[3] Such effects do not pass unnoticed within the imperialist powers themselves. The study *The Political Economy of American Foreign Policy* refers to some of the effects of economic liberalism on the underdeveloped countries with this comment:

> However, as the example of the United States suggests, this is probably not the way their resources would have been used had these countries been fully independent and had local enterprise existed capable of managing its own development. [p. 29]

And Alfred Marshall, for one, observes: "The brilliant genius and national enthusiasm of List stand in contrast to the insular narrowness and self-confidence of the Ricardian school ... [for] ... he showed that in Germany and still more in America, many of its indirect effects [free trade, in the early nineteenth century] were evils ... "[4] But by and large, the dominant world powers easily manage to construct a self-image of benevolence and rationality, the United States not excepted.

The unification of the world economy by American-based multinational corporations poses a threat to national sovereignty, but more significantly, to the possibility for social progress within even the more powerful societies. The problem is, quite naturally, of deep concern to organized labor. The head of one of Great Britain's largest unions, Hugh Scanlon, has recently discussed "the power of international corporations to hamstring and browbeat the interests of organized labour." He cites *Fortune* magazine on the scale of these institutions:

> The hard financial core of capitalism is composed of not more than 60 firms, partnerships or corporations, owned or controlled by 1000 men ... In fact recent forecasts claim that in 25 years 200 multinational firms will completely dominate production and trade and account for over 75 per cent of the total corporate assets of the capitalist world.[5]

The scale of these institutions is such, he writes, that they can "obtain an overwhelming bargaining power with any government." Furthermore, their power and ability to transfer operations from one country to another can be used as a weapon against labor — as an example he cites the recent Ford strike, when the threat to transfer operations from England to Belgium was used in exactly this way. Evidently, only an international labor organization (with, as Scanlon emphasizes, "real grass roots on the shop floor") could begin to deal with this threat, which surely is severe.

In the less developed societies other means are employed to prevent balanced independent development. The imperial powers have consistently exploited and exacerbated ethnic rivalries and hostilities, and have tried to develop native elites that would control the local population while enriching themselves through their relations with the imperial power. Josue de Castro observes that "productive forces [are] strangled by the domination of alienated [i.e., Western-educated] elites, whose interests do not coincide with those of the disinherited masses."[6] The goal of the imperial power is to create a class of bureaucrats and a colonial bourgeoisie that will collaborate in the administration and exploitation of the country. As Keith Buchanan points out, citing de Castro's remark, "Such elite groups today constitute one of the heaviest millstones around the necks of some of the emerging Southeast Asian peoples." Nominal political independence may have little or no effect on the underdevelopment caused by colonial dependence. Buchanan observes:

> In this prolongation of dependent and "underdeveloped" status the new elites, the colonial bourgeoisie created by the European restructuring of colonial societies, play an essential role; this, as we have seen, is a group which profited by, still profits by, the exploitation of the colonial peoples — their fellow-countrymen. This group, which now controls effective-political power in Southeast Asia, has neither the vision nor, for obvious reasons, the desire to strike out and create, through the medium of planned societies based on a humanistic socialism, a fuller and more autonomous life for their people; only in Cambodia is there a dedicated attempt to follow this path. [No more — N.C.] And since these countries are now an area on which the conflict between the West and the Soviet Bloc is projected, the whole military establishment of the West, and its associated economic, cultural and political mechanisms, is used to buttress the elite groups who rule them. These groups are kept in power as a barrier against the changes the creation of a decent society would involve, against the changes we for some reason fear, and the aid we give is used too often to create a Potemkin-facade of prestige development (Bangkok or Kuala Lumpur offer classic examples of this) behind which the stagnation of whole areas continues.[7]

The social and economic effects of such tendencies in Southeast Asia are reviewed in a recent paper by two Yale University economists.[8] Surveying the situation in the Philippines, Thailand, Malaya, and Singapore, they note

> the persistence of virtual stagnation in the hinterland, in which the majority of the people live, in contrast to the rapid growth of the metropoli: Bangkok, Manila, and Kuala Lumpur. Widening inequality is also visible within the metropoli in the form of industrial dualism: an organized and heavily protected manufacturing sector coexists with a large crafts sector where most of the urban people are employed or where there exists disguised unemployment.

Despite political independence, there is "increased dependency on the goods and the technology of the West." Many of the recently developed consumer-goods industries are, furthermore, subsidiaries of multinational corporations. Economic policies favor consumer goods for the privileged, while a pool of cheap labor provides services for the middle and upper classes. While the countryside stagnates, the overcrowded cities decay behind the facade of wealth. A recent United Nations report notes that "the conjunction of rapid population growth . . . with widespread unemployment and family poverty has led to a further precipitous decline in urban living conditions, which in many large Asian cities have reached a stage of depression and disorder that practically defies description."[9] To cite one illustrative example, in Bangkok, a superficially affluent metropolis of three million, most people have no sanitation facilities, while color television is now available throughout the country. Bangkok, Bell and Resnick comment, "has become less and less a part of Thailand and more a part of the West." Of course the process has been accelerated by the American use of Bangkok as a rest-and-recreation center for the Vietnam war, and Thailand in general as a sanctuary for the attack on the countries of Indochina. The corruption of Bangkok is, in fact, immediately evident even to the casual visitor. Furthermore, "about half of the increase of the gross domestic product from 1965 to 1967 was attributable to military spending by the U.S. within Thailand, which has only further lopsided the pattern of development," and, incidentally, led to considerable fears among the Thai elite concerning the future, in the event of an American de-escalation of the war.[10]

Needless to say, this subservience to foreign interests breeds corruption on a vast scale. To cite just one example, the previously cited review of "The Korean Question" by an anti-Communist Korean journalist living in Japan[11] maintains that the present Park administration has earned the worst reputation of any Korean government with regard to political corruption and injustice. Kim claims that "a foreign credit of $10 million shrinks to $6 million before it becomes available for its intended purpose: 20 per cent of the original amount goes to political funds and another 20 per cent disappears in bribes for government officials from low-echelon clerks up to ministers." The same observations hold for other less developed Asian countries that remain within the "integrated world system" of modern capitalism.

The vested interest in American imperialism that is developing in such countries as Japan, South Korea, Thailand, and Singapore is also a potentially dangerous feature of modern American imperialism in Southeast Asia. American power modifies the social and economic structure of countries that become partners in its Asian wars, and consequently threatens true independence in complex ways. Even the aid program has this effect. In 1967, Michael Leifer wrote: "The urban elite [of Cambodia] – accustomed to a high standard of living sustained by American aid – is now finding it difficult to adjust to economic austerity" caused by the termination of this program in 1963 on Sihanouk's initiative.[12] Similarly, the termination of American military assistance led to disaffection among the military. This disaffection of the military and the urban elite was a contributing factor to the coup of March 18, 1970, which toppled Sihanouk and plunged Cambodia into a civil war, and the Indochina war. (See the comments by Keith Buchanan cited above, pages 19–20, and Chapter 3, below.)

The American crusade against Communism is in part an effort to prevent independent economic development, but, as Joan Robinson also noted, it functions in other ways as well. It provides the psychological climate in which a continuing public subsidy can be provided to technologically advanced sectors of American industry for "maintenance of a huge war machine." Only a population that fears for its survival can be induced to consent to this subsidy, which has become a central factor in the American postwar economy. This, indeed, was the primary economic lesson of World War II. New Deal measures had smoothed many of the rough edges of the great depression, but had not succeeded in bringing it to an end. The depression was overcome by wartime government spending, and this lesson was not lost on those who own and manage the economy. Business historian Alfred Chandler describes the economic lessons of World War II as follows:

> The government spent far more than the most enthusiastic New Dealer had ever proposed. Most of the output of the expenditures was destroyed or left on the battlefields of Europe and Asia. But the resulting increased demand sent the nation into a period of prosperity the like of which had never before been seen. Moreover, the supplying of huge armies and navies fighting the most massive war of all time required a tight, centralized control of the national economy. This effort brought corporate managers to Washington to carry out one of the most complex pieces of economic planning in history. That experience lessened the ideological fears over the government's role in stabilizing the economy.

The ensuing Cold War, the crusade against Communism, carried further the depoliticization of American society and created the psychological climate in which the government is able to intervene, in part through fiscal policies, public works, and public services, but very largely through war spending, to preserve "economic health." The government acts as "a coordinator of last resort" when "managers are unable to maintain a high level of aggregate demand."[13] Charles E. Wilson, president of General Motors, was undoubtedly motivated in part by a sense of economic realism when he proposed a "permanent war economy" in 1944.[14] As another business historian writes, enlightened corporate managers, far from fearing government intervention in the economy, view "the New Economics as a technique for increasing corporate viability."[15] And the primary technique of intervention is, quite naturally, war spending. Indeed, it is not easy, with the best will, to imagine other forms of government-induced production that will not harm but will rather enhance the interests and power of the private empires that control the economy, that are endlessly expandable, and that will, at the same time, be tolerated by the mass of the population, which has to foot the bill.

The managers of the publicly subsidized war industries are pleasingly frank about the matter. Bernard Nossiter has published a remarkable series of articles in which he reports a number of interviews with representatives of this system of militarized state capitalism. Samuel F. Downer, financial vice-president of the LTV Aerospace Corporation, explained in the following words why "the post-war [i.e., post-Vietnam war] world must be bolstered with military orders":

It's basic. Its selling appeal is defense of the home. This is one of the greatest appeals the politicians have to adjusting the system. If you're the President and you need a control factor in the economy, and you need to sell this factor, you can't sell Harlem and Watts but you can sell self-preservation, a new environment. We're going to increase defense budgets as long as those bastards in Russia are ahead of us. The American people understand this.[16]

Of course, those bastards aren't exactly ahead of us in this deadly and cynical game, but that is only a minor embarrassment to the thesis. In times of need, it is always possible to call upon Dean Rusk, Hubert Humphrey, and other luminaries to warn of the billion Chinese, armed to the teeth and setting out on world conquest.

Many commentators have noted the dependence of the American economy on Third World resources, particularly nonferrous metals, as one factor in explaining the American crusade against independent national development.[17] These resources are required, to a large extent, for war production. Harry Magdoff notes that "three quarters of the imported materials included in the stockpile program come from the under-developed areas." He illustrates this dependence by an analysis of critical materials needed for jet engines. The strategic character of the materials is a factor, along with general considerations of profitability and control, in making the American government wary of trusting to trade relations with independent nations to acquire its needed raw materials.

Military power is needed to control the empire. The empire is seen as a necessity to guarantee military power. Militarization of the economy is a primary factor in maintaining "economic health." The threat of war, the constant "danger" of domestic insurgency in many parts of the world, helps maintain the appropriate psychological climate of psychosis and conformism. Such mutually supporting factors create a system that is highly resistant to change, despite its irrationality and the costs it imposes on the citizenry (almost 70 per cent of taxes now are used to pay for past, present, and future wars), not to speak of the threat to continued survival.

The role of the Cold War in this system as a technique of domestic control should not be overlooked. Of course, Russian imperialism is not an invention of American ideologists. It is real enough, as the Hungarians and Czechs can testify. What is an invention is the uses to which it was put, for example, by Dean Acheson in 1950[18] or Walt Rostow a decade later, when they pretended that the Vietnam war was an example of Russian imperialism; or by the Johnson administration in 1965 when it justified the Dominican intervention with reference to the "Sino-Soviet military bloc"; or by "an entire generation of leaders" who, as Townsend Hoopes puts it, were "conditioned by the tensions of the Cold War years" and thus could not perceive that the triumph of the national revolution in Vietnam would not be "a triumph for Moscow and Peking"[19] — a most remarkable blindness on the part of literate men; or by Eugene Rostow, who, in a recent book that was widely praised by American liberals,[20] outlined the series of challenges to world order in the modern era: Napoleon, Kaiser Wilhelm, Hitler — and continuing in the postwar world (among others), general strikes in France and Italy, the civil war in Greece,[21] and the attack on South Vietnam where, he writes, *Russia* "has put us to severe tests" in its efforts to spread Communism by the sword.

One can continue indefinitely. I mean to suggest that the Cold War is highly functional for the American elite as well as for its Soviet counterpart, who, in a similar way, sends its armies into Czechoslovakia to ward off Western imperialism. It serves to provide an ideology for empire and to mobilize support for the government-subsidized system of military state capitalism. It is predictable, then, that opportunities to end the Cold War will be side-stepped, and that challenges to Cold War ideology will be bitterly resisted.

In many ways, American society is indeed open and liberal values are preserved. However, as the poor and the black know well, the liberal veneer can be thin. Mark Twain once wrote: "It is by the goodness of God that in our country we have those three unspeakably precious things: freedom of speech, freedom of conscience, and the prudence never to practice either of them."[22] Those who lack the prudence may well pay the cost.

A crucial element of the evolving postwar system is the increasing centralization of control in the economy and political life of the postwar world. A recent report by the staff of the Federal Trade Commission notes: "By the end of 1968, the 200 largest industrial corporations controlled over 60 per cent of the total assets held by all manufacturing corporations." In 1941, the same amount of power was spread over a thousand corporations. The report notes further that the top two hundred corporations are partially linked with one another and with other corporations in ways that may prevent or discourage independent behavior in market decisions.[23] These corporations are, furthermore, increasingly becoming international in the scope of their operations.

At the same time, in every parliamentary democracy, the role of parliament in policy formation is diminishing. The House Armed Services Committee described the role of Congress as "that of a sometimes querulous but essentially kindly uncle who complains while furiously puffing on his pipe but who finally, as everyone expects, gives in and hands over the allowance."[24] Careful studies of civil-military decisions show that this is an accurate perception. Harold Stein, Professor at the Woodrow Wilson School of Princeton University, writes that since World War II

> the basic determination of foreign-military policy, of military expenditures and organization, and of weapons has been made by civilians in the Executive Branch, usually with the President in active control. Congress has exercised an occasionally restraining but never a guiding hand.[25]

Senator Arthur Vandenberg, twenty years ago, expressed his fear that the American Chief Executive would become "the number one war lord of the earth."[26] That has since occurred. The clearest example, perhaps, was President Johnson's decision to escalate the war in Vietnam in February 1965, in cynical disregard of the expressed will of the electorate.[27] The recent invasion of Cambodia is a further step in this erosion of parliamentary power, so blatant that it has finally called forth significant gestures of senatorial opposition. These incidents reveal with perfect clarity the role of the public, acting through the parliamentary system, in decisions about peace and war.

Furthermore, these processes of centralization of control in economic and political life are closely related, by virtue of the interpenetration of the executive branch of the government and the corporate elite. Richard Barnet cites his study of the men "who have set the framework of America's national-security policy." Most of the top four hundred decision makers, he writes, "have come from executive suites and law offices within shouting distance of one another in fifteen city blocks in New York, Washington, Detroit, Chicago, and Boston."[28]

In general, democratic decision-making in a capitalist democracy is severely limited by the very fact that the commercial, financial, and industrial systems — the central institutions of the society — are in law and in principle excluded from public control or participation, except in the indirect ways in which any system of authority, no matter how autocratic, must be responsive to the public will. The tendencies toward concentration of power just noted, and now commonly discussed, further underscore the fundamental incompatibility of democracy and capitalism, particularly in its modern centralized form. The reliance of this system on production for war with the ideological mobilization of the population that is required, the paranoid fears that must be induced if the system is to be viable, simply indicates the severity of the current American crisis – a world crisis, given American power.

II

The people of Indochina have, for twenty years, been the victims of the American crisis. For twenty years, the United States has been attempting to maintain Western control over Indochina, first by support of the French, and then, when they proved inadequate to the task, through its own efforts. During this period there have been many modifications of tactics, and even occasional revision of goals as earlier hopes proved unrealizable. At first, there were recognizable and clearly presented material interests that motivated the American intervention in Indochina. I shall return to some of these later on. As time progressed and American involvement deepened, ideological factors became increasingly dominant. By now, a rational calculation of material interest would presumably dictate that the United States abandon Indochina to its own people, and influential segments of the American corporate elite itself are urging that this venture be "liquidated," as bad business, if for no other reason. Unfortunately, the anti-Communist crusade, so deeply rooted in the American system of postwar imperial state capitalism, cannot be turned on and off at will. Only a political leader of great courage and skill could extricate the United States from Indochina, even if the will were there. Hence even if the dominant segments of American society decide that the war is no longer a paying proposition, there is no guarantee that they will be able to bring this particular case of "anti-Communist" aggression to an end – and they are far from having reached this decision, it appears. Even today the hope remains that a military victory can be achieved, if only domestic protest can be stilled. There is little indication of any change of strategy, though new tactics are being proposed to achieve the long-range goal of dominating Indochina. . . .

III

The American war in Indochina has been based on two principles: physical destruction in areas that are beyond the reach of American troops, and the use of what are euphemistically called "population control measures" in areas that can be occupied by American forces or the forces that they train, supply, advise, and provide with air and artillery support. Since 1959 forced relocation has been undertaken to concentrate the population. Population removal through defoliation began in 1961, according to one Vietnamese eyewitness.[29] Long reports that "It proved easier to order fliers to spray crops from the air than to send in ground troops to force the people out by setting fire to their fields and houses." Later, population removal was carried out largely by air and artillery bombardment, particularly after the establishment of vast free-fire zones. To put the matter in the simplest and most dispassionate terms, massacre and forced evacuation of the peasantry, combined with rigorous control over those forced under American rule, is the essence of American strategy in Vietnam.[30]

The facts are easily established, and the reasons are also fairly clear: there is no other technique that can be effective against a "people's war." The reasons for the success of the "people's war" are also not obscure. Years ago the strongly anti-Communist Australian reporter Denis Warner, who knows Southeast Asia well, observed that "in hundreds of villages all over South-East Asia the only people working at the grass roots for an uplift in people's living standards are the Communists."[31] In his judgment, this is a "monstrous trick," but his judgment does not seem to be shared by the peasants of Vietnam. United States government documents suffice to show the effects of this grass-roots work, which forced the United States to resort to violence and terror.[32]

Observing the American response to the "people's war," one recalls once again the Philippine campaign at the turn of the century. For example, when President Theodore Roosevelt gave orders to pacify Samar, General "Jake" Smith ordered that Samar be transformed into "a howling wilderness." "I want no prisoners," he ordered.[33] "I wish you to kill and burn; the more you burn and kill the better it will please me."[34]

For a clear explanation of the theory behind the American strategy in Vietnam, one can turn to an important essay by Professor Samuel Huntington, Chairman of the Department of Government of Harvard University and Chairman of the Council on Vietnamese Studies of the

Southeast Asia Development Advisory Group (SEADAG).[35] He writes: "In an absent-minded way the United States in Vietnam may well have stumbled upon the answer to 'wars of national liberation.' " The answer to such wars is "forced-draft urbanization and modernization which rapidly brings the country in question out of the phase in which a rural revolutionary movement can hope to generate sufficient strength to come to power." He presents a more detailed description of "the answer" we have stumbled upon in a comment on Sir Robert Thompson's contention that People's Revolutionary War is immune to "the direct application of mechanical and conventional power." This Professor Huntington denies:

> In the light of recent events, this statement needs to be seriously qualified. For if the "direct application of mechanical and conventional power" takes place on such a massive scale as to produce a massive migration from countryside to city, the basic assumptions underlying the Maoist doctrine of revolutionary war no longer operate. The Maoist-inspired rural revolution is undercut by the American-sponsored urban revolution.

He also notes that the Viet Cong remains "a powerful force which cannot be dislodged from its constituency so long as the constituency continues to exist."

These comments, no doubt accurate, provide a succinct explanation for American strategy. Since the Viet Cong is a powerful force which cannot be dislodged from its constituency so long as the constituency continues to exist, the United States command has resorted to military force, causing the migration of rural population to refugee camps and urban slums where, it is hoped, the Viet Cong constituency can be properly controlled. . . .

The American involvement in Indochina is tragic for all concerned. It is deeply rooted in global American policies that have persisted, without serious change, since World War II and that are still operative today. Given the anti-Communist obsessions that have so distorted and narrowed American life, the easiest course for any political leader will be to adjust tactics and try once again, quite apart from the underlying material interests that once clearly motivated the American intervention and still are not without force, quite apart from the pressure of the military and others with a vested interest in policies that, once undertaken, are difficult to abandon. This being so, public apathy and limited, intermittent concern may be all that are required to guarantee that we shall find ourselves at war with Asia.

The people of Asia are, of course, the pitiful victims of these policies. But the United States will not escape. It is unlikely that we can continue indefinitely on this mad course without severe domestic depression and regimentation. For those who hope to rule the world, to win what some scholars like to call "the game of world domination,"[36] American policies in Southeast Asia may appear rational. To the citizens of the empire, at home and abroad, they bring only pain and sorrow. In this respect we are reliving the history of earlier imperial systems. We have had many opportunities to escape this trap and still do today. Failure to take advantage of these opportunities, continued submission to indoctrination and indifference to the fate of others, will surely spell disaster for much of the human race.

NOTES

1. *New York Times,* May 6, 1967. Cited in a perspective article by Paul Mattick, "The American Economy," *International Socialist Journal,* February 1968.

2. Cited by Clairmonte, *Latin America.*

3. See, for example, Clairmonte, *Economic Liberalism and Underdevelopment.* Also, Andre Gunder Frank, *Capitalism and Underdevelopment in Latin America* (New York, Monthly Review Press, 1967); *Latin America: Underdevelopment or Revolution* (New York, Monthly Review Press, 1970).

4. Cited in Clairmonte, *Economic Liberalism and Underdevelopment,* p. 66. Marshall is speaking of Friedrich List, who, inspired by the protectionist policies of Alexander Hamilton and others, urged that industrializing Germany reject the economic liberalism advocated by industrially dominant Great Britain. The obvious example of the advantages of extrication from the imperial economic system is Japan, which alone of the Asian nations prior to World War II succeeded in maintaining its independence and developing a self-sustaining industrial economy.

5. "International Combines Versus the Unions," *Bulletin* of the Institute for Workers' Control, Vol. 1, No. 4, 1969. Address: 45 Gamble Street, Forest Road West, Nottingham.

6. "La formation humaine – elé da développement," *Le Monde diplomatique,* March 1968.

7. "Southeast Asia – Predeveloped or Underdeveloped?" in *Looking North: Readings in Asian Geography,* published by the Manawatu Branch, New Zealand Geographical Society, undated.

8. Peter F. Bell and Stephen A. Resnick, "The Contradictions of Post-war Development in Southeast Asia," *The Journal of Contemporary Asia* (London), Vol. 1, No. 1 (June 1970). I quote from a preprint of this forthcoming essay.

9. *UN Review of the Social Situation in the ECAFE Region* (Bangkok, 1970), cited by Bell and Resnick.

10. See the "Economic Survey of Asia and the Pacific," *New York Times,* January 17, 1969, the article headed *Thais see peace as a mixed blessing.* The survey notes that "an end to the fighting [in Vietnam] would pose a grave threat to Thailand's economy." And if the Americans decide to maintain their military presence in Thailand, "the Thais will be faced with the even more difficult choice between a continued boom and further deterioration of their traditional society."

11. Kim Sam-kyu, *op. cit.*

12. *Cambodia: The Search for Security* (New York, Frederick A. Praeger, 1967), p. 8. See also Daniel Roy, "Le coup de Phnom-Penh," *Le Monde diplomatique,* April 1970, for further discussion.

13. Alfred D. Chandler, Jr., "The Role of Business in the United States: A Historical Survey," *Daedalus,* Winter, 1969.

14. Cited by Richard Barnet, *The Economy of Death* (New York, Atheneum Publishers, 1969), p. 116, an excellent and concise study of the evolution of this system.

15. Joseph Monsen, "The American Business View," *Daedalus,* Winter, 1969.

16. Bernard Nossiter, *Washington Post,* December 8, 1968.

17. See, for example, Claude Julien, *L'Empire américain* (Paris, Bernard Grasset, 1968): Harry Magdoff, *op. cit.;* Gabriel Kolko, *The Roots of American Foreign Policy* (Boston, Beacon Press, 1969).

18. On Acheson's role, see the excellent review article by Ronald Steel, *New York Review,* February 12, 1970.

19. "The Nuremberg Suggestion," *Washington Monthly,* January 1970. For similar statements, see Hoopes', *The Limits of Intervention* (New York, David McKay Co., 1969).

20. *Law, Power and the Pursuit of Peace* (Lincoln, University of Nebraska Press, 1968).

21. It will be recalled that the British conquered Greece from its own population and that the United States took over when the British could no longer afford to sustain domestic repression in the country, while Stalin refused to support the guerrillas and, in fact, repeatedly urged them to desist. For discussion, see Gabriel Kolko, *Politics of War;* Richard Barnet, *Intervention and Revolution.*

22. Quoted by Howard Zinn, *Disobedience and Democracy: Nine Fallacies on Law and Order* (New York, Vintage Books, 1968). p. 75.

23. *Economic Concentration,* Hearings before the Subcommittee on Antitrust and Monopoly of the Committee on the Judiciary, United States Senate, 91st Congress, 1st Session (1969), Part 8A. See also pages 17f. above.

24. Quoted by Arthur S. Miller, "Toward the 'Techno-corporate' State? – An Essay in American Constitutionalism," *Villanova Law Review,* Vol. 14, No. 1 (Fall, 1968), p. 43, from H. R. Rep. No. 1406, 87th Congress, 2d Session (1962), p. 7.

25. Introduction to Stein, ed., *American Civil-Military Decisions.* For further discussion of this process and its roots in the planning role of the executive under state capitalism, see Michael Kidron, *Western Capitalism Since the War* (London, Weidenfeld & Nicolson, 1963).

26. Quoted by LaFeber, *op. cit.,* p. 79.

27. A decision that was apparently advocated by unanimous decision of the President's advisers even prior to the election. See James Thomson's remarks in Richard M. Pfeffer, ed., *No More Vietnams? The War and the Future of American Foreign Policy* (New York, Harper & Row, 1969), published for the Adlai Stevenson Institute of International Affairs; and in "How Could Vietnam Happen?" *Atlantic Monthly,* April 1968, reprinted in Robert Manning and Michael Janeway, eds., *Who We Are: An Atlantic Chronicle of the United States and Vietnam 1966-1969* (Boston, Little, Brown and Co., 1969).

28. *The Economy of Death,* p. 97. The role of the law firms that cater to corporate interests as representatives of the general interest of the corporate elite, rather than of some specific segment of it, has been widely discussed in recent years. For more discussion of these matters see Gabriel Kolko, *The Roots of American Foreign Policy;* Ralph Miliband, *The State in Capitalist Society* (London, Weidenfeld &

Nicolson, 1969); David Horowitz, ed., *Corporations and the Cold War* (New York, Monthly Review Press, 1969).

29. Ngo Vinh Long, "The Vietnam War and Its Implications for Southeast Asia," speech given on March 27, 1970, at the Conference of Southeast Asian Students at Indiana University, reprinted in *Thòi-Báo Gà,* No. 9 (April 1970), a journal of Vietnamese students in the United States, 76a Pleasant Street, Cambridge, Mass. Mr. Long was part of a land-survey expedition in 1959-1963 which, he reports, took him to virtually every part of the country.

30. For many references and citations, see my *American Power and the New Mandarins;* Edward S. Herman, *"Atrocities" in Vietnam: Myths and Realities* (Boston, Pilgrim Press, 1970); *In the Name of America* (Annandale, Va., Turnpike Press, 1968), published by Clergy and Laymen Concerned About Vietnam; the material presented below; and other sources too numerous to mention.

31. *The Last Confucian: Vietnam, South-East Asia and the West* (A Penguin Special; London, Angus & Robertson, 1964), p. 312.

32. For many references, see my *American Power and the New Mandarins.* For a serious and, in my opinion, persuasive analysis see Mark Selden, "The National Liberation Front and the Transformation of Vietnamese Society," *Bulletin of Concerned Asian Scholars,* Vol. 2, No. 1 (October 1969), and a more extended version: "People's War and the Transformation of Peasant Society: China and Vietnam," in Friedman and Selden, eds., *America's Asia;* and also Gérard Chaliand, *The Peasants of North Vietnam,* (Harmondsworth, Eng., Penguin Books, 1969).

33. Compare the report in the *New York Times,* March 28, 1970: "Four young infantry officers said under oath today that United States Army policy, as they understand it, is not to take prisoners in combat operations in Vietnam."

34. Cited in Teodoro A. Agoncillo and Oscar M. Alfonso, *History of the Filipino People* (Quezon City, Malaya Books, 1967), p. 272. General Smith was later court-martialed and retired from the service. No action was taken against those who ordered the pacification of Samar. The parallel between the Philippine and Vietnam campaigns is, incidentally, frequently noted by Philippine nationalists. See, for example, Renato Constantino's introduction to James H. Blount, *The American Occupation of the Philippines* (Quezon City, Malaya Books, 1968); Hernando J. Abaya, *The Untold Philippine Story* (Quezon City, Malaya Books, 1968).

35. "The Bases of Accommodation," *Foreign Affairs,* Vol. 46, No. 4 (July 1968).

36. Walter Isard, in Isard, ed., *Vietnam: Some Basic Issues and Alternatives* (Cambridge, Mass., Schenkman Publishing Company, 1969), a publication of the Peace Research Society (International) in which various scholars try to develop policies that will assist American leaders in more effective use of American power, this being a legitimate objective for value-free scientists because of the underlying axiom that the foreign policy of the United States has been "characterized" by "good-intentioned leaders and policy makers."

Part IV

COLONIALISM AND IMPERIALISM

It is staggering to realize that the United States presently and for the past fifty years has consumed over sixty percent of the world's natural resources while constituting less than six percent of the world's population. To take a longer view, the industrialized nations of the world have for four hundred years lived in the mouth of luxury compared to the rest of the world and largely at their expense.

It is conventional to explain the underdevelopment of the nonindustrialized societies as stemming from characteristics of those societies. Such a view is completely misleading. To speak of nonindustrialized nations as though they existed apart from and independent of the industrialized nations is to ignore the events of the last five hundred years. Since the fifteenth century, when the commercial centers of Europe began to expand and take into their orbit the cities of Spain, Portugal, Africa and later America, Oceania, Asia and Eastern Europe, the fate of the underdeveloped nations has been determined by the policies and decisions of the developed. It is not Africa's feudalism or Latin America's rapidly expanding population that accounts for these nations' underdevelopment. What accounts for it is that the Western cities that possessed superior war-making technology established control over the nonindustrialized nations by the use of violence, force, and coercion. Since the reason for establishing this control was to provide raw materials and manpower (including slaves) for the economic development of the West, the policies implemented by the Western nations assured that the technologically undeveloped nations would in fact remain that way. Without technological development, which makes possible an increase in a nation's wealth, poverty is a built-in characteristic of the nonindustrialized world.

The articles in this section describe the sources of underdevelopment. Paul Baran provides a general statement on the causes of economic backwardness. Jean Paul Sartre and Frantz Fanon describe the changing mood of the peoples in nonindustrial societies, and the concluding articles by Andre Gunder Frank and William Pomeroy describe how imperialistic, neocolonial policies perpetuate the conflict inherent between the interests of the haves and the have-nots of the world.

TOWARDS A MORPHOLOGY OF BACKWARDNESS

Paul Baran

The gearing of policies and opinion in the West to the support of big business in its concerted effort to preserve its positions in the backward countries, and to sabotage their economic development, reflects itself in official pronouncements no less than in economic writings. Thus President Eisenhower defined the aims of American foreign policy as "doing whatever our Government can properly do to encourage the flow of private investment abroad. This involves, as a serious and explicit purpose of our foreign policy, the encouragement of a hospitable climate for such investment in foreign countries."[1] This view was echoed by Mr. C.B. Randall, the Chairman of the Commission on Foreign Economic Policy, who insists that "a new and better climate for American investment must be created" — rejoicing at the same time over the fact that "happily this is being recognized and such countries as Turkey, Greece, and Panama have led the way in modernizing their corporate laws and creating the right sort of atmosphere for our investment."[2] And with what might be called truly "disarming brutality" the big business position was expressed by August Maffry, Vice-president of the Irving Trust Company and one of Wall Street's most influential economists. In a special report prepared for the United States Department of State, he calls for "total diplomacy" in the service of the American foreign investment drive. "The improvement in investment climate in friendly countries by more direct measures should be the objective of a total and sustained diplomatic effort by the United States. . . . All agencies of the U.S. Government concerned with foreign economic development should exercise constant vigilance for discriminatory or other actions by foreign governments adversely affecting the interests of American investors and employ all possible diplomatic pressures to forestall or remedy them." Not too choosy about methods, he further suggests: "There is still another and a very promising way in which the U.S. Government can assist in achieving better conditions for investment in foreign countries. This is by aiding and abetting by all available means the efforts of private investors to obtain concessions from foreign countries in connection with specific proposed investments. . . . Once concessions have been won through combined private and official efforts in a particular case, then the way is open to generalize them for the benefit of all other private investors."[3]

Since "American private investment abroad is largely concentrated in mining investments, notably in the petroleum field," and since "it is probably substantially true that in the absence of very special circumstances no American private capital will now venture abroad unless the prospects are good that . . . the returns will amortize the investments within five years or so,"[4] it can be readily visualized what kind of governments in the underdeveloped countries are needed for such investments to be assured of the required hospitality. And it is no more difficult to perceive what type of regime and what variety of social and political forces in the underdeveloped countries have to be furthered by "total diplomacy" and by the application of "more direct measures" if the "right sort of atmosphere" for foreign investment is to be created in the raw-materials-rich parts of the backward world. . . .

The principal obstacle to rapid economic growth in the backward countries is the way in which their potential economic surplus is utilized. It is absorbed by various forms of excess consumption of the upper class,[5] by increments to hoards at home and abroad, by the maintenance of vast unproductive bureaucracies and of even more expensive and no less redundant military establishments.[6] A very large share of it – on the magnitude of which more is known than on that of others – is withdrawn by foreign capital. That the profits earned by foreign interests in the underdeveloped countries are very high, indeed considerably higher than the returns on home investments, is well known. A recently published, extraordinarily interesting study provides an excellent survey of the profits realized by British business in underdeveloped countries.[7] While the material there assembled abounds with examples of firms having for periods of more than forty years average profits in the order of 50 percent per annum and more, "the facts presented may be summarized in a few words: (1) of the more than 120 companies . . . whose dividend records have been presented in the various tables, only 10 failed to make average annual returns of more than 10 percent over periods of from one to several decades on the face value of their ordinary shares, and only 17 failed during their most prosperous five years to pay aggregate dividends at least equivalent to their capital; (2) 70 companies made aggregate payments during their most flourishing half-decade amounting to more than twice their capital, and . . . more than a fourth of the group recouped their entire capital in a single year or less; (3) the returns 1945–1950 suggest that the years of lush dividends have not vanished."

A comparison of the dividends paid by (1) Dutch corporations mainly operating in the Netherlands with those paid by (2) Dutch corporations mainly operating through branches or subsidiary companies in the Netherlands East Indies is no less suggestive.[8]

Year	Dividends of Group 1 (percent)	Dividends of Group 2 (percent)
1922	4.8	10.0
1923	4.2	15.7
1924	4.5	22.5
1925	5.0	27.1
1926	5.2	25.3
1927	5.6	24.8
1928	5.6	22.2
1929	5.4	16.3
1930	4.9	7.1
1931	2.2	3.0
1932	2.1	2.5
1933	2.2	2.7
1934	2.1	3.3
1935	2.0	3.9
1936	3.3	6.7
1937	4.5	10.3

Similarly Belgian investments in the Belgian Congo yielded returns considerably in excess of those earned by Belgian companies at home. "Net profits of corporations operating mainly in the Congo averaged 16.2

per cent of their combined share and reserve capital during the years 1947-1951, as against 7.2 per cent for corporations operating in Belgium."[9]

Nor is the impression different if we compare the earnings of United States' enterprises operating in underdeveloped countries with those recorded on domestic investment.[10]

Year	Ratio of earnings to book value in underdeveloped countries (percent)	Ratio of earnings to book value in the United States (percent)
1945	11.5	7.7
1946	14.3	9.1
1947	18.1	12.0
1948	19.8	13.8

Correspondingly remittances to foreign capital claim considerable parts of the underdeveloped countries' aggregate foreign receipts. Thus in 1949 investment income payments as percent of current foreign receipts were 5.0 in India, 8.5 in Indonesia, 6.5 in Egypt, 10.0 in Mexico, 8.6 in Brazil, 17.1 in Chile, 17.7 in Bolivia, 34.3 in Northern Rhodesia, 53.1 in Iran — to name only some of the most important countries.[11]

Where the situation is nothing short of outrageous — matched perhaps only by what happens to the economic surplus of the oil-producing countries — is in the British colonial empire. These areas, the population of which has undoubtedly the world's lowest per capita income, have been made by Britain's "paternalistic" government (Labor as well as Conservative) to *support* throughout the entire postwar period the United Kingdom's incomparably higher standard of living. In the years 1945 through 1951 the colonies were forced under innumerable pretexts to accumulate no less than 1 billion pounds of sterling balances. Since these represent the difference between the colonies' receipts from abroad and their payments to other countries, this billion pounds constitutes the colonies' capital *export* to Britain! In the measured words of the author on whose excellent paper the above is based, the colonies' "investment of £1,000 million in Britain does not accord well with commonly held ideas on the desirable direction of capital flow between countries at different levels of economic development. There is a belief that British colonial policy has been pursued with great financial generosity. The colonies' needs were great 'so the British taxpayer came to the rescue.' It is thought that the United Kingdom, since the war, has given large sums of money to help the colonies. One purpose of this paper has been 'to test the order of thought by the order of things.' "[12]

As was stressed before in a different connection, the importance of the underdeveloped countries' payments abroad to their economic development is not adequately measured by whatever proportion of their national income those payments may represent. The paramount significance of the transfers becomes clear only if it is realized what share of the underdeveloped countries' *economic surplus* is removed in this way. Small wonder that "many underdeveloped countries feel that this is too high a price to pay for capital"[13] – particularly once it is seen how small a contribution, if any, foreign capital makes to economic growth in the host countries. . . .

NOTES

1. State of the Union Message, 1953.

2. *A Foreign Economic Policy for the United States* (Chicago, 1954), Chapter II; the list of the countries that rated this special commendation is rather noteworthy. It could be extended to include Franco's Spain, Syngman Rhee's Korea, Chiang Kai-shek's Formosa, Castillo's Guatemala, and a few other similarly development-minded parts of the "free world."

3. "Program for Increasing Private Investment in Foreign Countries" (mimeographed, New York, 1952), pp. 10-12.

4. Jacob Viner, "America's Aims and the Progress of Underdeveloped Countries," in *The Progress of Underdeveloped Areas* (B.F. Hoselitz, ed.) (Chicago, 1952), p. 184.

5. This is a horse of a different color from "an increase in the tension, impatience and restlessness which cause an upward shift in the consumption function, and which acts as an impediment to savings," attributed by Professor Nurkse to the operation of the "demonstration effect" of higher living standards in the advanced countries. In the face of mass starvation of the overwhelming majority of the people inhabiting the backward areas, and of the waste and extravagance of their capitalist stratum visible to the naked eye, it is nothing short of mockery to "hesitate' – as Professor Nurkse does – "to make any class distinction in this connection," and to speak of some "national" propensity to consume. *Problems of*

Capital Formation in Underdeveloped Countries (Oxford, 1953), pp. 65, 68, 95.

6. The nature of the statistical information gathered and made available by the governments of underdeveloped capitalist countries is – not surprisingly – such as to render the assessment of these quantities extremely difficult. Dr. Oshima's previously cited study attempts – to my knowledge, for the first time – at least partly to fill this gap for those countries for which the data can be pieced together.

7. J.F. Rippy, "Background for Point Four: Samples of Profitable British Investments in the Underdeveloped Countries," *Journal of Business of the University of Chicago* (April 1953).

8. J. Tinbergen and J.J.J. Dalmulder in *De Nederlandsche Konjunktuur* (August 1939), p. 122, cited in Erich Schiff, "Direct Investments, Terms of Trade, and Balance of Payments," *Quarterly Journal of Economics* (February 1942), p. 310.

9. United Nations, *The International Flow of Private Capital, 1946-1952* (1954), p. 26.

10. H.J. Dernburg, "Prospects for Long-Term Foreign Investments," *Harvard Business Review* (July 1950), p. 44. A rough calculation on the basis of data supplied in S. Pizer and F. Cutler, "International Investments and Earnings," *Survey of Current Business* (August 1955), leads to the conclusion that since 1949 this discrepancy has significantly increased.

11. D. Finch, "Investment Services of Underdeveloped Countries," International Monetary Fund, *Staff Papers* (September 1951), p. 84. It should be noted that in a number of countries these percentages are considerable lower in 1949 than they were before the Second World War. This is due to postwar exchange controls that have in a number of countries prevented the outflow of investment income. How much of the amounts thus blocked will be reinvested by their owners in the blocking countries, and how much will be taken out as soon as regulations permit, is obviously impossible to say.

12. A.D. Hazlewood, "Colonial External Finance Since the War," *Review of Economic Studies* (December 1953), pp. 49 ff. Mr. Hazlewood's first quotation is from the official government publication *Introducing the Colonies* (1949), p. 58.

13. United Nations, *Measures for the Economic Development of Underdeveloped Countries* (1951), par. 225.

ON THE WRETCHED OF THE EARTH
Jean Paul Sartre

Not so very long ago, the earth numbered two thousand million inhabitants: five hundred million men, and one thousand five hundred million natives. The former had the Word; the others had the use of it. Between the two there were hired kinglets, overlords and a bourgeoisie, sham from beginning to end, which served as go-betweens. In the colonies the truth stood naked, but the citizens of the mother-country preferred it with clothes on: the native had to love them, something in the way mothers are loved. The European élite undertook to manufacture a native élite. They picked out promising adolescents; they branded them, as with a red-hot iron, with the principles of western culture; they stuffed their mouths full with high-sounding phrases, grand glutinous words that stuck to the teeth. After a short stay in the mother country they were sent home, whitewashed. These walking lies had nothing left to say to their brothers; they only echoed. From Paris, from London, from Amsterdam we would utter the words "Parthenon! Brotherhood!" and somewhere in Africa or Asia lips would open ". . . thenon! . . . therhood!" It was the golden age.

It came to an end; the mouths opened by themselves; the yellow and black voices still spoke of our humanism but only to reproach us with our inhumanity. We listened without displeasure to these polite statements of resentment, at first with proud amazement. What? They are able to talk by themselves? Just look at what we have made of them! We did not doubt but that they would accept our ideals, since they accused us of not being faithful to them. Then, indeed, Europe could believe in her mission; she had hellenized the Asians; she had created a new breed, the Greco-Latin Negroes. We might add, quite between ourselves, as men of the world: "After all, let them bawl their heads off, it relieves their feelings; dogs that bark don't bite."

A new generation came on the scene, which changed the issue. With unbelievable patience, its writers and poets tried to explain to us that our values and the true facts of their lives did not hang together, and that they could neither reject them completely nor yet assimilate them. By and

---

From Sartre's Introduction to Frantz Fanon, *The Wretched of the Earth*. Reprinted by permission of Grove Press, Inc., New York, and MacGibbon and Kee, London. Copyright © 1963 by Presence Africaine.

large, what they were saying was this: "You are making us into monstrosities; your humanism claims we are at one with the rest of humanity but your racist methods set us apart." Very much at our ease, we listened to them all; colonial administrators are not paid to read Hegel, and for that matter they do not read much of him, but they do not need a philosopher to tell them that uneasy consciences are caught up in their own contradictions. They will not get anywhere; so, let us perpetuate their discomfort; nothing will come of it but talk. If they were, the experts told us, asking for anything at all precise in their wailing, it would be integration. Of course, there is no question of granting that; the system, which depends on overexploitation, as you know, would be ruined. But it's enough to hold the carrot in front of their noses, they'll gallop all right. As to a revolt, we need not worry at all; what native in his senses would go off to massacre the fair sons of Europe simply to become European as they are? In short, we encouraged these disconsolate spirits and thought it not a bad idea for once to award the Prix Goncourt to a Negro. That was before '39.

1961. Listen: "Let us waste no time in sterile litanies and nauseating mimicry. Leave this Europe where they are never done talking of Man, yet murder men everywhere they find them, at the corner of every one of their own streets, in all the corners of the globe. For centuries they have stifled almost the whole of humanity in the name of a so-called spiritual experience." The tone is new. Who dares to speak thus? It is an African, a man from the Third World, an ex-"native". He adds: "Europe now lives at such a mad, reckless pace that she is running headlong into the abyss; we would do well to keep away from it." In other words, she's done for. A truth which is not pleasant to state but of which we are all convinced, are we not, fellow-Europeans, in the marrow of our bones?

We must however make one reservation. When a Frenchman, for example, says to other Frenchmen "The country is done for" — which has happened, I should think, almost every day since 1930 — it is emotional talk; burning with love and fury, the speaker includes himself with his fellow-countrymen. And then, usually, he adds "Unless . . ." His meaning is clear; no more mistakes must be made; if his instructions are not carried out to the letter, then and only then will the country go to pieces. In short, it is a threat followed by a piece of advice and these remarks are so much the less shocking in that they spring from a national intersubjectivity. But on the contrary when Fanon says of Europe that she is rushing to her doom, far from sounding the alarm he is merely setting out a diagnosis. This doctor neither claims that she is a hopeless case — miracles have been known to exist — nor does he give her the means to cure herself. He certifies that she is dying, on external evidence, founded on symptoms that he can observe. As to curing her, no; he has other things to think about; he does not give a damn whether she lives or dies. Because of this, his book is scandalous. And if you murmur, jokingly embarrassed, "He has it in for us!" the true nature of the scandal escapes you; for Fanon has nothing in for you at all; his work — red-hot for some — in what concerns you is as cold as ice; he speaks of you often, never to you. The black Goncourts and the yellow Nobels are finished; the days of colonized laureats are over. An ex-native, French-speaking, bends that language to new requirements, makes use of it, and speaks to the colonized only: "Natives of all underdeveloped countries, unite!" What a downfall! For the fathers, we alone were the speakers; the sons no longer even consider us as valid intermediaries: we are the objects of their speeches. Of course, Fanon mentions in passing our well-known crimes: Sétif, Hanoï, Madagascar: but he does not waste his time in condemning them; he uses them. If he demonstrates the tactics of colonialism, the complex play of relations which unite and oppose the colonists to the people of the mother country, it is for his brothers; his aim is to teach them to beat us at our own game.

In short, the Third World finds *itself* and speaks to itself through his voice. We know that it is not a homogeneous world; we know too that enslaved peoples are still to be found there, together with some who have achieved a simulacrum of phoney independence, others who are still fighting to attain sovereignty and others again who have obtained complete freedom but who live under the constant menace of imperialist aggression. These differences are born of colonial history, in other words of oppression. Here, the mother country is satisfied to keep some feudal rulers in her pay; there, dividing and ruling she has created a native bourgeoisie, sham from beginning to end; elsewhere she has played a double game: the colony is planted with settlers and exploited at the same time. Thus Europe has multiplied divisions and opposing groups, has fashioned classes and sometimes even racial prejudices, and has endeavoured by every means to bring about and intensify the stratification of colonised societies. Fanon hides nothing: in order to fight against us the former colony must fight against itself: or, rather, the two struggles form part of a whole. In the heat of battle, all internal barriers break down; the puppet bourgeoisie of businessmen and shopkeepers, the urban proletariat, which is always in a privileged position, the lumpen-proletariat of the shanty towns – all fall into line with the stand made by the rural masses, that veritable reservoir of a national revolutionary army; for in those countries where colonialism has deliberately held up development, the peasantry, when it rises, quickly stands out as the revolutionary class. For it knows naked oppression, and suffers far more from it than the workers in the towns, and in order not to die of hunger, it demands no less than a complete demolishing of all existing structures. In order to triumph, the national revolution must be socialist; if its career is cut short, if the native bourgeoisie takes over power, the new State, in spite of its formal sovereignty, remains in the hands of the imperialists. The example of Katanga illustrates this quite well. Thus the unity of the Third World is not yet achieved. It is a work in progress, which begins by the union, in each country, after independence as before, of the whole of the colonised people under the command of the peasant class. This is what Fanon explains to his brothers in Africa, Asia and Latin America: we must achieve revolutionary socialism all together everywhere, or else one by one we will be defeated by our former masters. He hides nothing, neither weaknesses, nor discords, nor mystification. Here, the movement gets off to a bad start; there, after a striking initial success it loses momentum; elsewhere it has come to a standstill, and if it is to start again, the peasants must throw their bourgeoisie overboard. The reader is sternly put on his guard against the most dangerous will o' the wisps: the cult of the leader and of personalities, western culture, and what is equally to be feared, the withdrawal into the twilight of past African culture. For the only true culture is that of the Revolution; that is to say, it is constantly in the making. Fanon speaks out loud; we Europeans can hear him, as the fact that you hold this book in your hand proves; is he not then afraid that the colonial powers may take advantage of his sincerity?

No; he fears nothing. Our methods are out-of-date; they can sometimes delay emancipation, but not stop it. And do not think that we can change our ways; neo-colonialism, that idle dream of mother-countries, is a lot of hot air; the "Third Forces" don't exist, or if they do they are only the tin-pot bourgeoisies that colonialism has already placed in the saddle. Our Machiavellianism has little purchase on this wide-awake world that has run our falsehoods to earth one after the other. The settler has only recourse to one thing: brute force, when he can command it; the native has only one choice, between servitude or supremacy. What does Fanon care whether you read his work or not? It is to his brothers that he denounces our old tricks, and he is sure we have no more up our sleeves. It is to them he says: "Europe has laid her hands on our continents, and we must slash at her fingers till she lets go. It's a good moment; nothing can happen at Bizerta, at Elizabethville or in the Algerian *bled*[1] that the whole world does not hear about. The rival blocks take opposite sides, and hold each other in check; let us take advantage of this paralysis, let us burst into history, forcing it by our invasion into universality for the first time. Let us start fighting; and if we've no other arms, the waiting knife's enough."

NOTE

1. Up-country in North Africa (Transl).

CAPITALISM AND UNDERDEVELOPMENT IN LATIN AMERICA
Andre Gunder Frank

Agriculture is in crisis. Everyone agrees. And the crisis of agriculture is the crisis of Latin America and of Brazil. But what about the sources, nature and solution of the crisis? The standard Western bourgeois view is that Latin American agriculture is feudal and that it is this feudal structure of agriculture which prevents economic development. The consequent solution proposed, following the Western example, is to destroy feudalism and substitute capitalism. Curiously, this explanation of "feudalism" is almost equally widespread among Marxists. According to their analysis, feudalism persists at least in large sectors of the agricultural countryside, although these are being progressively penetrated by capitalism. And these Marxists propose essentially the same solution for the crisis as their bourgeois antagonists: Accelerate and complete the capitalization of agriculture.

The purpose of this study is to suggest that the causes and explanation of the agricultural crisis must be sought not in feudalism, but in capitalism itself. The Brazilian economy, including its agriculture, is part of a capitalist system. It is the development and functioning of this system which produce both development and underdevelopment and which account for the terrible reality of agriculture in Brazil — and elsewhere. . . .

Really to understand underdeveloped agriculture, we must understand underdevelopment. And for this, we must investigate the development of that underdevelopment. Yes, *development of underdevelopment* — because underdevelopment, as distinct perhaps from *un*development, did not pre-date economic development; nor did it spring up of itself; nor did it spring up all of a sudden. It developed right along with economic development — and it is still doing so. It is an integral part of the *single* developmental process on this planet during the past five centuries or more. Unfortunately, attention has hitherto been paid almost exclusively to the economic development part of the process — maybe because our science, both its bourgeois and its Marxist branches, developed in the metropolis along with economic development itself.

It is not possible of course to elaborate here a whole theory of underdevelopment, but it is essential to take note of some fundamentals of the process. The first is that this process took place under a single dominant form of economic and political organization known as mercantilism, or mercantile capitalism. A second fundamental is that each step of the way this form of organization concentrated economic and political power, and also social prestige, to an extremely high degree — what has come to be known as monopoly. Thirdly, the effects have been widespread, one might say universal; and while they have been quite different from one place and group to another, they have everywhere been extremely unequal. It is the third factor (universality) which lends to the second (concentration) its importance. For concentration also exists, for instance, in feudalism. But feudalism concentrates land in each separate feud rather than in any wider economy; whereas monopoly in the modern sense refers to concentration in a universally interrelated whole. Further, it is this combination of universal relations with monopoly which necessarily produces inequality, not only of the monopolized factor but of other relations as well. Fourthly, we are dealing here with a *process:* It continues, and so do its effects. Thus, inequality is still increasing (cf. Myrdal 1957), and so are both economic development and underdevelopment.

Capitalist development has involved monopolization of land and other forms of capital, and of labor, commerce, finance, industry and technology — among other things. In different times, in different places, monopoly has taken various forms and effects in adapting to differing circumstances. But while it is important to distinguish peculiarities, such as those of Brazilian agriculture, it is still more important to keep in sight fundamentally similar aspects. Above all, it is important to take into account, where possible, how other parts of the capitalist process in the world determine the one under study, and vice versa.

The development/underdevelopment duality or contradiction of capitalism of course receives its greatest attention today on the international level of industrialized countries and underdeveloped countries. The European metropolis began seriously accumulating capital several centuries ago. Its expanding mercantilist system was spread to other continents, where it imposed forms of economic organization differing in place and time according to circumstance. In the American elevation running from the Sierra Madre in the north across the Isthmus to the Andes, it found highly organized empires of civilized peoples – with existing mineral wealth ready to be taken home. In Africa, it found human labor which it then used to open up the Latin American lowlands, notably Brazil. This expansion not only contributed to the economic development of the metropolis; it left its marks on other peoples, the effects of which we are still witnessing today. Among the Aztecs and the Incas whole civilizations were destroyed. But, although capitalism did penetrate these lands and tie them to metropolitan forces that have determined their fate, some of their people found partial protection by retreating into a mountainous isolation. In Brazil, a whole new society was implanted, mixing three races and countless cultures, all as grist for the expanding metropolitan capitalist mill. Whatever institutional forms were transplanted or grew up in the New World, their content inevitably was mercantilist- or capitalist-determined.

Later, when metropolitan industrialization and urbanization began to demand more raw materials and foodstuffs, the now underdeveloped regions were called upon – that is, forced – to supply that part which the metropolitan primary producers could not produce, or were thus spared from having to produce. Countries like India and China, which had not yet been thus exploited, received their turn in the imperialist phase when their rural industries, if not their agriculture directly, were destroyed so that they might more effectively absorb the metropolis's surplus industrial goods. In our day, the capitalized metropolis is investing its capital in producing technology and synthetics which substitute for some raw materials, and even produce surpluses of other primary products (wheat, etc.), which the now-specialized primary producing countries are also forced to absorb. Throughout, the peripheral countries have been the tail which has been wagged by the metropolitan capitalist dog: They developed underdevelopment, particularly underdeveloped agriculture, while the metropolis developed industry. Current analyses of this process may be found in Baran (1957), Myrdal (1957) and Lacoste (1961).

This simultaneous development of unequal wealth and poverty may also be seen between regions of a single country. The relationship between the North and South in the United States, and in Brazil between the South and the Northeast, is fundamentally the same as that between the metropolis and its underdeveloped regions. But the Northeast's relation to the South is a supplement to, not a substitute for, its relation with the metropolitan world; that world has not ceased to exist and can never have its effects undone.

The Brazilian Northeast, one of the world's poorest and most underdeveloped regions, has a per capita income about one fourth that of the South; Piauí, its poorest state, one tenth that of Guanabara, the seat of Rio de Janeiro (*Desenvolvimento & Conjuntura* 1959/4: 7-8). The Northeast (including Sergipe and Bahia), with 32 percent of Brazil's inhabitants, in 1955 earned 75 billion cruzeiros out of the national total of 575 billion. And the income at the disposal of its inhabitants was even less, since the area shows an outflow of capital to other regions (*Desenvolvimento & Conjuntura* 1957/2: 18-19). In fact, the capital-poor and starving agricultural Northeast earns foreign exchange which is spent for the capitalization and welfare of other regions, from which it in turn imports the foodstuffs which represent 30 to 40 percent of its regional imports (*Desenvolvimento & Conjuntura* 1959/4: 71). Even its expenditure on maintaining and educating its young people goes to the development of other regions, for its most productive workers migrate to areas of greater opportunity.

It is enlightening to examine the historical course of the Northeast's underdevelopment. During the sugar era its coast was the leading sector; and its interior was the sugar export sector's peripheral, underdeveloping, cattle-raising meat supplier – as the sugar sector was itself an underdeveloping periphery of the European metropolis. With the decline of the Northeast's sugar fortunes, the entire Northeast became fully underdeveloped. The subsequent rise of the national metropolis in São Paulo further decapitalized the Northeast, as it has much of the rest of the economy. There are Paulistas who say that São Paulo is the locomotive that draws twenty-one cars (the twenty-one states); they neglect to add that these are its fuel-supplying coal cars. To regard the one region as more "feudal" and the other as more "capitalist," however, serves only to obscure their common capitalist structure, which generates this inequality between them.

This development/underdevelopment duality or contradiction of capitalist society is universally accompanied by monopoly concentration of resources and power. In the United States, the contradiction appears in the large cities and metropolitan areas, between regions like North and South, between sectors like industry and agriculture, within sectors in industry. In agriculture, 10 percent of the farms in 1950 produced 50 percent of the output, whereas 50 percent of the farms produced 10 percent of the output – while 1 million of the 5 million farm families live at a mere subsistence level. And the United States never underwent feudalism in any form. Western European industry exhibits at once the most advanced technology, incorporated in international cartels, alongside factories which are more family than business and artisan shops that take us back to the Middle Ages. We find the same thing in all parts of the Brazilian economy, as in the urban properties of Porto Alegre in which 0.5 percent of the population accounts for 8.6 percent of the proprietors who among them own 53.7 percent of the real estate (*A Classe Operária* 1963).

AMERICAN NEO-COLONIALISM IN THE PHILIPPINES
William J. Pomeroy

The controversy over a Philippine policy, and over the whole question of colonial possession to which it was related, has been called one of the "great debates" in American history. It has also been one of the least understood debates, and one not easily nor finally resolved. Aspects and features of it, in fact, in other forms, have persistently reappeared in American life, and continue to do so until the present time.

From 1898 onwards, this great debate was over whether the expansion of American trade and investment outside the borders of the United States should occur with or without the customary imperialist possession of colonies. Involved essentially in the outcome was the development of what has come to be known as "neo-colonialism," a system in which all the advantages and pertinent features of colonial domination are maintained in an exploited country without its outright possession as a colony.

From its evolvement in the 19th century, modern imperialism did not always find it necessary, or possible, to resort to colonial possession of an area that it exploited. The "sphere of influence" that operated often in regions where rival imperialist countries were more or less evenly matched (as for some time in China or in Latin America) had many of the aspects associated with neocolonialism. In the main, however, the term gained its application in countries that were once colonies but where political "independence" has been converted into more or less of a facade behind which the domination of foreign monopolies and strategic interests continues.

Although often argued in moral terms, the great debate, as conducted by the anti-colonialists in the United States, had this as its ultimate, if not clearly stated, aim. The granting of Philippine independence was not a matter of the moral principle of freedom for Filipinos winning out over an immoral principle of colonial subjugation for Filipinos, any more than the emancipation of Negro slaves in the United States in 1863 could be equated with freedom for black Americans. Filipinos in 1970 have still not overcome the limitations on their freedom that the concept of "stable government" laid down in the Jones Act of 1916 embodied. It was a neo-colonial "stable government," committed to protection of American interests, that was handed independence in the Philippines in 1946.

It is not always realized that the Spanish-American War, which precipitated the great debate and which has always been associated with the outright seizure of colonies by the United States, produced a model of neo-colonialism at the same time that it brought traditional-type colonies under the American flag. The neo-colonial model was Cuba, where American monopolies (especially the sugar monopoly) gained a protected sphere of operations masked by a form of independence subject to U.S. intervention and control. Significantly, anti-colonialists, from members of the Anti-Imperialist League to domestic sugar and tobacco growers, worked long and hard, not for complete Filipino freedom but for the Philippines to come into the same relationship to the United States as Cuba.

This was the essence of the position adopted by the antiimperialist movement. Although it had humanitarian voices within it, the hard, practical colonial legislation that it supported, from the Organic Act of 1902 to the Jones Act of 1916 to the Tydings McDuffie Philippine Independence Act of 1934, satisfied, through compromise, the economic needs of domestic sectional interests, the market and investment needs of overseas expansion, and the military-strategic needs connected with the latter.

The "anti-imperialists," by and large, were not opposed to the expansion of overseas markets and investments. Some of them like Edward Atkinson, believed that the allegedly critical need for this was greatly exaggerated, and favored a much more intensive development of the potentialities of the home market. This did indeed occur; it modified the imperialist urge but it did not expunge it. In the main, however, it was felt by "anti-imperialists" that overseas expansion could be achieved without the burden of owning colonies, through superior American production and competitiveness, through manipulation of tariffs, or at most through protectorates in which direct colonial responsibility would not have to be assumed nor concessions made in the American market for a colonial people.

In the case of the Philippines, anti-imperialist views on the expense and the overall unprofitability of colonies were clearly substantiated in the long term. A complete balance sheet on the Philippines up to the date of independence has never been drawn up, but it is possible to construct its broad outline.

William Howard Taft, who claimed that military costs in the Philippines were part of general American defense needs and should not be counted as colonial expenses as such, insisted that the only actual costs of occupation were a sum of $3.5 million appropriated by the U.S. Congress on March 3, 1903 for relief needs in the colony and for conducting a Philippine census.[1] However, it was officially estimated by Elihu Root that "equipment, supplies and military operations" between May 1, 1898 and April 1902 in the Philippines (i.e., during the conquest of the colony) came to $170.3 million.[2] Annual garrison and naval costs from 1902 onwards averaged between $6 million and $50 million,[3] and to this must be added the costs of fortifications, the initial stage of these, from 1906-1912, amounting to $10 million;[4] in 1923 accumulated costs of this type were put at $140 million.[5] It would no doubt be safe to say that military costs of conquest, suppression, fortification and garrison maintenance totalled at least $500 million by the time an Independence Act was voted by the U.S. Congress (a figure existing prior to the incalculable expenditure of reconquering the islands from Japan and rehabilitating them as a result of World War II).[6]

In terms of trade, in the 30 years of colonial possession prior to the beginning of the Great Depression of the 1930s, Philippine exports to the United States exceeded imports of American goods by nearly $400 million (up to 1927, $1.2 billion vs $900.1 million). . . .[7]

All the wars fought by the United States in this century have been waged outside the boundaries of the nation, in the interests of overseas investments and markets. In World War I it was to protect the loan capital made available to the Allied side. In World War II it was to protect and to expand the entire international stake, at the expense of rival fascist imperialisms in Europe and Asia alike.

The moves made by American imperialism in Asia and the western Pacific in the period after World War II, including the Korean War and the Vietnam War, have had a great similarity to the aggressive expansionism of 1898. In both periods a key target was the illimitable Chinese market. Whereas in the earlier period this goal was frustrated by Japanese and other rival imperialists, with U.S. capability proving to be over-extended, in the latter period American imperialism had won overwhelming supremacy over its rivals and had tremendous power to exploit the victory. In 1946 the United States seemed poised to realize its dreams of half a century.[8]

Militarily, the concept of the holding action (which did not stand up to the Japanese conquest of the Philippines early in 1942) had been converted after World War II into the policy of building a powerful ring of bases on the island rim of Asia and on its shores. This went infinitely far beyond the original Mahan idea of naval facilities and coaling stations. New military base-colonies were created out of Okinawa, Guam and other central Pacific islands, out of Korea and South Vietnam, while Japan, Formosa and the Philippines were dotted with huge base complexes of an aggressive character.

In this situation, the impulse for conquest and for scarcely-disguised colonial-type aggression, in an even more virulent form, has once again come to the fore. It has been augmented by an aspect of American surplus production not present in the era of 1898: military production, on which a large part of the U.S. economy has been made dependent, and for which war is the market. The colonial wars in Korea and Vietnam, in an important respect, were an outlet for surplus arms production and have been used to support a semblance of prosperity in the United States. The result, however, has been an overextension of American capability, and diminishing returns from an extremely costly policy.

Both the Korean War of 1950-1954 and the Vietnam War beginning in 1961 produced serious debates within American ruling circles over the profitability of these imperialist ventures, debates with an echo of those occurring early in the century. The enormous overseas expenditures connected with the Vietnam War in particular undermined the whole American international trade and balance of payments position, seriously affecting other areas of imperialist operations. A new and more profound anti-imperialist movement in the United States came into being as part of the new debate, with mass features as well as dissent in capitalist and middle-class sectors. It is paralleled by a trend in ruling circles for a reemphasis on indirect neo-colonial methods. When an analysis of the contemporary period is made, it will bear a marked resemblance to the period of debate over imperialist policy following the Spanish-American War. (Clashes between military and civil concepts of policy, authority and administration have also occurred in a repeated pattern, the MacArthur-Truman dispute in the Korean War, the "hawk" and "dove" antagonism in the Vietnam War, and the frequent Pentagon-State Department rifts being much like echoes of the Otis-Schurman and MacArthur-Taft differences during the Philippine conquest.)

As the staggering cost of the Vietnam War mounted, one of the main issues that arose was the inability of American resources to take care of the needs both of the home market and of militaristic imperialist adventures abroad. A "poverty program" and a "reconstruct the cities program" clashed with the spending of enormous sums for overseas expansion. The old struggle between domestic and foreign interests reappeared in a new form.

The controversy in the 1960s, curiously enough, has been associated with a frustration almost identical to that which blunted the imperialist drive across the Pacific in 1898: the withering of hopes to exploit the China market and other parts of Asia. Unfortunately for American imperialism, a new rival did emerge to supplant Japan in challenging its drive for domination: the national liberation movements of China, Korea, Vietnam, Indonesia, the Philippines and elsewhere. In a much more thorough fashion, by popular revolution, the China market was again taken from the American grasp. In the new situation, coupled with the failure of present-day colonial wars, American imperialism attempts to fashion new methods of retaining its positions, including even more subtle techniques of neo-colonialism.

American neo-colonialism, often attributed to the sheer power of American production and of the American dollar, has been shaped by contradictions encountered by American imperialism both abroad and at home. As the contradictions continue, and as they are more fully understood by the American people and others, the great debate over the course of American imperialist policy will continue to echo both within and beyond the borders of the United States.

NOTES

1. Dennett, *Americans in Eastern Asia,* 418-20, 272, 285.

2. Pratt, "The Large Policy of 1898," 230, 224.

3. Edwardes, *Asia in the European Age,* 93.

4. Regidor and Mason, *Commercial Progress in the Philippine Islands.*

5. Conant, *The United States in the Orient,* 79, 171.

6. A variety of estimates were made as to the costs of the Philippine conquest and retention. Senator George Hoar claimed in 1901 that the cost was $600 million, and was not refuted. The *New York Evening Post* estimated it at $308.4 million on March 6, 1907. Cong. James L. Slayden of Texas inserted an estimate of $284.4 million in the *Congressional Record* of February 25, 1909. Carl Crow, in his book *America and the Philippines,* 1914, stated that suppressing the "insurrection" cost $300 million.

7. Conant, "The Economic Basis of Imperialism," 327.

8. Curiously enough, the inheritors of the "Empire Days" have some of the same names: a new General MacArthur, son of the former military governor of the Philippines, came to act as a proconsul in Asia: a new Henry Cabot Lodge, son of the imperialistic senator, came to act as a spokesman for the new expansionists.

Part V

RACE AND RACISM

It is quite common, as the article by van den Berghe in this section points out, for social groups to think of themselves as superior to other groups. Racism, however, is not always a part of this ingroup feeling of superiority (ethnocentrism). And although racism has existed in many societies it remained for Western man through the colonization of the world to spread racism to all corners of the earth.

The belief that men other than whites were genetically inferior was a most convenient perspective for Western capitalism to perpetuate. Obviously it is much easier on one's conscience to exploit, undermine, and kill people if they are viewed as inferior.

There is, of course, a response from those who are defined as inferior. For many years American social scientists devised experiments and conducted surveys to show that the black man had accepted the prevailing white definition of black inferiority. It is doubtful that these studies were accurate in their portrayal. We know now, for example, that many of the strongest forces in American black culture have been antiwhite movements that have praised the virtues of the black man and exposed the demonic character of the white. For the southern black, the "shuffle" and "head scratch" of "Uncle Tom" were doubtless effective for manipulating "whitey," but such gestures were mistakenly interpreted as bespeaking an acceptance by the black man of his inferior status.

In any event these days are passed. E. Essien-Udom, from his personal research, provides a description in the article concluding this section of some of the Black Nationalist movements that have grown up in America in the face of the white man's racism.

ORIGINS AND DISTRIBUTION OF RACISM

Pierre L. van den Berghe

Until a few years ago it was not intellectually respectable among many American social scientists to ask the question: How did a social phenomenon get started? This ahistorical and antievolutionary attitude was a reaction against the simplistic, unilinear evolutionism of the late nineteenth century. Such questions were intrinsically unanswerable, I was told as a graduate student, either because they were of the "chicken and the egg" variety or because the origins of social institutions were lost in the night of time, hence any attempt at historical reconstruction was unscientific and speculative.

First, it is important to stress that racism, unlike ethnocentrism, is not a universal phenomenon. Members of all human societies have a fairly good opinion of themselves compared with members of other societies, but this good opinion is frequently based on claims to cultural superiority. Man's claims to excellence are usually narcissistically based on his own creations. Only a few human groups have deemed themselves superior because of the content of their gonads. Of course, racist cultures have also been ethnocentric, and some peoples have held the theory that their cultures were superior because of their superior genetic pool. But the reverse is not true: many, indeed most, societies have exhibited ethnocentrism without racism.

On the other hand, the contention that racism is a unique invention of nineteenth-century Western European culture and its colonial offshoots

From Pierre L. van den Berghe, *Race and Racism,* N.Y.: John Wiley, 1967. Reprinted by permission.

in the Americas, Australia, Africa, and Asia is also untrue. Racism, as might be expected of such a crude idea, has been independently discovered and rediscovered by various peoples at various times in history. For example, in the traditional kingdoms of Rwanda and Burundi in the Great Lakes area of central Africa the Tutsi aristocracy (about 15 per cent of the population) ruled over the Hutu majority and a small group of Twa. The three groups are physically distinguishable: the Twa are a Pygmoid group of shorter stature and somewhat lighter complexion than the Negroid Hutu; the Tutsi, although as dark as the Hutu, are by far the tallest group and have distinctly non-Negroid features. Of course, miscegenation over three centuries of Tutsi domination has somewhat blurred these physical distinctions, but, nevertheless, physical characteristics, notably height, play a prominent role in the Tutsi claim to superiority and political domination.

The Muslim emirates of Northern Nigeria, where a Fulani aristocracy conquered the local Hausa in the first decade of the nineteenth century, provide another illustration of non-Western racism, albeit only a mild manifestation. Thus M.G. Smith writes about one of the vassal states of Sokoto in northern Nigeria: "In Zaria also, social significance is given to color distinctions; value is placed on lightness of skin as an attribute of beauty, and as a racial character, and a host of qualitative terms reflect this interest, such as *ja-jawur* (light-copper skin), *baki* (dark), *baki kirim,* or *baki swal* (real black), and so forth. The Fulani rulers of Zaria distinguish on racial grounds between themselves and their Hausa subjects, stressing such features as skin color, hair, and facial form, and also make similar distinctions among themselves, since past miscegenation has produced wide physical differences among them"[18].

Allowing, then, for the independent discovery of racism in a number of societies, it remains true that the Western strain of the virus has eclipsed all others in importance. Through the colonial expansion of Europe racism spread widely over the world. Apart from its geographical spread, no other brand of racism has developed such a flourishing mythology and ideology. In folklore, as well as in literature and science, racism became a deeply ingrained component of the Western *Weltanschauung*. Western racism had its poets like Kipling, its philosophers like Gobineau and Chamberlain, its statesmen like Hitler, Theodore Roosevelt, and Verwoerd; this is a record not even remotely approached in either scope or complexity by any other cultural tradition. Therefore, in this book, we shall concentrate on Western racism.

Let us ask again the question of the origin of racism in the specific context of the Western tradition. Two major ways of answering the question are in terms of necessary antecedent conditions and efficient causes. The most important necessary (but not sufficient) condition for the rise of racism is the presence in sufficient numbers of two or more groups that look different enough so that at least some of their members can be readily classifiable. In addition to their physical differences, these groups also have to be culturally different (at least when they first met) and in a position of institutionalized inequality for the idea of inherent racial differences to take root. It seems that only when group differences in race overlap at least partly with dissimilarities in status and culture are these two sets of differences held to be causally related to one another.

These conditions are most clearly met when groups come into contact through migration, of which the most common types are the following:

1. Military conquest in which the victor (often in numerical minority) establishes his political and economic domination over an indigenous group (e.g., the European powers in tropical Africa, starting in the 1870s).

2. Gradual frontier expansion of one group which pushes back and exterminates the native population (e.g., European expansion in North America or Australia), as contrasted with the "dominating symbiosis" of type 1.

3. Involuntary migration in which a slave or indentured alien group is introduced into a country to constitute a servile caste (e.g., the slave regimes of the United States, Brazil, and the West Indies).

4. Voluntary migration when alien groups move into the host country to seek political protection or economic opportunities (e.g., Puerto Rican, Mexican, or Cuban immigration to the United States mainland or West Indian immigration into Britain).

These various forms of migration, singly or in combination, account for most of the interracial societies created by Western powers and indeed probably also for most non-Western societies in which racism is present. However, the migration (whether peaceful or military, voluntary or involuntary) of culturally and physically different groups does not tell the whole story. Indeed, there have been many cases in which these conditions were met but in which racism did not develop. This is true despite the fact that such pluralistic societies are often rigidly stratified and characterized by acute ethnic competition and conflict. Thus, for example, the Spanish conquest of the New World, brutal as it was, gave rise to only a mild form of racism toward Indians, although religious bigotry and ethnocentricism were dominant traits of the Spanish outlook. Similarly, the Aryan invasion of India, although it probably marked the beginnings of the Hindu caste system, does not appear to have brought about racism. Some scholars argue that mild racism exists in India and underlies the origin of the caste system. *Varna* (the broad division into four groups of castes: Brahmin, Kshatriya, Vaisya, and Sudra) literally means "color"; Hinduism uses the same kind of color symbolism as the Judeo-Christian tradition, associating evil with black and good with white; and there is a mild esthetic preference for lighter skin in modern Indian culture. But this is very much of a limiting case.

Given the necessary and facilitating conditions for the development of racism, what are the efficient causes of it? It seems probable that in each historical case in which racism appeared its causal antecedents have been different. Here, I shall try to answer the question only with reference to Western racism, a difficult enough problem in itself. A number of fragmentary answers have been advanced by various social scientists, most of them ascribing causal priority according to their theoretical predilection. Thus to a psychologist the ultimate source or "seat" of racism is personality, and causation must be sought in terms of the dynamics of frustration and aggression, or the "authoritarian personality." We shall return to the psychological aspects of racism, but our primary concern at present is with the *social* level of explanation.

Vulgar Marxism has a monocausal theory on the origin of racism; racism is part of the bourgeois ideology designed especially to rationalize the exploitation of nonwhite peoples of the world during the imperialistic phase of capitalism. Racist ideology thus becomes simply an epiphenomenon symptomatic of slavery and colonial exploitation. In the modern American context vulgar Marxists have interpreted racism as a capitalist device to divide the working class into two hostile segments for better control. Others, more inclined to assign causal priority to the realm of ideas, trace the origins of racism to the current of social Darwinism and the reaction against eighteenth-century environmentalism.

Western racism is a fairly well-defined historical phenomenon, characteristic of a distinct epoch; it came of age in the third or fourth decade of the nineteenth century, achieved its golden age approximately between 1880 and 1920, and has since entered its period of decline, although, of course, its lingering remains are likely to be with us at least for the next three or four decades. To be sure, racist ideas were occasionally expressed in the eighteenth century and even before. Thus Thomas Jefferson wrote in his *Notes on Virginia* (1782): "This unfortunate difference of color, and perhaps of faculty, is a powerful obstacle to the emancipation of these people [i.e., Negroes]." In various places Jefferson described Negroes in the following terms: "In music they are more generally gifted than the whites." "They seem to require less sleep." They secrete less by the kidneys, and more by the glands of the skin, which gives them a very strong and disagreeable odor." Even the Spanish of the sixteenth and seventeenth centuries, who have a reputation for lack of racism, did exhibit it in mild form, but it was almost invariably intertwined with, and secondary to, ethnocentrism.

The era of the Enlightenment which immediately preceded the growth of racism was strongly environmentalist (i.e., the belief was that both the physical and social environment determined human behavior to a greater extent than heredity), and Jefferson himself never resolved this intellectual dilemma to his satisfaction. He continuously wavered between racist and social "explanations" of group differences. Racist thinking in the Anglo-Saxon world, in Germany, and to a lesser extent in other European countries was in the ascendancy in the 1830s and 1840s; throughout the second half of the century it retained the status of a firmly established, respectable orthodoxy, and it received the accolade of science, both natural and social, in the United States, Canada, Britain, Australia, Germany, and to some degree in the Low Countries and France. Two great classics of racist literature are Arthur de Gobineau's *Essai sur l'Inégalité des Races Humaines,* published in 1853–1855, and in 1911, Houston Stuart Chamberlain's *The Foundations of Nineteenth Century.* Lesser luminaries like Adolf Hitler and Theodore Roosevelt also penned substantial contributions to the field, but, unlike their armchair predecessors, applied their ideas with a considerable degree of success.

Any social explanation of the genesis of Western racism must, I believe, take three main factors into account.

1.   Racism was congruent with prevailing forms of capitalist exploitation, notably with slavery in the New World and incipient colonial expansion in Africa. There is no question that the desire to rationalize exploitation of non-European peoples fostered the elaboration of a complex ideology of paternalism and racism, with its familiar themes of

grownup childishness, civilizing mission, atavistic savagery, and arrested evolution. However, any simple, direct, causal relationship that makes racism an epiphenomenal derivative of the system of production is unsatisfactory. European chattel slavery antedated the development of racist thinking; it was not until the nineteenth century that racism became a well-defined ideology distinguishable from ethnocentrism. Of course, the dehumanizing effect of slavery on both slave and owner facilitated the view of the Negro as a beast of burden without culture, and racism was a convenient rationalization for both slavery and colonialism. Yet both slavery and colonialism existed, as far as we know, without an appreciable amount of racism; therefore racism cannot be accounted for purely as a consequence of slavery and colonialism.

2.   Racism was congruent with the new Darwinian current of thought in the biological sciences [19]. Notions of stages of evolution, survival of the fittest, hereditary determinism, and near constancy of the gene pool (except for rare mutations) were all eagerly applied to *homo sapiens* and adopted by the bourgeois social science of the late nineteenth century, represented by such figures as Herbert Spencer and William Graham Sumner. Social Darwinism and organicism (i.e., the notion that society is analogous to biological organisms) also dovetailed with the economic liberalism of the early nineteenth century. Although John Stuart Mill and other early liberals were explicitly antiracists, *laissez-faire* was later reinterpreted as a mandate not to interfere with any form of human inequality and suffering. The poor were poor because they were biologically inferior; Negroes were slaves as a result of natural selection which had found the best place for them. Thus philanthropy, abolitionism, or any other attempt to interfere with "nature" could only debilitate the superior race by favoring inferior people (who already had the nasty habit of reproducing like rabbits, perhaps to compensate for their deservedly high mortality rate).

3.   The egalitarian and libertarian ideas of the Enlightenment spread by the American and French Revolutions conflicted, of course, with racism, but they also paradoxically contributed to its development. Faced with the blatant contradiction between the treatment of slaves and colonial peoples and the official rhetoric freedom and equality, Europeans and white North Americans began to dichotomize humanity between men and submen (or the "civilized" and the "savages"). The scope of applicability of the egalitarian ideals was restricted to "the people," that is, the whites,

and there resulted what I have called *"Herrenvolk* democracies," – regimes such as those of the United States or South Africa that are democratic for the master race but tyrannical for the subordinate groups [20]. The desire to preserve both the profitable forms of discrimination and exploitation and the democratic ideology made it necessary to deny humanity to the oppressed groups. It is only an apparent paradox that the lot of the slave has typically been better in aristocratic societies (like colonial Latin America or many traditional African kingdoms that practiced domestic slavery) than in *Herrenvolk* democracies like the United States.

BLACK NATIONALISM IN AMERICA

E.U. Essien-Udom

Marcus Garvey, the 'Black Moses', was born in Jamaica on 17 August 1887. As an African nationalist, he strongly differed from Noble Drew Ali. Garvey identified the problems of American Negroes with the problem of colonialism in Africa. He believed that until Africa was liberated, there was no hope for black people anywhere. He not only travelled extensively in the Latin American countries but in 1912 he journeyed to London to learn what he could about the condition of Negroes in other parts of the British Empire. While in London he associated himself with an Egyptian author, Duse Mohammed Ali, publisher of the *Africa Times and Orient Review.* Through this association, meeting with African and West Indian students, African nationalists, sailors, and dock workers, and reading, he delved deeply into the condition of Africans under colonial rule. In addition, he developed an interest in the condition of Negroes in the United States. He was profoundly influenced by Booker T. Washington's autobiography, *Up From Slavery:*

> I read *Up From Slavery* by Booker T. Washington, and then my doom – if I may so call it – of being a race leader dawned upon me . . . I asked: 'Where is the black man's Government? Where is his King and his Kingdom? Where is his President, his country, and his

From E.U. Essien-Udom, *Black Nationalism*, London: Penguin Books, 1962. Reprinted by permission.

ambassador, his army, his navy, his men of big affairs?' I could not find them, and then I declared, 'I will help to make them.'

In the summer of 1914 Garvey returned to Jamaica with a vision of 'uniting all the Negro peoples of the world into one great body to establish a country and Government absolutely their own'. He envisaged the coming of 'a new world of black men, not peons, serfs, dogs, and slaves, but a nation of sturdy men making their impress upon civilization and causing a new light to dawn upon the human race'.

On 1 August 1914 he established the Universal Negro Improvement Association and African Communities League, with the motto: 'One God! One Aim! One Destiny!' In 1915 Garvey was in communication with Booker T. Washington, who agreed to confer with him, and on 23 March 1916 he arrived in New York's Harlem. Washington was dead by this time. A year later Garvey established a branch of the Universal Negro Improvement Association (U.N.I.A.) in Harlem. In two months he built up a new organization of about 1,500 members. Five years later the membership had increased to 'several' million Negroes in the United States, the West Indies, Latin America, and Africa. No exact information on the total membership of the movement has been compiled, but figures ranging from one million to six million have been suggested by various writers. For 1923, during the Black Star Line trials in which Garvey was involved, the following figures for some divisions of the movement were revealed: New York City, 30,000; Chicago, 9,000; Philadelphia, 6,000; Cincinnati, 5,600-6,000; Detroit, 4,000; Washington, D.C., 700; Jamaica, 5,000; Guatemala, 3,000.

Garvey's ideology was both nationalist and racial. His nationalist objective was the redemption of Africa for 'Africans abroad and at home'. He advocated racial purity, racial integrity, and racial hegemony. He sought to organize Negroes in the United States into a vanguard for Africa's redemption from colonialism and hoped eventually to lead them back to Africa. The major instrument for the achievement of these objectives was economic cooperation through racial solidarity. He believed that if the Negroes were economically strong in the United States, they would be able to redeem Africa and establish a world-wide confraternity of black people. Above all, he believed that the Negroes of the world, united together by the consciousness of race and nationality, could become a great and powerful people. The following excerpts give a general idea of Garvey's teachings:

We are too large and great in numbers not to be a great people, a great race and a great nation. I cannot recall one single race of people as strong numerically as we are who have remained so long under the tutelage of other races. The time has now come when we must seek our place in the sun. . . . Without Africa, the Negro is doomed even as without America the North American Indian was lost. We are not preaching any doctrines to ask all the Negroes of Harlem and of the United States to leave for Africa. The majority of us may remain here, but we must send our scientists, our mechanics, and our artisans, and let them build railroads, let them build the great educational and other institutions necessary, and, when they are constructed, the time will come for the command to be given, 'Come Home!'. . . Africa must be linked to the United States, to South and Central America, to the West Indies by vessels which will unite in fraternal ties the ebony-hued sons of Ethiopia in the Western Hemisphere with their brothers across the sea. . . . If you cannot live alongside the white man in peace, if you cannot get the same chance and opportunity alongside the white man, even though you are his fellow citizen; if he claims that you are not entitled to this chance or opportunity because the country is his by force of numbers, then find a country of your own and rise to the highest position within that country. . . . The hour has come for the Negro to take his own initiative. . . . Any race that has lost hope, lost pride and self-respect, lost confidence in self in an age like this, such a race ought not to survive. Two hundred and fifty years we have been a race of slaves; for fifty years we have been a race of parasites. Now we propose to end all that. No more fear, no more cringing, no more sycophantic begging and pleading; the Negro must strike straight from the shoulder for manhood rights and for full liberty. Destiny leads us to liberty, to freedom; that freedom that Victoria of England never gave; that liberty that Lincoln never meant; that freedom, that liberty, that will see us men among men, that will make us a great and powerful people. . . . Race amalgamation must cease; any member of this organization who marries a white woman is summarily expelled.

The Universal Negro Improvement Association and African Communities League was the organization for the propagation of his teachings. On 1 August 1920 Garvey convened in New York an International Convention of the Negro People of the World at which he called upon the delegates 'to work towards the one glorious end of a free, redeemed, and mighty nation. Let Africa be a bright star among the constellation of nations.'

The 1920 convention was marked by pomp and fanfare. Garvey was elected the provisional president of Africa and also President-General and Administrator of the Universal Negro Improvement Association. As head of the African republic he envisaged, his official title was 'His Highness, the Potentate' and his honorarium $22,000 per year. The eighteen members of the 'High Executive Council' were to receive from $3,000 to $10,000 per year. After the 'Provisional Government' had been formed and sworn in, Garvey conferred peerages and knighthoods upon them.

Garvey's economic programme included the establishment of the Black Star Steamship Company (which included four ill-fated ships) and the Negro Factory Corporation. He sent to the Republic of Liberia a commercial and industrial mission which consisted of fifteen technicians. These enterprises were complete failures because of incompetence, mismanagement, and other difficulties. The other auxiliaries of the movement were: the African Orthodox Church, the Universal African Legion, the Universal Black Cross Nurses, the Universal African Motor Corps, the Juvenile, and the Black Flying Eagles, all equipped with officers and uniforms. A weekly newspaper which Garvey edited, *The Negro World,* was the main propaganda organ.

The Negro Political Union was established in 1924 to 'consolidate the political union of the Negro through which the race would express its political opinion'. This was Garvey's latter-day adventure into the domestic politics of the United States. During the presidential election of 1924 Garvey issued a list of approved candidates and came out strongly in support of Calvin Coolidge, the Republican presidential nominee. In New York City, Garvey supported a white Tammany nominee against a Negro candidate for Congress from the Harlem district. In Chicago, the Union gave its support to the Negro candidate, who later admitted that the Garveyites had 'worked like Trojans' and had been 'a material factor' in his campaign.

Garvey combined business enterprises with nationalist agitation. It was in connexion with his business activities that he got into difficulties with the United States government, which led to his imprisonment on 8 February 1925, after being convicted of using the mails to defraud. Garvey's followers to this day believe that he was framed by 'Negro Uncle Toms' and whites who were threatened by his success in organizing the Negro masses. President Coolidge commuted the sentence late in 1927. In December of the same year Garvey was deported as an undesirable alien.

While in the federal penitentiary at Atlanta, Georgia, Garvey sent the following message to his followers:

> If I die in Atlanta my work shall then only begin, but I shall live, in the physical or spiritual, to see the day of Africa's glory. When I am dead wrap the mantle of the Red, Black, and Green around me, for in the new life I shall rise with God's grace and blessing to lead the millions up the heights of triumph with the colours that you well know. Look for me in the whirlwind or storm, look for me all around you, for, with God's grace, I shall come and bring with me countless millions of black slaves who have died in America and the West Indies and the millions in Africa to aid you in the fight for Liberty, Freedom and Life.

After deportation Garvey returned to Jamaica and then went to London, where he died in 1940. He tried to revive the movement, but never again was the Universal Negro Improvement Association what it had been before 1925. Today Garvey is 'Our Saint' to his strict followers. Garveyites are still active in Harlem, Chicago, and other cities, but the movement remains split, small in membership, and organizationally weak. In New York the African Nationalist Pioneer Movement is one neo-Garvey group which continues to keep his memory alive on the streets of Harlem. The group, under the leadership of Carlos A. Cooks, has been trying to raise money to build a hall in memory of Garvey.

Liberty Hall, the Garveyites' centre in Chicago in the twenties, no longer exists. But Garveyites still meet to discuss, among other things, the 'redemption of Africa'. There are at least four factions still in existence, each claiming to represent the purest of Garvey's teachings.

NOBLE DREW ALI 'REINCARNATED'

It has already been indicated that upon the death of Noble Drew Ali, one W.D. Fard claimed that he was Drew Ali reincarnated. Fard founded a Temple in Detroit in 1930. He is said to have declared, 'I am W.D. Fard, ... and I came from the Holy City of Mecca. More about myself I will not tell you yet, for the time has not yet come. I am your brother. You have not yet seen me in my royal robes.' Master Fard proclaimed that his mission was to secure 'freedom, justice, and equality' for his 'uncle' living in the 'wilderness of North America, surrounded and robbed completely by the cave man'. 'The Uncle of W.D. Fard' became the symbolic term for all Negroes of North America. The white man was referred to as the 'cave man', 'satan', or the 'Caucasian devil'. According to Bontemps and Conroy, Fard maintained that he was racially identical with North American Negroes, 'in spite of the fact that he is said to have been born in Mecca, the son of a wealthy member of the Koreish tribe of which the Prophet Muhammad was a member'. He is reputed to have been educated in England and at the University of Southern California in Los Angeles, and to have been trained for a diplomatic career in the service of the Kingdom of Hehaz. He has been described as 'light coloured', with an 'oriental cast of countenance'.

Fard used various names: Walli Farrad, Professor Ford, Farrad Mohammed, F. Mohammed Ali, and even God, Allah. He is said to have peddled silks and raincoats from door to door in 'Paradise Valley', the Negro neighbourhood of Detroit. It has been estimated that between 1930 and 1934, Fard recruited eight thousand followers among Detroit Negroes. The rapid growth of the first Temple was accompanied by the establishment of various subsidiary organizations, among which was the University of Islam for the training of 'Moslem' youth and families in the 'knowledge of our own' as distinct from that of the 'civilization of the Caucasian Devils'.

Having thoroughly organized the Detroit Temple, W.D. Fard seems to have 'receded into the background, appearing very seldom to his followers during his final months in Detroit', and this mysterious aloofness fostered the belief that he was indeed the 'Supreme Ruler of the Universe' or as he called himself, the 'God, Allah'. Apparently, not all his followers believed in his divinity, and 'controversy over this was one of the several causes of dissension in the movement'. As a direct consequence of an internal dispute, the Chicago branch of the Nation of Islam was established in the latter part of 1933 or early 1934. W.D. Fard left Detroit in 1933, 'disappearing altogether as far as any authoritative record is concerned'. Some of his Detroit followers immediately identified him with Allah and claimed that he had returned to the Holy City of Mecca. Others continued to regard him simply as the Prophet. A split occurred, and 'that faction favourable to the deification of W.D. Fard assumed "Temple People" as a name, severed all connexions with the parent group, and eventually set up its headquarters in Chicago under Elijah Muhammad whose original name had been "Robert Poole".' The Detroit Temple is now called Muhammad's Temple of Islam, No. 1.

PROPHET FARD IN CHICAGO

Little is known of Fard's activities in Chicago. Police investigation of a courtroom riot in 1935, which involved members of the 'Allah Temple of Islam', identified the leader of the 'coloured cult' as 'W.D. Fard, or Fard Muhammed, or Elijah Mohammed'.

There is no certain knowledge as to the identity of Master Wallace Fard Muhammad. An Arab was thought to be the founder and leader of the 'Allah Temple of Islam' between 1930 and 1933 after the breach developed between the Moors and those who believed that 'Prophet' Fard was Noble Drew Ali reincarnated. The second split, which came over the question of whether or not Prophet Fard was the 'God, Allah', led to the rise and leadership of Elijah Muhammad. Bontemps and Conroy have indicated that there was a man by the name of W.D. Fard. The Chicago police investigation of the courtroom incident suggests that Prophet Fard was also known as 'Fard Muhammad or Elijah Muhammad'. Muhammad claims that Master W.D. Fard or Wallace Fard Muhammad came from Mecca, Arabia, and that he was with the Mahdi at the airport when he was deported. Aside from this account, there is no evidence of who Prophet Fard was, where he came from, or what happened to him. Muhammad's own account and those of others are examined in later chapters.

THE NATIONALIST TRADITION IN CHICAGO

During the first wave of intensive nationalist agitation — about 1915 to 1930 — the Garvey and Moorish movements gained a large number of adherents in Chicago. However, neither received the support of the majority of the people in the Chicago Negro community. The Moorish movement, at the peak of its success, had about two to three thousand followers in Chicago, according to a former follower of Drew Ali. The combined strength of all nationalist groups by 1925 seems to have been close to 10 per cent of the total Chicago Negro population (109,458) in 1920. Of the two or three other nationalist groups in Chicago, a group of Negroes who styled themselves 'Abyssinians' seems significant.

The existence of the 'Abyssinians' in Chicago drew public attention for the first time in a dramatic shooting and killing of two persons on Sunday afternoon, 20 June 1920. This incident followed a parade and a ceremony at which the Abyssinians deliberately burned two United States flags. A Negro patrolman was wounded and several other persons were injured. Grover C. Redding, who is reputed to have been the leader, and his colleague, Oscar McGavick, were indicted for murder by a grand jury.

A study by the Chicago Commission on Race Relations describes the Abyssinian movement as 'an illegitimate offspring' of the Garvey movement. The *Chicago Tribune* sought to link the Abyssinian incident with 'Racial "reds" ' and also with the writings of W.E.B. DuBois.

The back-to-Abyssinia movement was semi-religious and nationalistic, and Redding was both a secular and religious leader. He claimed that he was a prophet and a native of Ethiopia. In addressing the court at his trial, Redding stated the following as his mission:

> My mission is marked in the Bible. Even if they have captured me, some other leaders will rise up and lead the Ethiopian back to Africa. The Bible says, 'So shall the King of Assyria lead away the Egyptian prisoners and the Ethiopian captives, young and old . . . to the shame of Egypt.' The Ethiopians do not belong here and should be taken back to their own country. Their time was up in 1919. They came in 1619. The Bible has pointed out that they were to appear in three hundred years. The time is up. The burning of the flag last Sunday night by me was a symbol that Abyssinians are not wanted in this country. That was the sign the Bible spoke of.

The prophetic role is particularly attractive to the leaders of the black masses. Lower-class Negroes are somewhat 'superstitious' and the leaders can exploit their religious susceptibilities. However, most of these leaders have no significant social status and prestige which would lend credibility and legitimacy to their leadership.

The belief of the Abyssinians that they are Ethiopians and not Negroes is an obvious device to avoid the label 'Negro' with all its connotations of inferiority. To differentiate themselves from their 'Negro-ness' became a means of escaping the abuse and insults of the whites. For a dollar, a member could purchase an Abyssinian flag, a small pamphlet containing a prophecy relating to the return of the dark-skinned people of Africa, a so-called treaty between the United States and Abyssinia, and a picture of the 'Prince of Abyssinians'. In addition, a member could sign up to return to Ethiopia in order that he might fill any one of forty-four positions, such as chemist, civil engineer, mechanic, chicken farmer, teacher, cartoonist, etc.

Aside from these pedestrian goals, concrete activities to realize the back-to-Abyssinia objective are not apparent. The esoteric teachings of the

Abyssinians emphasized their connexion with the 'source' of civilization — curiously enough, Israel via Ethiopia — and the expectation
of their redemption after the apocalypse when 'God's chosen people will
be all right'. This assertion of a connexion with the 'sacred' as well as with
the source of civilization were means of enhancing self-esteem and status.
Perhaps the mainstay of the movement was its preachment of hatred for
the white man and its rejection of the pejorative label 'Negro'. The
Abyssinian movement received little support from Negroes and now seems
to have entirely disappeared, superseded by other organizations interested
in Negro repatriation to Ethiopia.

BLACK NATIONALISM IN DECLINE: 1930-45

The decline of black nationalist appeal began in the late nineteen twenties
and continued until the end of the Second World War. The splits which
occurred in both Marcus Garvey's and Noble Drew Ali's movements
weakened the possibility of a 'united nationalist front'. Secondly, a
number of separatist nationalist movements were begun, but only one of
them has, since the last war, been able to make an impression on the Negro
community. The inception of the Nation of Islam belongs to this period.

The Peace Movement of Ethiopia, in the Garvey tradition, was
founded at a meeting in Chicago in 1932. The group conducted a vigorous
campaign for Negro repatriation to Africa and urged that Negroes support
Mississippi Senator Theodore G. Bilbo's Negro Repatriation Bill in 1939.
Garvey supported the scheme in an editorial in the *Black Man,* published
in London. Garvey's followers in Chicago and members of the Peace
Movement launched an abortive march on Washington in support of the
measure.

Members of the Peace Movement, as well as the Moors, the Iron
Defense Legion (a few uniformed black fascists), and the Pacific
Movement of the Eastern World are said to have been sympathetic to the
Japanese during the war. In Chicago a leading member of the Peace
Movement was sentenced to the federal penitentiary for advising Negroes
to resist the draft and for propagating pro-Japanese sentiments. The Peace
Movement continues to function, although its membership is small.

The Ethiopian World Federation Council, Incorporated, was formed
on 25 August 1937 by Dr. Maluku E. Bayen, a nephew of Emperor Haile
Selassie. Dr. Bayen was sent to the United States as a special envoy to
solicit aid from people of Ethiopian descent for Ethiopia during the

Italo-Ethiopian War. The Chicago branch was formed on 27 May 1938. The aims of the Federation include the promotion of 'love and goodwill among Ethiopians at home and abroad, and thereby to maintain the integrity and sovereignty of Ethiopia . . .' . Chapters of the Council are scattered throughout the United States, according to an officer of the local branch in Chicago. The Federation holds regular religious meetings and relies on the same biblical references to 'Ethiopia' as the Abyssinians of the early twenties. It is semi-religious and nationalistic.

The National Movement for the Establishment of the Forty-Ninth State was founded in Chicago during this period by Oscar C. Brown, a Negro lawyer and businessman. This movement was essentially political in ideology. Unlike Garvey, he sought political 'self-determination' for Negroes by the establishment of a Negro state within the United States. The movement received no support from Negroes, and unlike those linked with an idea of 'self-determination' for Negroes in Africa or the religiously oriented ones, it was short-lived.

Present-day quasi-nationalistic organizations in Chicago, in addition to those previously mentioned, include the following: the Joint Council of Repatriation; World Wide Friends of Africa; American Economic League; the Garvey Club; Royal Ethiopian Jews; Washington Park Forum; and the United African Federation Council. Membership in some of these organizations is too small to justify extensive comment.

The World Wide Friends of Africa, known also as the House of Knowledge, was founded in the nineteen thirties. Its director, F.H. Hammurabi, believes that 'a race without knowledge of its history is like a tree without roots'. Hammurabi sponsors a number of weekly activities to encourage Negroes 'to know themselves, their nation and the world'. Negroes visit the House of Knowledge on Saturdays and Sundays to seek information, read, listen to lectures, or simply see educational films.

The American Economic League is primarily interested in urging Negroes to invest in Africa. A representative of the League, at a meeting of the United African Federation Council in December 1958, stressed that 'the time is fast approaching when Negroes must go back to Africa', although 'there is no room in Africa for lazy American Negroes'.

The Joint Council of Repatriation is interested in Negroes' return to Africa. Its members stand solidly behind a bill (similar to the Bilbo Bill) to aid persons emigrating to Liberia, which was introduced in the United States Senate in January 1951 by the late Senator Langer. The Council is known to favour repatriation programmes of such segregationist and fascist groups as the American Party led by Lincoln Rockwell, Commander of the American Party of the World Union of Free Enterprise Socialists.

On 1 December 1958 the United African Federation Council was founded, and this statement was issued:

> All African groups and organizations, united together for general council, of people of African descent. To improve historical, economical, and general welfare.
>
> Object: To promote love, harmony, and understanding among people of African descent at home and abroad, to better their conditions educational, religious. To send technical aid and representation to Africa for economical, educational, and business purposes for all free states in the Continent of Africa.

Seventeen organizations which have some interest in Africa were invited, but only six appeared at the meeting. The provisional president of the Federation, Winston G. Evans, explained that:

> Many organizations arise in this Chicago among the Negroes and die out. A government never dies out and that is the kind of organization which we want. The existing organizations are numerically weak. The so-called 'big-shots' among the Negroes have no interest whatsoever in the masses of the Negroes. Why should they organize and demand the City Council to bring Dr. Nkrumah, or Haile Selassie, or Tubman to the South Side when they know that they can buy their way downtown? Now is our time to unite in this U.S.A. as Ghana and Guinea. The French and British empires are going down. One nation goes down and another rises up. So it is with race.
>
> In New York City, Mr.____(a Harlem black nationalist who is connected with the African Stock Exchange Association Development Corporation) informed me that the Jews are trying their best to break up all African nationalist organizations. The Jew wants you to stay in this country so that he can continue to exploit the Negro. The Jews will raise a million dollars for the NAACP. Why not raise the same amount for resettling those Negroes who wish to return to Africa? That amount would build a sizeable town in Africa. We must look to Africa for our redemption. The Repatriation Bill is still up in Congress. The Negroes continue to feel content in spite of the conditions in America. Our only economic resource consists of the churches, funeral homes and policy. Our ministers get richer and richer. All the rich ministers of course make frequent visits to 'the Holy land' – Africa. They return learning nothing from the people

out there about how to organize for freedom. . . . For all the money the Negro churches have collected there is no economic result coming from it.

African history is not taught to Negro children. We must give them this message. They are ashamed of Africa. A white kid is not. He learns the vital products of Africa and can name them. The Negro child knows only about monkeys.

His comment on Negro leadership reveals the hostility of the nationalists towards the educated Negro:

We should not wait for everyone to make up his mind. Do not expect the lawyers, doctors, and the rest of the Negro middle class here. But wait, once you have the membership, the lawyers and doctors will be here, and if you have the money, they will become members. They never start any movement themselves. They are joiners. They join the whites and the Negroes alike.

These observations represented the general feeling of members at the meeting.

SUMMARY: CHARACTERISTICS OF BLACK NATIONALISM

The movements we have examined exhibit common characteristics as well as differences. Their common origins are the cultural alienation and social estrangement of the urban Negro masses from the white society, the absence of a 'great Negro ethos' capable of inspiring them to work together for the ends they seek, and the confusion, apathy, frustration, and disillusionment which arise in their attempt to adjust to these conditions. Consequently, Negroes tend to perceive white society as a monolith united in opposition to their advancement and therefore as not susceptible to fundamental change through rational persuasion, let alone through coercion. They become overwhelmed by a feeling of total powerlessness.

Those who do not succumb completely to this feeling of hopelessness tend to develop a distrust for existing institutions and conventional modes of action. This distrust and antagonism towards existing institutions (white or Negro) is common to the nationalist movements, reflected in their negative attitude towards political participation, conventional Negro education, the Negro church, and hence Christianity, traditional modes of Negro social protest and action, Negro middle-class leadership, and the intellectuals. Some hostility may even be displaced from the 'sacred'

Christian whites to a more vulnerable minority such as the Jews. Their attitude was perhaps best summed up in an interview with S.A. Davis who is Chairman of the Advisory Board of the Joint Council of Repatriation, and an active participant in nationalist activities:

> As long as the Negro is in America there is no hope for him. The white man takes one Negro and kills the aspirations of a million others. The white man has successfully made the Negro into an individualist for himself, and denied a nation of his own to the Negro. The Negro's worst enemy is his religion. The acceptance of Christianity killed his nationalism. Christianity is his worst poisonous enemy. There are over 700 denominations among Negroes and yet the Negroes have not founded a single denomination of their own. They get together to serve white gods. The Negro will never unite until the religious struggle is won.

> Ask a Negro what his problem is, he says, unity. He agrees with you, but that is all. His case in America is hopeless. The NAACP is the Big Niggers' organization. It was founded by whites, the bosses are whites and Jews – the biggest thief there ever was. The Big Niggers, the NAACP, don't want Langer's Bill passed. The Jews don't want it passed. The Big Niggers want to get jobs here. They are not nationalists. They have no national programme. They are not interested in the plight of the masses. The Big Niggers as a class don't think. Of course they get their diplomas and stand around like any other Negro for a job from the white man. Once a Negro reaches college level he is no good for anybody. They were brought here slaves, have remained slaves, and will remain slaves.

The nationalists tend to become preoccupied with the means of overcoming their sense of powerlessness, but in their preoccupation with the means, the end of building up black power appears to become less important because it seems either unattainable or utopian. Hence, they call upon superhuman or divine intervention for its realization. This phenomenon permeates the teachings of the more religiously oriented nationalist movements and, as we shall see, it is quite important in the end-doctrines of Muhammad.

The preoccupation with means and the relegation of ends to a superhuman agency is important for understanding the relationship between the exoteric and esoteric doctrines of black nationalism. It accounts in large measure for the part religion plays in black nationalism, so that even Garvey, whose nationalism was more secular than religious had to accommodate it:

It is foolish for us to believe that the world can settle itself on chance. It is for man and God to settle the world. God acts indifferently and His plan and purpose is generally worked out through the agency of human action. In His directed, inspired prophecy He promised that Ethiopia's day would come, not by the world changing towards us, but by our stretching out our hands unto Him. It doesn't mean the mere physical test, but the universal and independent effort to surround ourselves with the full glory of man.

RACIAL REDEMPTION

Concern with racial redemption is an important esoteric component of nationalism. The nationalists tend to perceive black redemption as a struggle between 'good' and 'evil' in which God is on their side. This image of the world leads to an intense feeling of persecution, since it necessarily divides the world into 'friends' and 'enemies':

It seems that the whole world of sentiment is against the Negro, and the difficulty of our generation is to extricate ourselves from the prejudice that hides itself beneath, as well as above, the action of an international environment.

And also:

Let us pray for our enemies, whosoever they be! Let us all over the world pray daily for God's handling of our enemies! . . . let us in silent prayer for thirty seconds send up our supplications and appeal to God for the correction of those who oppose us even against His divine will that we should stretch out our hands to Him.

Surely God will answer our prayers against the wicked and unjust and strengthen us for the great work that must be done in His name and to His glory. Remember our duty is to be firm in faith.

THE QUEST FOR IDENTITY AND POWER

Theoretically, black nationalism is a special type of political behaviour. The nationalists, like most people, feel a need of attachment to some power centre, but this need is not satisfied in existing society. In an interview, Paul Robeson expressed the significance of Africa to him as a centre of black power:

I think a good deal in terms of the power of black people in the world. . . . That's why Africa means so much to me. As an American Negro, I'm proud of Africa as one of those West Coast Chinese is proud of China.

Now that doesn't mean that I'm going back to Africa, but spiritually I've been a part of Africa for a long time.

Yes, this black power moves me. Look at Jamaica. In a few years the white minority will be there on the sufferance of black men. If they're nice, decent fellows they can stay.

Yes, I look at Senator Eastland and say, 'So you think you are powerful here? If only I could get *you* across the border.'

Although I may stay here the rest of my life, spiritually I'll always be part of that world where the black man can say to these crackers, 'Get the hell out of here by morning.'

If I could get a passport, I'd just like to go to Ghana or Jamaica, just to sit there for a few days and observe this black power.

The black nationalists define the power centre in many ways. On the whole, they tend to disassociate themselves from the power centre of the ruling white society. Some think of it in religious or utopian terms, and God or Allah becomes that power centre. The downtrodden feel particularly gratified by the knowledge that they enjoy a special relationship with the omnipotent or with the sacred. It is also perceived in relation to an ancient kingdom, a present African state, or a powerful black kingdom yet to come. Hence, some nationalists are particularly fond of Ethiopia, Egypt, Morocco, or the Sudan. In general, they tend to disassociate themselves from sub-Saharan Africa because it has been disparaged by the whites as uncivilized and without culture.

Related to the need for attachment to a power centre is the desire for a non-white tradition and civilization. The 'Ethiopians' attach themselves to the Coptic Christian tradition, the Muslims to Arabic civilization, and some to the 'Moorish' or 'Asiatic' peoples. The Garveyites identify themselves with 'Africans at home', and essentially with their West African origins, although Garvey himself used 'Ethiopian' as a symbolic term for all of black Africa. These movements seek to legitimize their attachment to these traditions by placing the black race in an exalted position in some very remote past. They entail a rejection of the 'Negro heritage' in America, and of their 'Negro-ness', supposedly hated by the whites. Thus the nationalists tend to view the Negro heritage in America as a period of discontinuity in the particular tradition to which they attach themselves, or as a period of God's chastisement of the black race, or simply as part of a divine plan for the redemption of the race.

The dichotomy between means and ends, the peculiar relationship between exoteric and esoteric forms of black nationalism, enables us to explain the lack of interest in political participation among the black nationalists. It restrains the nationalists' hostility towards existing institutions from finding expression in extra-constitutional means for changing or modifying the political institutions of the United States. In fact, the nationalists have generally pursued a policy of self-imposed 'political exile' and have not made any effort to use the vote to attain their objectives. This fact of political inaction, with the exception of a few minor incidents, is particularly important for understanding the attitude towards the state of the black nationalists.

The exoteric forms of black nationalism are the 'means' for coping with the material, cultural, moral, and psychological problems which are purported to impede the advancement of the Negro masses. In esoteric terms, the Negro has 'fallen' from the grace of God and, in the eyes of the 'civilized' world, he is universally held in contempt. In other words, the nationalists take the view that the Negro is psychologically and spiritually 'sick'. The task of the nationalists is to 'reclaim the fallen' and to bring them 'a new life, pride and love of race'. Consequently, they insist that the Negro can transcend his 'Negro-ness', which is held in contempt by both his friends and foes, only by radically asserting his racial identity. To do this Garvey advocated the necessity to

> ... create for ourselves a central ideal and make our lives conform to it in the singling out of a racial life that shall know no end. ... We need the creation of a common standard among ourselves that will fit us for companionship and equitable competition with others.

MESSIANIC LEADERSHIP

The nationalists' emphasis on racial redemption and reclamation of the 'fallen' calls for a messianic style of leadership. The leader is a national messiah. He may deliberately create this image of himself, but, apparently, he believes intuitively that he is the chosen 'vessel' for the redemption of his people. His followers share this image of the leader. The messianic leader legitimizes his mission — social protest and action — on the ground that he received his 'commission' directly from God. His mission is further confirmed by the historical and prevailing social conditions which afflict the masses. His personal qualifications need not be consistent with conventional standards of competence and knowledge, but his ability to articulate and project the problems of the oppressed, to identify himself with them, and his sincerity and devotion to the 'cause' are indispensable.

The messianic phantasy has exercised a powerful fascination on the imagination of peoples in different societies and cultures. It has a special appeal for the politically and socially oppressed. This phantasy has had, therefore, an appeal for some Negroes, who then tend to perceive their plight as analogous to the biblical account of the children of Israel in Egypt. Accordingly, God will deliver them in the same manner that the Jews are said to have been delivered. This belief appears to soothe their temporal miseries, and is made credible by the New Testament doctrine of the Second Coming of Christ with which they are familiar. Negroes have traditionally sought the 'promised land' – from the slave to the free North before the Emancipation; from Mississippi to New York, Detroit, Chicago, or San Francisco; from New York to Paris, Mexico, or Rome; from the separate Negro church to Islam, Judaism, and Voodooism.

Expectation of a messianic remedy for social ills makes the prophet-leader particularly attractive to the oppressed masses. The degree to which black nationalist leaders indulge in the theme of racial redemption and the means by which it is to be attained have given rise to two styles of leadership. The tradition represented by Noble Drew Ali appealed to the Negro's religious susceptibilities and sought to improve the status of the Negro masses through its own version of Islam. Garvey appealed to their economic plight and pointed to the political inferiority of the black race throughout the world. Garvey's declared aim was not only to improve their economic position in the United States but also to unite them into a 'vanguard for Africa's redemption'. Both appealed to history in order to justify their movements, Drew Ali abstracting a history of the Negro people from the Holy Bible, and through his interpretations, bequeathing to his followers a body of racial theology which is religious and nationalistic in content. Garvey appealed essentially to social or 'secular' history. The Negroes, he said, are Africans abroad, and they must seek to discover their greatness in that continent. Both believed in racial 'purity' and racial separation. However, Garvey believed that racial cooperation was desirable, and appealed to the 'conscience' of white America in support of his programme. Both sought to create a 'central ideal' for the race (at least for American Negroes). The nationalists differ on this point. Drew Ali had a firm faith in Islam as the central ideal.

Garvey believed the focus was Africa, although it seems doubtful that he actually wanted all his followers to emigrate there:

> ... After Marcus Garvey had returned millions to Africa spiritually, he had done his work. It was finished in the real sense. I believe if Garvey had lived, he would have studied the conditions in Africa even more than in the New World and he would have realized that the return to Africa had taken place – that the black man in the New World could make a greater contribution to Africa by remaining in America, rather than migrating.
>
> ... People misunderstood him. As a matter of fact, the term, back-to-Africa, was used and promoted by newspapers, Negro newspapers mostly, to ridicule Garvey. There was no back-to-Africa movement except in a spiritual sense.

The consequence of the disagreement among the black nationalists on what the central ideal shall be has given rise to sectarianism among them. Their past performance in this respect hardly justifies their appeal for a 'United Front of Black Men'.

The creation of a central ideal by these movements is further complicated by the social and cultural environment in which they function. The nationalists are confronted, as are other Negroes, with the problem of attraction to and revulsion from the existing white society. This problem is highlighted by some of the behaviour patterns of the nationalists. It is interesting to note that in spite of Garvey's hostility to imperialist Britain he was attracted to the British tradition of peerages and knighthoods. Even an ardent black nationalist shared the stereotypes towards the 'backward tribes' of Africa that are fostered by the whites. There are many examples of this nature in the behaviour patterns of the black nationalists. Thus the creation of a central ideal for the race is hampered by the fact that withdrawal from the object which one rejects is never complete. The sense of cultural incompleteness and the subtle attractions to the centre of white power become a problem for black nationalists. This may be explained as a consequence of the interaction with American society; the practical result for a viable nationalism is that the sense of cultural incompleteness and attractions to the centre of white power tend to undermine and dissipate black nationalist sentiments even among the Negro masses.

In spite of the difficulties and disagreements indicated here, the black nationalist organizations we have examined are united in their rejection of the proposition that in time the Negro problem in the United States will be satisfactorily resolved. They assert that the only satisfactory and permanent solution to the problem of black-white relations is the separation of Negroes from a white majority and the establishment of a 'Negro homeland' politically controlled by a black majority.

The Nation of Islam advocates this point of view and in its ideology seeks to integrate the religious and the secular traditions. Meanwhile, the Nation of Islam offers its members a sense of identity and seeks to mobilize them for spiritual, moral, social, and economic reforms within the Negro ghettoes of the urban North.

Part VI

CRIME, DEVIANCE, AND THE LAW

Even a cursory review of the criminal law statutes reveals the tangle of human actions that are contained within the legal definition of a crime. It is a crime in many states to sell retail goods on Sunday. Even so august a body as the Supreme Court of the United States has held that the state of Maryland was quite proper to arrest and punish employees of a retail store who sold cheese and assorted items on Sunday. In many states it is a crime to distribute literature that tells women how to avoid pregnancy. Youths are prohibited from smoking, hanging around rail yards, and talking back to their parents — and in some cases these acts are legally delinquent until such persons reach twenty-one years of age.

The problem of determining what constitutes a criminal act is even more confusing if we develop a historical perspective. It was once a crime punishable by death to wander from one town to another without written permission of your employer. Furthermore it was *not* a crime to take another man's life if you found the man flirting with your wife. Today it is not a crime for the state to kill someone who has given state information to a foreign government. A policeman can kill someone who appears to be attempting to escape arrest, even if the alleged offense is as minor a matter as stealing a television set.

The point of listing these things — and the list could, of course, be expanded indefinitely — is to underline the fact that what constitutes "crime", "delinquency," or even "insanity" is not uniform from time to time or from place to place. The study of crime, then, must involve as a starting point the study of the institutions that define some acts as criminal and others as not.

161

Frank Tannenbaum surveys the traditional approaches to the study of deviance and shows how these approaches have often failed to point out the basic fact that no one is deviant unless they or their behavior is so defined. Tannenbaum also argues persuasively that a key part of the process of becoming deviant is the dramatization of "evil" on the part of those in a position to label others.

Karl Marx argues, in a short essay, that crime is produced in much the same way and for the same reasons that any other useful enterprise is produced in capitalist societies. He also traces the origin of criminal and deviant behavior to the state. The final article, by Chambliss and Seidman, explores the role of bureaucracy in the deviance-defining process. This article also stresses the relationship between power and the definition of criminal or deviant behavior.

CRIME AND THE LAW

Frank Tannenbaum

THE SEARCH FOR A SCAPEGOAT

Criminology has been the happy hunting ground for all kinds of theories. The dramatic quality of criminal behavior has challenged attention and called forth explanation. Its very deviations from the accepted and approved have required elucidation and judgment. The community has ever had to do something about the criminal, and theory served as a justification of social policy as well as an interpretation of its genesis.

From age to age the conduct of society toward the criminal has differed in accordance with the underlying assumption of the prevailing theory. The outstanding characteristic of all criminological discussion has been the assumption that there was a qualitative difference between the nature of the criminal and that of the noncriminal. This probably was inevitable; to find the unsocial and the social identical in nature was to strain all the evidence. All things done despite being forbidden and condemned were done by the unsocial or criminal. They were addicted to the vice which the virtuous shunned. The criminal or unsocial committed theft, robbery, arson, murder; they showed regard for neither God nor man. The conduct of these deviates illustrated the perversity of their beings.

This contrast was sharpened by the prepossession of social theorists with the overshadowing conflict between absolute good and absolute evil. This battle, personified by God on one side and the Devil on the other,

From Frank Tannenbaum, *Crime and the Community*, New York, Columbia University Press, 1938. Reprinted by permission.

made the distinction clear and judgment easy. Regardless of the changes that criminological theory has undergone, this underlying contrast has persisted under one or another cover, under one or another disguise. The terminology has changed, but the original idea has persisted. "Good" may have become translated into "normal," and "evil" may have come to be described as "abnormal" in one of its many current variants, but, after all, the change in fundamental attitude is not great. The contrast in absolutes still pervades the air of criminological discussion.

During the Middle Ages the notion that evil action was proof of possession by the Evil One seemed both obvious and consistent with the entire accepted view of the world and its ways, and was descriptive of the motives of human conduct. This belief has long persisted, and even today it has not entirely disappeared from the common judgment of ordinary folk when they condemn the evil-doer. In fact the idea of possession found its way into the North Carolina State Constitution as late as 1862. "To know the right but still the wrong to pursue proceeds from a perverse will brought about by the seductions of the evil one." The "Rationalism" of the seventeenth and eighteenth centuries, their belief in reason, their notions of equality, their rejection of theological theories of causation as a means of explaining human conduct, led them to describe evil-doing in terms of choice rather than in terms of "possession" or "seduction" by the evil one. All men were assumed to be both reasonable and wise about their own interests, and if one chose to do evil it was because of the pleasure it would bring him. Evil-doing became evil choice for the sake of the pleasure it provided. Like the earlier doctrine, the explanation was consistent with a current view of the universe.

This theory from the period of the French Revolution, generally identified for criminology with the name of the Italian criminologist, Beccaria, has had a profound influence upon both law and practice in dealing with the criminal.

> Our substantive criminal law is based upon a theory of punishing the vicious will. It postulates a free moral agent, confronted with a choice between doing right and doing wrong, and choosing freely to do wrong[1]

As it affected children and the insane this view broke down, but its influence upon our legal system has been very great indeed.

The development of modern science, the growing practice of

measurement, the science of statistics, the development of the theory of evolution, and especially the growth of the sciences of anthropology and psychology have sharply influenced criminological discussion.

The controversies which these new additions to social theory have aroused have dealt, in criminology, mainly with *how* the good were to be distinguished from the evil. "Possession" and "seduction" had given way to the "rational" choice to do evil. This in turn was to give way to a series of other explanations. The Positive School of Criminology, so called as distinguished from the Classical (which is the name given to the theories that arose out of the French Revolution), found the evidence of the distinction between the good and the evil in the physical characteristics of the criminal. Lombroso, who is the recognized father of the Positive School of Criminology, has had a wide and persistent influence upon attitudes toward the criminal. His view has been described as "the proposition that a man's mode of feeling and the actual conduct of his life are in turn determined by and find expression in his physical constitution,"[2] and that these constitutions were so variable that the "assassins, ravishers, incendiaries, and thieves could be distinguished according to physical characteristics not only from the general population, but also from each other."[3] The various constitutions were in a measure anthropological throwbacks:

> Such a man as this is a reversion to an old type savage, and was born by accident in the wrong century. He would have had a sufficient scope for his bloodthirsty propensities and been in harmony with his environment in a barbaric age or at the present day in certain parts of Africa.[4]

These throwbacks were differentiated by projecting ears, thin beard, insensitiveness to pain, projecting frontal eminences, large jaws, square and protruding chin, and a number of other items. For our purpose here it is sufficient to point out that the proof of criminality now became a matter of external evidence. It seems incredible, although it is true, that in 1890 Havelock Ellis said in his book on the criminal, "The greater number of tattooed criminals are naturally found among recidivists and instinctive criminals, especially those who have committed crimes against the person,"[5] as if being tattooed were one of the evidences of criminality in addition to purely physical deformities. The fact that this adduced knowledge about the criminal is merely a proof of a somewhat naïve anthropology and physiology as well as an uninformed description of primitive people is beside the point. The fact that it had wide acceptance and that remnants of it are still to be seen in circles seriously dedicated to the study of the criminal is important.[6]

The development of psychology on one hand, and the annihilating attack upon the naïve "morphological" theories of the Lombrosian school by Goring on the other hand, shifted the ground once more from external to internal evidence of criminality. In the meantime the general sophistication had reduced "the devil" and "possession" to a series of concepts that served the old purpose under a new name or names. The new way of identifying criminality was now more fully aided by a statistical technique almost as naïve as the older morphological and anthropological technique had been. Instead of measuring heads, ears, nose and arm length, it now became the rule to measure intelligence. Apart from the fact that a definition of "intelligence" was no more easily formulated than one of "possession," the game of classifying criminals according to psychological terminology went merrily on for a number of years. It has since been shown that, whatever "intelligence" is, it has no demonstrated relationship to crime, and it has also been shown that the "intelligence" testers seem to test their particular techniques against each other rather than the thing they are testing. But the fact remains that the proof adduced was used to "identify the criminal" in terms as naïve and full of faith as those of the older evidence, as, for example, when Dr. Henry H. Goddard said, "It is no longer to be denied that the greatest single cause of delinquency and crime is low-grade mentality, much of it within the limits of feeble-mindedness."[7] Criticisms of this view since about 1915 have reduced its pretensions, but have not entirely eliminated its hold upon either theorists or practitioners in their dealing with the criminal.

Under the influence of recent psychological thought a new body of theories was developed to describe not the mental but the emotional deficiency of the criminal. A new series of tests and devices were brought into play to show that the criminal was not normal. The difference between the older concepts of "good" and "evil" has now become one between "normal" and "abnormal," and the insistence that the criminal must exhibit the evidence of his shortcomings has been shifted from intellectual to psychiatric phenomena.

We are not concerned here with a review of criminological theory. It is sufficient to say here that the theories advanced by the endocrinologists who have asserted that criminals "are either of subnormal mentality or of faulty mental or nervous constitution,"[8] or of the eugenists who claim that eugenics "supplies the most effective and permanent solution to the problems . . . of combating disease, disability, defectiveness, degeneracy, delinquency, vice and crime,"[9] have no greater validity than the theories they attempt to supersede.

The criminological theorist has tended to set off the criminal from the rest of the population in terms that would make the difference qualitative.[10] These attitudes have something of absolutism, and their imputation to the man of the physical or psychological deficiency that shows how he is distinguished from his fellows has something of the definiteness and inevitableness of the theories of damnation and predestination. The impact of the idea of "law" in the physical sciences has in this branch of the social sciences led to a crude assumption of definiteness, separateness, difference, in terms so absolute as to be final. The imputation of physical or psychic abnormality has this crude "scientific" basis, that it derives from measurement, testing, calculation. It permits the use of statistical tables and mathematical formulae. The fact that the qualities measured are intangible, that the traits examined may be irrelevant, has not prevented the process from finding wide acceptance and considerable acclaim, and in some instances even legislative sanction.

The issue here, however, is not the adequacy of the method but rather the fact that all through criminological theory has run the notion of good and bad in the older days and "normal" and "abnormal" in the current period. In each period the criminal has been set off from his fellows. This was indicated by Professor Root when he said:

> None is so repentant a sinner as to share the blame with the criminal. If we can localize the blame in the individual we can exact vengeance with precision and satisfaction. The more we can make it appear that all the causes for delinquency have their origin within the individual victim the more we may feel self-elation, the less danger there is of negative self-feeling. Writers of melodramas know this full well. The villain, in order to make us get the full satisfaction out of our positive self-feeling, must be bad with everyone else on the stage oozing goodness from every pore. He must be bad in spite of us; it is highly disconcerting to have him one of us.[11]

The underlying causes may be deeper than that: they may lie in the inability to accept deviation from the "normal." The projection of the idea of normal or good is merely the passing of a moral judgment upon our own habits and way of life. The deviate who is a communist, a pacifist, a crank, a criminal, challenges our scheme of habits, institutions, and values. And unless we exclude him and set him apart from the group, the whole structure of our orderly life goes to pieces. It is not that we do not wish to be identified with him: we cannot be identified with him and keep our own world from being shattered about us. The question of values is fundamental. Just because we appreciate the habits, ways, and institutions by which we live, we seem driven to defame and annihilate those activities and individuals whose behavior challenges and repudiates all we live by. Under these circumstances the theories of the criminologists are understandable. They have imputed an evil nature to the evil-doer, whatever the terms upon which that nature was postulated — possession by the devil, deliberate evil-doing, physical stigmata, intellectual inferiority, emotional instability, poor inheritance, glandular unbalance. In each case we had a good explanation for the "unsocial" behavior of the individual, and it left unchallenged our institutional set-up, both theoretic and practical.

THE MEANING OF BEHAVIOR

In each case these theories rest upon the individual criminal, almost as if he were living in a vacuum and his nature were full-blown from the beginning. Even the mildest of the current theories assumes that the criminal is an unsocial creature because he cannot "adjust" to society. Parsons represents this point of view when he says that the findings "seem to indicate that the bulk of crime is committed by persons who are unable to adjust themselves to society with a sufficient degree of success to meet the requirements of the law."[12] The facts seem to point to just the opposite conclusion. The criminal is a social human being, he is adjusted, he is not necessarily any of the things that have been imputed to him. Instead of being unadjusted he may be quite adjusted to his group, and instead of being "unsocial" he may show all of the characteristics we identify as social in members of other groups. The New York Crime Commission says, "He is adjusted to his own social group and violently objects to any social therapy that would make him maladjusted to it."[13]

Crime is a maladjustment that arises out of the conflict between a group and the community at large. The issue involved is not whether an individual is maladjusted to society, but the fact that his adjustment to a special group makes him maladjusted to the large society because the group he fits into is at war with society.

The difficulty with the older theory is that it assumed that crime was largely an individual matter and could be dealt with when the individual was dealt with. Instead, most delinquencies are committed in groups; most criminals live in, operate with, and are supported by groups. We must face the question of how that group grew up into a conflict group and of how the individual became adjusted to that group rather than to some other group in society. The study of the individual in terms of his special physical or psychical idiosyncrasies would have as much bearing on the question why he became a member of a criminal group as it would on the question why he joined the Ku Klux Klan, was a member of a lynching bee, joined the I.W.W., became a member of the Communist or Socialist party, joined the Seventh Day Adventists or the Catholic Church, took to vegetarianism, or became a loyal Republican. The point is that a person's peculiar physical or psychic characteristics may have little bearing on the group with which he is in adjustment.

The question is not how a criminal is distinguished in his nature from a non-criminal, but how he happened to be drawn into a criminal group and why that criminal group developed that peculiar position of conflict with the rest of society. The important facts, therefore, are to be sought in his behavior history.

Criminal behavior originates as part of the random movement of children in a world of adults, a world with attitudes and organized institutions that stamp and define the activities of the little children. The career of the criminal is a selective process of growth within that environment, and the adult criminal is the product and summation of a series of continued activities and experience. The adult criminal is usually the delinquent child grown up.

The delinquent child is all too frequently "the truant of yesterday."[14] The truant is the school child who found extra-curricular activities more appealing and less burdensome than curricular ones. The step from the child who is a behavior problem in school to the truant is a natural one; so, too, is the step from truancy to delinquency, and that from delinquency to crime. In the growth of his career is to be found the important agency of the gang. But "the majority of gangs develop from the spontaneous play-group."[15]

The play group becomes a gang through coming into conflict with some element in the environment. A single illustration will indicate the process.

> The beginning of the gang came when the group developed an enmity toward two Greeks who owned a fruit store on the opposite corner. The boys began to steal fruit on a small scale. Finally they attempted to carry off a large quantity of oranges and bananas which were displayed on the sidewalks, but the Greeks gave chase. This was the signal for a general attack, and the fruit was used as ammunition. The gang had a good start from this episode.[16]

But even after the gang has been formed, in its early stages its activities are not necessarily delinquent, and delinquent and non-delinquent activities may have the same meaning for the children. "We would gather wood together, go swimming, or rob the Jews on Twelfth Street."[17] The conflict may arise from play.

> We did all kinds of dirty tricks for fun. We'd see a sign "Please keep the street clean," but we'd tear it down and say, "We don't feel like keeping it clean." One day we put a can of glue in the engine of a man's car. We would always tear things down. That would make us laugh and feel good, to have so many jokes.[18]

Or the jokes may be other ways of annoying people. "Their greatest fun consists in playing tag on porches and having people chase them."[19] Or it may be more serious annoyance: "such as throwing stones at windows of homes and ridiculing persons in the street who are known as 'odd characters.' "[20] Even a murder may arise out of the ordinary by-play of two gangs of young boys in rivalry.

> Dey picked on us for two years, but even den we wouldn't a shot if "Stinky" – the big guy and the leader of the Elstons – hadn't jumped out of his dugout in a coal pile Saturday and waved a long bayonet wid a red flag on one end of it and an American flag upside down on de udder and dared us to come over de tracks.[21]

Once the gang has been developed, it becomes a serious competitor with other institutions as a controlling factor in the boy's life. The importance of the gang lies in its being the only social world of the boy's own age and, in a sense, of his own creation. All other agencies belong to elders; the gang belongs to the boy. Whether he is a leader or just one of the pack, whether his assigned rank has been won by force or ingenuity or represents a lack of superior force or ingenuity, once that rank is established the child accepts it and abides by the rules for changing it.

Children are peculiarly sensitive to suggestion.

> It is known that young people and people in general have little resistance to suggestion, that fashions of thought and fashions of dress spread rapidly through conversation and imitation, and that any form of behavior may be normalized through conversation and participation of numbers.[22]

In the boy's gang, conversation, gossip, approval, participation, and repetition will make any kind of behavior whatsoever normal.

The gang is important, because the reaction of others is the source of the greater part of the individual's conduct. Conduct is learned in the sense that it is a response to a situation made by other people. The smile, the frown, approval and disapproval, praise and condemnation, companionship, affection, dislike, instruments, opportunities, denial of opportunities, are all elements at hand for the individual and are the source of his behavior. It is not essential that the whole world approve; it is essential that the limited world to which the individual is attached approve. What other people think is the more important because what they think will express itself in what they do and in what they say; and in what they do or say, in the way they look, in the sound of their voices, in the physical posture that they assume, the individual finds the stimuli that call out those particular attitudes that will bring the needed and desired approval from his immediate face-to-face companionship. It is here that we must look for the origin of criminal behavior. It is here, largely, that the roots of conduct difficulties are to be found. What one learns to do, one does if it is approved by the world in which one lives. That world is the very limited world which approves of the conduct one has learned to seek approval for. The group, once it becomes conscious of itself as an entity, tends to feed and fortify itself in terms of its own values. The contrast with the rest of the world merely strengthens the group, and war merely enhances its resistance.

THE GROUP AND THE COMMUNITY

Once the differentiation of the gang has taken place, it becomes a competitor for the child's allegiance, and wins in a certain number of cases.

The growing child in a modern large city is exposed to a variety of conflicting stimuli, interests, and patterns. Not only are there differences between the family, the school, the church, and the street gang, but the family itself may be representative of a series of differences between parents and children, between father and mother, between older and younger children. The pattern is uneven, the demands are contradictory. What is approved in one place is derided and condemned in another.

Behavior is a matter of choice as to whose approval you want. And whose approval you want may be determined by such invisible and subtle influences as whom you like, who has given you pleasure, who has commended you. Conflicting demands for the growing child's loyalty are the source of much of the difficulty.

The fact that the gang wins in many instances does not reflect upon the children. It reflects upon the other agencies that are competing for the child's adherence. Of a dozen children who have come into conflict with the other groups in the community and have given their loyalty to the gang instead, the victory of the gang may have had a different cause in each case.

The family by its internal weakness may have been a contributory factor. The father or mother or an older brother may have been delinquent, or there may have been sharp conflict of opinions and attitudes in the family, or constant bickering and incompatibility between the parents, or the father may have been dead and the mother forced away from home so that the children were left unsupervised, or an ignorant and poverty-stricken mother may have encouraged the child to bring in food or money whether earned or stolen, or the father may have been a drunkard and given to seriously mistreating the child and breaking down the loyalty and unity which are essential to the slow maturation of systematic habit formation. In these and innumerable other examples that might be cited of family inadequacy we have a source for the acceptance by the child of his playmates and gang affiliates *as a substitute for the home.* Gang membership under these circumstances may be a perfectly natural reaction and a seeking for fun, contentment, and status. That the fun may take on delinquent forms is another matter, and depends on the opportunities for such uses of leisure within the environment as make delinquency an alternative, or by-product, of gang activity.

If the family itself is a unit and well co-ordinated, it still may contribute to delinquency by forcing upon the child an incompatible pattern. The dislike of the pattern, again, may arise from many different reasons, none of which are in themselves evidence of moral turpitude or psychical deficiency on the part of the child.

The objections to going to school may arise from lack of good hearing, from poor eyesight, from undernourishment, from being left-handed, from dislike for the teacher because of favoritism, from being taken away from playmates because the family moves, from lack of interest in intellectual pursuits, from being either too big or too small for the grade, from undue competition with other children within the family, from a desire for excitement which the school does not provide, from having poor clothes and being ashamed to go to school, from a too rapid maturing, from a too slow development, from losing a grade because of illness, or from any number of other causes. That is, even in a "good" family, where moral standards are rigid, habits regular, ambitions high, there may still be adequate cause for the child to fall out of the pattern of the family interest because there are insufficient insight and sympathy for his needs, with the consequent conversion of the difficulty into conflict.

Truancy may in some degree have its roots in physical defect.

"Thus, only 2.9 per cent of normal school children were suffering from malnutrition, whereas 26.2 per cent of truants were undernourished. Seven and three-tenths per cent of normal school children had defective vision, whereas 20.1 per cent of truants were so handicapped. Forty-nine and four-tenths per cent of normal children had defective teeth, whereas 91.2 per cent of truants had bad teeth."[23]

The physical defect may not be a direct cause of truancy, but it may contribute to that disgust with the school which may be directly responsible for truancy. "These are children in whom a definite attitude of dislike or even of disgust toward school has been built up."

If the deviation could be compensated by having its need met, then the conflict might never arise and the competition of the gang would not be serious. But ordinarily it is not met.

> Under our system of compulsory education we force into schools many, many children who would otherwise have been kept, or at least allowed to stay, at home — the "delicate" child, the excessively shy child, the child with some obvious defect, the child who does not care especially for books or activities that appeal only to the intellect. Now we make all of these children attend school, but we have not yet adapted our educational system to their needs.[24]

The difficulties of the child who is forced out of step in the school system, either through poor health or through lack of aptitude for scholastic endeavor, are met by the school authorities in terms of conflict, discipline, and tradition.

> This group has been regarded by school teachers and administrators as more or less of an enigma, because these children stand out so decidedly from their playmates as being free from the domination of school discipline. Threats, punishment, hearings at the Bureau of Attendance, pleas of parents, frequently even commitments to the truant school do not seem to be successful in breaking up this attitude of unyielding resistance to compulsory schooling. It is because the truant is usually such an enigma to the average school administrator that he arouses so much ire. The response of the school administrator to the problem of truancy takes very little cognizance of the specific factors which have entered into the individual case of truancy. His response is in terms of an established tradition.[25]

Another source of failure of the other agencies within the community to fulfill the demands made upon them for winning the loyalty and cooperation of the child who ultimately becomes delinquent may have no direct relation to the family or to the school, but be the results of the environment. The family may live in such crowded quarters as to force the child into the street to such an extent that street life takes the place of family life. The family may be living in a neighborhood where houses of prostitution are located; where gangsters gather; where there is a great deal of perversion of one sort or another; where street pilfering is a local custom; where there is hostility to the police; where there is race friction and warfare; where the children, without the knowledge of their parents, may find means of employment in illicit ways such as acting as procurers for prostitutes or as messengers and go-betweens for criminals; where they can observe the possession of guns, the taking of dope; where they can hear all sorts of tales and observe practices or be invited to participate in practices, or become conscious of habits, attitudes, morals, which are entirely in conflict with the teaching, habits, and points of view of the family in which they live. And because the family under these conditions may be an inadequate instrument for the purpose of supervising and co-ordinating all the child's activities, the family may lose the battle for the imposition of its own standards just because there was a lack of time, energy, space, for the doing of the things that needed to be done or for the provision of the room that the children required for the development of their normal play life.

The activities which are taken as a substitute for those provided by the community may be innocent enough in themselves. The New York Crime Commission found that the activities of truants, as a rule, were not delinquent activities: the children flew pigeons, went fishing, rode in the subway and the "L," went to the movies, went to a park, shot craps, collected junk, went to work, peddled fruit, went auto riding with older boys, hitched on the backs of wagons, delivered wetwash, and stole lead pipe for sale. These activities, we see, were for the children an adequate substitute for the school which they did not particularly enjoy; instead of doing required things which were not particularly attractive to them — they almost all liked mechanical shop work but were generally indifferent to purely intellectual endeavor — these children turned to the endless opportunities for adventure in the city streets. Here they are free of physical restraint, can avoid any authority they do not wish to acknowledge; may use their wits and legs and voices for objectives they themselves set.

But these and other activities carried on during truancy or in spare time are carried on in a group. The gang tends to dominate the children's activities as soon as conflict arises. And conflict arises frequently over issues much less conspicuous than stealing. In the congested neighborhoods where most of the young delinquent gangs arise, the elements of conflict between the old and the young are natural and difficult to avoid. The old want peace, security, quiet, routine, protection of property. The young want just the opposite: chiefly room, noise, running about, unorganized mischief, fighting, shouting, yelling.

The crowded homes provide no place for the children, and therefore force them into the streets for play. Not only the homes are congested, but the streets are, too. In densely populated sections children engaged in even the mildest activities seem in the way. The absence of open spaces on the one hand and the conflict of interests on the other provide many occasions for opposition, dispute, and difference.

Gang KK. This group of 12 boys, ranging in age from 12 to 15 years, were all American-born. They were fond of athletics and had made a habit of playing hand-ball against the rear wall of a moving picture theatre. Their yells disturbed the patrons of the theatre, and the management frequently ordered them away from the premises. They left, but returned. Finally, in anger, the movie proprietor called a patrol wagon and had them loaded into it. They were arraigned in the Children's Court, but discharged. None of these boys had previous court records. They consisted partly of boys who lived in the immediate neighborhood, and partly of former residents, who still kept up their intimacy with the group.[26]

Here is an illustration of the difficulty in its simplest form. It is no crime to play handball against a wall. Nor is it a crime to yell and shout while the playing proceeds. In fact, the shouting, yelling, rough-housing, are an integral part of the game. It would be no game at all if this loud verbalization could not go on. The patrons are watching a picture and the noise disturbs them. The owner wants to keep his customers. A natural conflict has arisen, and no compromise is possible: the children cannot promise not to play or shout, the patrons cannot help being annoyed. The alternative is a different place to play. But a different place may not exist; there may be only one available wall and ground in the neighborhood. The children are arrested. A definition of evil has been created, a court record has been set up. The beginning of a career may have been marked. A differentiation has now been created which would never have arisen if the interests of the children were as highly considered as those of the patrons of the theater or of the owner. The children needed space and a wall; these should have been provided in some form that would not involve the children with the court, the police, the patrol wagon, with which they had had no previous contact.

The process of gang formation may be stimulated also by the natural efforts of parents to maintain their own social standards in a continual process of classification, of separation of the "good" and the "bad," the right and the wrong. Parents carry their attitudes over to their children by talk, gossip, approval, condemnation, punishment, and reward. A system of values, judgments, differentiations, and classifications makes itself felt very early in the children's lives, and may have any number of grounds: religious, racial, economic, social, professional, and occupational. The more differentiation in the community, the greater the heterogeneity of the population, the less internal unity and sympathy, the greater the ease with which gangs are formed. In a sense, therefore, the gangs derive from the natural conflict that exists within the community itself.

Gangs are not merely spatial relationships — blocks, neighbor-hoods — but they are social relationships. The Irish gangs, the Jewish gangs, the Italian gangs, the Polish gangs, the gangs of English-speaking and non-English-speaking members of the community, are all evidence of the range of conflict within which the individual finds an outlet, recognition, and companionship.

A MATTER OF DEFINITION

In the conflict between the young delinquent and the community there develop two opposing definitions of the situation. In the beginning the definition of the situation by the young delinquent may be in the form of play, adventure, excitement, interest, mischief, fun. Breaking windows, annoying people, running around porches, climbing over roofs, stealing from pushcarts, playing truant — all are items of play, adventure, excitement. To the community, however, these activities may and often do take on the form of a nuisance, evil, delinquency, with the demand for control, admonition, chastisement, punishment, police court, truant school. This conflict over the situation is one that arises out of a divergence of values. As the problem develops, the situation gradually becomes redefined. The attitude of the community hardens definitely into a demand for suppression. There is a gradual shift from the definition of the specific acts as evil to a definition of the individual as evil, so that all his acts come to be looked upon with suspicion. In the process of identification his companions, hang-outs, play, speech, income, all his conduct, the personality itself, become subject to scrutiny and question. From the community's point of view, the individual who used to do bad and mischievous things has now become a bad and unredeemable human being. From the individual's point of view there has taken place a similar change. He has gone slowly from a sense of grievance and injustice, of being unduly mistreated and punished, to a recognition that the definition of him as a human being is different from that of other boys in his neighborhood, his school, street, community. This recognition on his part becomes a process of self-identification and integration with the group which shares his activities. It becomes, in part, a process of rationalization; in part, a simple response to a specialized type of stimulus. The young delinquent becomes bad because he is defined as bad and because he is not believed if he is good. There is a persistent demand for consistency in character. The community cannot deal with people whom it cannot define. Reputation is this sort of public definition. Once it is established, then unconsciously all agencies combine to maintain this definition even when they apparently and consciously attempt to deny their own implicit judgment.

Early in his career, then, the incipient professional criminal develops an attitude of antagonism to the regulated orderly life that he is required to lead. This attitude is hardened and crystallized by opposition. The conflict becomes a clash of wills. And experience too often has proved that threats, punishments, beatings, commitments to institutions, abuse and defamation of one sort or another, are of no avail. Punishment breaks down against the child's stubbornness. What has happened is that the child has been defined as an "incorrigible" both by his contacts and by himself, and an attempt at a direct breaking down of will generally fails.

The child meets the situation in the only way he can, by defiance and escape — physical escape if possible, or emotional escape by derision, anger, contempt, hatred, disgust, tantrums, destructiveness, and physical violence. The response of the child is just as intelligent and intelligible as that of the schools, of the authorities. They have taken a simple problem, the lack of fitness of an institution to a particular child's needs, and have made a moral issue out of it with values outside the child's ken. It takes on the form of war between two wills, and the longer the war lasts, the more certainly does the child become incorrigible. The child will not yield because he cannot yield — his nature requires other channels for pleasant growth; the school system or society will not yield because it does not see the issues involved as between the incompatibility of an institution and a child's needs, sometimes physical needs, and will instead attempt to twist the child's nature to the institution with that consequent distortion of the child which makes an unsocial career inevitable. The verbalization of the conflict in terms of evil, delinquency, incorrigibility, badness, arrest, force, punishment, stupidity, lack of intelligence, truancy, criminality, gives the innocent divergence of the child from the straight road a meaning that it did not have in the beginning and makes its continuance in these same terms by so much the more inevitable.

The only important fact, when the issue arises of the boy's inability to acquire the specific habits which organized institutions attempt to impose upon him, is that this conflict becomes the occasion for him to acquire another series of habits, interests, and attitudes as a substitute.

These habits become as effective in motivating and guiding conduct as would have been those which the orderly routine social institutions attempted to impose had they been acquired.

This conflict gives the gang its hold, because the gang provides escape, security, pleasure, and peace. The gang also gives room for the motor activity which plays a large role in a child's life. The attempt to break up the gang by force merely strengthens it. The arrest of the children has consequences undreamed-of, for several reasons.

First, only some of the children are caught though all may be equally guilty. There is a great deal more delinquency practiced and committed by the young groups than comes to the attention of the police. The boy arrested, therefore, is singled out in specialized treatment. This boy, no more guilty than the other members of his group, discovers a world of which he knew little. His arrest suddenly precipitates a series of institutions, attitudes, and experiences which the other children do not share. For this boy there suddenly appear the police, the patrol wagon, the police station, the other delinquents and criminals found in the police lock-ups, the court with all its agencies such as bailiffs, clerks, bondsmen, lawyers, probation officers. There are bars, cells, handcuffs, criminals. He is questioned, examined, tested, investigated. His history is gone into, his family is brought into court. Witnesses make their appearance. The boy, no different from the rest of his gang, suddenly becomes the center of a major drama in which all sorts of unexpected characters play important roles. And what is it all about? about the accustomed things his gang has done and has been doing for a long time. In this entirely new world he is made conscious of himself as a different human being than he was before his arrest. He becomes classified as a thief, perhaps, and the entire world about him has suddenly become a different place for him and will remain different for the rest of his life.

THE DRAMATIZATION OF EVIL

The first dramatization of the "evil" which separates the child out of his group for specialized treatment plays a greater role in making the criminal than perhaps any other experience. It cannot be too often emphasized that for the child the whole situation has become different. He now lives in a different world. He has been tagged. A new and hitherto non-existent environment has been precipitated out for him.

The process of making the criminal, therefore, is a process of tagging, defining, identifying, segregating, describing, emphasizing, making conscious and self-conscious; it becomes a way of stimulating, suggesting, emphasizing, and evoking the very traits that are complained of. If the theory of relation of response to stimulus has any meaning, the entire process of dealing with the young delinquent is mischievous in so far as it identifies him to himself or to the environment as a delinquent person.

The person becomes the thing he is described as being. Nor does it seem to matter whether the valuation is made by those who would punish or by those who would reform. In either case the emphasis is upon the conduct that is disapproved of. The parents or the policeman, the older brother or the court, the probation officer or the juvenile institution, in so far as they rest upon the thing complained of, rest upon a false ground. Their very enthusiasm defeats their aim. The harder they work to reform the evil, the greater the evil grows under their hands. The persistent suggestion, with whatever good intentions, works mischief, because it leads to bringing out the bad behavior that it would suppress. The way out is through a refusal to dramatize the evil. The less said about it the better. The more said about something else, still better.

> The hard-drinker who keeps thinking of not drinking is doing what he can to initiate the acts which lead to drinking. He is starting with the stimulus to his habit. To succeed he must find some positive interest or line of action which will inhibit the drinking series and which by instituting another course of action will bring him to his desired end.[27]

The dramatization of the evil therefore tends to precipitate the conflict situation which was first created through some innocent maladjustment. The child's isolation forces him into companionship with other children similarly defined, and the gang becomes his means of escape, his security. The life of the gang gives it special mores, and the attack by the community upon these mores merely overemphasizes the conflict already in existence, and makes it the source of a new series of experiences that lead directly to a criminal career.

In dealing with the delinquent, the criminal, therefore, the important thing to remember is that we are dealing with a human being who is responding normally to the demands, stimuli, approval, expectancy, of the group with whom he is associated. We are dealing not with an individual but with a group.

In a study of 6,000 instances of stealing, with reference to the number of boys involved, it was found that in 90.4 per cent of the cases two or more boys were known to have been involved in the act and were consequently brought to court. Only 9.6 per cent of all the cases were acts of single individuals. Since this study was based upon the number of boys brought to court, and since in many cases not all of the boys involved were caught and brought to court, it is certain that the percentage of group stealing is therefore even greater than 90.4 per cent. It cannot be doubted that delinquency, particularly stealing, almost invariably involves two or more persons.[28]

That group may be a small gang, a gang of children just growing up, a gang of young "toughs" of nineteen or twenty, or a gang of older criminals of thirty. If we are not dealing with a gang we may be dealing with a family. And if we are not dealing with either of these especially we may be dealing with a community. In practice all these factors — the family, the gang, and the community — may be important in the development and the maintenance of that attitude towards the world which makes a criminal career a normal, an accepted and approved way of life.

Direct attack upon the individual in these circumstances is a dubious undertaking. By the time the individual has become a criminal his habits have been so shaped that we have a fairly integrated character whose whole career is in tune with the peculiar bit of the environment for which he has developed the behavior and habits that cause him to be apprehended. In theory isolation from that group ought to provide occasion for change in the individual's habit structure. It might, if the individual were transplanted to a group whose values and activities had the approval of the wider community, and in which the newcomer might hope to gain full acceptance eventually. But until now isolation has meant the grouping in close confinement of persons whose strongest common bond has been their socially disapproved delinquent conduct. Thus the attack cannot be made without reference to group life.

The attack must be on the whole group; for only by changing its attitudes and ideals, interests and habits, can the stimuli which it exerts upon the individual be changed. Punishment as retribution has failed to reform, that is, to change character. If the individual can be made aware of a different set of values for which he may receive approval, then we may be on the road to a change in his character. But such a change of values involves a change in stimuli, which means that the criminal's social world must be changed before he can be changed.

THE SCAPEGOAT IS A SNARE AND A DELUSION

The point of view here developed rejects all assumptions that would impute crime to the individual in the sense that a personal shortcoming of the offender is the cause of the unsocial behavior. The assumption that crime is caused by any sort of inferiority, physiological or psychological, is here completely and unequivocally repudiated.

This of course does not mean that morphological or psychological techniques do not have value in dealing with the individual. It merely means that they have no greater value in the study of criminology than they would have in the study of any profession. If a poor IQ is a bad beginning for a career in medicine, it is also a poor beginning for a career in crime. If the psychiatrist can testify that a psychopath will make an irritable doctor he can prove the same for the criminal. But he can prove no more. The criminal differs from the rest of his fellows only in the sense that he has learned to respond to the stimuli of a very small and specialized group; but that group must exist or the criminal could not exist. In that he is like the mass of men, living a certain kind of life with the kind of companions that make life possible.

This explanation of criminal behavior is meant to apply to those who more or less consistently pursue the criminal career. It does not necessarily presume to describe the accidental criminal or the man who commits a crime of passion. Here perhaps the theories that would seek the cause of crime in the individual may have greater application than in attempting to deal with those who follow a life of crime. But even in the accidental criminal there is a strong presumption that the accident is the outcome of a habit situation. Any habit tends to have a background of social conditioning.

> A man with the habit of giving way to anger may show his habit by a murderous attack upon some one who has offended. His act is nonetheless due to habit because it occurs only once in his life. The essence of habit is an acquired predisposition to *ways* or modes of response, not to particular acts except as, under special conditions, these express a way of behaving. Habit means special sensitiveness or accessibility to certain classes of stimuli, standing predilections and aversions, rather than bare recurrence of specific acts. It means will.[29]

In other words, perhaps the accidental criminal also is to be explained in terms such as we used in discussing the professional criminal.

NOTES

1.   Roscoe Pound, *Criminal Justice in America,* pp. 33-34. New York, 1930.

2.   Hans Kurella, *Cesare Lombroso, A Modern Man of Science,* p. 18. London, 1911.

3.   Morris Ploscowe, "Some Causative Factors in Criminality," National Commission on Law Observance and Enforcement, No. 13, *Report on the Causes of Crime,* Vol. I, p. 21. Washington, D.C., 1931.

4.   Philip Archibald Parsons, *Crime and the Criminal,* p. 41 (quoting Hack Tuke, *Case of Congenital Moral Defect*). New York, 1926.

5.   Havelock Ellis, *The Criminal,* p. 194. London, Fifth Edition, 1910.

6.   See Chapter VIII for evidence of the persistence of such views.

7.   Henry H. Goddard, *Human Efficiency and Levels of Intelligence,* p. 73. Princeton, 1920.

8.   Max G. Schlapp and Edward H. Smith, *The New Criminology,* p. 119. New York, 1928.

9.   Report of the President of the American Eugenics Society, June 26, 1926, p. 18.

10. The environmentalist school does not fall within this classification.

11. William T. Root, Jr., *A Psychological and Educational Survey of 1916 Prisoners in the Western Penitentiary of Pennsylvania,* p. 10. 1927.

12. Parsons, op. cit., p. 46.

13. State of New York. Report of the Crime Commission, 1930. Legislative Document (1930) No. 98, p. 243.

14. State of New York. Report of the Crime Commission, 1927. Legislative Document (1927) No. 94, p. 285.

15. Frederic M. Thrasher, *The Gang,* p. 29. Chicago, 1927.

16. Thrasher, op. cit., p. 29.

17. Ibid., p. 36.

18. Ibid., pp. 94-95.

19. New York Crime Commission, 1927 Report, p. 371.

20. Ibid., p. 370.

21. Thrasher, op. cit., p. 180.

22.   William I. Thomas and Dorothy S. Thomas, *The Child in America,* p. 164. New York, 1928.

23.   New York Crime Commission, 1927 Report, p. 287.

24.   White-Williams Foundation: Five Years' Review for the Period Ending December 31, 1921, p. 8.

25.   New York Crime Commission, 1927 Report, p. 285.

26.   State of New York. Report of the Crime Commission, 1928, p. 620. Legislative Document (1928) No. 23.

27.   John Dewey, *Human Nature and Conduct,* p. 35. New York, 1922.

28.   Clifford R. Shaw and Earl D. Myers, "The Juvenile Delinquent," *The Illinois Crime Survey,* pp. 662-663. Chicago, 1929.

29.   Dewey, op. cit., p. 42.

THE PRODUCTIVITY OF CRIME
Karl Marx

A philosopher produces ideas, a poet poems, a clergyman sermons, a professor compendia, and so on. A criminal produces crimes. If we look a little closer at the connection between this latter branch of production and society as a whole, we shall rid ourselves of many prejudices. The criminal produces not only crimes, but also criminal law, and with this also the professor who gives lectures on criminal law, and in addition to this the inevitable compendium in which this same professor throws his lectures onto the general market as "commodities." This brings with it augmentation of national wealth, quite apart from the personal enjoyment which – as a competent witness, Herr Professor Roscher, tells us – the manuscript of the compendium brings to the originator himself.

The criminal moreover produces the whole of the police and of criminal justice, constables, judges, hangmen, juries, etc.; and all these different lines of business, which form equally many categories of the social division of labor, develop different capacities of the human spirit, create new needs and new ways of satisfying them. Torture alone has given

From *Theories of Surplus Value*, vol. I, pp. 375-6 (Foreign Languages Publishing House, Moscow).

rise to the most ingenious mechanical inventions, and employed many honorable craftsmen in the production of its instruments.

The criminal produces an impression, partly moral and partly tragic, as the case may be, and in this way renders a "service" by arousing the moral and aesthetic feelings of the public. He produces not only compendia on Criminal Law, not only penal codes and along with them legislators in this field, but also art, belles lettres, novels, and even tragedies, as not only Müllner's *Schuld* and Schiller's *Räuber* show, but also Sophocles' *Oedipus* and Shakespeare's *Richard the Third*. The criminal breaks the monotony and everyday security of bourgeois life. In this way he keeps it from stagnation, and gives rise to that uneasy tension and agility without which even the spur of competition would get blunted. Thus he gives a stimulus to the productive forces. While crime takes a part of the superfluous population off the labor market and thus reduces competition among the laborers – up to a certain point preventing wages from falling below the minimum – the struggle against crime absorbs another part of this population. Thus the criminal comes in as one of those natural "counterweights" which bring about a correct balance and open up a whole perspective of "useful" occupations.

The effects of the criminal on the development of productive power can be shown in detail. Would locks ever have reached their present degree of excellence had there been no thieves? Would the making of bank-notes have reached its present perfection had there been no forgers? Would the microscope have found its way into the ordinary sphere of commerce (see Babbage) but for trading frauds? Doesn't practical chemistry owe just as much to adulteration of commodities and the efforts to show it up as to the honest zeal for production? Crime, through its constantly new methods of attack on property, constantly calls into being new methods of defense, and so is as productive as strikes for the invention of machines. And if one leaves the sphere of private crime: would the world-market ever have come into being but for national crime? Indeed, would even the nations have arisen? And hasn't the Tree of Sin been at the same time the Tree of Knowledge ever since the time of Adam?

In his *Fable of the Bees* (1705) Mandeville had already shown that every possible kind of occupation is productive, and had given expression to the line of this whole argument:

That which we call Evil in this World, Moral as well as Natural, is the grand Principle that makes us Sociable Creatures, the solid Basis, the

Life and Support of all Trades and Employments without exception ... there we must look for the true origin of all Arts and
Sciences; and ... the moment, Evil ceases, the Society must be
spoil'd if not totally dissolved. (2nd edition, London, 1723, p. 428).

Only Mandeville was of course infinitely bolder and more honest than
the philistine apologists of bourgeois society.

POVERTY AND THE CRIMINAL PROCESS

William J. Chambliss and Robert B. Seidman

The shape and character of the legal system in complex societies can be
understood as deriving from the conflicts inherent in the structure of these
societies which are stratified economically and politically. Generally, the
legal system in its normative strictures and organizational operations will
exhibit those norms and those practices that maintain and enhance the
position of entrenched powerholders. Those broad principles underlying
the legal order are ramified in and attenuated by the organizational aims of
complex societies. The logical structure and its empirical implications,
uncovered in our analysis of law, order, and power, may be set forth as a
set of propositions. We begin with propositions about the relationship
between a group's norms and the law:

Propositions

1. One's "web of life" or the conditions of one's life affect one's values
   and (internalized) norms.

2. Complex societies are composed of groups with widely different life
   conditions.

3. Therefore, complex societies are also composed of highly disparate
   and conflicting sets of norms.

4. The probability of a group's having *its* particular normative system
   embodied in law is *not* distributed equally among the social groups

From William J. Chambliss and Robert B. Seidman, *Law, Order, and
Power*, Reading, Mass.: Addison-Wesley, 1971.

but, rather, is closely related to the group's political and economic position.

5. The higher a group's political or economic position, the greater is the probability that its views will be reflected in the laws.

According to these first five propositions, then, the law will differentially reflect the perspectives, values, definitions of reality, and morality of the middle and upper classes while being in opposition to the morality and values of the poor and lower classes. Given this twist in the content of the law, we are not surprised that the poor should be criminal more often than the nonpoor. The systematically induced bias in a society against the poor goes considerably farther than simply having values incorporated within the legal system which are antithetical to their ways of life. Since, in complex societies, the decision to enforce the laws against certain persons and not against others will be determined primarily by criteria derived from the bureaucratic nature of the law-enforcement agencies, we have the following propositions which explain what takes place within these agencies and the kinds of decisions they are likely to make:

1. The legal system is organized through bureaucratically structured agencies, some of which are primarily norm-creating agencies and others of which are primarily norm-enforcing agencies.

2. The formal role-expectation for each official position in the bureaucracy is defined by authoritatively decreed rules issuing from officials in other positions who themselves operate under position-defining norms giving them the power to issue such rules.

3. Rules, whether defining norm-creating positions or norm-applying positions, necessarily require discretion in the role-occupant for their application.

4. In addition, the rules are for a variety of reasons frequently vague, ambiguous, contradictory, or weakly or inadequately sanctioned.

5. Therefore, each level of the bureaucracy possesses considerable discretion as to the performance of its duties.

6. The decision to create rules by rule-creating officials or to enforce rules by rule-enforcing officials will be determined primarily by criteria derived from the bureaucratic nature of the legal system.

7. Rule-creation and rule-enforcement will take place when such creation or enforcement increases the rewards for the agencies and their officials, and they will not take place when they are conducive to organizational strain.

8. The creation of the rules which define the roles of law-enforcing agencies has been primarily the task of the appellate courts, for which the principal rewards are in the form of approval of other judges, lawyers, and higher-status middle-class persons generally.

9. The explicit value-set of judges, lawyers, and higher-status middle-class persons generally is that which is embodied in the aims of legal-rational legitimacy.

10. Therefore, the rules created by appellate courts will tend to conform to the requirements of legal-rational legitimacy and to the specific administrative requirements of the court organization.

11. The enforcement of laws against persons who possess little or no political power will generally be rewarding to the enforcement agencies of the legal system, while the enforcement of laws against persons who possess political power will be conducive to strains for those agencies.

12. In complex societies, political power is closely tied to social position.

13. Therefore, those laws which prohibit certain types of behavior popular among lower-class persons are more likely to be enforced, while laws restricting the behavior of middle- or upper-class persons are not likely to be enforced.

14. Where laws are so stated that people of all classes are equally likely to violate them, the lower the social position of an offender, the greater is the likelihood that sanctions will be imposed on him.

15. When sanctions are imposed, the most severe sanctions will be imposed on persons in the lowest social class.

16. Legal-rational legitimacy requires that laws be stated in general terms equally applicable to all.

17. Therefore, the rules defining the roles of law-enforcement officials will require them to apply the law in an equitable manner.

18. Therefore, to the extent that the rules to be applied are potentially applicable to persons of different social classes, the role-performance

of law-enforcement officials may be expected to differ from the role-expectation embodied in the norms defining their positions.

Taken as a unit, these propositions represent the basis of a theory of the legal process in complex societies. It is a theory derived essentially from the facts of the operation of criminal law — facts gathered by a large number of researchers into the criminal-law process at each level of the operation.

POVERTY AND THE LEGAL SYSTEM

The empirical data and the propositions based on them make it abundantly clear that the poor do not receive the same treatment at the hands of the agents of law-enforcement as the well-to-do or middle class. This differential treatment is systematic and complete. It includes the practice by the police and prosecuting attorneys of choosing to look for and impose punishments for offenses that are characteristically committed by the poor and ignoring those committed by the more affluent members of the community. Where offenses are equally likely to be committed by persons from different social classes (such as gambling), the police will look for these crimes in the lower-class neighborhoods rather than in middle- or upper-class neighborhoods. For example, in almost every American community, medical doctors, dentists, and practicing attorneys are the groups most actively engaged in placing bets with bookmakers. This is so not because of the inherently corrupt tendencies of people in these professions but rather because these people can hide substantial amounts of their income and thus avoid paying taxes on that income. They can then afford to gamble with this tax-free money and declare it as gains only when they substantially increase their wealth. They cannot simply spend the money they do not declare, since to do so would mean living at a much higher level than could be justified by their acknowledged income which makes good grounds for being prosecuted for income tax evasion. Hence, professional groups are the most important financial backers of many forms of gambling. Yet the police virtually never attempt to discover this practice and punish the professional people who are gambling, nor do they very often curtail the activities of those who take the bets (except, of course, where these operations are part of a criminal organization, which subject we shall take up shortly). By contrast, persons who bet on or sell policy numbers (a typically lower-class form of

gambling) are often subject to arrest and prosecution. Similarly, middle-
and upper-class suburbanites who play poker in their own homes are never
sought out or prosecuted for gambling (though in most states there are
statutes prohibiting this game). But lower-class persons who shoot dice in
the alley or hallway of their apartment house (the apartment itself is of
course too small to permit such activities) are constantly in jeopardy of
legal intervention. To reduce the visibility of gambling, the devotees may
be willing to pay someone a "cup" or the "pot" in order to use their
apartment for a game. To do so, however, makes the entire group
vulnerable, since this solution to the problem of finding space in which to
gamble simultaneously increases the ability of the police and prosecutor to
make the game appear as one run by "professional gamblers," thereby
justifying arrest and prosecution. As we shall see, in most communities in
the United States, there is a substantial amount of highly organized
gambling activity which takes place with the complicity of the police and
the prosecuting attorney's office. The purveyors of these enterprises are
generally immune from prosecution. It is ironically the games between
friends and acquaintances in lower-class areas which are likely to be chosen
for prosecution; similar games among middle- and upper-class members of
the community are ignored, as are games handled by truly professional
gamblers.

   That the selective enforcement by policing agencies is not merely a
function of what is most pressingly needed by the society is clearly
indicated by a comparison of civil rights law-enforcement and the
enforcement of laws prohibiting the use of "dangerous drugs." On the one
hand, although riots and general discontent are rampant in the urban areas
where black ghettos are concentrated, the laws which prohibit discrimination in employment, unions, and housing, consumer fraud, housing
violations, and other protections for the poor are effectively ignored at
every level of the government, federal, state, and local. By contrast,
despite the preponderance of scientific evidence demonstrating that the
smoking of marijuana is a relatively harmless pastime (less harmful, most
experts agree than drinking alcohol), laws prohibiting marijuana smoking
are enforced vigorously. With respect to unfair employment, housing, and
labor practices, enforcement would involve the enforcement agencies in
conflicts with politically powerful groups. The federal government, for
example, would be involved in serious conflict with the politically
powerful trade unions if the section of the National Labor Relations Act
prohibiting discrimination in unions were enforced. And if sanctions were

inflicted for discrimination in employment, as it can be under Title VII of the Civil Rights Act of 1964, the federal and state governments would be at loggerheads with many of the nation's leading corporations. It is to avoid such clashes that only fourteen of some eight thousand complaints received by the Department of Justice between 1965 and 1968 complaining of discrimination in employment resulted in litigation.[1]

On the other hand, since marijuana smokers were, until quite recently, concentrated among the poor black and Chicano (Mexican-American) populations in the United States, these laws could be enforced at the will of the enforcement agencies and indeed they were. Recently, the spread of marijuana and other "drugs" to middle- and upper-class youths has increased the population of "criminals" substantially. It has also brought into public view some of the problems of selective enforcement which characterize America's legal process. It is possible that this increased visibility of police activities will bring about changes in policy and law. It is unlikely, however, that these changes will substantially alter the tendency of the legal system to select for enforcement laws dealing with acts of the poor.

Since 1941 there has been a constant stream of executive orders prohibiting discrimination in employment by any company holding government contracts. The latest order, Executive Order 11236 issued in 1965, is one of the most stringent. Despite the increased stringency of these executive orders, and despite the fact that most of the companies holding government contracts are covered by these orders, *there has never been a single contract with the government canceled nor sanctions applied because of job discrimination by the employer,*[2] though there are administrative board findings clearly showing discrimination in employment by companies holding government contracts.

By way of digression, this is an appropriate place to point out that it is because of the very great and real gap between "laws" and "enforcement" that the generally held ideal of a "fair" and "just" system of law can be maintained despite widespread tendencies subverting these goals. For few people would be so cynical as to doubt the sincerity of an executive order decrying discrimination in employment and providing for the cancelation of contracts with companies who engage in such practices. Yet the truth of the matter is that the order is totally meaningless; if the sanctions are never imposed and if the enforcement agencies do not seek out violators, it is apparent that the executive order does nothing – it is a rhetorical ritual, empty of content, whose principal significance is the acknowledgment of the need to placate dissentors. It succeeds indeed only in providing a false sense of the inherent justice of the system.

Perhaps the best way to grasp the all-encompassing nature of the differential treatment of the poor in the American legal system is through case studies. The intensive patrol by the police in slum areas presents a constant threat to everyone in the community, whether they are engaged in illegal activities or not.[3]

Case 1

Ralph worked the four-to-twelve shift in a factory. After work one night he decided to work on his car before going to sleep. Since he had no garage, the only place to work on the car was in the street. He was working on the engine, with the hood up when a policeman stopped and asked him what he was doing. He explained that he was fixing his car. The policeman asked to see his driver's license and registration card. Ralph showed these and the policeman left. Within five minutes another policeman had stopped and essentially the same scene took place. Five minutes after the second policeman left, a third patrol car turned the corner and asked Ralph what he was doing. According to the policeman and Ralph the conversation went like this:
Officer: Whatcha doing to the car, son?
Ralph (angrily): I'm stealin' the motherfucker.

Ralph was arrested and taken to the station. Later he was released after questioning by the lieutenant.

If a policeman suspects that someone had done something wrong, then the pattern of discriminatory treatment of the poor continues. The following case, adapted from the President's Crime Commission Report,[4] is illustrative of the kinds of problems encountered by the poor as they make their way from arrest through trial and conviction:

Case 2

Defendant A is spotted by a foot-patrol officer in the skid-row district of town, weaving along the street. When the officer approaches him, the man begins muttering incoherently and shrugs off the officer's inquiries. When the officer seizes his arm, A breaks the hold violently, curses the officer and the police. The patrolman puts in a call for a squad car, and the man is taken to the precinct station where he is booked on a double charge of drunkenness and disorderly conduct.

In the stationhouse

Defendant A's belt is removed to prevent any attempts at suicide; he is then put in the drunk tank to sober up.

His cellmate lies slumped and snoring on the cell's single steel bunk, sleeping off an all-day drunk, oblivious to the shouts . . . There are at least two men in each 4 X 8 foot cell and three in some . . . The stench of cheap alcohol, dried blood, urine and excrement covers the cell block. Except for the young man's shouts, it is quiet. Most of the prisoners are so drunk they gaze without seeing, unable to answer when spoken to. There are no lights in the cells, which form a square in the middle of the cell block. But the ring of naked light bulbs on the walls around the cell block throw the light into the cells, each of which is equipped with a steel bunk. There are no mattresses. "Mattresses wouldn't last the night," a policeman explains. "And with prisoners urinating all over them, they wouldn't be any good if they did last." The only sound in the cell block is the constant flowing of water through the toilets in each cell. The toilets do not have tops, which could be torn off and broken. Every half hour or so a policeman checks to see if the inmates are "still warm."

After sobering up, a drunk or disorderly can usually leave the lockup in four or five hours if he is able to post the collateral ($10-$25). No matter how many times he has been arrested before, he will not have to appear in court if he chooses to forfeit the collateral. The drunk without money stays in jail until court opens the next morning. At 6 a.m., the police vans come to collect the residue in the precinct lockups and take them to the courthouse cell blocks to await a 10 a.m. arraignment.

Preliminary hearing and arraignment

Defendant A, charged with drunkenness and disorderly conduct, is brought into court from the bullpen in a shuffling line of dirty, beat, unshaven counterparts, many still reeking of alcohol. Each spends an average of 90 seconds before the judge, time for the clerk to intone the charge and for the judge to ask if he desires counsel and how he pleads. Rarely does a request for counsel or a "not guilty" break the monotony of muttered "guilty" pleas. Lawyers are not often assigned in police courts, and anyone who can afford his own counsel will already have been released from jail on bond – to prepare for trial at a later date or to negotiate with the city prosecutor to drop the charges.

Occasionally, an unrepresented defendant will ask for trial. If the arresting officer is present, he will be tried on the spot. There are no jury trials for drunkenness. The policeman will testify that the man was "staggering," "his breath smelled of some sort of alcoholic beverage," his speech was "slurred," "his eyes were bloodshot and glassy." The man may protest that he had only a few drinks, but there are no witnesses to support his testimony, no scientific evidence to establish the level of alcohol in his blood at the time of arrest, no lawyers to cross-examine the officer. If the defendant pleads not guilty and hopes he can get counsel (his own or court-assigned), he may have his trial postponed a week or two. Meanwhile, he must make bond or return to jail.

Police-court sentencing is usually done immediately after a plea. A few courts with alcoholic rehabilitation court clinics may screen for likely candidates – those not too far along on the alcoholism trail – in the detention pens. Counsel, when available, can ask for a presentence report, but delay in sentencing means jail or bail in the meantime. On a short-term offense it is seldom worth it. Other kinds of petty offenders – disorderlies, vagrants, street-ordinance violators – follow a similar route in court. Guilty pleas are the rule. Without counsel or witnesses, it is the defendant's word against that of the police. Even when counsel is present, defense efforts at impeachment founder on the scanty records kept by the police in such petty offenses. The only defense may be the defendant's word, which is suspect if he has a record, or hard-to-find "character witnesses" without records from his slum neighborhood.

Because the crime is more serious, the poor defendant accused of a felony fares even worse than one who is accused of a misdemeanor. Frequently the difference between a misdemeanor and a felony charge is the result of police work to a greater extent than it is a result of the defendant's criminal act. The following case from Chambliss' research is illustrative.

Case 3

Louie, a black militant active in organizing the black community in a middle-sized western city, had failed to pay two traffic tickets. One ticket was for running a stop sign (at three miles an hour); another was for driving without a tail light on his car. A warrant was issued for his arrest. The police pursued him into the night and confronted him at 11:00 p.m. with the warrant. He was approaching his car when the policeman commanded him to place his hands on the top of his car and allow them to search him. He did so, and as he took the stance with his legs spread apart, the policeman kicked his legs to make him spread them apart more widely. After searching him, the policeman handcuffed him and began pushing him across the street to the police car. The policeman also pushed him as he started into the car, causing Louie to hit his head against the top of the automobile.

A friend of Louie's, Dan, was in a nearby cafe when someone came in and told him Louie was being arrested. Dan confronted the officer and demanded to know what Louie was being arrested for. The policeman informed Dan that if he wanted to accompany them to the police station to see that Louie was not mistreated he could. Dan entered the car and went with Louie and the policeman to the station.

Dan and Louie argued vehemently at the police station and accused the police of being "white racists" and of arresting them because they were black. Louie was shoved down to the floor and taken by force into the elevator and to the jail. Dan began to leave the station but was informed that he, too, was under arrest for "obstructing arrest." Dan tried to leave and was forcefully restrained. The police filed charges as follows:

Louie: charged with resisting arrest, public intoxication, and disorderly conduct (all misdemeanors).

Dan: charged with public intoxication, disorderly conduct, resisting arrest, and battery against a police officer.

The last charge, battery against a police officer, is a felony in the state and, as such, carried with it a possible prison sentence. The alleged battery came about when Dan "threw a pendulum which he was wearing around his neck at a police officer." The policeman claimed to have had his hand nicked by the pendulum.

Bail for Louie was set at $650. He was immediately released when friends posted bond, by paying a bail bondsman $65, which of course is never returned no matter what the result of the trial. Dan could not be bailed out until the hearing the next day, since a hearing is necessary to set the bail in felony cases. Since the arrest occurred on Friday, Dan had to spend the entire weekend in jail.

Friends contacted a lawyer. Dan and Louie insisted they were innocent. The lawyer agreed to talk to the district attorney. The lawyer they hired was with one of the best-known firms in the city. He arranged a bargain with the prosecuting attorney so that in exchange for a guilty plea to the disorderly conduct charges (and a possible six-months jail sentence or up to $1000 fine) the prosecution would drop the other charges. Louie and Dan said they wanted to plead not guilty. The lawyer then informed them that (a) if they pleaded guilty to the lesser offense, his fee would be $500, but (b) if they chose to plead not guilty and the case went to trial (which it probably would), his fee would be a minimum of $1500. He also told them that if they wished, they could ask for a court-appointed lawyer, and he acknowledged that court-appointed lawyers were sometimes excellent.

Ultimately, the men were able to raise $1500 (by a campaign for funds to defend themselves), and the case went to trial. Within two days of testimony the entire case was dismissed without ever going to the jury on the ground that the prosecution did not have sufficient evidence for bringing the case to court. At the hearing, the judge criticized the prosecution and pointed out the expense that the county had incurred. He failed to make note of the expense it had caused Louie and Dan. The two men who were accused of crimes which they did not commit and which were escalated by police because the latter's insensitivity and belligerence had elicited harsh words from Louie and Dan, were exonerated. But the whole episode cost them over two thousand dollars (the lawyer's fee turned out to be two thousand instead of fifteen hundred) and several nights in jail.

Case 4

The previous case contrasts sharply with that of Joe, who was arrested for disorderly conduct and malicious mischief against personal property. Joe was a black man who had been sharing an apartment with two white men. The three of them had an argument, and Joe broke some furniture in the apartment and cussed out his roommates. He moved from the apartment two days later, and one of the former roommates pressed charges. Joe was arrested. He spent the night in jail until he raised $125 to pay the bail bondsman (again, not refundable no matter what the outcome of the trial) so he could be released. The bondsman would *not* have been willing to provide bond except for the fact that Joe's employer signed the bond and put his home up for collateral. Joe asked for and was assigned a court-appointed lawyer. The lawyer encouraged Joe to plead guilty to whatever the prosecutor would offer. Joe refused. The lawyer requested that he be withdrawn from the case because he was "about to go on vacation." A new lawyer was appointed. Joe went to the new lawyer's office, and explained what had happened. He told the lawyer that he had witnesses that the property damages consisted of only a plate and that he had not assaulted anyone. The second lawyer suggested that he see still another lawyer, and the court appointed a third one. Each lawyer encouraged Joe to plead guilty. None of them acknowledged that he was being accused unjustly. Meanwhile, the man who had filed the original charge withdrew it and asked the prosecuting attorney's office to drop the charges.

The prosecuting attorney's office refused to do so and determined to pursue the case. After several weeks of postponement, indecision, and changing lawyers, during which no one would give Joe the satisfaction of telling him that he could perhaps win in a court fight, Joe pleaded guilty because, in his words, "I'm tired of all this fucking around, Chambliss." He was sentenced to three months in the county jail. As a consequence, he lost his job and had to drop out of a remedial reading program in which he was enrolled.

For the indigent, free representation by a lawyer is available in two ways: the court may appoint a lawyer chosen from a list supplied by the local bar association or, in states and communities with a public defender system, an indigent defendant may be assigned a public defender. In both instances, whether or not the defendant is indigent and therefore eligible for a court-appointed lawyer or a public defender is a question that must be decided by the judge. Standards of indigency are in no way prescribed and vary considerably from one judge to another:

Case 5

The defendant was charged with petty larceny. He had allegedly stolen a $19.95 sleeping bag from Sears department store. He was brought to the courtroom handcuffed after spending a night in jail awaiting his preliminary hearing. The judge asked if he could afford a lawyer.

Def: No sir, I would like to have one appointed by the court.
Judge: It's up to me to decide whether or not you should have one appointed by the court. Do you work?
Def: Yes Sir.
Judge: What do you do?
Def: I make sandals.
Judge: How much do you earn making sandals?
Def: About $40 a month.
Judge: Can you live on $40 a month?
Def: (nods yes)

Judge: Do you own any personal property?
Def: No.
Judge: Any musical instruments?
Def: Yes, a sitar.
Judge: How much does a sitar cost?
Def: I paid $150 for it.
Judge: O.K., you can sell your sitar and hire your own attorney. Hearing is set for tomorrow at 11:00 a.m.
Def: How can I sell it and get a lawyer while I'm in jail?
Judge: You'll have to work that out for yourself.

But even when the indigent is assigned a free lawyer, as the case of Joe illustrates, the court-appointed lawyer will conscientiously pursue the best interests of his client only if he can put professional duty without reward of money or status ahead of other more lucrative employment. Even where the state provides public defenders, as was pointed out earlier, the tendency is for the public defender simply to become a pawn of the prosecuting attorney's office. In any event, it is a simple maxim that the best disposition of a poor defendant from the standpoint of the practicing attorney, public defender, prosecuting attorney, judge, police – indeed, everyone in the legal system – is to convince the defendant in one way or another that he should plead guilty to something and throw himself on the mercy of the court. Given the disadvantageous position of the impoverished when confronted with the legal system, it is not surprising that most defendants are coerced into doing just that. It is unlikely that many of them are met with the mercy they plead for.

NOTES

1. William F. Ryan, "Uncle Sam's betrayal," *The Progressive*, May 1968, pp.25-28.

2. *Ibid.*, p. 25.

3. Field notes of William J. Chambliss.

4. President's Commission on Law Enforcement and Administration of Justice, *Task Force Report: The Police*, U.S. Government Printing Office, 1967.

Part VII
THE QUALITY OF LIFE

In the fervor of the late nineteen sixties two words came to dominate the discussion of modern man's plight: pollution and alienation. In general, the "quality of life" became a theme that was exploited and discussed by politicians, professors, and soothsayers. These themes are not brand new, of course, but the discussion of them has taken on a new urgency. The signs of discontent with the present way of life in industrial societies go deeper than high suicide, divorce, alcoholism and murder rates. The seeds of discontent are everywhere apparent to even the most optimistic observer: indeed, even Hubert Humphrey sees some cause for concern.

The article by Baran and Sweezey points to the irrational character of the capitalist economic system. This irrational character, they argue, is destructive of a qualitatively satisfying life for most of the people who must live within its boundaries. Erich Fromm develops this theme with more specific application to the psychological well-being of modern man. A biologist, William Murdoch, ends the section with an article on the relationship between environmental pollution and the power structure of modern societies. It is a sceptical conclusion, suggesting that change is likely to be unsuccessful unless it can be made to work in the interests of the decision-making elites.

THE IRRATIONAL SYSTEM

Paul A. Baran and Paul M. Sweezy

It is of the essence of capitalism that both goods and labor power are typically bought and sold on the market. In such a society relations among individuals are dominated by the principle of the exchange of equivalents, of *quid pro quo,* not only in economic matters but in all other aspects of life as well.

Not that the principle of equivalent exchange is or ever has been universally practiced in capitalist society. As Marx showed so convincingly in the closing chapters of the first volume of *Capital,* the primary accumulation of capital was effected through violence and plunder, and the same methods continue in daily use throughout capitalism's dependent colonies and semi-colonies. Nevertheless the ideological sway of *quid pro quo* became all but absolute. In their relations with each other and in what they teach those over whom they rule, capitalists are fully committed to the principle of *quid pro quo,* both as a guide to action and as a standard of morality.

This commitment reflected an important step forward in the development of the forces of production and in the evolution of human consciousness. Only on the basis of equivalent exchange was it possible to realize the more rational utilization of human and material resources which has been the central achievement of capitalism.[1] At the same time, it must never be forgotten that the rationality of *quid pro quo* is specifically capitalist rationality which at a certain stage of development

From Paul A. Baran and Paul M. Sweezy, *Monopoly Capital*, Monthly Review Press, 1966.

becomes incompatible with the underlying forces and relations of production. To ignore this and to treat *quid pro quo* as a universal maxim of rational conduct is in itself an aspect of bourgeois ideology, just as the radical-sounding assertion that under socialism exchange of equivalents can be immediately dispensed with betrays a utopian view of the nature of the economic problems faced by a socialist society.[2]

But even during the life span of capitalism itself, *quid pro quo* breaks down as a rational principle of economic and social organization. The giant corporation withdraws from the sphere of the market large segments of economic activity and subjects them to scientifically designed administration. This change represents a continuous increase in the rationality of the parts of the system, but it is not accompanied by any rationalization of the whole. On the contrary, with commodities being priced not according to their costs of production but to yield the maximum possible profit, the principle of *quid pro quo* turns into the opposite of a promoter of rational economic organization and instead becomes a formula for maintaining scarcity in the midst of potential plenty. Human and material resources remain idle because there is in the market no *quid* to exchange against the *quo* of their potential output. And this is true even though the real cost of such output would be nil. In the most advanced capitalist country a large part of the population lives in abysmal poverty while in the under-developed countries hundreds of millions suffer from disease and starvation because there is no mechanism for effecting an exchange of what they could produce for what they so desperately need. Insistence on the inviolability of equivalent exchange when what is to be exchanged costs nothing, strict economizing of resources when a large proportion of them goes to waste – these are obviously the very denial of the rationality which the concept of value and the principle of *quid pro quo* originally expressed.

The obsolescence of such central categories of bourgeois thought is but one symptom of the profoundly contradictory nature of monopoly capitalism, of the ever sharpening conflict between the rapidly advancing rationalization of the actual processes of production and the undiminished *elementality* of the system as a whole.[3] This conflict affects all aspects of society. While rationality has been conquering ever new areas of consciousness, the inability of bourgeois thought to comprehend the development of society as a whole has remained essentially unchanged, a faithful mirror of the continuing elementality and irrationality of the capitalist order itself.

Social reality is therefore conceived in outlived, topsy-turvy, and fetishistic terms. Powerless to justify an irrational and inhuman social order and unable to answer the increasingly urgent questions which it poses, bourgeois ideology clings to concepts that are anachronistic and moribund. Its bankruptcy manifests itself not so much in the generation of new fetishes and half-truths as in the stubborn upholding of old fetishes and half-truths which now turn into blatant lies. And the more these old fetishes and half-truths lose whatever truth content they once possessed the more insistently they are hammered, like advertising slogans, into the popular consciousness.

The claim that the United States economy is a "free enterprise" system is a case in point. At no time was enterprise really free in the sense that anyone who wanted to could start a business of his own. Still the concept conveyed an important aspect of the truth by pointing up the difference between the relative freedom of competitive capitalism on the one hand and the restrictions imposed by the guild system and the mercantilist state on the other. Having long ago lost this limited claim to truthfulness and referring as it now does to the freedom of giant corporations to exercise undisturbed their vast monopoly powers, "free enterprise" has turned into a shibboleth devoid of all descriptive or explanatory validity.

Of a similar nature is the incessant repetition that the political regime in the United States today is a democracy. In the United States, as in all other capitalist countries, the property-less masses have never been in a position to determine the conditions of their lives or the policies of the nation's government. Nevertheless as long as democracy meant the overthrow of monarchial despotism and the ascent to power of a relatively numerous bourgeoisie, the term focused attention on a major change in the life of society. But what is left of this truth content in a society in which a tiny oligarchy resting on vast economic power and in full control of society's political and cultural apparatus makes all the important political decisions? Clearly the claim that such a society is democratic serves to conceal, not to reveal, the truth.

Or consider religion which still bulks large in the dominant ideology. That the religious perception of the world is and always has been false consciousness need not be belabored, nor that Christianity and other organized creeds have served to rationalize and justify conquest, exploitation, and inhumanity. And yet there is no doubt that in the past religious consciousness has partaken of truth by fostering the development of knowledge and the arts of civilization. It was the Roman Catholic Church which acted as the guardian of language, scholarship, and historical thought in Europe's darkest centuries; and modern science took shape in a centuries-long struggle between faith and reason. How different is the role of religion today! The more obviously it has succumbed to rationalism and the more manifestly it has ceased to exercise influence on people's thoughts and actions, the more strident has become the sales effort for this ingredient of the dominant ideology. The slogan "Jesus Saves" on innumerable roadside billboards, the massive advertising activities of neighborhood churches, the cartelized exhortations to join any of the unbiquitously available ecclesiastical institutions, the spiritual messages poured into millions of homes by the mass media of press and airwaves — all these have little to do with people's faith and morals, and still less with their perception of reality. What are being offered for sale in the religious marketplace are recipes for acquiring the "power of positive thinking" or attaining "peace of mind" — on the same footing as liquor and tranquilizing pills, ocean cruises and summer resorts.

Bourgeois ideology is no longer a world outlook, a *Weltanschauung*, which attempts to discern order in the existing chaos and to discover a meaning in life. It has turned into a sort of box of assorted tools and gimmicks for attaining the central goal of bourgeois policies. And this goal — which in its younger days the bourgeoisie defined in terms of material progress and individual freedom — is more and more explicitly limited to one thing only: preservation of the status quo, alias the "free world," with all its manifest evils, absurdities, and irrationalities.

It is of course impossible to advance a reasoned defense of this status quo, and indeed the effort is seldom made any more. Instead of taking the form of a demonstration of the rationality and desirability of monopoly capitalism, the defense increasingly focuses on the repudiation of socialism which is the only real alternative to monopoly capitalism, and on the denunciation of revolution which is the only possible means of achieving socialism. All striving for a better, more humane, more rational society is held to be unscientific, utopian, and subversive; by the same token the existing order of society is made to appear not only as the only possible one but as the only conceivable one.

The contradiction between the increasing rationality of society's methods of production and the organizations which embody them on the one hand and the undiminished elementality and irrationality in the functioning and perception of the whole creates that ideological wasteland which is the hallmark of monopoly capitalism. But we must insist that this is not, as some apologists of the status quo would have us believe, "the end of ideology"; it is the displacement of the ideology of rising capitalism by the ideology of the general crisis and decline of the world capitalist order. That its main pillar is anti-Communism is neither accidental nor due to a transient conjunction of political forces, any more than is the fact that the main content of the political and economic policies of modern capitalism is armaments and Cold War. These policies can only be *anti;* there is nothing left for them to be *pro.*

2

Adam Smith saw in the division of labor the key to the wealth of nations, and he was of course right. Many before and after him saw a darker side, and they were right too. In Marx's words, "the division of labor seizes upon not only the economic but every other sphere of society and everywhere lays the foundation of that all-engrossing system of specializing and sorting men, that development in a man of one single faculty at the expense of all other faculties, which caused A. Ferguson, the master of Adam Smith, to exclaim: 'We make a nation of helots, and have no free citizens.' "[4]

The great social critics of the nineteenth century, from Owen and Fourier through Marx and Engels, were all moved by a sense of outrage at this profoundly dehumanizing effect of the capitalist division of labor. And much as their visions of the good society differed, they all had one thing in common: conditions must be created to foster the development of whole human beings, "free citizens," in possession of all their faculties and capable of realizing their full potentialities. Some thought in romantic terms, of a return to a supposedly lost Golden Age. Others, of whom Marx and Engels were by far the most influential, saw the solution in the maximum development through scientific and technological advance of the productivity of human labor. As Marx expressed it in a well known passage in the *Critique of the Gotha Program,* it would be only

> when the enslaving subordination of the individual to the division of labor, and with it the antithesis between mental and physical labor, has vanished; when labor is no longer merely a means of life but has become life's principal need; when the productive forces have also increased with the all-round development of the individual, and all the springs of cooperative wealth flow more abundantly — only then

will it be possible completely to transcend the narrow outlook of bourgeois right and only then will society be able to inscribe on its banners: From each according to his ability, to each according to his needs!

Marx thought that such a high degree of labor productivity could be realized only in a "higher stage of communist society." We can now see that this was an illusion, that from the point of view of raising the productivity of labor, capitalism had a much greater potential than Marx, or for that matter contemporary bourgeois social scientists, imagined. The giant corporation has proved to be an unprecedentedly effective instrument for promoting science and technology and for harnessing them to the production of goods and services. In the United States today the means already exist for overcoming poverty, for supplying everyone with the necessities and conveniences of life, for giving to all a genuinely rounded education and the free time to develop their faculties to the full – in a word for escaping from that all-engrossing system of specializing and sorting men of which Marx wrote.

In fact, of course, nothing of the sort has happened. Men are still being specialized and sorted, imprisoned in the narrow cells prepared for them by the division of labor, their faculties stunted and their minds diminished. And a threat to their security and peace of mind which already loomed large in Marx's day has grown in direct proportion to the spreading incidence and accelerated speed of technological change under monopoly capitalism.

> Modern industry never looks upon or treats the existing form of a production process as final. The technical basis of industry is therefore revolutionary, while all earlier modes of production were essentially conservative. By means of machinery, chemical processes, and other methods, it leads to continual changes not only in the technical basis of production, but also in the function of the laborer, and in the social combinations of the labor-process. At the same time, therefore, it revolutionizes the division of labor within the society, and incessantly transfers masses of capital and of work-people from one branch of production to another. Large-scale industry by its very nature therefore necessitates changes in work, variability of function, universal mobility of the laborer; on the other hand, in its capitalistic form, it reproduces the old division of labor with its ossified particularities. We have seen how this insurmountable contradiction robs the worker's situation of all peace, permanence, and security; how it constantly threatens, by taking away the

instruments of labor, to snatch from his hands his means of subsistence, and, by suppressing his particular subdivided task, to make him superfluous. We have seen, too, how this contradiction works itself out through incessant sacrifices by the working class, the most reckless squandering of labor power, and the devastations caused by social anarchy.[5]

To bring this statement up to date one need only add that the scale of industry has grown incomparably bigger during the past century, that with the advent of automation and cybernation its technical basis has become far more revolutionary, and that the suppression of particular subdivided tasks has never taken place in so many areas of industry and with such startling speed.

NOTES

1. Max Weber went so far as to celebrate the introduction of double-entry bookkeeping, that classical outgrowth of the *quid pro quo* principle, as marking a major milestone of social history.

2. Marx emphasized in his *Critique of the Gotha Program* that the principle of equivalent exchange must survive in a socialist society for a considerable period as a guide to the efficient allocation and utilization of human and material resources. By the same token, however, the evolution of socialism into communism requires an unremitting struggle *against* the principle, with a view to its ultimate replacement by the ideal "From each according to his ability, to each according to his need." In a fully developed communist society, in which social production would be organized as in one vast economic enterprise and in which scarcity would be largely overcome, equivalent exchange would no more serve as the organizing principle of economic activity than at the present time the removal of a chair from one's bedroom to one's sitting room requires charging the sitting room and crediting the bedroom with the value of the furniture. This is obviously not to imply that the communist society of the future can dispense with rational calculation; what it does indicate is that the nature of the rationality involved in economic calculation undergoes a profound change. And this change in turn is but one manifestation of a thoroughgoing transformation of human needs and of the relations among men in society.

3. Throughout this chapter we use the words elemental and elementality to characterize a society which is governed as though by great natural

forces, like wind and tide, to which men may seek to adjust but over which they have no control.

4. *Capital,* Volume 1, Chapter 14, Section 4.

5. *Capital,* Volume 1, Chapter 13, Section 9.

MAN IN CAPITALISTIC SOCIETY

Erich Fromm

QUANTIFICATION, ABSTRACTIFICATION

In analyzing and describing the social character of contemporary man, one can choose any number of approaches, just as one does in describing the character structure of an individual. These approaches can differ either in the depth to which the analysis penetrates, or they can be centered around different aspects which are equally "deep," yet chosen according to the particular interest of the investigator.

In the following analysis I have chosen the concept of *alienation* as the central point from which I am going to develop the analysis of the contemporary social character. For one reason, because this concept seems to me to touch upon the deepest level of the modern personality; for another, because it is the most appropriate if one is concerned with the interaction between the contemporary socioeconomic structure and the character structure of the average individual.[1]

We must introduce the discussion of alienation by speaking of one of the fundamental economic features of Capitalism, the process of *quantification* and *abstractification.*

The medieval artisan produced goods for a relatively small and known group of customers. His prices were determined by the need to make a profit which permitted him to live in a style traditionally commensurate with his social status. He knew from experience the costs of production, and even if he employed a few journeymen and apprentices, no elaborate system of bookkeeping or balance sheets was required for the operation of his business. The same held true for the production of the peasant, which required even less quantifying abstract methods. In contrast, the modern business enterprise rests upon its balance sheet. It cannot rest upon such concrete and direct observation as the artisan used to figure out his profits. Raw material, machinery, labor costs, as well as the product can be expressed in the same money value, and thus made comparable and fit to appear in the balance equation. All economic occurrences have to be strictly quantifiable, and only the balance sheets, the exact comparison of economic processes quantified in figures, tell the manager whether and to what degree he is engaged in a profitable, that is to say, a meaningful business activity.

This transformation of the concrete into the abstract has developed far beyond the balance sheet and the quantification of the economic occurrences in the sphere of production. The modern businessman not only deals with millions of dollars, but also with millions of customers, thousands of stockholders, and thousands of workers and employees; all these people become so many pieces in a gigantic machine which must be controlled, whose effects must be calculated; each man eventually can be expressed as an abstract entity, as a figure, and on this basis economic occurrences are calculated, trends are predicted, decisions are made.

Today, when only about 20 per cent of our working population is self-employed, the rest work for somebody else, and a man's life is dependent on someone who pays him a wage or a salary. But we should say "something," instead of "someone," because a worker is hired and fired by an institution, the managers of which are impersonal parts of the enterprise, rather than people in personal contact with the men they employ. Let us not forget another fact: in precapitalistic society, exchange was to a large extent one of goods and services; today, all work is rewarded with money. The close fabric of economic relations is regulated by money, the abstract expression of work – that is to say, we receive different quantities of the same for different qualities; and we give money for what we receive – again exchanging only different quantities for different qualities. Practically nobody, with the exception of the farm population, could live for even a few days without receiving and spending money, which stands for the abstract quality of concrete work.

Another aspect of capitalist production which results in increasing abstractification is the increasing division of labor. Division of labor as a whole exists in most known economic systems, and, even in most primitive communities, in the form of division of labor between the sexes. What is characteristic of capitalistic production is the degree to which this division has developed. While in the medieval economy there was a division of labor let us say between agricultural production and the work of the artisan, there was little such division within each sphere of production itself. The carpenter making a chair or table made the whole chair or the whole table, and even if some preparatory work was done by his apprentices, he was in control of the production, overseeing it in its entirety. In the modern industrial enterprise, the worker is not in touch with the whole product at any point. He is engaged in the performance of one specialized function, and while he might shift in the course of time from one function to another, he is still not related to the concrete product *as a whole*. He develops a specialized function, and the tendency is such, that the function of the modern industrial worker can be defined as working in a machinelike fashion in activities for which machine work has not yet been devised or which would be costlier than human work. The only person who is in touch with the whole product is the manager, but to him the product is an abstraction, whose essence is exchange value, while the worker, for whom it is concrete, never works on it as a whole.

Undoubtedly without quantification and abstractification modern mass production would be unthinkable. But in a society in which economic activities have become the main preoccupation of man, this process of quantification and abstractification has transcended the realm of economic production, and spread to the attitude of man to things, to people, and to himself.

In order to understand the abstractification process in modern man, we must first consider the ambiguous function of abstraction in general. It is obvious that abstractions in themselves are not a modern phenomenon. In fact, an increasing ability to form abstractions is characteristic of the cultural development of the human race. If I speak of "a table," I am using an abstraction; I am referring, not to a specific table in its full concreteness, but to the genus "table" which comprises all possible concrete tables. If I speak of "a man" I am not speaking of this or that person, in his concreteness and uniqueness, but of the genus "man," which comprises all individual persons. In other words, I make an abstraction. The development of philosophical or scientific thought is based on an increasing ability for such abstractification, and to give it up would mean to fall back into the most primitive way of thinking.

However, there are *two* ways of relating oneself to an object: one can relate oneself to it in its full concreteness; then the object appears with all its specific qualities, and there is no other object which is identical with it. And one can relate oneself to the object in an abstract way, that is, emphasizing only those qualities which it has in common with all other objects of the same genus, and thus accentuating some and ignoring other qualities. The full and productive relatedness to an object comprises this polarity of perceiving it in its uniqueness, and at the same time in its generality; in its concreteness, and at the same time in its abstractness.

In contemporary Western culture this polarity has given way to an almost exclusive reference to the abstract qualities of things and people, and to a neglect of relating oneself to their concreteness and uniqueness. Instead of forming abstract concepts where it is necessary and useful, everything, including ourselves, is being abstractified; the concrete reality of people and things to which we can relate with the reality of our own person, is replaced by abstractions, by ghosts that embody different quantities, but not different qualities.

It is quite customary to talk about a "three-million-dollar bridge," a "twenty-cent cigar," a "five-dollar watch," and this not only from the standpoint of the manufacturer or the consumer in the process of buying it, but as the essential point in the description. When one speaks of the "three-million-dollar bridge," one is not primarily concerned with its usefulness or beauty, that is, with its concrete qualities, but one speaks of it as of a commodity, the main quality of which is its exchange value, expressed in a quantity, that of money. This does not mean, of course, that one is not concerned also with the usefulness or beauty of the bridge, but it does mean that its concrete (use) value is *secondary* to its abstract (exchange) value in the way the object is experienced. The famous line by Gertrude Stein "a rose is a rose is a rose," is a protest against this abstract form of experience; for most people a rose is just *not* a rose, but a flower in a certain price range, to be bought on certain social occasions; even the most beautiful flower, provided it is a wild one, costing nothing, is not experienced in its beauty, compared to that of the rose, because it has no exchange value.

In other words, things are experienced as commodities, as embodiments of exchange value, not only while we are buying or selling, but in our attitude toward them when the economic transaction is finished. A thing, even after it has been bought, never quite loses its quality as a commodity in this sense; it is expendable, always retaining its exchange-value quality. A good illustration of this attitude is to be found in a report of the Executive Secretary of an important scientific organization as to how he spent a day in his office. The organization had just bought and moved into a building of their own. The Executive Secretary reports that during one of the first days after they had moved into the building, he got a call from a real estate agent, saying that some people were interested in buying the building and wanted to look at it. Although he knew that it was most unlikely that the organization would want to sell the building a few days after they had moved in, he could not resist the temptation to know whether the value of the building had risen since they had bought it, and spent one or two valuable hours in showing the real estate agent around. He writes: "very interested in fact we can get an offer for more than we have put in building. Nice coincidence that offer comes while treasurer is in the office. All agree it will be good for Board's morale to learn that the building will sell for a good deal more than it cost. Let's see what happens." In spite of all the pride and pleasure in the new building, it had still retained its quality as a commodity, as something expendable, and to which no full sense of possession or use is attached. The same attitude is obvious in the relationship of people to the cars they buy; the car never becomes fully a thing to which one is attached, but retains its quality as a commodity to be exchanged in a successful bargain; thus, cars are sold after a year or two, long before their use value is exhausted or even considerably diminished.

This abstractification takes place even with regard to phenomena which are not commodities sold on the market, like a flood disaster; the newspapers will headline a flood, speaking of a "million-dollar catastrophe," emphasizing the abstract quantitative element rather than the concrete aspects of human suffering.

But the abstractifying and quantifying attitude goes far beyond the realm of things. People are also experienced as the embodiment of a quantitative exchange value. To speak of a man as being "worth one million dollars," is to speak of him not any more as a concrete human person, but as an abstraction, whose essence can be expressed in a figure. It is an expression of the same attitude when a newspaper headlines an obituary with the words "Shoe Manufacturer Dies." Actually a *man* has died, a man with certain human qualities, with hopes and frustrations, with a wife and children. It is true that he manufactured shoes, or rather, that he owned and managed a factory in which workers served machines manufacturing shoes; but if it is said that a "Shoe Manufacturer Dies," the richness and concreteness of a human life is expressed in the abstract formula of economic function.

The same abstractifying approach can be seen in expressions like "Mr. Ford produced so many automobiles," or this or that general "conquered a fortress"; or if a man has a house built for himself, he says, "I built a house." Concretely speaking, Mr. Ford did not manufacture the automobiles; he directed automobile production which was executed by thousands of workers. The general never conquered the fortress; he was sitting in his headquarters, issuing orders, and his soldiers did the conquering. The man did not build a house; he paid the money to an architect who made the plans and to workers who did the building. All this is not said to minimize the significance of the managing and directing operations, but in order to indicate that in this way of experiencing things, sight of what goes on concretely is lost, and an abstract view is taken in which one function, that of making plans, giving orders, or financing an activity, is identified with the whole concrete process of production, or of fighting, or of building, as the case may be.

The same process of abstractification takes place in all other spheres. The New York *Times* recently printed a news item under the heading: "B.Sc. + PhD = $40,000." The information under this somewhat baffling heading was that statistical data showed that a student of engineering who has acquired his Doctor's degree will earn, in a lifetime, $40,000 more than a man who has only the degree of Bachelor of Sciences. As far as this is a fact it is an interesting socio-economic datum, worth while reporting. It is mentioned here because the way of expressing the fact as an equation between a scientific degree and a certain amount of dollars is indicative of the abstractifying and quantifying thinking in which knowledge is experienced as the embodiment of a certain exchange value on the personality market. It is to the same point when a political report in a news magazine states that the Eisenhower administration feels it has so much "capital of confidence" that it can risk some unpopular measures, because it can "afford" to lose some of that confidence capital. Here again, a human quality like confidence is expressed in its abstract form, as if it were a money investment to be dealt with in terms of a market speculation. How drastically commercial categories have entered even religious thinking is shown in the following passage by Bishop Sheen, in an article on the birth of Christ. "Our reason tells us," so writes the author, "that if anyone of the claimants (for the role of God's son) came from God, the least that God could do to support His Representative's claim would be to preannounce His coming. Automobile manufacturers tell us when to expect a new model."[2] Or, even more drastically, Billy Graham, the evangelist, says: "I am selling the greatest product in the world; why shouldn't it be promoted as well as soap?"[3]

The process of abstractification, however, has still deeper roots and manifestations than the ones described so far, roots which go back to the very beginning of the modern era; to the *dissolution* of any *concrete frame of reference* in the process of life.

In a primitive society, the "world" is identical with the tribe. The tribe is in the center of the Universe, as it were; everything outside is shadowy and has no independent existence. In the medieval world, the Universe was much wider; it comprised this globe, the sky and the stars above it; but it was seen with the earth as the center and man as the purpose of Creation. Everything had its fixed place, just as everybody had his fixed position in feudal society. With the fifteenth and sixteenth centuries, new vistas opened up. The earth lost its central place, and became one of the satellites of the sun; new continents were found, new sea lanes discovered; the static social system was more and more loosened up; everything and everybody was moving. Yet, until the end of the twentieth century, nature and society had not lost their concreteness and definiteness. Man's natural and social world was still manageable, still had definite contours. But with the progress in scientific thought, technical discoveries and the dissolution of all traditional bonds, this definiteness and concreteness is in the process of being lost. Whether we think of our new cosmological picture, or of theoretical physics, or of atonal music, or abstract art — the concreteness and definiteness of our frame of reference is disappearing. We are not any more in the center of the Universe, we are not any more the purpose of Creation, we are not any more the masters of a manageable and recognizable world — we are a speck of dust, we are a nothing, somewhere in space — without any kind of concrete relatedness to anything. We speak of millions of people being killed, of one third or more of our population being wiped out if a third World War should occur; we speak of billions of dollars piling up as a national debt, of thousands of light years as interplanetary distances, of interspace travel, of artificial satellites. Tens of thousands work in one enterprise, hundreds of thousands live in hundreds of cities.

The dimensions with which we deal are figures and abstractions; they are far beyond the boundaries which would permit of any kind of concrete experience. There is no frame of reference left which is manageable, observable, which is adapted to *human dimensions*. While our eyes and ears receive impressions only in humanly manageable proportions, our concept of the world has lost just that quality; it does not any longer correspond to our human dimensions.

This is especially significant in connection with the development of modern means of destruction. In modern war, one individual can cause the destruction of hundreds of thousands of men, women and children. He could do so by pushing a button; he may not feel the emotional impact of what he is doing, since he does not see, does not know the people whom he kills; it is almost as if his act of pushing the button and their death had no real connection. The same man would probably be incapable of even slapping, not to speak of killing, a helpless person. In the latter case, the concrete situation arouses in him a conscience reaction common to all normal men; in the former, there is no such reaction, because the act and his object are alienated from the doer, his act is not *his* any more, but has, so to speak, a life and a responsibility of its own.

Science, business, politics, have lost all foundations and proportions which make sense humanly. We live in figures and abstractions; since nothing is concrete, nothing is real. Everything is possible, factually and morally. Science fiction is not different from science fact, nightmares and dreams from the events of next year. Man has been thrown out from any definite place whence he can overlook and manage his life and the life of society. He is driven faster and faster by the forces which originally were created by him. In this wild whirl he thinks, figures, busy with abstractions, more and more remote from concrete life.

ALIENATION

The foregoing discussion of the process of abstractification leads to the central issue of the effects of Capitalism on personality: the phenomenon of alienation.

By alienation is meant a mode of experience in which the person experiences himself as an alien. He has become, one might say, estranged from himself. He does not experience himself as the center of his world, as the creator of his own acts — but his acts and their consequences have become his masters, whom he obeys, or whom he may even worship. The alienated person is out of touch with himself as he is out of touch with any other person. He, like the others, is experienced as things are experienced; with the senses and with common sense, but at the same time without being related to oneself and to the world outside productively.

The older meaning in which "alienation" was used was to denote an insane person; *aliéné* in French, *alienado* in Spanish are older words for the psychotic, the thoroughly and absolutely alienated person. ("Alienist," in English, is still used for the doctor who cares for the insane.)

In the last century the word "alienation" was used by Hegel and Marx, referring not to a state of insanity, but to a less drastic form of self-estrangement, which permits the person to act reasonably in practical matters, yet which constitutes one of the most severe socially patterned defects. In Marx's system alienation is called that condition of man where his "own act becomes to him an alien power, standing over and against him, instead of being ruled by him."[4]

But while the use of the word "alienation" in this general sense is a recent one, the concept is a much older one; it is the same to which the prophets of the Old Testament referred as *idolatry*. It will help us to a better understanding of "alienation" if we begin by considering the meaning of "idolatry."

The prophets of monotheism did not denounce heathen religions as idolatrous primarily because they worshiped several gods instead of one. The essential difference between monotheism and polytheism is not one of the *number* of gods, but lies in the fact of self-alienation. Man spends his energy, his artistic capacities on building an idol, and then he worships this idol, which is nothing but the result of his own human effort. His life forces have flown into a "thing," and this thing, having become an idol, is not experienced as a result of his own productive effort, but as something apart from himself, over and against him, which he worships and to which he submits. As the prophet Hosea says (XIV, 8): "Assur shall not save us; we will not ride upon horses; *neither will we say any more to the work of our hands, you are our gods;* for in thee the fatherless finds love." Idolatrous man bows down to the work of his own hands. *The idol represents his own life-forces in an alienated form.*

The principle of monotheism, in contrast, is that man is infinite, that there is no partial quality in him which can be hypostatized into the whole. God, in the monotheistic concept, is unrecognizable and indefinable; God is not a "thing." If man is created in the likeness of God, he is created as the bearer of infinite qualities. In idolatry man bows down and submits to the projection of one partial quality in himself. He does not experience himself as the center from which living acts of love and reason radiate. He becomes a thing, his neighbor becomes a thing, just as his gods are things. "The idols of the heathen are silver and gold, the work of men's hands. They have mouths but they speak not; eyes have they, but they see not; they have ears but they hear not; neither is there any breath in their mouths. They that make them are like them; so is everyone that trusts in them." (Psalm 135).

Monotheistic religions themselves have, to a large extent, regressed into idolatry. Man projects his power of love and of reason unto God; he does not feel them any more as his own powers, and then he prays to God to give him back some of what he, man, has projected unto God. In early Protestantism and Calvinism, the required religious attitude is that man *should* feel himself empty and impoverished, and put his trust in the grace of God, that is, into the hope that God may return to him part of his own qualities, which he has put into God.

Every act of submissive worship is an act of alienation and idolatry in this sense. What is frequently called "love" is often nothing but this idolatrous phenomenon of alienation; only that not God or an idol, but another person is worshiped in this way. The "loving" person in this type of submissive relationship, projects all his or her love, strength, thought, into the other person, and experiences the loved person as a superior being, finding satisfaction in complete submission and worship. This does not only mean that he fails to experience the loved person as a human being in his or her reality, but that he does not experience *himself* in his full reality, as the bearer of productive human powers. Just as in the case of religious idolatry, he has projected all his richness into the other person, and experiences this richness not any more as something which is his, but as something alien from himself, deposited in somebody else, with which he can get in touch only by submission to, or submergence in the other person. The same phenomenon exists in the worshiping submission to a political leader, or to the state. The leader and the state actually are what they are by the consent of the governed. But they become idols when the individual projects all his powers into them and worships them, hoping to regain some of his powers by submission and worship.

In Rousseau's theory of the state, as in contemporary totalitarianism, the individual is supposed to abdicate his own rights and to project them unto the state as the only arbiter. In Fascism and Stalinism the absolutely alienated individual worships at the altar of an idol, and it makes little difference by what names this idol is known: state, class, collective, or what else.

We can speak of idolatry or alienation not only in relationship to other people, but also in relationship to oneself, when the person is subject to irrational passions. The person who is mainly motivated by his lust for power, does not experience himself any more in the richness and limitlessness of a human being, but he becomes a slave to one partial striving in him, which is projected into external aims, by which he is "possessed." The person who is given to the exclusive pursuit of his passion for money is possessed by his striving for it; money is the idol which he worships as the projection of one isolated power in himself, his greed for it. In this sense, the neurotic person is an alienated person. His actions are not his own; while he is under the illusion of doing what *he* wants, he is driven by forces which are separated from his self, which work behind his back; he is a stranger to himself, just as his fellow man is a stranger to him. He experiences the other and himself not as what they really are, but distorted by the unconscious forces which operate in them. The insane person is the *absolutely alienated* person; he has completely lost himself as the center of his own experience; he has lost the sense of self.

What is common to all these phenomena — the worship of idols, the idolatrous worship of God, the idolatrous love for a person, the worship of a political leader or the state, and the idolatrous worship of the externalizations of irrational passions — is the process of alienation. It is the fact that *man does not experience himself as the active bearer of his own powers and richness, but as an impoverished "thing," dependent on powers outside of himself, unto whom he has projected his living substance.*

As the reference to idolatry indicates, alienation is by no means a modern phenomenon. It would go far beyond the scope of this book to attempt a sketch on the history of alienation. Suffice it to say that it seems alienation differs from culture to culture, both in the specific spheres which are alienated, and in the thoroughness and completeness of the process.

Alienation as we find it in modern society is almost total; it pervades the relationship of man to his work, to the things he consumes, to the state, to his fellow man, and to himself. Man has created a world of man-made things as it never existed before. He has constructed a complicated social machine to administer the technical machine he built. Yet this whole creation of his stands over and above him. He does not feel himself as a creator and center, but as the servant of a Golem, which his hands have built. The more powerful and gigantic the forces are which he unleashes, the more powerless he feels himself as a human being. He confronts himself with his own forces embodied in things he has created, alienated from himself. He is owned by his own creation, and has lost ownership of himself. He has built a golden calf, and says "these are your gods who have brought you out of Egypt."

What happens to the *worker?* To put it in the words of a thoughtful and thorough observer of the industrial scene: "In industry the person becomes an economic atom that dances to the tune of atomistic management. Your place is just here, you will sit in this fashion, your arms will move x inches in a course of y radius and the time of movement will be .000 minutes.

"Work is becoming more repetitive and thoughtless as the planners, the micromotionists, and the scientific managers further strip the worker of his right to think and move freely. Life is being denied; need to control, creativeness, curiosity, and independent thought are being baulked, and the result, the inevitable result, is flight or fight on the part of the worker, apathy or destructiveness, psychic regression."[5]

The role of the *manager* is also one of alienation. It is true, he manages the whole and not a part, but he too is alienated from his product as something concrete and useful. His aim is to employ profitably the capital invested by others, although in comparison with the older type of owner-manager, modern management is much less interested in the amount of profit to be paid out as dividend to the stockholder than it is in the efficient operation and expansion of the enterprise. Characteristically, within management those in charge of labor relations and of sales — that is, of human manipulation — gain, relatively speaking, an increasing importance in comparison with those in charge of the technical aspects of production.

The manager, like the worker, like everybody, deals with impersonal giants: with the giant competitive enterprise; with the giant national and world market; with the giant consumer, who has to be coaxed and manipulated; with the giant unions, and the giant government. All these giants have their own lives, as it were. They determine the activity of the manager and they direct the activity of the worker and clerk.

The problem of the manager opens up one of the most significant phenomena in an alienated culture, that of *bureaucratization.* Both big business and government administrations are conducted by a bureaucracy. Bureaucrats are specialists in the administration of things *and of men.* Due to the bigness of the apparatus to be administered, and the resulting abstractification, the bureaucrats' relationship to the people is one of complete alienation. They, the people to be administered, are objects whom the bureaucrats consider neither with love nor with hate, but completely impersonally; the manager-bureaucrat must not feel, as far as his professional activity is concerned; he must manipulate people as though they were figures, or things. Since the vastness of the organization and the extreme division of labor prevents any single individual from seeing the whole, since there is no organic, spontaneous co-operation between the various individuals or groups within the industry, the managing bureaucrats are necessary; without them the enterprise would collapse in a short time, since nobody would know the secret which makes it function. Bureaucrats are as indispensable as the tons of paper consumed under their leadership. Just because everybody senses, with a feeling of powerlessness, the vital role of the bureaucrats, they are given an almost godlike respect. If it were not for the bureaucrats, people feel, everything would go to pieces, and we would starve. Whereas, in the medieval world, the leaders were considered representatives of a god-intended order, in modern Capitalism the role of the bureaucrat is hardly less sacred — since he is necessary for the survival of the whole.

Marx gave a profound definition of the bureaucrat saying: "The bureaucrat relates himself to the world as a *mere object* of his activity." It is interesting to note that the spirit of bureaucracy has entered not only business and government administration, but also trade unions and the great democratic socialist parties in England, Germany and France. In Russia, too, the bureaucratic managers and their alienated spirit have conquered the country. Russia could perhaps exist without terror — if certain conditions were given — but it could not exist without the system of total bureaucratization — that is, alienation.[6]

What is the attitude of the *owner* of the enterprise, the capitalist? The small businessman seems to be in the same position as his predecessor a hundred years ago. He owns and directs his small enterprise, he is in touch with the whole commercial or industrial activity, and in personal contact with his employees and workers. But living in an alienated world in all other economic and social aspects, and furthermore being more under the constant pressure of bigger competitors, he is by no means as free as his grandfather was in the same business.

But what matters more and more in contemporary economy is big business, the large corporation. As Drucker puts it very succinctly: "In fine, it is the large corporation – the specific form in which Big Business is organized in a free-enterprise economy – which has emerged as the representative and determining socioeconomic institution which sets the pattern and determines the behavior even of the owner of the corner cigar store who never owned a share of stock, and of his errand boy who never set foot in a mill. And thus the character of our society is determined and patterned by the structural organization of Big Business, the technology of the mass-production plant, and the degree to which our social beliefs and promises are realized in and by the large corporations."[7]

What then is the attitude of the "owner" of the big corporation to "his" property? It is one of almost complete alienation. His ownership consists in a piece of paper, representing a certain fluctuating amount of money; he has no responsibility for the enterprise and no concrete relationship to it in any way. This attitude of alienation has been most clearly expressed in Berle's and Means' description of the attitude of the stockholder to the enterprise which follows here: "(1) The position of ownership has changed from that of an active to that of a passive agent. In place of actual physical properties over which the owner could exercise direction and for which he was responsible, the owner now holds a piece of paper representing a set of rights and expectations with respect to an enterprise. But over the enterprise and over the physical property – the instruments of production – in which he has an interest, the owner has little control. At the same time he bears no responsibility with respect to the enterprise or its physical property. It has often been said that the owner of a horse is responsible. If the horse lives he must feed it. If the horse dies he must bury it. No such responsibility attaches to a share of stock. The owner is practically powerless through his own efforts to affect the underlying property.

"(2) The spiritual values that formerly went with ownership have been separated from it. Physical property capable of being shaped by its owner could bring to him direct satisfaction apart from the income it yielded in more concrete form. It represented an extension of his own personality. With the corporate revolution, this quality has been lost to the property owner much as it has been lost to the worker through the industrial revolution.

"(3) The value of an individual's wealth is coming to depend on forces entirely outside himself and his own efforts. Instead, its value is determined on the one hand by the actions of the individuals in command of the enterprise – individuals over whom the typical owner has no control, and on the other hand, by the actions of others in a sensitive and often capricious market. The value is thus subject to the vagaries and manipulations characteristic of the market place. It is further subject to the great swings in society's appraisal of its own immediate future as reflected in the general level of values in the organized market.

"(4) The value of the individual's wealth not only fluctuates constantly – the same may be said of most wealth – but it is subject to a constant appraisal. The individual can see the change in the appraised value of his estate from moment to moment, a fact which may markedly affect both the expenditure of his income and his enjoyment of that income.

"(5) Individual wealth has become extremely liquid through the organized markets. The individual owner can convert it into other forms of wealth at a moment's notice and, provided the market machinery is in working order, he may do so without serious loss due to forced sales.

"(6) Wealth is less and less in a form which can be employed directly by its owner. When wealth is in the form of land, for instance, it is capable of being used by the owner even though the value of land in the market is negligible. The physical quality of such wealth makes possible a subjective value to the owner quite apart from any market value it may have. The newer form of wealth is quite incapable of this direct use. Only through sale in the market can the owner obtain its direct use. He is thus tied to the market as never before.

"(7) Finally, in the corporate system, the 'owner' of industrial wealth is left with a mere symbol of ownership while the power, the responsibility and the substance which have been an integral part of ownership in the past are being transferred to a separate group in whose hands lies control."[8] . . .

The process of *consumption* is as alienated as the process of production. In the first place, we acquire things with money; we are accustomed to this and take it for granted. But actually, this is a most peculiar way of acquiring things. Money represents labor and effort in an abstract form; not necessarily *my* labor and *my* effort, since I can have acquired it by inheritance, by fraud, by luck, or any number of ways. But even if I have acquired it by *my* effort (forgetting for the moment that *my* effort might not have brought me the money were it not for the fact that I employed men), I have acquired it in a specific way, by a specific kind of effort, corresponding to my skills and capacities, while, in spending, the money is transformed into an abstract form of labor and can be exchanged against anything else. Provided I am in the possession of money, no effort or interest of mine is necessary to acquire something. If I have the money, I can acquire an exquisite painting, even though I may not have any appreciation for art; I can buy the best phonograph, even though I have no musical taste; I can buy a library, although I use it only for the purpose of ostentation. I can buy an education, even though I have no use for it except as an additional social asset. I can even destroy the painting or the books I bought, and aside from a loss of money, I suffer no damage. Mere possession of money gives me the right to acquire and to do with my acquisition whatever I like. The *human* way of acquiring would be to make an effort qualitatively commensurate with what I acquire. The acquisition of bread and clothing would depend on no other premise than that of being alive; the acquisition of books and paintings, on my effort to understand them and my ability to use them. How this principle could be applied practically is not the point to be discussed here. What matters is that the way we acquire things is separated from the way in which we use them.

The alienating function of money in the process of acquisition and consumption has been beautifully described by Marx in the following words: "Money . . . transforms the real human and natural powers into merely abstract ideas, and hence imperfections, and on the other hand it transforms the real imperfections and imaginings, the powers which only exist in the imagination of the individual into real powers. . . . It transforms loyalty into vice, vices into virtue, the slave into the master, the master into the slave, ignorance into reason, and reason into ignorance. . . . He who can buy valour is valiant although he be cowardly. . . . Assume *man* as *man*, and his relation to the world as a human one, and you can exchange love only for love, confidence for confidence, etc. If you wish to enjoy art, you must be an artistically trained person; if you wish to have influence on other people, you must be a person who has a really stimulating and furthering influence on other people. Every one of your relationships to man and to nature must be a definite expression of your *real, individual* life corresponding to the object of your will. If you love without calling forth love, that is, if your love as such does not produce love, if by means of an *expression of life* as a loving person you do not make of yourself a *loved person*, then your love is impotent, a misfortune."[9] . . .

In an alienated society the mode in which people express their will is not very different from that of their choice in buying commodities. They are listening to the drums of propaganda and facts mean little in comparison with the suggestive noise which hammers at them. In recent years we see more and more how the wisdom of public relations' counsels determines political propaganda. Accustomed to make the public buy anything for the build-up of which there is enough money, they think of political ideas and political leaders in the same terms. They use television to build up political personalities as they use it to build up a soap; what matters is the effect, in sales or votes, not the rationality or usefulness of what is presented. This phenomenon found a remarkably frank expression in recent statements about the future of the Republican Party. They are to the effect that since one cannot hope the majority of voters will vote for the Republican Party, one must find a personality who wants to represent the Party – then *he* will get the votes. In principle this is not different from the endorsement of a cigarette by a famous sportsman or movie actor. . . .

NOTES

1. As the reader familiar with the concept of the marketing orientation developed in *Man for Himself* will see, the phenomenon of alienation is the more general and underlies the more specific concept of the "marketing orientation."

2. From *Colliers'* magazine, 1953.

3. *Time* magazine, October 25, 1954.

4. K. Marx, *Capital.* cf. also Marx-Engels, *Die Deutsche Ideologie* (1845/6), in K. Marx, *Der Historische Materialismus, Die Früh-schriften*, S. Landshut and D. P. Mayer, Leipzig, 1932, II, p. 25.

5. J. J. Gillespie, *Free Expression in Industry*, The Pilot Press Ltd., London, 1948.

6. Cf. the interesting article by W. Huhn, "Der Bolschevismus als Manager Ideologie" in Funken, Frankfurt V, 8/1954.

7. Cf. Peter F. Drucker, *Concept of the Corporation*, The John Day Company, New York, 1946, pp. 8, 9.

8. Cf. A. A. Berle and G. C. Means, *The Modern Corporation and Private Property*, The Macmillan Company, New York, 1940, pp. 66-68.

9. "Nationalökonomie und Philosophie," 1844, published in Karl Marx' *Die Frühschriften,* Alfred Kröner Verlag, Stuttgart, 1953, pp. 300, 301. (My translation, E.F.)

THE QUALITY OF THE ENVIRONMENT

William W. Murdoch

As we grow richer in the U.S. the quality of our shared environment declines. One can even try to measure this by indices such as the clarity of the air, the dirtiness of the water we drink and swim in, the ratio of wilderness or National Park area to people and the fact that soon visits to National Parks may have to be rationed, the number of wildlife species lost or being lost, the number of feet of clean beachfront per person, the time spent in non-vacation trips in one's car, the average noise-level in the city, the increased probability of environmental disaster and so on. A few horror stories do not measure the decline, but they illuminate it. For example, the frequent warning to children in Los Angeles not to run, skip or jump on very smoggy days; smog in Yosemite valley; the fact that mothers' milk has so much DDT it would be banned from Interstate commerce.

The case is surely easy to make for the city dweller. Smog, noise, traffic, mental stress, all the apparently necessary trappings of a healthy economy. Mishan sees:

"The spreading suburban wilderness, the near traffic paralysis, the mixture of pandemonium and desolation in the cities, a sense of spiritual despair scarcely concealed by the frantic pace of life", and notes that

From William W. Murdoch, *Environment.* New York: Sinauer Associates, 1971. Reprinted by permission.

"such phenomena, not being readily quantifiable, and having no discernible impact on the gold reserves, are obviously not regarded as [economic] agenda".[1]

It might be said in reply that people choose to live in such conditions, they want this kind of life, therefore by definition wealth has brought them increased social welfare. Los Angeles, for example, is a rather unpleasant city, saved largely by what is left of its pleasant climate, yet it is one of the fastest growing in the U.S. Clearly people "choose" to come to Los Angeles. But in fact, people need jobs and they go where jobs are or where they think there is opportunity for economic success. Secondly, they have been led to believe that more money necessarily means a better life, and they go where there are higher paying jobs. That is, they make a choice based on misinformation. Madison Avenue has been assuring us for years that our sexual potency is directly related to the various consumer goods we own, and we do not choose impotency. It is inaccurate to say that people have chosen to live in a city such as Los Angeles, rather than some very different kind of city, since in fact there exists essentially no choice. Almost all of our cities have the same problems as does Los Angeles. But surely there must be other models than that collection of villages being slowly suffocated by a miasma of freeways and highways and the resultant smog: a city fit for (air conditioned) cars to crawl through but not for people to live in.

The matter of where people choose to live illustrates that, contrary to myth, increasing collective wealth does not necessarily increase individual choice. As Mishan has said: "As the carpet of increased choice is being unrolled before us by the foot, it is simultaneously being rolled up behind us by the yard".[1] Consider, for example, the restriction in one's freedom to choose a pattern of living. Because of the impact of the car (that bastion of economic growth) it is essentially impossible for most people to live close to work, to walk there or cycle there or to go by efficient public transport.

It would be foolish to blame all of the problems of urban life on population and economic growth. Clearly, major reasons for these problems include the fact that successive national administrations (and the voters) have placed higher priorities on military excursions and the space race than on the welfare of the poor, and in particular the poor black urban citizens, on educating people or on the quality of life generally. Other reasons include our stress on private consumption rather than public spending and quite simply poor planning and administration. Nevertheless, the spread of disamenities which has put a blight on urban life in general is directly attributable to the headlong rush of production and growth, and part of the physical and administrative problems of cities is attributable to their high growth rate.

One of the clearest illustrations of the possible inverse relation between national wealth and individual welfare is the supersonic transport (SST). By building SSTs, and flying them, we will increase the GNP, assuming that we don't concomitantly reduce production of other goods. It is difficult to see just who will benefit. A few businessmen will now be able to get from a traffic jam in New York to a traffic jam in London in possibly 2-1/2 hours less. But they will still take 2 or 3 days to adjust physiologically to the change in time zones. During the flight they will subject themselves to the potentially serious hazards of increased radiation.[2] They will subject some of the rest of the world to sonic booms (even if they fly only over the oceans which would be uneconomical for the airlines) and they will probably interfere with our weather.[3] SSTs will also aggravate the problem of scarce oil resources.[4] They would use about 2-1/2 times as much fuel per passenger mile as existing jet transports. It is projected that 600 jets will be in service by 1985 at which time they will consume about 11 percent of the projected world oil demand. As early as 1980 they would be using 3 times as much oil as the whole continent of Africa! It is even doubtful that the SST is a sound proposition economically; no corporation has been willing to finance the project, which will be 90 percent financed by the government (that is, by the public).[5] For most of us, on balance, the SST cannot possibly raise our quality of life and will quite probably reduce it.[6]

Now, it is clear that in fact we could go on increasing GNP for some time *and* improve the quality of our lives, by redirecting resources. Thus it has been estimated that we need $100 billion over the next five years just to get clean water. Governor Rockefeller of New York has guessed that the cities will need $30 billion per year, and a decent public transport system which would move people efficiently and use much less power would certainly run into several hundred billion dollars.

However, if we eventually convert to an ecologically sound system in which the population and the systems of production are in equilibrium with our environment, continual increase in cleaning up operations will not be necessary. As Heilbroner has pointed out, economic growth as western capitalists have come to know it would not continue long in an equilibrium society.[7]

IMPLICATIONS OF EQUILIBRIUM

Poverty and social inequity

The "environmental crisis" in the U.S. has been rightly recognized by some urban sociologists as the new fashionable concern of the affluent white middle class. They have pointed out that the poor, and especially the black urban poor have other priorities than clean air, clean beaches or some other irrelevancy such as a "balanced ecosystem". This is in spite of the fact that it is frequently the poor who suffer most from pollution. They cannot afford to move from airport flight patterns or from the smog- and lead-polluted freeway that runs past their house; it is poor farm laborers who suffer from acute pesticide poisoning in California and their children who are ill and dead from drinking water high in nitrates. However, the poor undoubtedly have their priorities right. One hardly will worry about the side effects of DDT if food itself is scarce; strontium-90 concentrates in milk, not corn; and why concern oneself about filthy beaches and overcrowded national parks if you never leave the ghetto to visit them?

Some sociologists and political scientists see the environment issue as a red herring, distracting us from the more important problems of war and racial and economic injustice. In particular they are worried about the "defection" of the youth from these causes, since whatever small gains have been made in the past decade in ameliorating the Vietnam War and racial inequality are owing largely to the efforts of the college generation of the '60s. Schaar and Wolin see the students' new concern for the environment as a retreat from politics by the very generation which became the most deeply political one in recent history. Nor is this retreat due simply to chance.[8] "It is not accidental that at the same time as the Nixon Administration is using environment to forge a new unity, it has been shelving, retarding, or neglecting most of the previous policies dealing with blacks, the poor, education, and the cities. . . . The Nixon consensus, by placating the silent majority, is also capitalizing upon the despair of the confused minority of activists who had struggled for racial justice and economic improvement and who now, by their commitment to nature, were tacitly conceding that racial and economic injustice were ineradicable facts of American society." By emphasizing in his State of the Union message (Jan. 22, 1970) that the environment was the special concern of youth, "Nixon captured the issue which might allow for peace between the political system and the younger generation". This peace, these commentators fear, will draw off the steam which powers the movement for social improvement.

In fact, the problem of economic injustice cannot be separated from environmental problems, and racial injustice derives in large part from economic inequality. For the rest, one has to hope that we can deal with more than one problem at a time. At least one point which these authors and others have made, that the environmental issue brings together the radicals and the establishment, the young and the old, "the hippies and the Hickels", promises success in attacking that issue, though it may also have its sinister aspects as they claim.

There need be no conflict between the aims of environmental equilibrium in our rich society and of increased social justice and affluence for the poor. Indeed, I contend that it is crucial that we achieve greater equality if we are to reach environmental equilibrium. The traditional way of making the poor richer, in theory, is to increase collective wealth, so that even the poor are dragged upwards. Of course, enormous inequality remains, generating economic competition among individuals and groups and producing more pressure for economic growth. Since it is important to remove such sources of economic competition in order to slow down the pressure for growth, the obvious solution is to have a more equitable distribution of wealth than we now have. It is difficult to see how one could achieve economic equilibrium in a free society without such economic equality. . . .

Population and the power structure

The current idea that the way to clear up pollution is to force industry to internalize its externalities through the price or market system is attractive.[9] For example, the price of every article could include the cost of its "disposal", or better, it should include the cost of readying the article for recycling. However, whether or not the present private enterprise, corporate capitalist system is suited to this mechanism is open to discussion.

First, a major function of the corporation is to grow.[10] If a sound environment implies a reduction and possible cessation of growth, it is questionable that the corporation can make the necessary metamorphosis. Corporations and those in favor of growth are likely to argue that we can have growth *and* a sound environment if only we develop a clean technology and resource substitutes. That is, they have tried and will continue to try to mold environmental issues so that they fit into the existing corporate model. Thus arguments about whether or not the "technological fix" is a feasible long term solution will remain central.

Second, the private corporation might well serve as a useful means of maintaining environmental quality if there were effective means of regulating its activities. In such an ideal situation, the people and therefore government might decide that a certain industrial activity was causing too much pollution. Government would therefore pass legislation defining the limits of acceptable pollution. This would be so low that the activity would stop or a clean one would be substituted. In other cases where an effluent tax existed this would lead to the installation of costly plants to reduce pollution and would increase the cost of the product. The regulation would be enforced by a regulating agency with adequate powers and nothing to lose by enforcing such regulations.

The reality of course is far from this ideal. The crux of the matter is that large corporations not only have the power to pollute, they have the economic and political power to prevent, delay and water down regulatory legislation. They also have the power and connections to ensure that the regulatory agencies don't regulate as they ought to. In theory this can all be sorted out, but in practice the system is most likely to be self-perpetuating.[11,12] The history of regulatory legislation against private industry with a view to increasing social welfare illustrates the problem. In the face of powerful evidence that poor automobile design kills people, Detroit has successfully delayed and emasculated car safety legislation for a decade. Another example is the coal industry which has successfully combatted legislation against pollution from sulfur oxide.[13]

Third, conceivably the leaders of private industry might be convinced of the worthiness of the cause of social welfare, including the value of a clean and stable environment. In this case they might be willing to internalize the externalities because they have well developed social consciences. This system has the same appeal as benevolent dictatorship, being benevolent oligarchy. The problem here is that all the evidence points to the conclusion that the safety and welfare of the public is not a prime concern of the leaders of private industry, notwithstanding recent advertisements to the contrary. A case in point is the lack of concern over car safety shown by Detroit — this in spite of the fact that the car industry has long had access to accident statistics from Cornell.[14] The same industry did so much foot-dragging on air pollution control that the Justice Department in January 1969 filed suit against 4 major auto manufacturers and their trade association on the grounds that they had conspired to delay the development and use of devices to control air pollution from automobiles. (The power of the companies is shown by the fact that the Federal government later agreed to settle the suit) by a consent decree which did not penalize the companies and sealed the grand jury records.[13] Pesticide sales pitches and the high pressure pesticide salesmen provide another example. An even more serious disregard of public safety occurs in the nuclear power industry.[14]

Alternative systems

It is by now passé to observe that the system in the U.S.S.R. is more similar to the U.S. than different from it. Decisions are taken there by a remote élite of ruling bureaucrats obtaining power not from property, but from their position in the political party. Certainly we would not expect such a totalitarian system to be responsive to the public or sensitive to environmental concerns. And from the environmental point of view the results in the U.S.S.R. are essentially the same as in the U.S. Both countries are hell-bent on economic growth. Since the U.S.S.R. is poorer, environmental problems are less severe there. But they are bad enough and will get worse as Russia becomes more industrialized. The Soviet Union's problems with pollution in Lake Baikal and the Caspian Sea are notorious by now. Even the caviar-producing sturgeon faces extinction.

The elaboration of alternative systems to corporate and state capitalism and totalitarian collectivism is the job of the social scientist, not the ecologist. However, such a system probably requires a population educated to environmental realities and a decision-making apparatus sensitive both to the desires of this population and to these environmental realities. Along these lines, it may be possible to learn something from a recent Swedish experiment.[15]

Sweden has already shown that it is sensitive to environmental problems. It has banned the sale of some species of fish from some lakes because of the fishes' high mercury content. It is looking hard at DDT levels in Baltic fish and may soon ban the sale of some fish from there. Sweden was the first nation to impose a ban on DDT, aldrin, dieldrin and other chlorinated hydrocarbons. Moreover, the Swedish government have recognized that even strict legislation against pollution is difficult to enforce unless the public is informed and involved. As a start towards this goal, the Ministry of Education arranged a few evening classes on the technical and legal aspects of pollution for 250,000 people. 10,000 of these people took an extra 2 weeks' instruction. The most interesting aspect is that, from this group, about 1000 people throughout Sweden were picked to "conduct public enquiries and, in general, agitate on behalf of pollution control". Whether or not this project will work remains to be seen — but it appears to be a sound idea. Indeed, why restrict such education and agitation to the problem of pollution?

The need to obtain a widespread and fairly sophisticated understanding of environmental problems is illustrated by a recent advertisement run by Chevron Oil Co. to market a gasoline additive (F-310, a polybutine amine) which is claimed to reduce exhaust pollution.[16] This new panacea for cleaner and purer air in fact works by cleaning up deposits on the carburetor and intake valve. The ad is quite misleading since only a small percentage of cars have dirty enough engines to make this a problem — such engines are a very minor facet of air pollution. A much worse aspect of the campaign, however, is the picture in the advertisement. A balloon is attached to the exhaust of the automobile; in the "before additive" picture it is full of black fumes (bad) in the "after additive" picture it is clear (good). But the poisonous and smog-producing exhaust emissions, carbon monoxide, nitrogen oxide, unburnt hydrocarbons are *colorless*. Thus the additive will do almost nothing to lower the levels of these pollutants and the advertisement misleads and confuses the public.

Clearly, we need a large education program in the subject of the environment. One might judge the success of such a program in ten years' time by asking a layman what he thinks of a project, let us say, to dam a large African river. If he answers that he would need to know, before answering, the dam's potential effects on the spread of schistosomiasis, on the local climate, on downstream agriculture, and on health, the number of people to be moved, the nature of their destination, on the possibilities of flooding and the possible dislocations of community life, one might feel rather encouraged. Of course if he wanted to see good evidence that the benefits would far outweigh any conceivable costs and to be assured that the people there understood the implications of the dam and wanted it, then one would certainly be optimistic.

I assume that a proper understanding of environmental issues and all their ramifications, is not only a prerequisite but a *precursor* of wise action. Wise action entails nothing less than a change of values, a sorting out of "standard of living" and "quality of life", and an evaluation of individual actions in a population setting. It then entails acting on the basis of such values. There are many reasons for being pessimistic about such a possibility. But there is surprising basis for optimism. A *Fortune* survey of opinion among the 8 million people between 18 and 24 who are or were in college showed that 40% no longer look on making money as a decent purpose for one's life.[17] Of course, inevitably our ideals deteriorate with age, but that 40% is a good beginning.

NOTES

1. Mishan, E.J. 1969. *The Costs of Economic Growth*. Penguin Books, Ltd., Harmondsworth, England.

2. Cook, E. 1971. "Ionizing Radiation," in *Environment: Resources, Pollution, Society*, ed. by William W. Murdoch. Sinauer, Stamford, Conn.

3. MacDonald, G.J.F. 1971. "Pollution, Weather and Climate," in *Environment: Resources, Pollution, Society*, ed. by William W. Murdoch. Sinauer, Stamford, Conn.

4. *The Observer*. August 30, 1970, pages 1 and 2.

5. Hohenemser, K. 1970. "Onward and Upward." *Environment 12* (4): 23-27.

6. Hardin, G. 1970. "To Trouble a Star." *Bulletin of the Atomic Scientists*; January 1970.

7. Heilbroner, R. 1970. "Ecological Armageddon." *New York Review of Books 14* (8): 3-9.

8. Schaar, J.H., and S.S. Wolin. 1970. "Where Are We Now?" *New York Review of Books 14* (9): 3-10.

9. Boulding, K.E. 1971. "Environment and Economics," in *Environment: Resources, Pollution, Society*, ed. by William W. Murdoch. Sinauer, Stamford, Conn.

10. Galbraith, K. 1968. *The New Industrial State*. New American Library, New York.

11. *The Nader Report*. 1970. A series of separate reports on a number of administrative agencies, for example: James S. Turner, The Chemical Feast, study group report on the Food and Drug Administration. Grossman, New York.

12. Carter, L.J. 1968. "Water Pollution: Officials Goaded in Raising Quality Standards." *Science 160*: 49-51.

13. Davies, J.C. 1970. *The Politics of Pollution*. Pegasus, New York.

14. Nader, R. 1965. *Unsafe at Any Speed*. Grossman, New York.

15. Greenberg, D.S. 1969. "Pollution Control: Sweden Sets Up an Ambitious New Program." *Science 166*: 200-201.

16. "Selling against Pollution." 1970. *New Scientist 47*: 323-324.

17. "Crisis of Affluence, A Center Report." 1970. *Center Magazine 3* (1): 72-83.

Part VIII

RESPONSES TO SOCIETAL PROBLEMS

Every industrialized nation is faced with the crisis of conflicts between students and the institutions of learning. In many countries these conflicts turn into open violent confrontations. Buildings are burnt, students are beaten and killed, authority is questioned, and institutions are challenged.

The first article in this section is an analysis of crowds by historian George Rudé. His analysis makes it quite clear that crowd behavior is a rational, goal-directed response to socially induced situations. The next article, by Martin Lagassick, describes a student revolt at the University of California, Santa Barbara. His careful detailing of the underlying and immediate events which brought about several days of violent confrontation between students and police sheds considerable light on the internal dynamics of crises of this kind. Lagassick also shows how the internal dynamics are linked to events that are taking place in the society at large.

The third article in this section is an analysis of the rise of fascism in Europe during the 1930's. Written by G.D.H. Cole, a political economist, it links the rise of fascism to economic crises in capitalist societies. Although fascism, or some related form of totalitarian government, is not the only solution to the periodic economic crises that plague capitalist societies, it is a solution which, because of its costs in human suffering, must be understood. This article is a major contribution to that understanding. In sum, the articles in this section analyze and describe some of the characteristic features of responses to the problems of industrial societies.

THE CROWD IN 'PRE-INDUSTRIAL' SOCIETY
George Rudé

What I am mainly concerned with here is the changing complexion or
'face' of popular movements from one type of society to another. And by
'face' I don't mean only the physical appearance of crowds, or even their
modes of behaviour. In addition to these I am also concerned with the
issues involved, the forms of action in which they engage, their leaders and
motives, and their social composition. My contention is, rather, that the
'crowd' or popular movements has to be studied as a historical
phenomenon, and not as a stereotype that is equally suited to any form of
society. Thus popular movements occurring in ancient times tended to be
different in kind from those of the Middle Ages; and these in turn tended
to have distinctive characteristics that separate them from those that have
arisen in 'pre-industrial' or industrial society.

By 'pre-industrial' I mean broadly the period – it may extend over a
hundred years or it may be more or it may be less – during which a
society is adapting itself to the changes brought about by rapid
industrialisation and at the end of which that society has (as in Britain in
the nineteenth century) become radically transformed, so that we may
speak of a new society – an 'industrial' society – as having come into
being. This 'pre-industrial', or transitional, period naturally arises (if it
arises at all) in different countries and different continents at different
times. In England and France, with which I am most directly concerned,

we may date it roughly from the early eighteenth century to about the 1840s (or, possibly, in France a little later). In Central Europe, Australia and North America, it followed shortly after; in Eastern and Southern Europe not till 1900; in parts of Africa and Asia and in Latin America during the present century; and there are still countries in Asia, Africa and the Pacific (not to mention the 'aboriginal' areas of Australia) where the process has not yet begun.

So I am arguing that in each of these societies – whether ancient, medieval, 'pre-industrial' or industrial – popular movements have had their own distinctive and particular characteristics; and in each case, it is the historian's job to sort these out and not be content with readymade all-embracing answers. Which are these distinguishing features in the case of movements arising in 'pre-industrial' societies as, for example, those of France and England in the eighteenth and early nineteenth century?

Broadly speaking, it is convenient to classify them under the following six heads:

First, the types of disturbance. In the earlier phases food riots predominate, and these occur more frequently in villages and market towns than in cities; while industrial disputes, though fairly frequent, play only a secondary role. This is understandable enough at a time when there were no national or durable trade unions, when bread accounted for something like half, or more, of the working-man's budget, and when even the wage-earner was more concerned with the price of bread than with the amount of money in his pay-packet. But with growing industrialisation and working-class organisation, the roles became reversed: the strike tends to take over and the food riot tends to recede into the background. Similarly, political issues, always tending to obtrude in *urban* riots, play a relatively insignificant role in the earlier phase; but they come in greater evidence (as in England and France) from the latter part of the eighteenth century. This was largely due to early Radicalism in England and to the French Revolution of 1789, and to the advent, in both countries, of a working-class movement and socialist ideas half a century later.

Secondly, the forms of action. Predominantly, these are of the 'direct-action' type: in cities, 'pulling-down' of houses and burning the villain-of-the-hour in effigy; in country districts, arson (and particularly, in Britain, in the 1830s and 1840s), machine-breaking, and the imposition of price control by riot – what the French call *laxation populaire*. In brief, violence applied to property, but not (and I shall comment on this later) to life and limb. In addition, in the course of revolution, there are armed rebellions (assuming a progressively more organised and sophisticated form, as in Paris after 1789). At the same time, more 'modern' or 'industrial' forms of action are by no means absent; such as petitions to Parliament, marches, and modern-type industrial disputes of a more-or-less peaceful character. But the prevailing form of protest is the violent assault on property.

Thirdly, 'spontaneity' and lack of organisation; and therefore, a common feature is the *transformation* of a disturbance from a relatively small beginning (say, a meeting of housewives outside a baker's shop) into a wholesale rebellion and attack on property. This 'spontaneity' applies even to a highly developed movement like the popular outbreaks of the French Revolution; but notably more to its opening than to its later stages. And, generally speaking, as trade unions and political parties develop, this element of 'spontaneity' (which, of course, was never complete) begins to recede.

Fourthly, leadership: a point that is closely associated with the last. The typical leader of the 'pre-industrial' popular movement, certainly in its more sophisticated manifestations (in urban riots, revolutions and rebellions) comes from 'without' rather than from 'within' the crowd. Where the typical rioter or rebel is a craftsman, a labourer or a peasant, he may be a small nobleman, a lawyer, a journalist or a government official. Strictly speaking, there may be three types of leader: the leader-in-chief, in whose name the crowd riots or rebels; the intermediate leader — a sort of N.C.O — who passes on the slogans or tells the rioters whose house has to 'come down'; and the most articulate or militant among the rioters themselves, whose leadership is purely local and purely temporary. Of these three, the last alone emerges from the 'crowd' itself. He may be an anonymous figure who rides on a white horse, brandishes a sword or blows a bugle; he may bear a pseudonym like the countless Rebeccas, Ned Ludds and Captain Swings of the early nineteenth century, or like Tom the Barber who led the anti-Irish rioters in London in the 1730s; or he may be known by his proper name like the local leaders of London's Gordon Riots and several of the real or alleged leaders of the early disturbances of the French Revolution in Paris. But, whether anonymous or not, his authority is purely temporary and, after the riot which thrust him forward, he sinks back again into the obscurity of the crowd. Two further points may be worth making here. One is that the leader-in-chief in whose name the crowd riots or rebels may be an involuntary leader, whose leadership has been quite literally thrust upon him. Louis XVI of France, for instance (like other French Kings before him), claimed no more personal responsibility for the activities of the peasants who burned down *châteaux* in his name than Luther did for the rebellious German peasants of 1525. The other point is that, with the rise of a working-class movement in both England and France in the 1830s, the temporary and anonymous (or near-anonymous) local leader tends to give way to a more permanent and articulate successor. So, by the 1830s, we find men emerging as leaders from the crowd itself, who are no longer occasional, sporadic and anonymous, but continuous and openly proclaimed. Such a man was George Loveless, the leader of the Dorchester labourers of 1834, who was transported to Australia as a labour militant and political Radical and returned to his homeland, with similar opinions, three years later.

Fifthly, the composition of the 'pre-industrial' crowd. This is the feature of popular disturbance that has perhaps been more neglected than any other – and probably even more by sociologists than by historians. The main point I want to make here is that the typical protesting crowd of this transitional 'pre-industrial' period is not confined, or largely confined, to a single class. This has not always been the case. I suppose that the typical medieval crowd was composed of craftsmen in cities and peasants in country districts; and, in industrial society, industrial workers have – until recent times, at least – perhaps played a predominant part in urban riots. In 'pre-industrial' society, however, the composition is noticeably – and no doubt significantly – *mixed*. By this I don't mean that all classes of the community are represented in more or less equal proportions. Members of the upper and 'middling' classes have never been particularly noted for their participation in riots or street demonstrations: a notable exception here, of course, are the younger people, in particular the students – though even they played an altogether insignificant role in the disturbances of the eighteenth century – and, in Britain, even in the nineteenth. It is 'mixed', therefore, only in relation to the 'lower set of people' (as they were called in the eighteenth century): that is, the cottagers, small freeholders, rural craftsmen, weavers, farm labourers and miners of the countryside; and, in the towns, the small shopkeepers and stall-holders, the master craftsmen and wage-earners (whether skilled or unskilled); those, in short, who, during the French Revolution, acquired the name of *sans-culottes*. The very term *sans-culottes* – meaning originally those who wore trousers and not breeches – denotes not a single class but an amalgam of classes: both small employers and workpeople who had a common interest in a cheap and plentiful supply of bread.

Sixthly, the Motives or ideology of disturbance, or what some sociologists have termed the 'generalised ideas' underlying all forms of collective behaviour. This is the most difficult and most elusive question of all, as it raises all sorts of problems that the historian may not be particularly well qualified to handle; all the more so as his visual sources of enquiry all too rarely provide him with any satisfactory answers. It was all very well for the historians of the nineteenth century – before the days of mass observation or social psychology – to say that men rioted or rebelled simply because they were hungry or because this or that political leader or party had given them a new vision of the world or a taste for political reform. But the historian of today is expected to probe more deeply and cannot get away with such easy generalisations. And having read Tocqueville and Marx (and possibly Freud and Durckheim), he can hardly fail to realise that human motivation is extremely complex. This complexity applies, of course, as much to ancient and medieval as to 'pre-industrial' and industrial society. But it does not mean that the same motives for certain types of collective behaviour are equally predominant at all times and in all places – even though so respectable a figure as Gustave Le Bon, the 'father' of crowd psychology (he was writing about sixty years ago), appears to have thought so. It is fairly evident, for example, that 'political' motivation (whether of the Right or Left) played a more important role in popular disturbance at some stages than at others. It played a considerable part, as we shall see, in the latter part of this 'pre-industrial' period in France and England, though it is certainly not a distinctive feature of the period as a whole.

What *is* the distinctive feature of the 'pre-industrial' crowd is, I believe, its attachment to the *traditional* ways (or believed traditional ways) of the old village community or urban craft and its violent reaction to the sort of changes promoted, in the name of 'progress', by governments, capitalists, corn-merchants, speculative landlords or city authorities. So we find the constant and continuous presentation of demands for the 'restoration' of 'lost' rights, such as the 'just wage' and the 'just price', and even (later in the period) the right to vote. This is, of course, only a part (though a very important part) of the whole picture. I will return to the wider question later.

So far, then, I have argued that the distinctive hall-marks of the 'pre-industrial' crowd (at least, in its Western European manifestations) are: (1) the prevalence of the rural food riot; (2) the resort to 'direct action' and violence to property; (3) its 'spontaneity'; (4) its leadership from 'without' the crowd; (5) its mixed composition, with the emphasis on small shopkeepers and craftsmen in the towns and weavers, miners and labourers in the village; and (6) its concern for the restoration of 'lost' rights. I am arguing, too, that these features are 'distinctive' in the sense that, by and large, they distinguish the 'pre-industrial' popular movement from those that occur in both earlier and later periods. But I am certainly not insisting that all movements of the 'pre-industrial' age conform to this pattern or 'model'; nor am I blinding myself to the obvious fact that many popular disturbances of later times share common features with them. If such exceptions were frequent enough, they would of course invalidate the whole case I am putting forward. I don't think they were; but I'll return to this point a little later.

Before doing so, I should like to discuss certain of these 'common features' a little more fully, once more drawing my illustrations mainly from the history of England and France.

To return first to the types of disturbance and the behaviour of crowds. I have already said that food riots were the most common type of popular disturbance and I have tried to explain why this should have been so. But it would be a mistake to assume that the whole period, in both France and England, was punctuated by an almost unbroken succession of food riots. This, for obvious reasons, was not the case. Food riots generally occurred, as one might suspect, in the wake of bad harvests and shortage which sent prices rocketing upwards, and they may be said to have been the direct outcome of a fear of famine rather of famine itself. (The great famine year of 1709 in France, for example, was not conspicuous for popular disturbance.) In their most characteristic form such riots were attended by popular price-fixing (or *taxation populaire*), which took the form of a violent invasion of markets, granaries, flour-mills and bakers' shops in the course of which the crowd, or its 'local' leaders, insisted that the baker, miller or farmer should reduce the price of his wheat or bread or flour to a 'just' or traditional level. Such movements made their appearance in England soon after Parliament passed the first Corn Law in 1660 and, in France, in the early part of the eighteenth century. In both countries the lean years were more frequent after 1760 than in the half-century before; and the 'peak' years for this type of rioting were, in

France, 1768, 1775, 1789 and the 1790s, and, in England, 1766, 1795 and 1800. In both, the French Revolution served as a watershed, tending to inject a political content into such disturbances where they did not exist (or hardly existed) before. So we must look for their most classic, simon-pure, non-political expression, to the great English corn riots of 1766 and the French of 1775. The latter took the form of a vast rural rebellion in which the small consumers invaded the markets, flour-mills and bakers' shops in half a dozen provinces and in Paris itself, imposing a reduced price on corn, flour and bread, which, owing to the potency of rumour and of the 'bush-telegraph' of the market far more than to any organised conspiracy, was remarkably similar within the whole area over which the riots progressively spread. Such movements gained a new lease of life from the French Revolution; and they survived, through a couple of further revolutions, until the early 1850s. In England, they barely survived the Napoleonic Wars. There the last great outbreak of popular price-fixing by riot took place in East Anglia in 1816; after that, they persisted only in remote parts of the country (in Cornwall as late as 1830); and gave way to machine-breaking, arson and, later, to rural trade unionism.

In England (rather more than in France), the other most common type of rural riot was the attack on enclosures and toll-gates which spanned a roughly similar period; though, in West Wales (as remote from the centre of things as Cornwall), the last great manifestation of this kind, the so-called Rebecca Riots, took place as late as the early 1840s, at a time when the People's Charter was already winning wide support in the industrial districts of England, Scotland and South Wales.

Industrial disputes, during this 'pre-industrial' period, were also attended, in their most typical form, by attacks on machinery or the destruction of the mill-owner's or coal-owner's house or personal possessions. This has generally been called 'Luddism'; but as Dr. Hobsbawm and others have pointed out, 'Luddism' had two sides to it: its purpose was not always to arrest the growth of machinery (though this was certainly the prevailing intention in the Luddite riots in Yorkshire and Lancashire in 1812); it was also a traditional method of bringing pressure on the employer to raise wages or improve the conditions of work: this was generally the idea in the machine-breaking activities of the miners and weavers in the years preceding the Industrial Revolution and was also the case with the frame-work knitters of the Midlands 'hosiery' counties in the Luddite outbreaks of 1811 and 1812. And in 1816, in 1822, and, above all, in 1830, the same method of settling what was primarily a wages dispute was adopted by the country labourers of East Anglia and the South of England. In 1830, the labourers fired stacks, extorted money, engaged in wages riots and — most characteristically — destroyed threshing machines in a score of counties. And so convinced were they of the justice of their cause that they exacted payment from the farmers for obliging them by breaking their machines. In Berkshire, the usual rate for breaking a threshing machine of a reasonable size was £2; and the treasurer of the Kintbury 'gang' of rioters, a bricklayer named Francis Norris, was found with £100 and a couple of receipts in his pocket when arrested by the troops.

So a common factor in most of these disturbances — whether food riots or industrial disputes, whether they were rural or urban — was violence to property. And this goes as much for riots taking place before, during and after the French Revolution, and even for a short while, at least, after the birth of a working-class movement and the emergence of socialist ideas in the 1830s. Why this violence? In the case of individuals, it might perhaps be claimed that violent behaviour then, as now, is a release from tension or a way of canalising innate aggressive instincts. But, whatever the merit of such explanations in regard to individuals, we are dealing here with collective behaviour and we cannot assume that the urges stimulating the crowd are identical with the urges prompting the individuals that compose it or that crowd behaviour is simply individual behaviour writ large. The old-fashioned historian was inclined to identify the two and attribute the violence of the crowd to the natural violence of the rather unsavoury persons who composed it. Similarly, an old-fashioned crowd psychologist like Gustave Le Bon, who quite obviously was appalled by all such collective manifestations and had acquired his knowledge of the French Revolution from Taine, believed that the crowds that took the Bastille and stormed the Tuileries were displaying a 'collective mentality' that reduced all those taking part to a common level of bestiality.

The historian, however, cannot afford to neglect the political and social aspects of the case. The eighteenth century crowd, in particular, could hardly fail to be corrupted by the example set them by their social betters. It was an age of brutal floggings, torture of prisoners and public executions: in London, the desiccated heads of the Jacobite rebels executed after the 'Forty-Five' still grinned down from Temple Bar in the early 1770s; and in Paris men were broken on the wheel before the City Hall to the accompaniment of the consoling incantations of officiating clergy. Babeuf, the later promoter of a so-called 'conspiracy of the Equals', deplored the lynching by the crowd of a handful of victims after the fall of the Bastille, but ascribed their savagery to the lessons learned from their social superiors. Besides, was there a practical and effective alternative to violence (I am no longer talking of its grosser forms, like lynching) at a time when those composing these crowds were not allowed to organise in trade unions and were, almost without exception, excluded from the vote? In theory, there were, of course, alternatives such as carrying petitions to Parliament or engaging in peaceful processions. This was sometimes done in capital cities; but this was not much good in villages or in the suburbs of the new industrial towns where most of the disturbances took place. So the obvious and the most effective form of action, in times of hardship or dispute, was to take the law into your hands (as in the case of food riots) or to strike at the employer where it hurt most: at his house, his mill, his mine or his machinery. And it is perhaps no coincidence that the great debate on the relative virtues of 'physical force' and 'moral force' should have taken place at the time of Chartism, when many workers saw for the first time the possibility of finding a viable alternative to violence in the winning of the vote.

But it is important to note that violence was overwhelmingly applied to property and not to persons. This was so, with certain important exceptions, even in the most violent phases of the French Revolution. In the year 1789, for example, the crowd that stormed the Bastille massacred the governor, a municipal officer and half a dozen Swiss Guards; and, in the months that followed, four persons (including a baker) were lynched in Paris, two Household Guards were shot dead at Versailles and three or four persons were reported killed in the peasant attacks on the *châteaux* in the summer. In all, a total of a little short of twenty victims of the crowd in the opening year of revolution. This contrasts sharply with the greater savagery of the crowd's opponents. In the Réveillon riots of April 1789, 'several hundred' (the exact number is not known) were killed by troops and three were hanged after the event. At the siege of the Bastille, 150 assailants were killed or wounded. Five were hanged as a result of the disturbances in the capital that followed; and, two years later, in the great demonstration in the Champ de Mars in Paris, the crowd took two victims in return for fifty. In the case of all the English (and Welsh and Scottish) urban and rural riots of the 1830s to 1840s, the toll of death was even more one-sided. From my (no doubt) incomplete and imperfect record of the twenty-odd major riots and disturbances taking place in Britain between the Edinburgh Porteous Riots of 1736 and the great Chartist demonstration of April 1848 in London, I have totted up the following score: the crowds killed a dozen at most; while, on the other side, the courts hanged 118 and 630 were shot dead by the troops. We are told that Japanese students today, armed with sticks and helmets, inflict a heavier toll of casualties on the police than is inflicted on them by their opponents; but this was evidently far from being the case in similar engagements in the eighteenth and early nineteenth centuries in France and England. In brief, all talk of the famous 'blood-lust' of the crowd is largely based on legend and a few selected episodes in the French Revolutionary Terror; but it is a legend that dies hard.

What also dies hard is the legend of the crowd as riffraff or *canaille*, or as a 'mob', 'foreigners', lay-abouts, or simply (to quote Dr. Dorothy George on the Gordon Riots) of 'the inhabitants of the dangerous districts who were always ready for pillage'. That historians should have helped to perpetuate this legend is perhaps hardly surprising. On the one hand, they have often had to cater for their own prejudices which reject the 'mob' (or *mobile vulgus*) as a squalid and dangerous intruder on the historical scene. On the other, they have had the more respectable justification of deriving their picture from that presented of the crowd by the great majority of contemporary observers, to whom the 'lower orders', particularly when engaged in acts of violent protest, readily appeared as gangs of criminals, drunkards or marauding 'strangers'. Doubtless for sound historical reasons, this picture tended to become less lurid and less one-sided by the early nineteenth century; but even in 1830, the 'Swing' labourers who fired stacks or broke threshing machines in the South of England were still being described in reports to the Home Office (often by clerical magistrates) as 'smugglers and deer-stealers', 'strangers dressed as labourers' (sometimes reported to be riding about in 'green gigs'), as 'the lowest description of persons' or 'men of indifferent character'. Usually these epithets fell wide of the mark, as these rioters, in particular, turn out, from the voluminous records that have survived in their case, to have been mainly respectable labourers and rural craftsmen of almost unimpeachable character: this, at least, is the general picture that emerges from the records relating to the 480 who were transported to Australia. And, similarly, the Parisians who stormed the Bastille and the Tuileries, though described by the historian Taine as cut-throats, vagrants, bandits and foreigners, are now fairly widely accepted as having been typical craftsmen, small employers and workmen of the Paris *faubourgs;* and generally of fixed abode and settled occupation.

A rather more refined variant of the 'crowd-as-mob' thesis is that put forward by M. Louis Chevalier in his book on the 'industrious and dangerous classes' of Paris in the 1830s and 1840s. From a wealth of sources, both literary and demographic, M. Chevalier paints a horrifying picture of the growth of Paris in the early nineteenth century, in terms of a growth of slums and overcrowding; and, with them, of crime, suicide, violence and prostitution. The main agents of this transformation are the 'nomads' or 'uprooted' who flock into the capital from the provinces and proceed, almost literally, to wage war on the old settled population. The 'industrious' and 'dangerous' classes turn out to be much the same; and the author infers – though he never specifically states – that these 'dangerous' and overcrowded districts were the nurseries not only of poverty and crime but also of riot and rebellion. If this was so, one would expect to find a fair sprinkling of criminals and down-and-outs among the rioters and rebels of the period – and more particularly in the revolutions of 1830 and 1848. Yet such studies as have been made on the subject by Pinkney, Tilly, Gossez and others do not bear this out; and the Parisian crowd of the 1830s and 1840s appears, when every allowance has been made for the changes brought about in certain occupations, to be remarkably similarly constituted to that of 1789 and 1793.

This is, of course, a bald generalisation; and it is not being suggested either that the crowd remained largely identical whatever the nature of the disturbance, or that it remained unchanged from one decade to another. In Paris, for example, political and para-military engagements like the assault on the Bastille and the Tuileries involved a far higher proportion of craftsmen than food riots, in which both women and unskilled workers were more conspicuously represented. And the French Revolution was an important turning point, after which nothing was ever quite the same as before, not only because it gave a new political dimension to riot (and this applies to riots of the Right as well as to those of the Left), but also because it drew a wider range of social forces into political, or semipolitical, activity. Not that political issues were entirely absent from rioting in the period up to the 1780s. The urban riot in big cities like London and Paris always tended to have political undertones; and in London, even before the early eighteenth-century riots of Anne's reign, the Common Council of the City had begun to serve as the political educator of the crowd in much the same way as the Paris Parlement, which did not scruple to clothe its appeal to uphold ancient privilege in popular terms, served to educate the French. In Paris, the big change came with the

Revolution, when the crowd took a sharp and decisive turn to the Left and the popular movement even gained a considerable degree of independence, not only in breaking loose from its former aristocratic allies but even to a large extent from its new-found *bourgeois* allies as well. In London, this happened in two stages: in the 1760s, the crowd attached itself to the City Radicals and the person of John Wilkes; after the revolution in France it began to throw up leaders and organisations of its own. And this whole process was vastly speeded up in both countries by the emergence of working-class movements and socialist ideas in the 1830s.

So we come back to the most complex question of all: that of ideology and motivation. The question: why did people riot or rebel? is a simple one, but, as I have said before, it has no simple answer. The best I can hope to do here is to indicate certain motives and attempt to classify them. But how? as short-term and long-term motives? As 'economic' and 'political'? as overt or submerged? as 'forward-looking' or 'backward-looking'? as 'progressive' or 'reactionary'? This is largely a matter of choice as one type of classification cannot claim to be intrinsically more suitable than any other. For myself, I prefer to distinguish broadly between motives that are 'indigenous' (that is, directly experienced) and those that are 'derived', or borrowed or adapted from another quarter. As I see it, 'indigenous' motives are of two kinds: there are those that are concerned with the immediate problems relating to the rioters' daily bread, such as wages and prices, enclosures, turnpikes, land; and I assume that in food riots, turnpike riots and wages movements such overt motives play a predominant, though by no means an exclusive, role. But there are also, both in this type of riot and in others, certain underlying ideas and traditional, or 'generalised', beliefs that, for lying partly submerged, are none the less important. Such is the 'levelling' instinct or the belief in a rough sort of social justice, which prompts the poor to settle accounts with the rich by smashing their windows or burning their property or destroying their fences; we find examples of this both in English rural riots of the 1830s and 1840s and in the London riots of the 1760s and 1780s. There was also the strong belief among both 'middling' classes and poor in England in the 'Englishman's birthright' and his right to certain basic freedoms (as in Good King Alfred's day!), which distinguished him from poor benighted foreigners, like Frenchmen or Spaniards who had to put up with Popery and Wooden Shoes; and it seems that the fear that these freedoms were being threatened served on occasion as a powerful stimulus to riot. Again, in countries of absolute monarchy like France or Russia, the King or Tsar was frequently seen in the guise of Protector of his People; and this belief was no doubt strong among the French peasants who rioted in the King's name for bread in 1664 and 1775 and against feudal dues in August 1789. Again, as I have mentioned earlier, there was a strong attachment among both English and French labourers and small consumers to the traditional principles of a 'fair price' and a 'fair wage' untouched by the new-fangled notions of supply and demand. And this may do a great deal to explain the peculiar tenacity with which crowds broke machines and imposed price-controls by riot.

On the other hand, political motives and beliefs came, as we have seen, to be of increasing importance after the French Revolution; and these were, in the first place at least, *derived* from outside sources; from the Common Council or Parlement, from Radical journalists and politicians, or from liberal aristocrats or revolutionary *bourgeois*. Such was the notion and slogan of 'liberty' absorbed by the London crowds in the 1760s; and such were the ideas of the Rights of Man and Popular Sovereignty which Rousseau passed on to the Parisian *sans-culottes* via the Parlement and the revolutionary journalists and orators of 1789. And, later, socialist ideas were similarly derived from Babeuf, Owen and Marx.

But though originally derived from outside, such ideas were given a particular twist in the course of their assimilation by the small masters, craftsmen and wage-earners, who adapted them, as it were, to their own social and political needs. This is particularly striking in the case of the *sans-culottes* in Paris, who gave new meanings to the ideas of 'equality', 'Liberty' and 'sovereignty' which were quite unacceptable to their Jacobin teachers.

And to formulate more clearly what I only hinted before: it was a feature of this 'pre-industrial' period that the predominant traditional and 'indigenous' beliefs, which played so important a part in the ideology of the eighteenth century crowd, were gradually rivalled or eclipsed by the new political ideas emanating from the French Revolution and the working-class movements of the 1830s and 1840.

Thus, in spite of my somewhat tentative 'model', the face of the crowd, far from being firmly fixed, was constantly changed as society moved from its 'pre-industrial' to its industrial phase; and there was certainly no sharp cutting-off point between the two. So we have recognisable points of transition that mark the passing-over from the earlier to the later type of society. Examples of this are found in the revolution of 1848 in France and Chartism in England. We see signs of the old 'pre-industrial' forms in the February stage of the 1848 revolution: in the initial alliance of classes between bourgeoisie and *sans-culottes* (reminiscent of 1789), in food riots, industrial 'Luddism', not to mention the frequent repetition of the slogans, organisations and ideas of the older revolution. On the other hand, there is a reaching forward to the newer industrial society (particularly in the June insurrection) in the armed clash between capital and labour, in the workingmen's clubs and socialist ideas, and in the emergence of new types of worker, such as railwaymen and engineers. Chartism, too, has a similar dual complexion. On the one hand, the six points of the People's Charter look back to a similar programme drawn up in Westminster in 1780; and Feargus O'Connor's Land Plan as a cure for industrial ills and the old-style 'house-breaking' riots in Staffordshire in 1842 are stamped with the traditions of a 'pre-industrial' society. On the other hand, the Chartist political organisation, the industrial aims of the miners and textile workers, and the activities of the Manchester 'turn-outs' in the 'Plug-Plot' riots of 1842 were new and 'forward-looking'.

Again, it may occur to the reader that there have been plenty of cases of 'pre-industrial'-type riots in our modern industrial society. In 1914, for example, German bakers' shops were attacked in London in much the same way as the Gordon rioters attacked the property of Roman Catholics and their reputed sympathisers in 1780. In Kalgoorlie, in Western Australia, striking miners in the 1930s wrecked pit-head machinery as their forbears in the Durham coalfields had done a hundred years before. The Japanese rice riots of 1918 were accompanied by the same sort of direct action and popular price control as the food riots in France and England in the eighteenth and early nineteenth centuries. Dr. Hobsbawm gives us plenty of illustrations of archaic and strictly non-'industrial' forms of popular protest in his book on twentieth century 'Primitive Rebels'. The Mexican Cristeros of 1936 hailed Christ the King and damned the radical *bourgeois* in a manner highly reminiscent of the Vendée peasants of 1793 and of the 'King and Church' movements in Spain, Italy and the Tyrol at the time of the Revolutionary and Napoleonic Wars. And what of the Negro rebellion that has been erupting in the northern cities of the United States since 1964? Hasn't this, in certain of its aspects at least, a distinct flavour of the 'pre-industrial' riot? I think the answer is yes. But why this should be so, and why Japanese rice-rioters should have behaved as they did at a time when Japan was already considered to have moved into its 'industrial' stage, I prefer to leave to my readers to work out for themselves.

ANATOMY OF A STUDENT REVOLT

Martin Legassick

Angry demonstrators rushed a branch of the Bank of America in Santa Barbara at 12:45 a.m. Thursday piling tables and chairs against the walls and setting them afire. No policemen or firemen attempted to enter the troubled area to fight the blaze, which spread to the bank itself, eventually burning the structure to the ground. Several hundred demonstrators stood back and watched the walls crumble.

— LOS ANGELES TIMES, February 26, 1970

As the news and pictures of the bank-burning spread across America, the University of California, Santa Barbara, stepped from the shadows: Isla Vista joined that list of left-wing "happenings" which stretched from Greensboro through to the Berkeley Free Speech Movement, Columbia, Chicago, People's Park . . . and Kent and Jackson State. On the morning after, the directors of the Bank of America fulminated against this "outrageous act of violence . . . and insurrection against the democratic process of the kind that leads to further violence, bloodshed and anarchy." In the Cook County jail, where Jerry Rubin, Tom Hayden and the five others of the Chicago "Conspiracy" trial were smarting under the contempt of court sentences that had climaxed the proceedings, there was rejoicing: justice, felt the Chicago Seven, was being taken to the streets. The bank-burning episode was indeed only the most dramatic of the events that rocked Santa Barbara from January to June 1970. Among the others were the beating of dozens of heads by police, over a thousand arrests in the course of three "riots" and three series of demonstrations, substantial damage to police vehicles and local realty offices, and a three-night reign of terror in Isla Vista by Los Angeles police, called in to an area declared in essence a "free strike zone" by local law enforcement, unable to subdue student rebellion. And, most important perhaps, on April 17 a 22-year-old economics major, Kevin Moran, was killed by a bullet from a police gun. All these events — and the bank-burning most of all — were greeted by the world outside with, most of all, surprise. How did such a sunny, sleepy backwater spring to the vanguard of student militance?

THE SANTA BARBARA BACKGROUND

One must begin with Isla Vista itself and the community of Santa Barbara which surrounds it. The town, founded as a Spanish mission site, lies in a narrow coastal plain between white sunny beaches and mountains, beyond which national forest extends north through a hundred miles of wilderness: as late as 1916 a stagecoach, perhaps the last in the West, still ran through these mountains to a railhead on the other side. The salubrious climate attracted the retired wealthy, conservatives from the Midwest and liberals from New England, who patronized huge and opulently baroque hotels in the early part of the century and then moved to large estates in Montecito or Hope Ranch. From this time there still lingers over Santa Barbara the patina of leisured unconcern, of quiet certainty of an undisturbed future, dulling and distorting the patterns of contemporary conflict. The county sheriff's office and jail is situated in a large neo-Spanish building, enclosing a green and fountained courtyard in which concerts have been held.

Transformation began after the Second World War. Santa Barbara College became a part of the University of California, which acquired — for ten dollars, it is rumored — a site on a military base fifteen miles from the town on the seaward side of the lemon- and avocado-groved Goleta Valley. As in Los Angeles and Orange County, orchards made way for progress. In their stead came research and development firms — General Electric's Tempo, Raytheon, General Motors, General Research, Systems Research, and two dozen others. County, city, university, and industry found mutual advantage in the ecological rape of the valley in the interests of the cold war economy. For the research firms the university was a source of expertise and equipment: even today employees of these firms have greater privileges at the university library than most students. For the university, the firms were a carrot with which to attract superior faculty — or rather, superior academic entrepreneurs for whom consulting and upward mobility into national decision-making circles was more important than scholarship or teaching. For the county power structure, R and D was an area of growth potential to supplement existing "industries" — agriculture, tourism, and often dubiously valuable medicine characteristic of retirement spots.

California, it is often said, has built its bizarre extremes and repulsive paradoxes on a lack of history and tradition. But California does not lack tradition: it has simply flaunted its traditions and denied its history.

Indians enslaved, expropriated and conquered by the Spanish, Spanish conquered by the Anglos, miners replaced by railway builders, by capitalist farmers, by defence industry . . . each has brutalized, thrown off its predecessors rather than absorbing them in fruitful osmosis. American ideology became Californian reality: man against nature, man for the present, and the future untempered by the past. The disguises with which man usually clothes his baser acts dissolve in California. If the state has produced a spate of actors as politicians it is because politicians *are* actors. Logic becomes basic: logic in action. Chicano's make good tomato-pickers, said the late Senator George Murphy, because "they're built closer to the ground." There will be a bloodbath, Governor Reagan warned student protestors . . . and soon there was a bloodbath. "I want to kill a nigger so damn bad I can taste it" said drunken off-duty San Francisco policeman Michael O'Brien after a row with his girlfriend and a minor car accident . . . and he killed one. With all organic bonds in space and time dissolved, anything can happen.

Thus in Santa Barbara the avocado groves gave way to acres of plastic tract housing, into which poured the lesser and greater technocrats of MesoAmerica. "Progress," like a centrifuge, flung to the peripheries the other elements of the Santa Barbara population. Downtown is a Chicano ghetto, many of its demoralized inhabitants able to trace their ancestry to the Spanish forefathers of the community. On the beachfront benches, in the bars along lower State Street, in tiny old houses along tree-lined sidewalks and up in the mountains live other rejects of Santa Barbara and the nation's present. There are alcoholic cowboys, still living the myths of the old West. And senior citizens of the lower middle class or lower still, lured by glossy brochures to the sun only to find that age without money can find no rest anywhere in a profit-oriented society. While Goleta Valley grows in population as fast as anywhere in the country, and Montecito boasts one of the highest per capita income levels, wealth and growth conceal, as always, poverty and despair.

THE GROWTH OF ISLA VISTA

Isla Vista, a small community of beach houses adjoining the military base, began to take its present form as the university underwent rapid expansion in the early 1960's. A Rockefeller Foundation plan to build cooperative student housing in the area was blocked by local real-estate interests who bought up the land and threw up street upon street of jerry-built apartments: a strong fist could punch through an interior wall of these buildings without much difficulty. Today the housing in I.V. is managed by some ten realty companies, six with offices in the community (though one sold out after the first "riot"). At least half the landlords live in Los Angeles or Ventura, thirty miles down the coast, though members of the UCSB administration and faculty also own I.V. property. The chancellor of the university, indeed, is a director of Goleta Savings and Loan Association which holds mortgages in I.V. Though there are no large-scale landlords, there is little incentive for owners or managers to maintain property. The investment is often a tax gimmick. And students are transients, usually present only nine months of the year, and with less incentive to overt complaint than a long-term tenant. The realty companies skim off profits and provide minimum services in return. The nine-month contracts are rigidly enforced, and exorbitant, and such complaints as occur are rarely or tardily remedied. Few students do not hold a grudge against realty companies and landlords.

The role of the university in housing matters is, to say the least, curious. The university housing office has a list of "approved housing" and could engage in blacklisting, but it has not done so. Indeed, when Isla Vista Realty, whose behavior had stimulated most complaints, was convicted in court of malpractice and had its license suspended – for fifteen days! – a member of the university administration testified on behalf of the company. Theoretically the student government, Associated Students, had more muscle; until recently, however, their lawyer was also the lawyer for Isla Vista Realty.

Isla Vista cannot be called a ghetto in any classical sense. Of its 13,000 or so inhabitants, some 9000 are students, the overwhelming majority from middle-class or higher status parentage. Indeed, one of the community's problems is lack of off-street parking facilities – and among student cars Mustangs and other more exotic breeds are not uncommon. Most people have expensive stereos, a large wardrobe, and in general an accumulation of material possessions that would leave students in Europe astounded. But Isla Vista is isolated, geographically, politically, socially, and its inhabitants feel themselves powerless: in this sense it is a ghetto. Apartments, services, and stores are over-priced and exploitive – but it is a nuisance to shop outside the area. Isla Vista is separated from the outside, the town of Goleta, by acres of fields (mainly university-owned) and by an airport: there are only three access roads, one of them through the campus. The business community is largely nonresident. There are, or were until recently, few registered voters – and registration drives were seriously hampered by local officials. The community is, in consequence, neglected by the county: transportation, recreation, sanitary services, street-cleaning, street-lighting, and emergency health facilities are nonexistent or atrocious in quality. A local underground newspaper managed to expose a reportedly fraudulent affair involving bribery, zoning, and land involving one of the County Board of Supervisors; other zoning violations abound. Perfect Park, adjoining the Bank of America and the only community park, was established only after considerable pressure and on leased land.

Consistent with its ghetto status, Isla Vista has not been neglected only in one "service" – law enforcement. In strictly legal terms, there are reasons for this. Since at least the "San Francisco summer" of 1967, dope has become Isla Vista's major community industry. Situated at a convenient half-way house between Mexico and San Francisco, Isla Vista has seen grass, hash, speed, opium, mescalin, acid, smack, cocaine, and every other natural or artificial "high" that can be sniffed, smoked, swallowed or shot pass through and remain. This had certain positive effects on lifestyles in the community (as I shall relate shortly) but it brought problems too. There are the smack-freaks and speed-freaks, spaced-out and withered forms who sprawl in and around the twenty-four-hour donut shop and the local pool hall nearby. There are the persistent rumors of Mafia infiltration of the dope market which follow such incidents as the knifing of a local dealer in a large apartment complex: and the Mafia is most interested in hard drugs. Rapes average ten a month or more, though since many are unreported it is hard to give an accurate figure; burglaries increase. Some of the problem is directly due to drugs; some comes from outsiders who see easy pickings in a community with free and easy values.

But if it was this milieu which attracted the attention of law enforcement, its contribution was to exacerbate rather than solve the problems. They certainly never succeeded, if they ever tried, in stamping out hard drugs or protecting the community from outside malfeasants. The county sheriff's department shrugged off reports of burglary and rape. Instead, the main crackdown came on marijuana. Over half the felony arrests in recent years in Santa Barbara County were for marijuana: there are few Isla Vistans who have not had a roommate, a neighbor, or a friend busted for dope – and most of these arrests were for possession or "possession of paraphernalia" rather than dealing. Sheriff's cars patrolled the streets at night, likely to stop and harass pedestrians; plainclothes "narks" circulated in the more frequented areas. Between 1967 and 1969 hard drugs and the police between them built up an atmosphere of tension in Isla Vista which crackled and hummed in the air. Increasingly, the overwhelming majority of the community came to see the police as objects of at least suspicion and mistrust. Law enforcement appeared to be directed selectively *against* the community rather than for its protection and service. Their pressing crime problems untackled, their harmless peccadillos vigorously acted against, residents came to see the police as the prime symbol of their oppression.

THE POLITICAL CULTURE OF ISLA VISTA

It was the new "youth culture" rather than the tradition of 1960's New Left activism which shaped the political culture of Isla Vista and the university. The New Left moved from politics to embrace the idea of "cultural revolution": Isla Vista moved in the other direction. Both movements, of course, sprang out of a reaction against that antiideological, materialistically oriented corporate liberalism characteristic of post-New Deal America and contemporary capitalism in general which Charles Reich has labeled Consciousness II.[1] The Depression, the war, the cold war, and McCarthyism left the generation of whites who grew up in the 1930's divided between an overwhelming majority who accepted as final ends material affluence and anticommunism, and a small, impotent, and cowed minority of left-liberals terrorized into privatism. The New Left grew out of the first hesitant moves of this minority back into civil-rights politics, and out of the blunders of a corporate liberalism overly self-confident but bereft of innovative ideas. In retrospect, the snub given to the Mississippi Freedom Democratic Party at the 1964 Democratic convention can be seen as marking the transition from black integrationism to black power, with the consequence that young whites were cast back from Southern or ghetto organising to their own cultural milieu. And, again in retrospect, the decision to commit massive military force in Vietnam in 1965 where the CIA had failed to counter the NLF, was an equal blunder for corporate liberalism.

Blacks and Vietnamese, in other words, helped along by the errors of the power structure, created the white New Left. Vietnamese protest led through teach-ins and demonstrations, through Carl Oglesby's "naming of the system" as corporate liberalism in the 1965 March on Washington,[2] to draft resistance, to Benjamin Spock, to the Oakland "Stop the Draft" week in October 1967. Meanwhile black power led through the ghetto rebellions and the paltry attempts at New Deal type reform programs, through cultural nationalism, to the Black Panther Party. The mediators were dead or defeated: Martin Luther King, Bobby Kennedy, Eugene McCarthy. The Free Speech Movement escalated into Columbia in 1968. The "San Francisco Summer" of 1967 became the street battles of Berkeley in 1968. By the time of the Democratic convention, what had appeared as a set of traditional issue-oriented protests, ineffectively infiltrated by sectarian ideologists, was in fact being transformed into a broad-based mass movement with a large number of shared assumptions. It began to pose a danger. "The New Leftists of the early Sixties" writes Tom Hayden, "and many of the black radicals as well, were preoccupied not with the danger of fascist repression but with that of liberal co-optation. We saw a power structure with such vast wealth and weaponry that it seemed beyond defeat . . . we seemed doomed to exist only as a marginal force."[3] It was at the Democratic convention, he continues, that he began to realize how wrong they had been. The failure of liberal co-optation, in fact, necessitated repression.

This new movement had its source, but also the base of its following, among youth and more particularly students. That its source was intellectual is not surprising; its emergence as a movement of mass appeal has yet to be explained. Perhaps it is, as Richard Flacks has written, that for the first time persons trained to the function of "intellectuals" have substantial numbers: there are indeed more students (6 million) than farmers (5 million) in the United States. But what is this function? Some regard the American university as little more than a haven for disguised unemployment in conditions of advanced capitalism, whereas others believe that the same advanced capitalist conditions necessitate the training of teachers, public administrators, technicians with skills that would previously have secured them elite status but now give a position nearer worker than manager. In either case the traditions of a university education and the equipment of the intellectual are being provided to those whose role in society is undergoing downward mobility. Indeed, historically it has been the function of the intellectual to explain production, to provide rationalisations and mystifications for mechanisms of exploitation, as also to develop new techniques of production. But, as Flacks has pointed out, there is another element in the heritage of the intellectual, inseparable from a training for these roles. It is the intellectual who has sustained bohemianism, the revolt against bourgeois values in the name of leisure, spontaneity, artistic appreciation, in the name of nature, taste, and culture, against efficiency, practicality, and market values. In the contemporary crisis, it would seem that these elements in the university heritage have come into conflict with a system of training which is increasingly standardised, mechanized, regimented, and alienating, under conditions which assure the student little or no creative future but that of a small cog in a large machine, and in which he is justifying or sustaining a system whose conflict with the antibourgeois aspects of his socialization is every day more pronounced.[4] One might add that generational conflict within the family has reinforced the tendencies. It is, studies have shown, the children of upper middle-class liberals who have been the activist vanguard of student revolt.[5] These parents were the generation who left politics to the benevolence of a reformist Federal government, and then retreated into privatism, and yet transmitted antibourgeois tendencies within the family. Their children have elevated to the public and political realm what the parents retained in the private, and denounce as hypocritical the gap between the practice of affluence and the theory of equality.

Isla Vista, I have said, did not participate in the intellectual realization of these issues in early 1960's New Left politics. If UCSB had an image at this time which extended beyond sun, sea, and surfing it was for fraternity activities which were, by all accounts, even wilder than usual.[6] Orgies, "gang-bangs," nude motorcycle riding, wild drinking — with all the cliqueishness, aggression, ambition, and male chauvinism which these involved — were characteristic. Yet, shorn of these aspects, this deviant subculture was a strong element in the lifestyle revolution which occurred in Santa Barbara as fraternity hegemony gave way to dope between 1965 and 1967.

It is impossible to exaggerate the role played by marijuana and the "new music" of the 1960's in the experience of Isla Vistans. They are constants of life of the order of beer and TV. As a citizen of Goleta said to the local paper in disgust, "you can't drive through Isla Vista without smelling marijuana in the streets."[7] From being a semisecret experience shared only with close friends, marijuana began from about 1967 to move into the open; and with it long hair and beards, a change in dress styles, and all the surface accoutrements of the "cultural revolution." Hippie petty capitalism sprang up: leather stores and head shops and craft shops of all kinds were added to book and record stores. An organic food store and restaurant, the Sun and Earth, became a community focus where sandwiches could be consumed in a garden of nasturtiums. "Street people" began to gravitate to the area from San Francisco and elsewhere. In its isolated and intimate geographic setting, Isla Vista acquired a shared experience of the "counterculture" which drew its people together against the world outside.

This shared experience was inward as well as outward. Whatever people's views on the benefits or evils of marijuana, few deny that it alters the structure of mental perception. Sensations of color, sound, time, taste, smell, feel are changed: the world and communication within it become, literally, different. All those tendencies which on a national or Western scale were encouraging a revolt against a sterile and misused intellect were enhanced in the atmosphere of California, which in denying history denied also the source of intellectual contemplation. Marijuana, with its encouragement of sensory experience, of wholes rather than roles, provided the means of escape from a barren academic training and the promised alienation of the future into a richer and warmer present. The journey inward to the mind was an implicit — and became an explicit — critique of a generation of parents who had been captivated by the outer and the material. The shared ritual of drugs, the passing around of the joint within a group, symbolized the restoration of the organic bonds between human beings to replace the artificial role-playing of capitalist society in its bureaucratic phase. The illegality directed fear outside, away from one's neighbor and to "them."

THE BEGINNINGS OF POLITICAL ACTIVITY

The marijuana culture did not lead directly to politics: though polls of the student body showed a strong majority of liberal to radical views these were not actively expressed. Vietnam marches, draft resistance, an underground newspaper, a short-lived Che Guevara Memorial Society were symptomatic, but engaged limited numbers. In the summer of 1967 a small group organized a temporarily successful "counter-nark" operation in Isla Vista, which kept watch on police activity. But those who despaired on the materialism and bureaucracy of the system were paranoid, cynical, and "escapist" about politics. Politics was a "bummer," or futile, or exposed one's private life to police prying. A pad and some bread were sufficient goals.

Things began to change toward the end of 1968. A mixture of disillusioned liberals, culture-freaks, and radicals began to thrash out their differences in a new chapter of Students for a Democratic Society (SDS). Meanwhile, those who had worked for Gene McCarthy — and they were many — found the massive antiwar vote in the California primary negated by Bobby's death, Daley's Gestapo, and a Democratic convention which nominated Humphrey.[8] The events which warned Hayden of the danger of fascism served to open a yawning gulf between the myth and reality of American democracy for naive UCSB students.

In the fall and throughout the 1968-1969 academic year, it was black students whose grit and determination gave momentum to the radical movement on most campuses. Such mass white support as was generated beyond the already committed few stemmed largely from liberal guilt. The different forces generating black and white student protest, indeed, continued to generate problems.[9] Accustomed to the tactics appropriate to an oppressed minority, the blacks were often accused of vanguardism and antimajoritarianism; less willing to follow through the logical consequences of their rhetoric, white students were on occasion accused by the blacks of "jiving." In the protest of 1970 warm egalitarian relationships developed between some white and black radicals. Yet the blacks were sensitive to the greater "exposure" that they suffered through participation in "white" political issues and resented the fact that white support for their own protest was never as large or sustained.

The initial move by the Black Student Union (BSU) in the fall of 1968 was to seize the UCSB computer center and threaten to destroy the computer unless their calls were met for an ethnic studies center and increased minority enrollment. By this one act, all things were opened for debate and conflict. The administration did not call in the police and agreed to negotiate ... thus opening up tension between itself and the Regents which was to condition future events. A faculty "Committee of 50" (later much larger in number) issued a statement, to be opposed by a more radical faculty group, on the merits of the black case and the nature of the university. Such faculty division contributed to greater student discussion of the same issues and implanted the beginnings of a division between students and faculty.

In February 1969, with their demands still unmet, the BSU joined with SDS and the Chicano students organization to "liberate" the student-financed University Center. The choice of a student-supported building, and the immediate creation in it of a "New Free University" (NFU) open to all comers and to be run on the basis of participatory democracy, was a significant departure from the classic sit-in at the administration building characteristic of other campuses. As such it completely disarmed the administration or the potential for right-wing student mobilization. Again no police were called: UCSB's first mass student action was left to take its own momentum. Blacks and browns gained – eventually – their demands, though in watered-down form. White students, in specific terms, gained nothing. Yet in less definable ways they had experienced the joy of collective action and the potential of student power. The NFU opened a utopian vision of a new kind of education, even if promise far exceeded practice and the practice was short-lived. "Radicalism" – its theory and its methods – gained credibility and legitimacy. A United Front slate (SDS-BSU-Chicano) won a majority in student government elections and radicals gained control of the student newspaper – though the BSU candidate for student president was rejected in favor of a more moderate black.

Most important of all, it was at the NFU that the particular *style* of UCSB radicalism began to take shape and gain legitimacy, though in this case only for a few short days before the culture-freaks departed to leave the terrain to more conventional organisers. Through the Yippie politics of put-on and through an anarchist millenarianism which translated "do your own thing" into political language as "liberate yourself now," New Left politics were linked with "lifestyle revolution." The politics of put-on were best represented by the class "On The Tactics and Practice of Guerrilla Warfare at UCSB and in the Santa Barbara Community," whose outline proclaimed as its purpose "to give the people who are already convinced that this government needs to be overthrown a method for overthrowing it" and which promised lectures on, *inter alia,* "disrupting UCSB through hit-and-run actions" and "how to get the community involved through terrorism."

> What are a few looted buildings compared to millions of looted lives?
> How can you build new buildings before you burn the old ones down?
> What would a quick bloodbath in the streets be compared to the blood that's already been shed more slowly in the ghettos and factories to give you this campus?
> What are you willing to die for?

The class met only once, composed equally, needless to say, of students and undercover police. A year later Mayor Yorty of Los Angeles still took this sort of thing seriously enough to brandish the course outline to a Santa Barbara audience.[10] But – and it was a tactical fact not yet well-realized by the activists – the exorcising of establishment fantasies transformed easily into reality. A month or so later some unknown person placed a bomb at an entrance to the Faculty Club and blew the caretaker to pieces early one morning.

The McLuhan generation, even its radical activists, have less time for linear activities than their forebears. But for Isla Vista in general and even for the radicals, such literary influences as existed were Tolksen, Kurt Vonnegut, Krishnamurti, Herman Hesse, the I Ching, and the ecological poetry of Gary Snyder, rather than Marcuse or Mills, let alone Marx, Mao, or the corpus of their interpreters. Student preoccupations, symbolized by the courses spontaneously developed at the NFU, were with astrology, Zen Buddhism, transcendental meditation; sensate and religous experience, in other words; mystery, magic, and messianism. "Liberation" was directed inward rather than outward: it seemed, after all, more possible that way. Consciously and unconsciously anarchism became a dominant strain in Isla Vista's political culture – an anarchism fortified, above all, by the ideals of Wilhelm Reich. The key to liberation, the cure for neurosis, lay in freeing the body rather than the mind, let alone the society. The abandonment of all inhibitions and restraints, the free enjoyment of experience, rather than the seizure of state power, was the revolutionary goal. Often it was assumed that everything irrelevant to this goal could and should be eliminated through simple physical destruction.

Beautiful in its utopian vision, this kind of anarchism tended towards nihilism or, with its emphasis on the senses and its disdain for the mind, to an individualist elitism. There was little room in it for the notion of institutions rather than buildings, for the notion of the ideological hegemony of those institutions requiring not only a counter-culture but a counter-ideology. After all, in its traditional forms radicalism involves dialogue – not the dialogue of liberalism which leads to compromise, concealment, mystification, but a dialogue which transforms and synthe-sizes through teaching and learning, and which aspires towards increased understanding. In the absence of organized teaching and learning there is nothing but "revolution by example." And while revolutionaries need to be exemplary, such activity alone supposes that among the followers it is only willpower and not understanding that is lacking. X bombs a building, in other words, and assumes that he is alone only because no-one else has the guts, rather than that they don't know why the action is necessary — or indeed have considered and tactically rejected it. The trend of "revolution by example" is to have contempt for those who do not act, and ultimately to see them as enemies rather than potential supporters.

Yet under advanced capitalism, where revolutionaries are trying to surpass and supersede industrial society rather than build it, to reject capitalism for its successes rather than its failures, anarchism is an essential ingredient of revolution. As Tom Nairn writes of France in May 1968, "it is no longer enough to say, with Lenin, that Marxists and anarchists can agree on distant aims — on the ultimate state of 'freedom' the revolution will bring about — but must disagree as to methods. Under advanced capitalism, where society is materially much closer to the possibility of 'freedom', means and ends are also necessarily much closer." Moreover, as he continues, the very fact that it is the bonds of ideological hegemony, of alienation and authority, rather than of material oppression, which are the enemy, "the immediate violent voice of release is that much more important psychologically, and is more of a genuine lever of revolution than previously."[11]

By the fall of 1969 two new ideological tendencies were added to the amalgam: ecology and women's liberation. Ecological thinking owed more to Gary Snyder than to the national antipollution bandwagon: its most "advanced" advocates propounded a worldview that rejected industry, rejected cities . . . indeed plunged into muddy historical and philosophical waters in seeking the origins of man's alienation not in class society, but in the practice of agriculture or in the use of tools or language! The appeal of the movement was stimulated by the January 1968 oil-spill in the Santa Barbara channel and by the university's plans to build a freeway through the slough adjoining the campus. "Establishment ecology" became increasingly discredited by such happenings as the appointment of a UCSB administrator to Nixon's Environmental Council, and the rumored relations between General Electric's Tempo R and D firm and the Santa Barbara Get Oil Out (GOO) organization. Matters were not improved in this respect in April 1971 when, with student disaffection at its height after the police shooting of an undergraduate, the UCSB information bulletin combined the police versions of this incident with such "cooptative" items as "UCSB Acts on Ecology Problems," and "UCSB Vehicles Switch to Propane."[12]

The flavor of women's liberation activity and theory took its cues, too, from the Isla Vista style. If Reich's celebration of the orgasm could become a vehicle for untrammeled sexual exploitation by males (make love to me to be free), his analysis of fascism could provide a critique of male aggressions. Indeed the emphasis of women was on the nature and quality of interpersonal relationships and new family structures. Besides winning for women a role in the leadership more commensurate with the energy and talents they possessed, women's liberation, therefore, along with ecological tribalism, began to contain Isla Vista anarchism within a healthier collectivism. The stress on interpersonal relationships could have degenerated into sensitivity sessions or a mindless peace-love-V-sign sloganism or been lost to Isla Vista with people drifting off to rural communes. Instead the tendency was to produce an organic solidarity among radicals transcending their overtly "political" meetings and acts, a collective consciousness diminishing the need for leadership and formal hierarchical organisation.

The overall effects of the Isla Vista style indeed resulted in a disdain for political theory, an orientation toward short and intense periods of activism followed by times of unrelieved pessimism and escapism, rather than sustained low-level commitment to "organizing." Meetings were spasmodic, rarely started on time, half in attendance were stoned; but sectarianism and personal hostility were remarkably absent. The latent divergences in political temperament and strategy were certainly there, but the ideology of "collectivism" prevented their emergence and held the radical community together through the intense year of 1969–70. Through the year, "collectivism" emerged into a *praxis;* attempting to avoid the pitfalls of anarchism or of Leninist vanguardism, groups of friends engaged in political projects but engaged equally in "struggle" with each other. And through the year, too, the Isla Vista movement began to think of the area as a potential collection of such collectives and urban communes, as a potential organic *community*.

THE "ALLEN CASE"

As a focus for the growing discontent of a body of people preoccupied above all with life-style and increasingly concerned with the nature of university education, there could have been no more stunning issue than the termination of the contract of anthropology professor William Allen. A UCSB alumnus, an ex-Marine, with a Ph.D. from Illinois, a bushy red beard and red hair, Allen was warm and generous in his manner, careless and energetic, a popular and empathic teacher. Distrusting bureaucracy and intensely sensitive to hypocrisy from his military days, his research on Peruvian Indians had moved, partly influenced by the changing student mood, in the direction of the ecological impact of imperialism on the "tribal society." His personality, his research, his students, and the sequence of events interacted with one another to push him to greater experimentation in teaching methods and more overt radicalism.

What transpired in the tenured faculty meetings which decided not to rehire Allen will never be known with certainty. The UCSB anthropology department had had a short but checkered history, with rapid turnover of faculty and rumors of ugly personal disputes: anthropology had also come to be something of a soft-option major, and the university was indeed supposed to have the largest number of anthropology majors in the world. A case could indeed have been made that Allen was not "outstanding" in traditional academic terms, but his formal credentials were as good as many UCSB faculty, including those within his comparatively undistinguished department who had gotten regular promotions. At best the matter was badly handled. Between the first intimations in June 1969 and the final decision late in the fall, department members said nothing official but circulated in private a number of different, sometimes contradictory, and on occasion defamatory rumors. Their ultimate point of defence, that tenured faculty could fire whom they pleased, betrayed an authoritarianism out of tune with the times and impinging on the interests of all nontenured faculty and students. At worst, the firing was on nonacademic grounds: politics or life-style. And this was how students saw it. Indeed in June 1969 the department chairman told me that Allen was being terminated because he behaved too much like a graduate student and was "personally incompatible" with other department members.

The initial protests came from students in the department: after the NFU the radicals had in fact moved to Isla Vista to agitate against realty companies and prepare for a rent strike. But by the middle of the fall term the inconsistencies and department prevarication were sufficiently obvious – and had emerged sufficiently in the campus newspaper *El Gaucho* – that the Radical Union, successor to SDS, showed interest. At the start of the winter quarter 8000 signatures or so, from 12–13,000 students, had been obtained on a petition calling for an open and impartial hearing on Allen's termination.

This demand was categorically refused by all the relevant bodies: the ostensible reason was that an open hearing would have breached the "confidentiality" of the case. In fact, since there were obviously ways in which a safety valve could have been operated, someone, somewhere, was vetoing compromise. Perhaps it was the regents. Perhaps it was the acting chancellor (standing in for an absent chancellor), an elderly historian who had been at the campus since its pre-university days. Perhaps it was his advisors. Perhaps it was one or two members of the anthropology department. At any rate, this administration error was compounded by another, trivial in itself. A rally in January for presenting the petition to the administration had dwindled by mid-afternoon to a few hundred people, circling the building in frustration that it had been locked in anticipation of a sit-in, expecting failure. The dean of men emerged from the building with some orders, got into an altercation with a student, and a scuffle developed. All student witnesses agreed that the dean hit a student with his bullhorn and was then hit back. The campus police, seeing the incident, charged from the building into the crowd, 90% of whom were unaware that anything had occurred. The sudden shock of what seemed like an unprovoked police attack swung the mood: people scattered, tripping over bicycles and each other, but then returned, angrily, to hurl shoes, rocks, bottles, a huge trash can, and a bicycle (wielded by a very "straight" student) through administration building windows, some already broken when the police charged.

The incident could have died. But now the crowd grew and developed into a party which surrounded the locked building during the night and next morning became again a demonstration trying unsuccessfully to prevent employees entering the building. Mediating teams were once more rebuffed — and at 10 a.m. the administration summoned outside police assistance to allow "free access" to the building. The police arrived that afternoon, ironically at the time when dispersing classes swelled an already large crowd into several thousands. As yet unused to demonstrations, the police executed a number of highly inept crowd-control maneuvers and cleared the area by 5 p.m. They remained guarding the building and its surroundings until the following Wednesday, five days later.

In the interim, rallies, marches around the police cordon, and demonstrations outside an academic senate meeting effectively drew interest from classes and generated an atmosphere of intense "politiciza-tion." The most characteristic event was a brief student takeover of the faculty club, an extravagant and bizarre modernistic building filled with exotic *objets d'art* like a twelfth century ceiling. Barricading it with furniture, the students "liberated" food and liquor and skinny-dipped in the pool while a bemused lunch-time faculty crowd looked on. One professor won an interested audience with a disquisition on the ceiling and why it should not be harmed. When the building was abandoned after rumors that the police "tac squad" was approaching, the furniture was restored to its proper place. The festive, warm-hearted, democratic atmosphere was symbolic of the entire protest.

If this was the mood, it was the Radical Union leadership which had kept it in being by "cooling" the crowd at each moment of tension. Thus it was with amazement that the participants discovered in the middle of the crisis that warrants had been issued for 19 RU leaders and that their houses had been raided at dead of night by plainclothes police. Of those charged, some had not been present at the demonstrations at the times charged; and their offences ("unlawful assembly", "failure to disperse") had been committed by thousands. The arrests were *political*, based on presumed beliefs and active RU membership rather than on offences. The intention was to cream off the leadership (which was later found to have been identified by an undercover agent in the RU) in the hope that activity would stop. Such an "outside agitator" theory is rarely if ever justified, and the Isla Vista political culture more than most ensured that protest continued under new "leadership."

Such incidents consequent on the intervention of the police were among the major causes of further student disenchantment. Inevitably the outside police committed dozens of petty violations of constitutional rights; inevitably they used just *that* much more force and brutal treatment than necessary to "control" the situation. All this was repellent to student liberals. But beyond that was the plain argument that the university, which they had heard so many times declare itself dedicated to reasoned dialogue, refused this, refused an open hearing, and abdicated its authority to that of the police, in other words, the state. Wishing more control over their lives in the university, students found themselves with less. Subject to the forces of the state, they began to grow more sympathetic to the idea that the university had been all along an instrument of the state.

THE FACULTY RESPONSE TO CRISIS

American university faculties have shown themselves notoriously conservative on issues of student rights, student power, and campus demonstrations: one poll showed a 30–40% drop in "liberal" attitudes on such issues. UCSB faculty were no exception though, cowed by Reagan and his "stacked" Board of Regents, they were perhaps an extreme case. But the causes were more long-term. The cold war political economy had created perhaps more than ever before in history a university dedicated to service of the state rather than scholarship: universities were sources of applied knowledge. A new breed of academic entrepreneurs had been formed, versed in grantsmanship rather than the humanistic quest, regarding knowledge as a commodity to be quantified, bought and sold, dispensed with attractive packaging. Such men were immensely threatened by the notion of egalitarian discussion and challenge of their "expertise."

Indeed the faculty was more than eager to dismiss the most fundamental challenges to the structure of modern knowledge as "anti-intellectualism." So, in one sense, it is. Students began to ask not only about the state of the contemporary American university, but about the system of Western values of which it was most proud, a system which had separated reason from feeling and elevated "objectivity," "detachment," and "specialization" into ends, which could tinker with "values" as if they were building blocks. How is it, asked students, that despite all this "knowledge" that is generated and applied – 90% of the world's scientists are alive today – that problems accumulate faster than they are solved, that solutions generate more suffering than they alleviate? Why are the faculty so "hooked" on the stimulus of the written word and so blind to the data of everyday common-sense experience . . . or is that not so easily footnoted? And if "detachment" means the ability to teach what you don't believe equally with what you do, where are the *selves* of our teachers, their emotions, their commitments?

Few on the faculty were prepared to deal intellectually with such issues. Instead the academic senate rallied against Allen, to the defence of the faculty as a guild. Here emotions did emerge – inviting student complaints of hypocrisy. As a sop to student opinion, the senate meetings were broadcast on the campus radio and some students could attend: they grew aghast at the way parliamentary procedure was used to stifle debate, at the paternal arrogance, the unimplementable rhetoric, and in some cases the plain reactionary paranoia. Significantly, the man who emerged as a leading faculty spokesman was Harry Girvetz, of impeccable "old liberal" credentials, rotund, with a debating style of dated eloquence replete with florid appeals to the heritage of Western civilization. A long-time faculty member, he was an erstwhile speechwriter and adviser to Governor Brown, a substantial property-owner, and an author of philosophical textbooks in the tradition of Sidney Hook. Girvetz had been prominent in framing the earlier Committee of 50 statement and was now favorably placed in the senate to prevent the Allen case from being discussed on its merits by pleading the "confidentiality" argument.

The faculty-administration strategy was to offer token concessions to students but on false premises. "Adversary relations", the Committee of 50 statement had asserted, "are alien to a . . . university community. While there are frictions . . . no . . . conflict of interests divides faculty, administration and students, and the few who argue the contrary are guilty of gross and even mischievous exaggeration."[13] By denying the central issue at stake and using *ad hominem* arguments against those who disagreed, such an attitude perpetuated lack of communication and conflict of interest. Thus the key issue of student voting power in institutions of university governance could never be seriously discussed, and the limits of reform emerged in a statement by the chancellor: students "are competent to make and report judgments about what happens to them as students in class . . . or living quarters . . . (this) is not to argue for the equal participation of all elements in all decisions or for a majority rule standard on all problems."[14]

Meanwhile William Allen, under the pressure of events, increasingly abandoned the vestiges of his "professional" role for that of activist, giving his enemies the opportunity of a *post facto* justification of his termination as a "malicious rabble-rouser." A faculty conduct committee accused him of "unprofessional conduct" on a number of dangerously ludicrous charges which were never brought to judgment. And the police arrested him on a series of trivial charges some of which were never proven, evoking student suspicion of a coordinated faculty-administration-police campaign to discredit him. In microcosm, whether as "conspiracy" or as an example of the ineluctable interplay of persons and interests under crisis, the case foreshadowed that of Angela Davis. The subtlety of the "strategy" as a measure against academic freedom was most ominously apparent in a statement at the time by Charles Hitch, president of the University of California: "In the university, above all other institutions of American society, we have a profound duty to resist and oppose shoddy thinking, lies, and rhetoric which flames and shocks but does nothing for the truth. . . . The university teacher has not only the obligations of his academic competence but the demand upon him to be the representative of whatever passes for mature wisdom in this troubled time. . . ."[15] Instead of being the forum for the freest debating of what constituted "mature wisdom" or "truth," the agency for changing society's conceptions of such things, the university, was constrained to be an agency of the societal *status quo*. It was encouraged to use its power rather than its reason against dissidents. With such dangerous notions floating around, and with outside forces ever ready to expose the so-called "shoddy thinkers," it is little wonder that Girvetz could appear on local TV and assure Reagan that the university was able to clean its own house.

THE BANK OF AMERICA BURNS

On campus, the Allen crisis moved from "the streets" to the committees. The focus of radical action returned to Isla Vista, flowering initially in deliberate attempts to spread the fusion of culture and politics. Parties and picnics, with rock bands, free wine, free dope, and IV-style politics sprang up in Perfect Park each weekend. The frustrations and anger generated by the Allen case mingled explosively with the tensions of the Isla Vista ghetto and its street people. On Monday, February 24, a man was arrested for an obscene gesture at a police officer. Next day a popular black student, misidentified, was arrested: as he was taken away, shouting, a crowd gathered. Keys of a police car were seized and the car's tires deflated. Some gasoline was poured under it. A plainclothesman grabbed someone in the crowd, who hit him. Friends came to his defence; a melee developed; more arrests were made. That evening a murmuring crowd gathered in the park and moved systematically around the business "loop," smashing realty company windows and finishing at the bank windows. Fires were set – but only in the streets – with mattresses and huge trash containers. But the atmosphere was little different from the faculty club sit-in or the Sunday park picnics. The cops did not come.

The next afternoon William Kunstler, lawyer in the Chicago conspiracy trial, which had just concluded, spoke in the campus stadium. Kunstler did not, as the establishment media claimed, incite what was to come. (It was equally plausible to argue, indeed, that police and local politicians had conducted the arrests to stimulate protest and secure votes for law and order in the elections later in the year.) Already, when

Kunstler arrived in the stadium, the student crowd was more enthusiastic and angry than had ever been seen on the campus and gave him an unprecedented ovation. For them he was a symbol of the conspiracy trial, of resistance to the intransigence and repression which they saw nationally and were experiencing now locally. More than this, he symbolised that faint but wished-for hope, a man over 30 who had grown in stature, courage, and radicalism as he confronted Judge Hoffman's courtroom fascism. His speech was the reverse of demagogic. It was measured. It counselled against violence, though it compared the "picayune" violence of student radicals with the massive and pervasive violence of the American power structure. It said little new, but it reached and moved the crowd by its biting yet warm wit, its strong reason inspired by passion, its fusion of personal and general. Kunstler captured, encapsulated and threw back the vibrations which he found when he arrived, vibrations of a mood which matched his own. In contrast to the early 1950's, repression was to be met by active and sustained resistance "in the streets, where they can see you . . ." and he and the crowd were both groping for the collective courage to undertake such a task. "Power to the People! Right on!" he concluded, and as the crowd rose, at least half raised their fists in response to his: a ritual of collective solidarity.

The audience drifted back in groups to Isla Vista. The police were there too: helmeted, riot-equipped, six to a car. A student carrying a jug of wine and pineapple juice – a common practice but apparently illegal – was seized. He resisted and was thrown to the ground and beaten by three officers. The police had again provided the spark. Rocks began to fly at police cars, which withdrew a few blocks, almost tauntingly, and inevitably drawing the crowd after them. Just as police vanished from the "Loop," someone came running from a store with a morning newspaper headlining the previous night's "riot." (The *Chicago Tribune* had blamed this on Kunstler's speech, not yet given!) The crowd laughed and chanted "Riot! riot! – let's show them a real one." The pattern of fires and rocks was repeated, with damage selective in the extreme: when a rock accidentally smashed the window of a psychedelic store, a collection to repair it was taken on the spot, and the local Christian center, sandwiched between two realties, was quite untouched.

Inevitably, this time, the crowd set the bank on fire. Probably about 8 p.m. a burning trash container was wheeled through the door to light the drapes and the plywood window boarding placed that morning over the broken windows, and flames began to billow from the entrance. About an hour later the police made an inept and abortive foray in insufficient numbers. They extinguished the fire, but were forced to withdraw, leaving behind a patrol car which was set to the flame with glee. As fires flickered in the streets and the car, people from the crowd dropped into the only store that remained open to buy ice cream or cigarettes or gum and then strolled across to peer into the smoking insides of the bank, while the more daring "liberated" whatever was movable in the bank. Later, more quietly but more systematically, the bank was set on fire again; this time it burnt itself to the ground.

Earlier in the evening police checkpoints at the IV access roads had warned motorists that they risked death if they entered the area. The Bank of America director's statement the next day echoed the refrain: "Just before midnight, with the angry crowd in a frenzy, the branch was set ablaze again. While police and fire officials were held at bay by an angry, rock-throwing mob, the bank was gutted by fire and totally destroyed . . . Numerous other fires were started. Windows were smashed and life and property threatened.[16] The "stimulation of a violent few" was cited as the cause.[17] They were entirely wrong. There was no "frenzy," no police or firemen there at the time to be held at bay, no violent few, no threat to life.

In the first place, nobody had *planned* the act. Indeed the Radical Union had a meeting on campus that evening, oblivious of what was about to transpire. Yet if spontaneous, it was inevitable. The events in Isla Vista harked back in one sense to the "direct action" of the eighteenth-century preindustrial crowd of which George Rudé has written so lucidly.[18] But they also expressed the antimaterialistic revolt of affluent postindustrial society. The bank was, as one demonstrator told the press, the "most capitalistic thing around." And, as Nairn has written, where the collective and creative spirit of such revolt is born, "nothing else is tolerable . . . in its heat there are no more abstract truths, or dreams bequeathed to the grandchildren. Alienation has become an insult, an obscenity. . . . The authentic wealth of human beings reduced material wealth instantly to a drab backcloth of objects."[19] For the people that night that "drab backcloth" was an excrescence, to be exorcised through destruction. If the act was not planned, yet it had been fantasized by the radicals — just as the girl at the end of *Zabriskie Point* fantasizes the destruction of objects in slow and gripping detail. This was fantasy become reality, imagination

become theater, the joyous wish fulfillment of Yippie politics characteristic of those rapidly politicized from liberalism or cultural revolution,
without the mental inhibitions of the labored radical organiser. As
someone said who was making a movie of the Allen demonstrations, "If
the bank hadn't burned, I wouldn't have had a climax."

Yet the action too was courageous, and it represented imagination in
harmony with rather than opposed to reason, creation with purposive
goals. If the bank was evil, it was also powerful. It is, quite literally, the
largest bank in the world. Its board of directors is a Who's Who of
California industry. It was the major conduit for the American military in
Saigon. A former board chairman had just submitted to the president a
report on U.S. "aid" strategies for the 1970's. It, and the industries it
financed, had been the focus of protests for racist hiring policies, for
opposing unionization of farmworkers, for destroying California's ecology.
In the 1930's it owned half the arable land in California and was reputed
to have covertly assisted antiunion vigilantes. Its federally insured student
loan program took high interest at no risk. The Isla Vista branch, it
emerged, was run at small profit to lure students into the B of A habit and
conduct market research on them. We are accustomed to regard such
institutions as immovable, unchangeable, indestructible. Hence the burning
of the bank, and the overreaction of its directors, even if only a symbolic
intrusion on power, had immense psychological repercussions. At the time
life, far from being "threatened," was made more precious by its contrast
with this "backcloth" which normally seemed far more permanent. And a
poll taken soon after revealed that at least 30% of UCSB students, even
against their better judgment, were glad the bank had burned.

How and why such a reversal of the "normal" values of capitalist
society takes place is hard to determine. This account has stressed above
all the local determinants and also the national mood of the students. But
though it would be hard to pin down the mechanisms of influence, there is
little doubt in my mind that the international mood was of importance
too. When Huey Newton coined the slogan, "The spirit of the people will
triumph over the man's technology," he encapsulated what the struggle of
the Vietnamese people against the mightiest state in human history
symbolised on the level of values. Without this faith, a seemingly utopian
reversal of our "normal" thought, but demonstrable in Vietnam, it is hard
to see how the bank could have burned . . . or how and why the activists
of Isla Vista fought back against the police in the ensuing days and
months.

POLICE COUNTER-ATTACK

Santa Barbara County, sunny and sleepy, had refused federal funds for "riot-control" training. The first police foray into Isla Vista that momentous night was a disaster. Outnumbered, surrounded, their vehicles and themselves in a crossfire of missiles, they retired to their first tactical defeat. A while later several unmarked patrol cars sped at high speed through scattering crowds and threw out tear gas: it was a tactic of provocative terrorism which was to be frequently used. When an augmented force returned, the bank was gutted and the crowds had disappeared.

Next day "a state of extreme emergency and disaster" was declared and a 6 p.m.–6 a.m. curfew ordered by Governor Reagan, who flew into Santa Barbara and called the protestors "cowardly little bums". But it was no deterrent. At 6 p.m. a crowd gathered in the park and lit a bonfire, gesturing obscenely to the helicopter which commanded dispersal. Police gathered just outside the community and came under rock attack from a few. About 9 p.m. the police moved in and within half an hour, with clubs and tear gas, hurling back rocks, they secured the business loop.

But this was only the beginning; demonstrators counterattacked. As the local paper reported:

> Officers were driven from the business loop by a mass of demonstrators carrying garbage can lids, beating them with rocks, and shouting like savages. [The noise in fact was the ululation from the final scene of *Battle of Algiers,* which had played just before in the local movie theater.] The demonstrators were reportedly shoulder to shoulder and about a block deep. "The mass came on like a cavalry charge," a witness said, "running at high speed directly at three groups of about 50 officers each." One Ventura unit was reportedly pinned against the wall of the Red Lion book store before getting free. The officers retreated more than three blocks to a UCSB parking lot adjacent to Isla Vista, where the demonstrators reportedly stopped. A sheriff's spokesman confirmed that officers had "gotten the hell out of there" when badly outnumbered.[20]

Driven out for the second time, the police reverted for the moment to tear gas and speeding cars. An M-76 grenade launcher mounted on the back of a pick-up barraged the community with tear gas shells clearly marked "Do not use against crowds." Meanwhile police cars had hit a student, Robert Brevig, throwing him forward and twenty feet through the air: he recovered, but the rumor that he had died instantly spurred the demonstrators to greater resistance at the time.

This was almost the last "pitched battle." The activists began to turn, spontaneously, to guerrilla warfare. The details are hard to piece together, though the campus radio sounded like an action in Vietnam. Helicopters whirred; tear gas canisters crunched; shouts, chants and small explosions merged to crescendo; newsmen left the air suddenly. On one occasion the manager of the campus radio was clubbed by police while calling in a live report from a phone booth. Police began to use captured slingshots as well as rocks and held arrested persons in front of them as shields; while the demonstrators threw back tear gas – even the shells – and began to use Molotov cocktails. On one occasion police chased demonstrators down a deadend street, to have their minds blown as people melted into side alleys and reemerged, ululating wildly, to cut them off. Eventually, with a renewed effort to charge to the police staging-post, the police withdrew. "Load up all prisoners. Clear the parking-lot and 10.19" was the order.[21] Three times, on two consecutive nights, police had been forced to withdraw. It was a victory for self-determination: Reagan was quite wrong in talking of "cowardly little bums."

RECOLONIZATION

At 2:30 a.m. the National Guard moved in to replace the police, and Isla Vista moved from hostility to fraternization. "IV I" as it came to be called, had ended. The police had demonstrably been unable to protect corporate property or control a defiant citizenry. Repacification, recolonization, was needed. The National Guard performed this task, sweeping the business area, with near-random arrests during curfew, treating the arrested as prisoners of war, made to stand for hours at the booking site (foolishly chosen at the bank), in plastic handcuffs tightened to impede circulation and with shotguns leveled.

But the "natives" remained restless. In March there was a minor disturbance downtown when Governor Reagan appeared on campaign. In Isla Vista itself the community rose in violence twice more. Once was in April, when the chancellor and the board of supervisors banned Jerry Rubin from the campus and county. "IV III" followed in June, unprecedentedly during exam week. Sparked by the issuing of seventeen indictments for the February bank-burning, it continued for six nights. (As in the Allen case, those indicted were named for their politics rather than on concrete evidence: two had been in jail when the bank was burnt.)

Through IV II and III the police grew more efficient, more violent, more random in their violence. The action, confined in IV I to the loop area, broadened to encompass the whole of IV. The activists grew more sophisticated in their tactics. The people of IV as a whole, in the first uprising largely hostile or neutral to the activists, swung more and more to their support against the police.

After IV I the university, in true colonial style, tried to establish institutions of social control in Isla Vista on a social base of liberal faculty, clergymen, and "moderate" students. The activists eventually gained control of these institutions, but meanwhile, when violence broke out again in April, the "moderates" tried to act as a self-policing agency: they surrounded the temporarily reconstructed bank to defend it from attack and transformed physical confrontation into angry debate. But the police did not trust these methods. On the first two nights of IV II the police erupted suddenly into the "verbal struggle." They used open dumptrucks in convoy – "Operation Wagon-Train" they called it – to circumvent the problems of fighting their way into the community; and they arrived at the bank without warning, shooting waves of tear gas . . . and with guns. On the first night six passers-by were wounded by birdshot. On the second night a young student, Kevin Moran, one of those who was protecting the bank, was shot dead by a police weapon. Undeterred, the police continued on the following nights to use birdshot and sudden massive force.

Such tactics were an unexpected escalation. Many had assumed that, whatever happened in black ghettos, police would not use firearms against the sons and daughters of the upper middle-class, especially in terrain like Isla Vista where a stray bullet could penetrate several flimsy apartment walls.[22] Indeed in IV I the only recorded gunfire was against a university employee who drove unknowingly through police lines . . . and later insisted that students had fired at him!

The police blamed the escalation on snipers in the community. Indeed for nearly three days the official police account was that Kevin Moran had been shot by a sniper, until it was finally conceded that one of their men had fired "by accident." Isla Vista believed overwhelmingly that the shooting was no accident and that the intended victim had been a radical. In the meantime news reporting was massively distorted, an act with which the university administration and, more surprisingly, the faculty connived. The *Los Angeles Times* story was typical: "Before dawn on Saturday, more than 250 peace officers from Santa Barbara, Ventura, and San Luis Obispo counties had spent hours exchanging gunfire with snipers in what Sheriff's Captain Fritz Patterson called 'pure unadulterated warfare' ". The university's "crisis bulletin" claimed that after Moran's death, "Sniper fire was frequent and widespread. . . . During this time, according to Sheriff Webster, the police did not fire a single shot." In gross violation of FCC regulations, the administration acquiesced in a request to take the campus radio off the air since "it was helping snipers to locate the moving groups of police."[23]

The "rush to judgment" by the supposedly critically-minded faculty was more shocking, and comprehensible only in terms of the complete separation of their cozy and comfortable life experiences from those of Isla Vista. After the bank-burning the "official" faculty statement had placed the responsibility "with those who initiated the recent state of anarchy," namely, the demonstrators: a contemporary student petition had at least the grace to condemn both police and protestors. The partisanship of the faculty was as obvious after Moran's death; taking its cue from the police, their statement assailed "criminal anarchists" and proto-Fascist "Red Guards," and left little doubt that Moran had been shot by a sniper.

In fact, though some students had guns, there is absolutely no evidence that any used them. Some weeks later a reporter from the local paper could track down not a single credible instance of sniper fire during IV II.[24] What happened, as later emerged, was as follows. When police had entered the area on Friday night a police officer Gosselin, part of an antisniper unit, jumped from his vehicle, observed persons on the steps of the bank, lined them up in his sights, and then "accidentally" pulled the trigger. He continued with his normal duties and reported the event only a number of hours later. For two and a half days after that, police stated that no weapons of that calibre had been fired by county police (Gosselin was a city policeman), and they issued a bulletin describing a man leaving the scene on a motorcycle. On Monday afternoon at a press conference the sheriff admitted that "a police officer's gun had accidentally discharged as he was disembarking from a dump truck" (itself not correct). And the local paper, to compound the enormity, headlined not this, but "TIMED FIREBOMB IS FOUND", a reference to an obvious Yippie hoax found in IV as the description of the device made plain.[25]

Despite public silence from officials, harsh words must have circulated after IV II. For in IV III, if firearms were used by police, it was surreptitiously and far from the media gaze. After all, tear gas canisters shot *at* people were not much less effective. But the overall thrust of recolonization was different. Able by then to secure the business loop with ease and finding their enemy activists scattered through the community, dispersing and regrouping, the police increasingly regarded their enemy as the community as a whole. Apartments had been broken into at random before. Arbitrary arrests had been made. Now, as a suit filed after the events on behalf of IV inhabitants claimed, "a systematic pattern of lawless enforcement of the law" was instituted: a campaign of "terror and brutality" with the intention of making the people "too cowed" to assert their constitutional rights and of reducing them to a "state of terrified compliance." Interim statistics showed that between June 6 and June 9 there were: 12 police threats of shooting suspects, 75 persons physically removed from homes and private property, 73 persons clubbed and beaten, in many cases without arrest, 53 reports of indiscriminate use of gas, unwarranted harassment, destruction of private property, and several instances of harassment of persons facing a private emergency. To that date, there had been 292 arrests.[26]

Individual reports gave a flavour of the situation: "We were marched through an area completely littered with broken glass. Three of us did not have shoes on. . . ." . . ."The father protested. They slapped him against the car and tied his hands with the plastic handcuffs. They threw him into the truck and told him to lie with his face in the sand. . . ." . . ."We were roughly searched and our house was ransacked. . . . Damage: movie camera and light, flash camera, bed tipped over, couch damaged, beer spilled and food smeared all over. . . ." "Two cars . . were stopped. Passengers . . were kicked in the solar plexus. Tires were slashed on one vehicle; the windows of the other broken." . . ."Officers broke down the door . . . a student was studying in the back room. He was threatened . . . kicked in the groin, clubbed. Officers broke all of the decorative bottles, candle-holders, etc. . . ."

"Police brutality", yes, but the very essence of law enforcement rather than its perversion as liberals believe. IV III was more blatant, more systematic, and casting a wider net: police victims included middle-aged homeowners and a Santa Barbara assistant district attorney. The aim was still recolonization, pursued more desperately. The intention struck me at my first experience of jail as the result of a massive nonviolent curfew violation which protested these acts. In jail, individual fantasy and paranoia are encouraged. When told to move, you move, walking fast, eyes in front, hands in pockets. An unguarded sentence, a wrong move at the wrong moment, and you go to solitary confinement. The situation is immediate and total: "rights" mean nothing, for they can be enforced only when you leave, and against the word of the law enforcer. The aim is to inculcate that unthinking and automatic obedience on which all tyranny is based. And the method is atomization. For you can test the boundaries of your surviving humanity and dignity only by experience. Should I claim this "right"? Should I protest such a violation of myself or another? And if someone else shouts an obscenity and the guard asks who did it . . . should we not *all* plead guilty? Or did he compromise us without our consent? Each decision involves heroism or cowardice . . . and each decision must be based on the degree to which one can trust ones fellow inmates and their support under conditions where mistrust is fostered. Arbitrary force, "police brutality," is precisely the weapon which transforms freedom, collectivity, trust, into obedience, atomization, mistrust . . . for when force *may* be exerted for no reason (but *may* not, if you are careful) you can become a passive zombie. Such conditions define a "total institution." And for a few days in June, Isla Vista became such a "total institution."[26]

THE POLITICS OF COLLECTIVE RESISTANCE

In contrast to the German Jews in the 1930's, in contrast to the Old Left and the liberals at the time of McCarthy, the New Left has refused to submit to "total institutions" and their imperatives: it has had an abundance, a superabundance, of courage. The first principles of resistance were techniques of survival, techniques to overcome that insidious coercive manipulation of the mind by illegitimate but immediate authority, techniques to prevent that breakdown in trust in your brother and sister when full communication with them is prevented. In this respect the Isla Vista political culture, substituting collective consciousness for more easily fractured organization, disdaining strategy in favor of the intuitive directions which that consciousness took, stressing above all camaraderie, solidarity with acts of personal liberation, had its advantages, in IV and in jail.

The first stages of the IV II and IV III uprisings involved attacks on the new temporary bank, though the self-policing moderates transformed these to verbal confrontations. The fires were put out but the debates raged. On several occasions, indeed, votes were taken on whether to burn the bank again . . . and usually the burners won. But only once was the bank again in danger, when police stopped a rock concert on the IV outskirts two hours early and the enraged audience of over 1000 marched to the bank and set about demolition: orders to the relevant police detachment to guard it had apparently gone astray. But it was sufficiently fireproofed that police arrived before extensive destruction had occurred.

For the most part conflict took place away from the loop; there was a tendency for activists to break into spontaneous residential groups clustered about street corners, and even smaller mobile affinity groups which could move from streets to alleyways to gardens, through and into apartments (for as police action escalated, the number of doors open to the activists grew). The huge burning trash cans thrown into intersections to slow down traffic became the symbol of resistance: later old cars were used. People would gather around them, curfew-defiers or the more active, peering the block or two to the police line, crouching into hiding as police vehicles passed and throwing rocks, bottles, or firebombs, offering a rapid barrage to any advancing force of occupation and then dispersing to regroup at a safer distance. As escalated police action made direct personal action risky, there was minor sabotage. Nails driven in the streets, boards with nails pointing in each direction, put at least thirty police tires out of action in IV III. Piano wire was strung across the streets at the elevation of the top of the dump trucks: the police countered with boards mounted to cut the wires. Crude oil on the streets intercepted police vehicles moving too fast.

Moran's death was the essential turning point in community attitudes, though the process had begun earlier. In IV I, for example, occupants of Francisco Torres, a block of student flats planned and built with the opulence of a luxury hotel by the owner, a major university benefactor, had given coffee and cookies to the police. But when National Guardsmen made three arrests in the lobby, the occupants organized the lights of the tall building to flash "pig" at the police. But it was among the student group that the administration hoped to use as a moderate "buffer" in Isla Vista that the most rapid radicalization took place. After Moran's death and the police negation of student attempts at self-policing, there began to appear all around the community messages of defiance in the windows, most prominent being the symbol "Z" from the film of that name. Moran's roommate, speaking at a memorial service on Isla Vista beach, stressed that Moran's opposition to violence did not mean he supported "the capitalist system." Reagan, local politicians, the media, and university officials assumed that opposition to violence meant opposition to radical goals: polls showed rather a broad basis of agreement on goals, with differences only over tactics.

The coalescence of radicals and liberal-moderates over goals was fostered by the student strike which sprang up after Cambodia and Kent State. As at other campuses, a liberal-radical student alliance pushed for "reconstitution" of the university and were strongly supported by a minority of faculty humanist-liberals, who had grown disgusted with the corporate-liberal majority faculty. Reagan's decision to close the campuses for four days "cooling off" caught the administration and faculty conservatives off guard: a "National Crisis" course was instituted and attracted nearly a quarter of the student body, and many "normal" requirements were eased or suspended. Students and faculty were able to experiment with "relevant" education, and to participate jointly in the structuring and control of courses and examinations: the principle was established that community action, *praxis*, was as valuable a learning experience as hearing a lecture or reading a book. Students examined the history of the Vietnam struggle, the national and local functioning of police, courts, public officials, and media, and went into the community to develop methods of approach to the "middle-class."[27]

Indeed, when the indictments for the February bank-burning were issued, the initial reaction came from the semistructured leadership network of the post-Cambodian crisis, largely distinct from the "old radicals," who tended to view the reconstitution as liberal co-option. Protest rallies on campus staged a reenactment of the bank burning and Moran's death by a guerrilla theater group; the bank was occupied by demonstrators and compelled by a "smoke-in" of cigarettes to close. That evening, inevitably, IV III began. The reign of police terror which ensued merely confirmed the suspicions of those participating in the "National Crisis" course. Many were moved to resist. The small and possibly apocryphal example of a group of girls who chewed gum all day and placed it on sidewalks at night to hinder police movements illustrates the spirit.

In one sense the "National Crisis" course was a larger, more sustained, more effective "New Free University." Similarly the sit-in called to defy the curfew on Wednesday, June 10, after two nights of police horror was a larger repeat of that initial curfew defiance four months earlier on the night following the bank-burning. Instead of a few hundred, there were 1500 largely different people, and with them nearly fifty faculty and older community members. (One, a former grand jury member, was charged with attempted murder when he slipped and tore the pocket of a deputy!) Police moved in and arrested 375 – all and more than all that the not-yet-completed new county jail could hold. As darkness fell, those who remained or had gathered late were pepper-gassed, and then systematically beaten on the head as they sat by the elite tactical unit from Los Angeles responsible for much of the brutality of the previous two nights. In jail the harassment continued. Some of the women arrested were forced to stand naked under scalding hot showers; others were maced in their cells. Not one arrestee was not confined in solitary, or beaten, or verbally abused, or overcrowded in a cell, or denied food, or prevented from making phone calls, or prevented from departure after bail had been posted. The county's only rational judge, hearing only a fragment of what had occurred, dismissed all the charges.

The police were defeated this time morally if not militarily. Yet they would not budge. The judge was challenged and precluded from hearing any more cases on Isla Vista. Sheriff Webster categorically denied any charges of brutality, in IV or jail, during IV III, and to the rising wave of liberal protest he counterposed some words of J. Edgar Hoover:

> Police-watchers and self-styled law-enforcement reformers have no place in our society. Their altruistic mouthings are a front and a sham, for they have already prejudged law enforcement as an enemy to their nihilistic cause. Their real objective is to intimidate and to harass police. They care nothing about public protection and orderly due process. They seek special privileges which place them above the law and commit abuses which encroach on the rights of others.[28]

This epitaph on liberalism, together with police actions during IV III, was as clear an indication as any that the path from Chicago in August 1968 to Washington in May 1969, when the president endorsed police lawlessness, lay through Isla Vista and doubtless many other such local struggles. It was, or should have been, an ominous sign to those who believe "abuses" can be rectified and needed reforms made without fundamental structural alterations in the society. But how would such changes come?

CONCLUSION

In the first six months of 1970 Isla Vista radicals had achieved much in terms of exposure of issues and radicalizing of consciousness, though at some cost, including one death, much pain, many arrests and trials. But the achievement was potentially greater. Isla Vista had been transformed from a ghetto to a self-conscious community. The solidarity brought by uprising, recolonization and resistance had been institutionalized in mundane 'but real forms: a food cooperative, a communal garden, a radical-controlled community council. During 1970–1971 these would be developed in an attempt to win control for people over their lives. In some ways, by some people, the activists began to appear as the "people's army," defending community self-determination and lifestyle against occupation from outside. The "liberation front" of which they were part may have been an imaginative rather than organized construct, but it embraced some among all sections of the community, from fraternities to junkies, from homeowners to transients.

The politics of Isla Vista drew on existing trends of "New Left" theory and practice: in some respects it drew not enough. The spirit of Yippiedom persisted in the "war games" held on campus in May between the "Americong" and "Vietwrong." Fighting with water, the two groups then combined to attack first the administration, and then bystanders – with the message that war allowed no onlookers. Jerry Rubin, appearing finally on campus, was escorted to the stadium in a jeep filled with Che-style guerrillas with plastic guns. But the response to Rubin's talk was cool – because in IV politics had become more serious than the mental liberation of Woodstock Nation. Similarly, though the discipline and militance of 1970 Weathermanism was appealing to some, the IV uprisings, spontaneous, springing from and fought on behalf of needs and demands of a defined local community, were a direct contradiction of the Weatherman notion that white Americans had none but reactionary needs, white skin privilege, and only an exemplary duty to support Third World revolutions by .destruction of the U.S. Indeed the December 1970 Weatherman statement admitting other tactics besides violence and recognizing that the white youth movement was its social base, was an *ex post facto* ratification of IV strategy.

For Isla Vista was Woodstock Nation and Weatherman come to a resting place in concrete territory. From ghetto, through community, for some Isla Vista came to be seen as a "liberated area," a base from which further struggle could be launched into the world beyond. Collectivism was the concept at the heart of this, but a strategy going beyond individual collectives that, like a Chinese box, could link modes of collective organization of varying sizes, intensities, and purposes. Indeed, the movement in Isla Vista anticipated the idea of "free territories" which

Tom Hayden was formulating theoretically over the same period. Such areas, argued Hayden, where people could "create amidst the falling ruins of this Empire a new, alternative way of life more in harmony with the interests of the world's people" were already latently in existence in Berkeley, Haight-Ashbury, Madison, and elsewhere.[29] They were soviets, red bases, guerrilla-liberated zones adapted to the context of youth revolt in America and advanced capitalist society. They were to incarnate popular power and the lifestyle of post-revolution, and yet to reach constantly outward toward change in the wider society.

Such institutions of dual power are, many revolutionaries would argue, an essential component of a mass revolutionary movement.[30] Yet in the form adumbrated in Isla Vista and given a theoretical shape by Hayden they have yet to prove themselves. I have little knowledge of events in Isla Vista during the last year (1970–1971) but a letter recently received from a student is indicative:

> During and following the "riots" my emotional reactions corresponded to my intellectual perceptions. The rhetoric of the left was no longer rhetoric, but an accurate portrayal of what was happening . . . in this sense I was radicalized. By comparison my reflections of (sic) those days seem like hollow frames, void of the energy which it took to make them. Certainly I've learned that it's difficult for me to voluntarily subject myself to the emotional pain and frustration associated with resisting and changing the conditions of injustice and socio-political-economic insanity. . . . The past year has shown me that money, "being in step," not "rocking the boat," etc., are ways of emotionally isolating oneself . . . from the travesty and insanity that goes on every day. For now, I'm left with the continual task of intellectually resisting. . . .[31]

It is possible that Berkeley, where a "radical coalition" was elected to the city government in April 1971, underpinned by a structure of collectives and communes who could mobilize broad support, may sustain the idea better. But one is reminded of the communal idea which flourished and died in the old Northwest in the first part of the nineteenth century. A historian has argued recently that these "utopian" communities were planted near the American frontier because of the prevailing belief that the institutions shaped at the frontier would automatically blossom from seeds into large-scale future trends.[32] When this determinist strategy of change failed, so did the experiments. As yet the "free territory" idea has no more convincing a strategy on the attainment of national power (or even, not to beg the question, the destruction of national power). On the scale of Isla Vista, or even Berkeley, the realization of fantasy can indeed succeed without substantial planned conscious activity. But it is doubtful whether, without considerable theory and practice, the progressive hegemony of such free territories can be achieved. Indeed, if life in Isla Vista is groovy and the cops not over-present, the incentives towards escapism (or purely "intellectual resistance") will be enhanced. "Youth communities" will then become yet another of the compartments which isolate oppressed Americans from each other and which prevent the full realization of the common interests of ethnic minorities, white workers, even white middle-class, as the American proletariat — those deprived of the ownership of the means of production — against the American ruling class.

NOTES

1. Charles Reich, *The Greening of America* (New York: 1969).

2. For this speech see *Liberation*, January 1966.

3. Tom Hayden, *The Trial* (prepublished in *Ramparts*, July 1970, 12).

4. This analysis draws, inter alia, from Ernest Mandel, "Where is America Going?" *New Left Review*, 54; Carl Oglesby in *Liberation*, August-September 1969; C. Lasch and E. Genovese, "The Education and the University We Need Now," *New York Review of Books*, October 9, 1969; R. Flacks, "The Revolt of the Young Intelligentsia: Revolutionary Class-Consciousness in Post-Scarcity America," in N. Miller and R. Aya, *Revolution Reconsidered* (forthcoming).

5. I draw here on an unpublished Ph.D. dissertation in sociology by Milton Mankoff, former assistant professor, UCSB.

6. A former student of mine, James Doukas, has published, or is about to publish, a history of Isla Vista which deals with this period.

7. Apart from personal observation-participation, this study has utilized as primary sources the *Santa Barbara News Press*, the *Los Angeles Times*, *El Gaucho* (the UCSB student newspaper), and *Probe*, an IV underground paper. Except where the reference is particularly crucial, I have not specifically footnoted to these sources.

8. In the California primary McCarthy and Kennedy between them obtained about 90% of the votes, and the pro-Humphrey slate only 10%.

9. On the question of the relations of the black and student movements, see particularly Oglesby in *Liberation*, August-September 1969, and Hayden, *op. cit.*

10. Yorty believed the syllabus dated from 1970 and not 1969!

11. Tom Nairn and Angelo Quattrocchi, *The Beginning of the End: France, May 1968* (London: 1968), 136-137.

12. UCSB Information Bulletin, April 23 and 24, 1970. So far as I am aware, this bulletin was first issued on April 20, reporting (or rather, misreporting) the events leading up to and following the death of Kevin Moran. See below.

13 This statement was first published in *El Gaucho*, February 28, 1969.

14. Chancellor's statement to academic senate meeting, February 1970.

15. Reprinted in *Los Angeles Times,* March 29, 1970.

16. *Santa Barbara News Press*, February 27, 1970.

17. In the ensuing months the directors ate, or reswallowed, their words. In June Louis B. Lundborg, the chairman, who had meanwhile appeared before the Senate Foreign Relations Committee opposing the Vietnam war, said that "while the actual burning of our Isla Vista branch may have been perpetrated by a violent few, there is no question that there was widespread agreement among the students . . . that the causes leading to the protest were both serious and legitimate . . . We are facing a real, honest-to-God disenchantment . . . there is a new value system emerging . . . our dealing with it will jar us out of most of the comfortable assumptions that we have grown up with all our lives . . ."(*Los Angeles Times*, June 21, 1970.)

18. See, for example, George Rudé, *The Crowd in History, 1730–1848* (New York: 1964).

19. Nairn, *op. cit.*, 125.

20. *Santa Barbara News Press*, February 27, 1970.

21. *Los Angeles Times*, February 27, 1970.

22. Of course, in 1969 James Rector had been shot dead in Berkeley by Alameda County sheriffs, but many regarded this as "exceptional": Kent State was still to come.

23. *Los Angeles Times*, April 19, 1970; UCSB Information Bulletin, April 20 and 21, 1970.

24. The dating of this article, in the *Santa Barbara News Press*, is missing from my files, though it must be May or (less likely) early June.

25. *Santa Barbara News Press*, April 21, 1970.

26. These statistics and the quotations following are taken from the Faculty-Clergy Observer Program report: this aspect of the Isla Vista situation subsequently received quite a lot of attention in local and national media.

26a. On this concept see, inter alia, E. Goffman, *Asylums*; S. Elkins, *Slavery*.

27. Out of this course came a creative cornucopia of essays, reports, tapes, and other items of a far higher standard than the student norm: a selection of these may hopefully be published.

28. *News Press*, June 21, 1970.

29. Tom Hayden, *op. cit.*, 54.

30. See, for example, J. Wilcox, "Two Tactics," *New Left Review*, 53.

31. Student paper in my possession, c. June 1971.

32. A.E. Bestor, Jr., "Patent-Office Models of the Good Society: Some Relationships Between Social Reform and Westward Expansion," *American Historical Review*, 58, 3, April 1953, 505-526. Bestor, it should be noted, distinguishes "utopianism," as mental and literary activity, from the *praxis* of what he calls "communitarianism."

THE NEW MIDDLE CLASSES AND THE RISE OF FASCISM
G.D.H. Cole

It is, of course, impossible to say where the capitalist class ends and the class below it — the *petite bourgeoisie* — begins. There are infinite gradations of wealth and social status at every point of the scale, from the greatest capitalists to the lowest-paid labourers and the chronically unemployed. But undoubtedly there is a real division, as real and important as the distinction which Marx drew in *The Communist Manifesto* between the *grande* and the *petite bourgeoisie*, but of a radically different nature. . . .

G.D.H. Cole, *The Meaning of Marxism*, Ann Arbor: University of Michigan Press, 1948. Reprinted by permission.

MIDDLE-CLASS POWER, ECONOMIC AND POLITICAL

The new *petite bourgeoisie*, despite its great and growing importance in the conduct of modern industries and services, has hitherto had very little influence over economic policy. Although it is the chief repository of technical and administrative competence and of inventive power, and thus plays the leading part in shaping the evolution of the forces of production, it has been able to act hitherto only under the orders of its great capitalist masters, who have been interested in its achievements only as means to the extraction of profit, rent and interest. Large-scale Capitalism has paid the piper, even if it has got the money largely from small investors; and large-scale Capitalism has accordingly called the tune. In capitalist societies the power over economic policy of the rising salaried groups of technicians and administrators has therefore been hitherto very limited indeed — despite all that has been written about Technocracy and the so-called "Managerial Revolution." But can the same be said of its political power?

I am aware that it is often argued that "economic power precedes and dominates political power," which is only a reflection of it, and that accordingly the new industrial middle class cannot call in its political influence to redress its economic subservience. At this point, however, we must beware of an ambiguity in the use of phrases. The "economic power" which this class lacks is the power to control economic policy. But it possesses potential economic power in a more vital and fundamental sense. It has the capacity to organise and carry on industry under its own control, without the aid of the great capitalists, if it can ensure either the co-operation or the subservience of the proletariat. It and the proletariat, and not the great capitalists, are the classes which to-day perform the functions indispensable for the carrying on of industry and the further development of production, to which indeed the authority exercised by the hierarchs of banking, investing and financial manipulation constitutes a serious obstacle. There is, accordingly, no barrier in the way of the creation of a successful political movement by the technicians and administrators on account of any lack in their understanding and mastery of the technical requirements of economic progress; and there is a positive foundation for such a movement in the form of economic power which is already theirs.

The unity and strength of the middle classes of the twentieth century are certain, if they are manifested at all, to take shape primarily in a political movement. Economically, they cannot act together as a class, but only in sections, often with conflicting aims and policies, because they lack a common relation to industry such as binds the wage-earners together, and are too much mixed up with ownership, both by direct shareholding and by participation in profits, as well as by family connections, to be able to take a clear line. Politically, on the other hand, they can act together, and have often done so with considerable effect, for the protection of the rights and privileged inequalities of the recipients of unearned incomes. They have done this sometimes against the rich, but more often against the enactment of expensive social legislation or the improvement of municipal services. They have been found banded together against high taxation on middle incomes, against high local rates, and against Trade Unions which threaten the maintenance of essential services, as in the British General Strike of 1926.

These forms of combination are, however, merely negative and unconstructive; and they are, in any advanced industrial society in which the peasants and farmers do not form a group powerful enough to determine the issue, unlikely to be effective in the long run. They have succeeded hitherto in France and in a number of countries, though not on the whole in Great Britain, in checking the growth of social services and in offering a resistance to the proletariat and at the same time restraining the political influence of large-scale Capitalism; for in such countries as France, Holland and Switzerland, peasants and urban *petite bourgeoisie* are still, despite the high finance of Paris and other great centres and the growth of the proletariat, economically powerful groups. Not even in these countries, however, is a purely negative policy likely to suffice for long to hold a balance between the main contending forces in society: nor is there any certainty that it can suffice much longer even in the United States. In highly industrialised societies, among which France still barely counts, in the long run the pressure of the proletariat for improved conditions is bound to overbear a purely negative policy of resistance, if the affairs of State continue to be conducted upon a basis of universal suffrage with reasonable freedom of elections and of political organisation.

MIDDLE-CLASS POLICIES

Accordingly, the middle classes, if they desire to preserve their cherished inequality, are in the long run compelled either to look for a constructive policy of their own or to acquiesce, on such terms as they can secure, in the policies of the capitalist class. Hitherto, they have for the most part preferred the latter of these alternatives, and have acted politically as well as economically as the faithful servants of large-scale Capitalism, getting in return an increasing supply of crumbs from the rich man's table. Acting in this way, they have often been strong enough to help the capitalist interest to prevail in elections, even under adult suffrage; but this electoral success, at any rate in the more highly industrialised countries, has been bought only at the price of concessions to the proletariat, which have of late increased in scale and cost, and have been paid for to a growing extent by heavier taxation of the middle classes. The difficulties of Capitalism between the wars at the same time increased the need for these services, by swelling the numbers of the unemployed, and added to the awkwardness of paying for them. The proletariat, in face of these difficulties, became more clamant for some form of Socialism, which threatened the privileges of the middle classes as well as of the class above them. The middle classes responded, to a small extent, by blaming the financiers and the financial machine for their troubles, but to a much greater extent by banding themselves together to resist the proletariat, of which they stood in more fundamental fear. For most sections of the middle classes still regarded it as preferable to remain in subordination to the capitalist system rather than run the risk of forfeiting their unequal privileges under Socialism. This was the ultimate rationale of the inter-war growth of Fascism, which naturally developed first and furthest in those countries in which Capitalism was most in difficulties, and the demand for Socialism had accordingly become most insistent. Middle-class fears of Socialism were no doubt often exaggerated, and they were of course deliberately worked upon by the use of modern propagandist techniques. There was, however, substance behind them, wherever the capitalist system did appear to be in imminent danger of sheer collapse.

THE RISE OF FASCISM

Where the middle classes set out to aid the capitalists to defeat the proletariat, they need some stronger weapon than their mere voting strength. In the advanced industrial countries which have been pressed hardest by the growing difficulties of Capitalism, this weapon has already proved its inadequacy as a means of resisting the gradual encroachment of democratic social reform. In these circumstances a large section of the middle classes may go Fascist, under whatever name, with the aid of parallel elements in the country districts. It may repudiate Parliamentarism, and clamour for authoritative government. But this cry for a form of dictatorship to keep the proletariat in its place cannot be effective if it is put forward as an open defence of the vested interests in present-day society; for the proletariat is too strong, and has too many allies scattered among the other classes, and among a considerable part of the middle classes prejudice in favour of Parliamentarism is too strong, for a naked appeal to violence on a basis of privileged self-interest to be successful in overbearing them. Fascism has, therefore, needed to assume the outward form of an alternative ideal to that of Socialism, appealing to sentiments as deeply rooted as those of democracy, and capable of attracting not only a considerable part of the middle classes, but also a substantial section of the proletariat itself.

This appeal was found in aggressive Nationalism, reinforced according to local conditions by any form of anti-foreigner complex likely to arouse a widespread response in the country concerned. All right-minded citizens were called upon, in the name of national honour and manhood, to take arms against the insidious propaganda of pacifism, against Jewish penetration, and against the open cosmopolitanism of the Socialist ideal. The sentiment of the class struggle was countered by an appeal to the sentiment of national solidarity against the rest of the world; and a specious ideal of national service and self-sacrifice was held up against the allegedly materialist objectives of Socialism. These ideologies, which would have been powerless by themselves, proved able to become great powers when they were made the allies of class-interest; and a section of the worst-off part of the proletariat, the "submerged tenth," reinforced by many of the long-term unemployed, who had been ground down to despair by the attrition of economic distress and saw little prospect of early relief in face of the deadlock reached between the capitalist and Socialist forces, was won over by large, vague hopes and promises of the rewards certain to accrue from a Fascist victory, not unaccompanied by advance bribes, to go over to the Fascist side.

Where this happened, and the working-class forces were divided, the path was made easy towards a Fascist victory. For the power of the proletariat depends essentially upon substantial unity among its leading elements. But, in the circumstances here described, disunity was pretty certain to arise. In face of the growing difficulties of Capitalism there were some who urged an immediate advance towards Socialism, by revolutionary methods if no other way were immediately open; whereas others held that it was necessary to wait until a majority had been won over to Socialism by constitutional methods of propaganda and electioneering. In most countries such a majority was by no means easy to secure, in face of the combined voting strength and the propagandist resources of the upper and middle classes reinforced by the agricultural interests; and, condemned to prolonged inaction under stress of serious economic adversity, enough of the proletariat became disillusioned at the slow progress of Socialism, especially where the Socialist cause was poorly led, to result in a disastrous division in the proletarian ranks. This provided the Fascists with their opportunity to jettison the substance of Parliamentarism, though they usually preferred to keep its shadow, and enabled them to institute some form of dictatorship in the name of the "national spirit."

WORKING-CLASS DISUNITY

Division in the ranks of the working class would have developed in any case; but it was both facilitated and deeply aggravated by ideological conflict. After 1917 the Soviet Union, as the one country in which the proletarian Revolution had been successfully made, exercised a powerful spell upon the minds of the workers — especially the younger workers — in every country. The Bolsheviks had carried through their Revolution in strict accordance with their interpretation of Marxism and, attributing the failure of parallel revolutions to occur in Western Europe largely to lack of correct Marxist leadership of the working-class movements of the West, were continually calling upon the workers of other countries to throw over their "reactionary" leaders and to rally behind the Communist Parties created in imitation of the Communist Party of the Soviet Union. The long ostracism of the Soviet Union by the capitalist countries and the news of the tremendous efforts in economic construction that were being put into the successive Five Year Plans made the Soviet Union appear as the key position in the world struggle for Socialism, and lent immense authority to whatever advice its leaders chose to tender to the working classes of the capitalist countries. At the same time the sharp contrast between the strict authoritarianism of the Soviet régime, based partly on the continuing conditions of 'cold war' and partly on the heritage of Czarist autocracy and centralisation in a vast, mainly pleasant country, and the relatively liberal and unbureaucratic traditions of the West rendered the Communist approach quite unacceptable to more than a small minority in Great Britain or in the 'smaller democracies' of the West, and resulted in disastrous divisions among the workers of Germany and of France. In Germany, which had long been a battleground between liberal and autocratic conceptions, and in France, where centralisation had been the historic weapon of the opponents of privilege ever since 1789, the working-class forces were split through and through. In the one case, these divisions prepared the way for Nazism: in the other, though no such extreme result has so far followed, the action both of the Trade Unions and of the whole Republic was paralysed, and there developed that fatal mood of disillusion and disorientation which lead up to the collapse of 1940 and is still following its unhappy course in the frustrations and tumults of the period since the liberation. If France is now facing de Gaulle, with an unpleasing likeness to the mood in which Germany once faced Hitler, the principal cause is to be found in the disunity of the French working-class movement; and the principal cause of this disunity is to be found in the ideological conflict between Soviet-based Marxism and the traditional Socialism of the West.

The consummation that was reached in 1933 in Germany and the consummation that appeared to be threatening France in 1948 were alike the outcome of extreme economic difficulty and dislocation; for nothing short of this would have served either to bring about the necessary division in the proletariat or sufficiently to unite the middle classes under the nationalist banner. Where economic difficulties are less pressing, parliamentary forms and methods are likely to be preserved, and, in countries where there is a strong parliamentary tradition, nothing worse is likely to happen than a setback to social reform, and perhaps a period of national "economy" and reaction under the aegis of a "national" Government that will not do more than nibble at the existing provision for the poorer classes. In such countries severe strain on the economic system is needed to bring Fascism or any variant of it to boiling point, and to secure the necessary support for a forcible overthrow of the parliamentary system in the interests of the propertied classes. British people, however, are apt to exaggerate the strength of parliamentary institutions in other countries, judging of them by their own, and to mistake what is only a façade of parliamentary government for a deeply-rooted social habit; whereas those whose experience of parliamentary institutions has been entirely of the sham varieties are apt to fall into the opposite mistake of regarding all parliamentary government as essentially a sham, a cloak for the operations of a hypocritical ruling class. These misunderstandings lead British people to pay an exaggerated respect to the profession of parliamentarist principles even where they have no real roots, and they similarly lead Soviet propagandists and their fellow-travellers to dismiss with contempt the adherance of Socialists anywhere to the methods of parliamentary government. Each side interprets everything in the light of its own experience; and a disastrous game of cross-purposes and mutual recriminations is the result.

THE REAL NATURE OF FASCISM

For British Socialists it is important never to forget that the strains of the inter-war years and of the war period were very much more severe in many other countries than they ever became in Great Britain, and that in most parts of Europe there was no deeply-rooted parliamentary tradition at all corresponding to the British tradition. It is not at all surprising that many Socialists outside Great Britain saw the crisis of Capitalism as a thorough fulfilment of Marx's prophecies, and were consequently attracted to Communism as preached from the Soviet Union. It is not even surprising, though it is lamentable, that some of them were induced by their belief in the inevitably impending doom of Capitalism to underrate the importance of Fascism, or even to suppose that a Fascist victory would help to prepare the way for Socialism by sweeping obsolete pseudo-democratic parliamentary institutions aside. This attitude, as we shall see, rested on a fundamental misunderstanding of the nature of Fascism, which was regarded as merely the final stage of Capitalism in decline. This complacent attitude towards the Fascist menace created a situation in which the working class, instead of uniting to destroy it, divided itself into warring factions, of which one set itself to defend the existing parliamentary system against Fascist attack, while the other stood aloof, hoping either to profit immediately by the conflict or, at any rate, to inherit the control of society when "Fascist Capitalism" speedily broke down through its failure to solve the inherent contradictions of capitalist production.

The truth, however, was that Fascism, far from being merely the final stage of Capitalism in decline, was a new social phenomenon of the greatest independent significance. Although it owed its rise mainly to economic distress, it was not in itself or in its driving force mainly an economic movement. It rested rather, like the mass-movements of earlier ages, on the will to domination and conquest, on the hope to escape from the oppression of circumstances by forceful aggression, and on the exaltation of the "national spirit" as a liberation from the restraints and inhibitions of a customary morality made irksome by adversity. It was no accident that Fascism's gods were tribal gods or that it revived, in modernised form, the ancient myth of the "god-warrior-king." These things were not merely trappings, put on for propagandist purposes: they were of Fascism's very essence. If there is in history an analogy to Fascism, it is to be looked for, not in the record of class-conflicts, but in the greatest migrations of warrior peoples which have again and again set the world in turmoil. Nowadays, whole peoples cannot migrate: the foundations of their living are too deeply rooted in the places they inhabit, and if they were to move *en masse* they could only starve. It was not, however, impossible for a modern people to seek *Lebensraum* without mass-migration – by conquering and subjecting, by levying tribute on the conquered, and even by bringing their enslaved victims to labour for them in the fields and factories of the Fascist homeland.

All this, it may be said, is an interpretation of Fascism in essentially economic terms. It is, and yet it is not. I agree that the roots of Fascism were in economic distress, and that economic purposes ranked high among its objectives. But I deny, not only that the appeal which gave it strength was mainly economic, but also – what is really the critical point – that it can be correctly interpreted *as a class-movement*, or simply as the last manoeuvre of Capitalism to avert the proletarian revolution.

FASCISM AND CAPITALISM

No doubt Fascism, where it has triumphed, has climbed to power only with the help of a powerful section of the capitalist class. Neither in Italy nor in Germany could the forces which destroyed the parliamentary State have been brought to the required strength without the financial backing of a sufficient number of great capitalists. The creation of a revolutionary force based mainly on the declassed middle classes, the soldiers of fortune out of a job, and the most helpless sections of the proletariat required a large amount of money, which could in practice be supplied only from the resources of large-scale Capitalism. The great capitalists would, of course, not have financed such a movement unless they had considered that it was calculated to serve their ends. The leaders of Fascism had, therefore, to give to the great capitalists pledges of intentions which these paymasters would regard as good, and had to promise to turn their weapons upon the proletariat and not upon "Big Business." In the earlier stages of Fascist development the armies of counter-revolution fought the proletariat as the allies and upholders of Capitalism, which was represented under the guise of social solidarity as an integral element in the greatness of the National State.

PETIT BOURGEOIS ATTITUDES

This alliance with large-scale Capitalism was by no means welcome to all the members of the *petite bourgeoisie* whom the Fascists were attempting to attract into their ranks. The small-scale producers and traders in this group had a fear of high finance and of rationalised enterprise which was second only to their dread of a proletarian victory. Farmers and peasants shared this attitude and wanted to fight for their own interests and not for large-scale Capitalism. Fascist programmes, therefore, usually contained many projects designed to appeal to *petit bourgeois* sentiment, and had often an anti-capitalist seasoning, even where Capitalism was in fact giving them its support. The support was given none the less, because many capitalists believed that, if once the proletariat could be thoroughly defeated, there would be no real difficulty in keeping in proper subjection the forces which had been used to compass its defeat.

There have been, indeed, at periods of less intense social conflict, middle-class groups which, unwilling to become the instruments of large-scale Capitalism in the fight against Socialism, have attempted to devise constructive programmes of their own. Such groups were to be found in Great Britain at the time of the Industrial Revolution; and J.C.L. de Sismondi's "New Economics" of 1819 were an attempt to give their aspirations a theoretical basis in opposition to the classical Political Economy. From the days when Marx, at the outset of his career, arraigned Sismondi and Proudhon as *petit bourgeois* reformers — indeed, from even earlier — this has always meant largely the formulation of projects of monetary reform. These projects have to some extent changed their nature with the changes that have occurred in the composition of the middle classes. In the time of Proudhon they were predominantly schemes for securing to the small-scale producers and traders a sufficient supply of credit to enable them to stand up to the competition of large-scale business and to the vicissitudes of the trade cycle. They retain this character to a great extent even to-day in the agricultural areas of Canada and the United States; but among industrial communities the emphasis has shifted in modern times from the small-scale producer to the consumer, and recent projects have been designed to bring about low prices for consumers' goods, or issues of free credit to consumers to enable them to buy the greatly enlarged product of which modern industry is technically capable, but of which it has appeared disastrously unable to dispose. Currency and credit cranks are to-day, as they were a century ago, foremost among those *petit bourgeois* reformers who want their class to put forward a programme of its own, in order to fight Socialism in its own interest and not for the benefit of the great capitalists.

TECHNOCRACY

Nowadays, side by side with the monetary reformers go the technocrats, who emphasise the creative rôle of scientist, inventor and technician in the advance of material wealth, and urge the claims of the new *petite bourgeoisie* of experts to reform and govern society by virtue of their technical and administrative competence. Both the monetary reformers and the technocrats often have the merit of generous sympathies, and of a desire to raise the general standard of life by setting free the vast forces of productivity which have been chained up by the capitalist system. They mostly aim, however, at reconciling the advent of the new age of plenty with the maintenance of privileges and economic and social superiority for the technical and administrative groups in society over the manual workers, whom they dismiss as too ignorant to rule, and they usually repudiate the conception of the class-struggle because it appears to threaten their superiority of income and status.

This attitude condemns these "radical" movements among the middle-class technicians and experts to sterility, for they cannot possibly make themselves strong enough to stand alone, or expect to rally the main body of the middle classes behind them. A large section of the middle classes, including the small-scale producers, the small traders, and the farmers, acutely dislikes technocracy, which it rightly regards as standing on the whole for mass-production and for the elimination of the independent "small man." The great capitalist financiers naturally repudiate the claims of their hired servants to call the tune; and the workers are naturally not at all attracted by the offer of a new set of masters to order them about. Intellectually, technocratic theories have little appeal to the proletariat, unless they can be combined with an appeal to sentiment; but such an appeal is inconsistent with the desire of the technocrats to hold on to their superior status. Accordingly, though in a number of countries technocrats and monetary reformers have temporarily commanded considerable followings, there has never been any real chance of their rallying behind them, at any rate in any developed industrial country, a sufficient following to enable them to put their notions to the test of practice. The monetary reformers have had their best chance in predominantly agricultural countries, such as Canada, especially in the prairie provinces where the farmers' movement is in a position, if it can become united, to dominate the political situation. But even where monetary reformers have won elections they have been able to achieve little; and in industrial countries such creeds as technocracy and credit reform can but create diversions: they cannot win power.

FASCISM AND THE MIDDLE CLASSES

In such countries the middle classes, when they are driven into political activity as a reaction to economic crisis, are apt to become the allies of large-scale Capitalism in the fight against Socialism. They see no hope of preserving their petty privileges without the support of the great capitalists. But, when these classes unite in the struggle against Socialism, it remains to be seen which of them will carry off the victory in the contest between them which is certain to follow if they achieve the rout of the Socialist forces. Large-scale Capitalism starts with the great advantage of being in possession of the field, and of being able to claim that any attempt to disturb its vested interest will result in economic dislocation and will menace both the consolidation of the victory over Socialism and the attainment of the Fascist objective of national strength as a means to national aggrandisement and predatory aggression. But the leadership of the Fascist forces, and the power of Fascism to spell-bind the people, is bound to rest not with the capitalists but with a motley group of perverted idealists, thugs, swashbuckling adventurers, careerists, thwarted aristocrats, and assertive militarists, whose chief bond of union is a hatred of democracy, and by no means a love for Capitalism; and the main body of their followers will necessarily consist of the middle-class elements and of those sections of the peasants and of the working class which have rallied to the Fascist appeal. These groups will claim the fulfilment of the promises made to them in the course of the struggle, while the section of the aristocracy which has thrown in its lot with Fascism will also clamour for the reward of its collaboration. In face of the difficulties of the economic situation, these conflicting claims will not be easy to satisfy; and the centralised, authoritarian State set up for the purpose of destroying Socialism will be an instrument which can readily be applied to the issuing of positive orders, in the name of the awakened Nation, to the capitalists themselves as well as to the defeated workers and to the middle classes. In these circumstances, a drastic régime of State control over industry will have to be instituted, so that the State, even if it seeks to respect the interests of the big capitalists as a class, will not scruple to lay rough hands on the individual capitalist who refuses to work in with its National Plan of economic reform. There will arise a State-controlled Capitalism which will no doubt serve to protect the interests of property-owners, both large and small, against the proletariat, but will afford this protection only to the extent to which the rights of property can be turned into instruments of national consolidation and reconciled with the discipline of the civil population. Consequently, within the Fascist ranks, there will be a struggle for the control of the new State which is to exert this authority over all the people.

FASCISM IS *NOT* A CLASS MOVEMENT

In this ensuing struggle, the victory goes neither to the great capitalists nor to the small. It does not go to any *class*; for Fascism, though it wages war upon the working class and uses other classes as its instruments, is not fundamentally a class-movement. Its claim to transcend classes is in a sense quite genuine; for it reaches back, behind the class-divisions of modern society, towards primitive conditions of tribal solidarity. It is not a *class* but a *horde*-movement, profoundly antagonistic to every rational form of social structure and therefore to the rational utilitarianism which lies at the root of capitalist enterprise as much as of every form of 'liberal' philosophy. It may no doubt be able to reconcile the great capitalists to accepting its domination; for it can offer them the retention of their wealth and the re-establishment of their direct authority over the workers in return for their acceptance of its ends. Far, however, from controlling Fascism, the great capitalists come to be controlled by it, and are compelled to subordinate their money-making impulses to the requirements of the Fascist State as an organiser of national aggression. As for the small property owners, they soon discover that their property rights and social privileges are left to them only to the extent to which they can be fitted in with the requirements of centrally organised national power, and that no pledges given to them in the course of the counter-revolution are of any validity when they come into conflict with the power plans of the totalitarian State. The technicians and administrators fare better, on the whole, than the rest of the middle classes; for Fascism has need of them for the detailed execution of its national projects, and they can most readily square their ambitions and interests with its ideology and thus act without sense of frustration as members of the Fascist hierarchy. Fascism and technocracy make good bed-fellows; for the *"Fuehrer* principle" in practice involves the placing of immense delegated authority in the hands of an official class made up largely of expert administrators and technicians. Under Fascism, however, the technician is compelled to subject his technical mastery to the requirements of the totalitarian State. He changes masters, and works no longer mainly to pile up profits for the capitalist, but to make the State strong for aggressive war. With the change he acquires the possibility of a higher status, through promotion, under the *Fuehrer*, into the ranks of the dominant *élite*.

The victory of Fascism in a single country thus sets up a new set of internal power-relations. It vests power, not in an economic class, but in a "god-warrior-king" who gathers round him a military, administrative and technical bureaucracy devoted under his inspiration to the service of national aggrandisement; and it subordinates all classes to this horde concept of national solidarity. It tramples most heavily upon the working classes, both because they are the principal rival of whom it is afraid, and because their desire for better living and greater security conflicts with its creed of national glory. It seeks guns before butter, whereas the working-class movements everywhere put butter before guns. Fascism, however, tramples also — albeit much less heavily — on the classes which have been its allies in its capture of power. It erodes the class of small capitalists to whom it has promised succour; and it subordinates even large-scale Capitalism to its quest for national aggrandisement. If the situation which ensues upon its victory could last, it might be able to reduce the elements thus subjected to it to a condition of equilibrium, such as the Italian Fascists romanticised in their static phantasy of the Corporative State. But Fascism is in fact essentially unstable because it looks outward upon other nations and can realise its nationalist aspirations only by subjecting them to its rule. Fascism, as long as it is contained within one country, involves unremitting preparation for wars of conquest, leading to actual war; and when war comes as a natural consequence of its aggression it must either win outright, and make other nations its helots, or go down to a defeat in which its power is utterly broken. Its ambitions being irrational and unlimited, it cannot come to terms with any other power: it cannot be appeased or contained. It must win or lose everything.

THE EFFECTS OF FASCISM

If it loses, there is left behind a most intractable legacy of spiritual and economic disaster. The beating of its swords into ploughshares would be a hard enough task even if it had not done its utmost to uproot from the midst of the nation all the elements to which such a task would appeal, and to destroy national faith in all decencies of behaviour and aspiration. As things are, it has scorched the soil of humanity, leaving only bitterness and frustration behind, save among the few who have been strong enough to resist the brutal reinforcements of the mass-appeal — nor are even those few unscathed. Economically, its legacy is mass-privation and that very ruin of the middle classes which it claimed to prevent. The re-building of either the economic or the political and social foundations of a defeated Fascist nation presents a terrible problem because the very conditions which it leaves behind can serve as a breeding-ground for new forms of Fascism much more easily than for any democratic or Socialist system.

On the other hand, if Fascism were to win, what would the outcome be? It is still worth while to consider the answer to this question, though for the time German, Italian and Japanese Fascism have gone down together in defeat. For the world may not have done yet with the Fascist danger, even if a recurrence of it is likely to take somewhat different forms. Victorious Fascism, in its Nazi form, would have meant a Europe of helot peoples condemned to labour for the *Herrenvolk*, or in its Japanese form a "Co-prosperity Sphere" of Asiatic helots. But that could not have been the end. Even if the Soviet Union had been overwhelmed and divided up, these two could neither have lived in the world side by side with an unsubdued American continent nor have kept the peace with each other. War upon war would have laid the whole world waste, each waged with more frightfulness than the one before; and all the time the processes of Fascist indoctrination would have been intensified and decent sentiment and morality more and more savagely rooted out from the minds of the young in every country.

But, up to the final disaster, would the *Herrenvolk* — German, Japanese, and probably American — have been living well or ill? From any standpoint that takes account of decent human values, obviously very ill indeed; but how, in a sheerly material sense? With the tribute of a prostrate world to draw upon, it would seem that the conquerors should have been able to wax fat, even if they spent much of their substance on policing their victims and on arming against each other. Nor could there be any inherent reason why a Nazi State, ruling over subject peoples, should suffer from unemployment on account of any inability to distribute the products of the labour either of its own people or of its foreign slaves. In full control of the use of its resources and of the distribution of incomes, it would be in a position to raise the standard of life of its people to any extent consistent with the proportion of its man-power devoted to war services, including the garrisoning of subject territories and preparation for actual war against its remaining rivals, as long as any were left.

COULD FASCISM SUCCEED?

It was, I am sure, a fatal error to suppose that Nazism, even if it triumphed in arms, would be bound speedily to break down because of its continued liability to the contradictions of Capitalism. The view that this would necessarily happen was based on the erroneous belief that Fascism was simply a form of Capitalism, and therefore could not escape from its contradictions. If, as I have tried to show, Fascism was not a form of Capitalism, but an essentially different system, using certain capitalist institutions for its own aggressive nationalist ends, there was no presumption that it would break down *from this cause*.

The real reason why Fascism would in all probability have been unable to endure was its inherent insatiability. In attempting to conquer the whole world, it could hardly have avoided tearing both the world and itself to pieces, and collapsing under the immense strain which its effort would have placed upon its own nation as well as upon every other.

This view is of course highly unacceptable to rigid Marxists because it involves recognising that non-economic factors can play a primary part in determining the course of history. I have suggested earlier that Marx's theory of history was thought out as a theory of the continuous development of civilisation regarded as a unified whole, and took no adequate account of the impact of external forces on the internal process of development. Indeed, if all the world were one civilisation, developing in a straight line from lower to higher forms, there would be no question of an external impact deflecting the course of its evolution. In fact, however, the world never has been covered by a single civilisation; and the course of development has again and again been diverted by the impact of one civilisation upon another, in the form of mass migrations and wars of conquest. What I am suggesting is that the Fascist aggressive totalitarian State is the modern equivalent of the great conquering migrations of earlier history, and though, like them, greatly affected by economic forces, can no more than they be explained in terms of classes or class-struggles. To say this is not at all to deny that class-struggle played an important part in the development of Fascism. But I am contending that this part was secondary, and that the mainspring of Fascism has to be sought elsewhere. The factor of class-conflict played in the rise of Fascism a part analogous to that secondary influence which Marx recognised as affecting the course of history within the general movement determined by economic forces. His mistake lay in concluding that, because all civilisations rest fundamentally on the use made of the powers of production, and change as these powers develop, therefore the mode of change must be always and universally the same. In other words, it lay in not merely treating class-struggles as the sole mode by which the development of the powers of production could be translated into terms of social structure, but also asserting that the evolution of the powers of production could not be either interrupted or deflected by any human agency.

This error arose directly out of the confusion which I have already noted in Marx's thought about the powers of production themselves. In failing to stress their dual character, as consisting not only of things usable by men but also of men's knowledge of their use, he obscured the important fact that the powers of production are fundamentally altered if the same *things* fall into the hands of *men* better or worse equipped with knowledge of their use, or with an essentially different attitude towards them. This is precisely what has happened in the past as the result of great migrations and wars of conquest; and that is why such movements form the great element of discontinuity in human history.

It may be answered that, even if this be true, it has no bearing on the question of the fundamental character of Fascism, because Fascism was an outgrowth of Capitalism, and the Fascists were equipped with the same knowledge of the use of things as their victims. Agreed. That is a valid reason for holding that the victory of Fascism would not have involved a break in the continuity of development of the powers of production. But I have not argued that it would have had this effect. What I am arguing is that the powers of production, though *a* fundamental factor in social development at all stages, are not always the sole major factor, and that there are other forces in men's natures that can operate as major causes in history. Fascism, even if it had triumphed, would not have involved a break in the development of man's technical mastery over nature (though it might have deflected it in a number of ways): what it would have involved would have been the advent as successor to Capitalism of a system other than Socialism, which Marx regarded as the only possible claimant. Fascist victory would have continued the development of the powers of production, but, instead of transferring power from the capitalists to the proletariat, would have handed it over to an exploiting national group, and replaced the subjection of the working class in each country by the subjection of whole peoples to the victor nation. This is where the situation would have been analogous to past conquests based on mass-migration of peoples. There would no doubt have been an element of class-conflict in it; but to attempt to explain it exclusively in terms of class-conflict involves travestying the facts.

Part IX
SOCIOLOGY AND SOCIAL POLICY

By its very nature the sociological enterprise has policy implications. One cannot describe social phenomena without selecting some things for study and ignoring others. By what we choose to study we necessarily choose "a side," as Howard Becker would put it.[1]

Noam Chomsky, the well-known linguist, argues forcefully that the social scientist has a special responsibility to stand outside the prevailing ideological and political debates of the society and to make an independent judgment. An independent judgment requires an independence from institutional control and influence. The "responsibility of intellectuals" then goes beyond that of merely trying to be "objective"; it demands a commitment in one's personal life as well as in one's work to the maintenance of freedom from institutional control whether that control comes from careers, research grants, university affiliation, or fear.

Sociology and sociologists are involved in social policy whether they like it or not. The issue is not whether sociology should be concerned with social policy; the issue is how we will react to the fact that sociological inquiry inevitably has social policy implications.

---

[1] See Howard Becker "Whose Side Are We On?" *Social Problems*, Vol. 14, Fall 1967. See also K.T. Erikson, "Sociology: That Awkward Age," *Social Problems*, Vol. 19, Spring 1972.

THE RESPONSIBILITY OF INTELLECTUALS

Noam Chomsky

Twenty years ago, Dwight Macdonald published a series of articles in *Politics* on the responsibilities of peoples, and specifically, the responsibility of intellectuals. I read them as an undergraduate, in the years just after the war, and had occasion to read them again a few months ago. They seem to me to have lost none of their power or persuasiveness. Macdonald is concerned with the question of war guilt. He asks the question: To what extent were the German or Japanese people responsible for the atrocities committed by their governments? And, quite properly, he turns the question back to us: To what extent are the British or American people responsible for the vicious terror bombings of civilians perfected as a technique of warfare by the Western democracies and reaching their culmination in Hiroshima and Nagasaki, surely among the most unspeakable crimes in history? To an undergraduate in 1945-46 — to anyone whose political and moral consciousness had been formed by the horrors of the 1930s, by the war in Ethiopia, the Russian purge, the 'China Incident', the Spanish Civil War, the Nazi atrocities, the Western reaction to these events and, in part, complicity in them — these questions had particular significance and poignancy.

With respect to the responsibility of intellectuals, there are still other, equally disturbing questions. Intellectuals are in a position to expose the lies of governments, to analyze actions according to their causes and motives and often hidden intentions. In the Western world, at least, they have the power that comes from political liberty, from access to information and freedom of expression. For a privileged minority, Western democracy provides the leisure, the facilities and the training to seek the truth lying hidden behind the veil of distortion and misrepresentation, ideology and class interest, through which the events of current history are presented to us. The responsibilities of intellectuals, then, are much deeper than what Macdonald calls the 'responsibility of peoples', given the unique privileges that intellectuals enjoy.

The issues that Macdonald raised are as pertinent today as they were twenty years ago. We can hardly avoid asking ourselves to what extent the American people bear responsibility for the savage American assault on a largely helpless rural population in Vietnam, still another atrocity in what Asians see as the 'Vasco da Gama era' of world history. As for those of us who stood by in silence and apathy as this catastrophe slowly took shape over the past dozen years, on what page of history do we find our proper place? Only the most insensible can escape these questions. I want to return to them, later on, after a few scattered remarks about the responsibility of intellectuals and how, in practice, they go about meeting their responsibility in the mid 1960s.

It is the responsibility of intellectuals to speak the truth and to expose lies. This, at least, may seem enough of a truism to pass without comment. Not so, however. For the modern intellectual, it is not at all obvious. Thus we have Martin Heidegger writing, in a pro-Hitler declaration of 1933, that 'truth is the revelation of that which makes a people certain, clear and strong in its action and knowledge'; it is only this kind of 'truth' that one has a responsibility to speak. Americans tend to be more forthright. When Arthur Schlesinger was aked by the *New York Times*, in November 1965, to explain the contradiction between his published account of the Bay of Pigs incident and the story he had given the press at the time of the attack, he simply remarked that he had lied; and a few days later, he went on to compliment the *Times* for also having suppressed information on the planned invasion, in 'the national interest', as this was defined by the group of arrogant and deluded men of whom Schlesinger gives such a flattering portrait in his recent account of the Kennedy administration. It is of no particular interest that one man is quite happy to lie in behalf of a cause which he knows to be unjust; but it is significant that such events provoke so little response in the intellectual community – no feeling, for example, that there is something strange in the offer of a major chair in humanities to a historian who feels it to be his duty to persuade the world that an American-sponsored invasion of a nearby country is nothing of the sort. And what of the incredible sequence of lies on the part of our government and its spokesmen concerning such matters as negotiations in Vietnam? The facts are known to all who care to know. The press, foreign and domestic, has presented documentation to refute each falsehood as it appears. But the power of the government propaganda apparatus is such that the citizen who does not undertake a research project on the subject can hardly hope to confront government pronouncements with fact.[2]

The deceit and distortion surrounding the American invasion of Vietnam is by now so familiar that it has lost its power to shock. It is therefore well to recall that although new levels of cynicism are constantly being reached, their clear antecedents were accepted at home with quiet toleration. It is a useful exercise to compare government statements at the time of the invasion of Guatemala in 1954 with Eisenhower's admission – to be more accurate, his boast – a decade later that American planes were sent 'to help the invaders'.[3] Nor is it only in moments of crisis that duplicity is considered perfectly in order. 'New Frontiersmen', for example, have scarcely distinguished themselves by a passionate concern for historical accuracy, even when they are not being called upon to provide a 'propaganda cover' for ongoing actions. For example, Arthur Schlesinger describes the bombing of North Vietnam and the massive escalation of military commitment in early 1965 as based on a 'perfectly rational argument': 'so long as the Vietcong thought they were going to win the war, they obviously would not be interested in any kind of negotiated settlement'.[4] The date is important. Had the statement been made six months earlier, one could attribute it to ignorance. But this statement appeared after months of front-page news reports detailing the UN, North Vietnamese and Soviet initiatives that preceded the February 1965 escalation and that, in fact, continued for several weeks after the bombing began, after months of soul-searching by Washington correspondents who were trying desperately to find some mitigating circumstances for the startling deception that had been revealed (Chalmers Roberts, for example, wrote with unconscious irony that late February 1965 'hardly seemed to Washington to be a propitious moment for negotiations [since] Mr. Johnson . . . had just ordered the first bombing of

North Vietnam in an effort to bring Hanoi to a conference table where bargaining chips on both sides would be more closely matched'[5]). Coming at this moment, Schlesinger's statement is less an example of deceit than of contempt – contempt for an audience that can be expected to tolerate such behavior with silence, if not approval.[6]

To turn to someone closer to the actual formation and implementation of policy, consider some of the reflections of Walt Rostow, a man who, according to Schlesinger, brought a 'spacious historical view' to the conduct of foreign affairs in the Kennedy administration.[7] According to his analysis, the guerrilla warfare in Indochina in 1946 was launched by Stalin,[8] and Hanoi initiated the guerrilla war against South Vietnam in 1958 (*The View from the Seventh Floor*, pp. 39 and 152). Similarly, the communist planners probed the 'free world spectrum of defense' in Northern Azerbaijan and Greece (where Stalin 'supported substantial guerrilla warfare' – *ibid.*, pp. 36 and 148), operating from plans carefully laid in 1945. And in Central Europe, the Soviet Union was not 'prepared to accept a solution which would remove the dangerous tensions from Central Europe at the risk of even slowly staged corrosion of communism in East Germany' (*ibid.*, p. 156).

It is interesting to compare these observations with studies by scholars actually concerned with historical events. The remark about Stalin's initiating the first Vietnamese war in 1946 does not even merit refutation. As to Hanoi's purported initiative of 1958, the situation is more clouded. But even government sources[9] concede that in 1959 Hanoi received the first direct reports of what Diem referred to[10] as his own Algerian war and that only after this did they lay down their plans to involve themselves in this struggle. In fact, in December 1958 Hanoi made another of its many attempts – rebuffed once again by Saigon and the United States – to establish diplomatic and commercial relations with the Saigon government on the basis of the status quo.[11] Rostow offers no evidence of Stalin's support for the Greek guerrillas: in fact, though the historical record is far from clear, it seems that Stalin was by no means pleased with the adventurism of the Greek guerrillas, who, from his point of view, were upsetting the satisfactory postwar imperialist settlement.[12]

Rostow's remarks about Germany are more interesting still. He does not see fit to mention, for example, the Russian notes of March-April 1952, which proposed unification of Germany under internationally supervised elections, with withdrawal of all troops within a year *if* there was a guarantee that a reunified Germany would not be permitted to join a

Western military alliance.[13] And he has also momentarily forgotten his own characterization of the strategy of the Truman and Eisenhower administrations: 'to avoid any serious negotiation with the Soviet Union until the West could confront Moscow with German rearmament within an organized European framework, as a *fait accompli*[14] – to be sure, in defiance of the Potsdam agreements.

But most interesting of all is Rostow's reference to Iran. The facts are that there was a Russian attempt to impose by force a pro-Soviet government in Northern Azerbaijan that would grant the Soviet Union access to Iranian oil. This was rebuffed by superior Anglo-American force in 1946, at which point the more powerful imperialism obtained full rights to Iranian oil for itself, with the installation of a pro-Western government. We recall what happened when, for a brief period in the early 1950s, the only Iranian government with something of a popular base experimented with the curious idea that Iranian oil should belong to the Iranians. What is interesting, however, is the description of Northern Azerbaijan as part of 'the free world spectrum of defense'. It is pointless, by now, to comment on the debasement of the phrase 'free world'. But by what law of nature does Iran, with its resources, fall within Western dominion? The bland assumption that it does is most revealing of deep-seated attitudes toward the conduct of foreign affairs.

In addition to this growing lack of concern for truth, we find, in recent statements, a real or feigned naiveté with regard to American actions that reaches startling proportions. For example, Arthur Schlesinger has characterized our Vietnamese policies of 1954 as 'part of our general program of international goodwill'.[15] Unless intended as irony, this remark shows either a colossal cynicism or an inability, on a scale that defies comment, to comprehend elementary phenomena of contemporary history. Similarly, what is one to make of the testimony of Thomas Schelling before the House Foreign Affairs Committee, 27 January 1966, in which he discusses the two great dangers if all Asia 'goes communist'?[16] First, this would exclude 'the United States and what we call Western civilization from a large part of the world that is poor and colored and potentially hostile'. Second, 'a country like the United States probably cannot maintain self-confidence if just about the greatest thing it ever attempted, namely to create the basis for decency and prosperity and democratic government in the underdeveloped world, had to be acknowledged as a failure or as an attempt that we wouldn't try again'. It surpasses belief that a person with even minimal acquaintance with the record of American foreign policy could produce such statements.

It surpasses belief, that is, unless we look at the matter from a more historical point of view, and place such statements in the context of the hypocritical moralism of the past: for example, of Woodrow Wilson, who was going to teach the Latin Americans the art of good government, and who wrote (1902) that it is 'our peculiar duty' to teach colonial peoples 'order and self-control ... [and] ... the drill and habit of law and obedience'. Or of the missionaries of the 1840s, who described the hideous and degrading opium wars as 'the result of a great design of Providence to make the wickedness of men subserve his purposes of mercy toward China, in breaking through her wall of exclusion, and bringing the empire into more immediate contact with western and Christian nations'. Or, to approach the present, of A.A. Berle, who, in commenting on the Dominican intervention, has the impertinence to attribute the problems of the Caribbean countries to imperialism – *Russian* imperialism.[17]

As a final example of this failure of skepticism, consider the remarks of Henry Kissinger in concluding his presentation in a Harvard-Oxford television debate on American Vietnam policies. He observed, rather sadly, that what disturbs him most is that others question not our judgment but our motives – a remarkable comment on the part of one whose professional concern is political analysis, that is, analysis of the actions of governments in terms of motives that are unexpected in official propaganda and perhaps only dimly perceived by those whose acts they govern. No one would be disturbed by an analysis of the political behavior of Russians, French or Tanzanians, questioning their motives and interpreting their actions in terms of long-range interests, perhaps well concealed behind critical rhetoric. But it is an article of faith that American motives are pure and not subject to analysis (see note 2). Although it is nothing new in American intellectual history – or, for that matter, in the general history of imperialist apologia – this innocence becomes increasingly distasteful as the power it serves grows more dominant in world affairs and more capable, therefore, of the unconstrained viciousness that the mass media present to us each day. We are hardly the first power in history to combine material interests, great technological capacity and an utter disregard for the suffering and misery of the lower orders. The long tradition of naiveté and self-righteousness that disfigures our intellectual history, however, must serve as a warning to the Third World, if such a warning is needed, as to how our protestations of sincerity and benign intent are to be interpreted.

The basic assumptions of the 'New Frontiersmen' should be pondered carefully by those who look forward to the involvement of academic intellectuals in politics. For example, I have referred to Arthur Schlesinger's objections to the Bay of Pigs invasion, but the reference was imprecise. True, he felt that it was a 'terrible idea', but 'not because the notion of sponsoring an exile attempt to overthrow Castro seemed intolerable in itself'. Such a reaction would be the merest sentimentality, unthinkable to a tough-minded realist. The difficulty, rather, was that it seemed unlikely that the deception could succeed. The operation, in his view, was ill-conceived but not otherwise objectionable.[18] In a similar vein, Schlesinger quotes with approval Kennedy's 'realistic' assessment of the situation resulting from Trujillo's assassination: 'There are three possibilities in descending order of preference: a decent democratic regime, a continuation of the Trujillo regime or a Castro regime. We ought to aim at the first, but we really can't renounce the second until we are sure that we can avoid the third.'[19] The reason why the third possibility is so intolerable is explained a few pages later: 'Communist success in Latin America would deal a much harder blow to the power and influence of the United States.' Of course, we can never really be sure of avoiding the third possibility; therefore, in practice, we will always settle for the second, as we are now doing in Brazil and Argentina, for example.[20]

Or consider Walt Rostow's views on American policy in Asia.[21] The basis on which we must build this policy is that 'we are openly threatened and we feel menaced by communist China'. To prove that we are menaced is of course unnecessary, and the matter receives no attention; it is enough that we feel menaced. Our policy must be based on our national heritage and our national interests. Our national heritage is briefly outlined in the following terms: 'Throughout the nineteenth century, in good conscience Americans could devote themselves to the extension of both their principles and their power on this continent', making use of 'the somewhat elastic concept of the Monroe doctrine' and, of course, extending 'the American interest to Alaska and the mid-Pacific islands. . . . Both our insistence on unconditional surrender and the idea of post-war occupation . . . represented the formulation of American security interests in Europe and Asia'. 'So much for our heritage. As to our interests, the matter is equally simple. Fundamental is our 'profound interest that societies abroad develop and strengthen those elements in their respective cultures that elevate and protect the dignity of the individual against the state'. At the same time, we must counter the 'ideological threat', namely 'the possibility that the Chinese communists can prove to Asians by progress in China that communist methods are better and faster than democratic methods'. Nothing is said about those people in Asian cultures to whom our 'conception of the proper relation of the individual to the state' may not be the uniquely important value, people who might, for example, be concerned with preserving the 'dignity of the individual' against concentrations of foreign or domestic capital, or against semifeudal structures (such as Trujillo-type dictatorships) introduced or kept in power by American arms. All of this is flavored with allusions to 'our religious and ethical value systems' and to our 'diffuse and complex concepts' which are to the Asian mind 'so much more difficult to grasp' than Marxist dogma, and are so 'disturbing to some Asians' because of 'their very lack of dogmatism'.

Such intellectual contributions as these suggest the need for a correction to de Gaulle's remark, in his *Memoirs,* about the American 'will to power, cloaking itself in idealism'. By now, this will to power is not so much cloaked in idealism as it is drowned in fatuity. And academic intellectuals have made their unique contribution to this sorry picture.

Let us, however, return to the war in Vietnam and the response that it has aroused among American intellectuals. A striking feature of the recent debate on Southeast Asian policy has been the distinction that is commonly drawn between 'responsible criticism', on the one hand, and 'sentimental', or 'emotional', or 'hysterical' criticism, on the other. There is much to be learned from a careful study of the terms in which this distinction is drawn. The 'hysterical critics' are to be identified, apparently, by their irrational refusal to accept one fundamental political axiom, namely, that the United States has the right to extend its power and control without limit, insofar as is feasible. Responsible criticism does not challenge this assumption, but argues, rather, that we probably can't 'get away with it' at this particular time and place.

A distinction of this sort seems to be what Irving Kristol has in mind, for example, in his analysis of the protest over Vietnam policy, in *Encounter,* August 1965. He contrasts the responsible critics, such as Walter Lippmann, the *New York Times* and Senator Fulbright, with the 'teach-in movement'. 'Unlike the university protesters', he maintains,

> Mr. Lippmann engages in no presumptuous suppositions as to 'what the Vietnamese people really want' — he obviously doesn't much

care – or in legalistic exegesis as to whether, or to what extent, there is 'aggression' or 'revolution' in South Vietnam. His is a *realpolitik* point of view, and he will apparently even contemplate the possibility of a *nuclear* war against China in extreme circumstances.

This is commendable, and contrasts favorably, for Kristol, with the talk of the 'unreasonable, ideological types' in the teach-in movement, who often seem to be motivated by such absurdities as 'simple, virtuous "anti-imperialism" ', who deliver 'harangues on the "power structure" ', and who even sometimes stoop so low as to read 'articles and reports from the foreign press on the American presence in Vietnam'. Furthermore, these nasty types are often psychologists, mathematicians, chemists or philosophers (just as, incidentally, those most vocal in protest in the Soviet Union are generally physicists, literary intellectuals and others remote from the exercise of power), rather than people with Washington contacts, who, of course, realize that 'had they a new, good idea about Vietnam, they would get a prompt and respectful hearing' in Washington.

I am not interested here in whether Kristol's characterization of protest and dissent is accurate, but rather in the assumptions that it expresses with respect to such questions as these: Is the purity of American motives a matter that is beyond discussion, or that is irrelevant to discussion? Should decisions be left to 'experts' with Washington contacts – that is, even if we assume that they command the necessary knowledge and principles to make the 'best' decision, will they invariably do so? And, a logically prior question, is 'expertise' applicable – that is, is there a body of theory and of relevant information, not in the public domain, that can be applied to the analysis of foreign policy or that demonstrates the correctness of present actions in some way that the psychologists, mathematicians, chemists and philosophers are incapable of comprehending? Although Kristol does not examine these questions directly, his attitudes presuppose answers, answers which are wrong in all cases. American aggressiveness, however it may be masked in pious rhetoric, is a dominant force in world affairs and must be analyzed in terms of its causes and motives. There is no body of theory or significant body of relative information, beyond the comprehension of the layman, which makes policy immune from criticism. To the extent that 'expert knowledge' is applied to world affairs, it is surely appropriate – for a person of any integrity, quite necessary – to question its quality and the goals that it serves. These facts seem too obvious to require extended discussion.

A corrective to Kristol's curious belief in the administration's openness to new thinking about Vietnam is provided by McGeorge Bundy.[22] As Bundy correctly observes, 'on the main stage ... the argument on Vietnam turns on tactics, not fundamentals', although, he adds, 'there are wild men in the wings'. On stage center are, of course, the President (who in his recent trip to Asia had just 'magisterially reaffirmed' our interest 'in the progress of the people across the Pacific') and his advisers, who deserve 'the understanding support of those who want restraint'. It is these men who deserve the credit for the fact that 'the bombing of the North has been the most accurate and the most restrained in modern warfare' — a solicitude which will be appreciated by the inhabitants, or former inhabitants, of Nam Dinh and Phu Ly and Vinh. It is these men, too, who deserve the credit for what was reported by Malcolm Browne as long ago as May 1965: 'In the South, huge sectors of the nation have been declared "free bombing zones", in which anything that moves is a legitimate target. Tens of thousands of tons of bombs, rockets, napalm and cannon fire are poured into these vast areas each week. If only by the laws of chance, bloodshed is believed to be heavy in these raids.'

Fortunately for the developing countries, Bundy assures us, 'American democracy has no enduring taste for imperialism', and 'taken as a whole, the stock of American experience, understanding, sympathy and simple knowledge is now much the most impressive in the world'. It is true that 'four-fifths of all the foreign investing in the world is now done by Americans' and that 'the most admired plans and policies ... are no better than their demonstrable relation to the American interest' — just as it is true, so we read in the same issue of *Foreign Affairs*, that the plans for armed action against Cuba were put into motion a few weeks after Mikoyan visited Havana, 'invading what had so long been an almost exclusively American sphere of influence'. Unfortunately, such facts as these are often taken by unsophisticated Asian intellectuals as indicating 'a taste for imperialism'. For example, a number of Indians have expressed their 'near exasperation' at the fact that 'we have done everything we can to attract foreign capital for fertilizer plants, but the American and the other Western private companies know we are over a barrel, so they demand stringent terms which we just cannot meet',[23] while 'Washington ... doggedly insists that deals be made in the private sector with private enterprise'.[24] But this reaction, no doubt, simply reveals once again how the Asian mind fails to comprehend the 'diffuse and complex concepts' of Western thought.

It may be useful to study carefully the 'new, good ideas about Vietnam' that are receiving a 'prompt and respectful hearing' in Washington these days. The United States Government Printing Office is an endless source of insight into the moral and intellectual level of this expert advice. In its publication one can read, for example, the testimony of Professor David N. Rowe, Director of Graduate Studies in International Relations at Yale University, before the House Committee on Foreign Affairs (see note 16). Professor Rowe proposes that the United States buy all surplus Canadian and Australian wheat, so that there will be mass starvation in China. These are his words: 'Mind you, I am not talking about this as a weapon against the Chinese people. It will be. But that is only incidental. The weapon will be a weapon against the Government; because the internal stability of the country cannot be sustained by an unfriendly Government in the face of general starvation.' Professor Rowe will have none of the sentimental moralism that might lead one to compare this suggestion with, say, the *Ostpolitik* of Hitler's Germany.[25] Nor does he fear the impact of such policies on other Asian nations, for example Japan. He assures us, from his 'very long acquaintance with Japanese questions', that 'the Japanese above all are people who respect power and determination'. Hence 'they will not be so much alarmed by American policy in Vietnam that takes off from a position of power and intends to seek a solution based upon the imposition of our power upon local people that we are in opposition to'. What would disturb the Japanese is 'a policy of indecision, a policy of refusal to face up to the problems [in China and Vietnam] and to meet our responsibilities there in a positive way', such as the way just cited. A conviction that we were 'unwilling to use the power that they know we have' might 'alarm the Japanese people very intensely and shake the degree of their friendly relations with us'. In fact, a full use of American power would be particularly reassuring to the Japanese, because they have a demonstration 'of the tremendous power in action of the United States . . . because they have felt our power directly'. This is surely a prime example of the healthy '*realpolitik* point of view' that Irving Kristol so much admires.

But, one may ask, why restrict ourselves to such indirect means as mass starvation? Why not bombing? No doubt this message is implicit in the remarks to the same committee of the Reverend R. J. de Jaegher, Regent of the Institute of Far Eastern Studies, Seton Hall University, who explains that like all people who have lived under communism, the North Vietnamese 'would be perfectly happy to be bombed to be free'.

Of course, there must be those who support the communists. But this is really a matter of small concern, as the Honorable Walter Robertson, Assistant Secretary of State for Far Eastern Affairs from 1953 to 1959, points out in his testimony before the same committee. He assures us that 'The Peiping regime . . . represents something less than 3 per cent of the population' (p. 402).

Consider, then, how fortunate the Chinese communist leaders are, compared to the leaders of the Vietcong, who, according to Arthur Goldberg, represent about 'one half of one per cent of the population of South Vietnam', that is, about one half the number of new Southern recruits for the Vietcong during 1965, if we can credit Pentagon statistics.[26]

In the face of such experts as these, the scientists and philosophers of whom Kristol speaks would clearly do well to continue to draw their circles in the sand.

Having settled the issue of the political irrelevance of the protest movement. Kristol turns to the question of what motivates it — more generally, what has made students and junior faculty 'go left', as he sees it, amid general prosperity and under liberal, Welfare State administrations. This, he notes, 'is a riddle to which no sociologist has as yet come up with an answer'. Since these young people are well-off, have good futures, etc., their protest must be irrational. It must be the result of boredom, of too much security, or something of this sort.

Other possibilities come to mind. It might be, for example, that as honest men the students and junior faculty are attempting to find out the truth for themselves rather than ceding the responsibility to 'experts' or to government; and it might be that they react with indignation to what they discover. These possibilities Kristol does not reject. They are simply unthinkable, unworthy of consideration. More accurately, these possibilities are inexpressible, the categories in which they are formulated (honesty, indignation) simply do not exist for the tough-minded social scientist.

In this implicit disparagement of traditional intellectual values, Kristol reflects attitudes that are fairly widespread in academic circles. I do not doubt that these attitudes are in part a consequence of the desperate attempt of the social and behavioral sciences to imitate the surface features of sciences that really have significant intellectual content. But they have other sources as well. Anyone can be a moral individual, concerned with human rights and problems; but only a college professor, a trained expert, can solve technical problems by 'sophisticated' methods. Ergo, it is only problems of the latter sort that are important or real. Responsible, nonideological experts will give advice on tactical questions; irresponsible 'ideological types' will 'harangue' about principle and trouble themselves over moral issues and human rights, or over the traditional problems of man and society, concerning which 'social and behavioral science' have nothing to offer beyond trivialities. Obviously, these emotional, ideological types are irrational, since, being well-off and having power in their grasp, they shouldn't worry about such matters.

At times this pseudoscientific posing reaches levels that are almost pathological. Consider the phenomenon of Herman Kahn, for example. Kahn has been both denounced as immoral and lauded for his courage. By people who should know better, his *On Thermonuclear War* has been described 'without qualification . . . [as] . . . one of the great works of our time' (Stuart Hughes). The fact of the matter is that this is surely one of the emptiest works of our time, as can be seen by applying to it the intellectual standards of any existing discipline, by tracing some of its 'well-documented conclusions' to the 'objective studies' from which they derive, and by following the line of argument, where detectable. Kahn proposes no theories, no explanations, no factual assumptions that can be tested against their consequences, as do the sciences he is attempting to mimic. He simply suggests a terminology and provides a façade of rationality. When particular policy conclusions are drawn, they are supported only by *ex cathedra* remarks for which no support is even suggested (e.g., 'The civil defense line probably should be drawn somewhere below $5 billion annually' to keep from provoking the Russians – why not $50 billion, or $5.00?). What is more, Kahn is quite aware of this vacuity; in his more judicious moments he claims only that 'there is no reason to believe that relatively sophisticated models are more likely to be misleading than the simpler models and analogies frequently used as an aid to judgment'. For those whose humor tends towards the macabre, it is easy to play the game of 'strategic thinking' à la Kahn, and to prove what one wishes. For example, one of Kahn's basic assumptions is that 'an all-out surprise attack in which all resources are devoted to countervalue targets would be so irrational that, barring an incredible lack of sophistication or actual insanity among Soviet decision makers, such an attack is highly unlikely'. A simple argument proves the opposite. Premise

1: American decision makers think along the lines outlined by Herman Kahn. Premise 2: Kahn thinks it would be better for everyone to be red than for everyone to be dead. Premise 3: If the Americans were to respond to an all-out countervalue attack, then everyone would be dead. Conclusion: The Americans will not respond to an all-out countervalue attack, and therefore it should be launched without delay. Of course, one can carry the argument a step further. Fact: The Russians, have not carried out an all-out countervalue attack. It follows that they are not rational. If they are not rational, there is no point in 'strategic thinking'. Therefore . . .

Of course this is all nonsense, but nonsense that differs from Kahn's only in the respect that the argument is of slightly greater complexity than anything to be discovered in his work. What is remarkable is that serious people actually pay attention to these absurdities, no doubt because of the façade of toughmindedness and pseudoscience.

It is a curious and depressing fact that the 'antiwar movement' falls prey all too often to similar confusions. In the fall of 1965, for example, there was an International Conference on Alternative Perspectives on Vietnam, which circulated a pamphlet to potential participants stating its assumptions. The plan was to set up study groups in which three 'types of intellectual tradition' will be represented: (1) area specialists; (2) 'social theory, with special emphasis on theories of the international system, of social change and development, of conflict and conflict resolution, or of revolution'; (3) 'the analysis of public policy in terms of basic human values, rooted in various theological, philosophical and humanist traditions'. The second intellectual tradition will provide 'general propositions, derived from social theory and tested against historical, comparative or experimental data'; the third 'will provide the framework out of which fundamental value questions can be raised and in terms of which the moral implications of societal actions can be analyzed'. The hope was that 'by approaching the questions [of Vietnam policy] from the moral perspectives of all great religions and philosophical systems, we may find solutions that are more consistent with fundamental human values than current American policy in Vietnam has turned out to be'.

In short, the experts on values (i.e., spokesmen for the great religions and philosophical systems) will provide fundamental insights on moral perspectives, and the experts on social theory will provide general empirically validated propositions and 'general models of conflict'. From this interplay, new policies will emerge, presumably from application of the canons of scientific method. The only debatable issue, it seems to me, is whether it is more ridiculous to turn to experts in social theory for general well-confirmed propositions, or to the specialists in the great religions and philosophical systems for insights into fundamental human values.

There is much more that can be said about this topic, but without continuing, I would simply like to emphasize that, as is no doubt obvious, the cult of the expert is both self-serving, for those who propound it, and fraudulent. Obviously, one must learn from social and behavioral science whatever one can; obviously, these fields should be pursued in as serious a way as is possible. But it will be quite unfortunate, and highly dangerous, if they are not accepted and judged on their merits and according to their actual, not pretended, accomplishments. In particular, if there is a body of theory, well tested and verified, that applies to the conduct of foreign affairs or the resolution of domestic or international conflict, its existence has been kept a well-guarded secret. In the case of Vietnam, if those who feel themselves to be experts have access to principles or information that would justify what the American government is doing in that unfortunate country, they have been singularly ineffective in making this fact known. To anyone who has any familiarity with the social behavioral sciences (or the 'policy sciences'), the claim that there are certain considerations and principles too deep for the outsider to comprehend is simply an absurdity, unworthy of comment.

When we consider the responsibility of intellectuals, our basic concern must be their role in the creation and analysis of ideology. And, in fact, Kristol's contrast between the unreasonable ideological types and the responsible experts is formulated in terms that immediately bring to mind Daniel Bell's interesting and influential essay on the 'end of ideology',[27] an essay which is as important for what it leaves unsaid as for its actual content. Bell presents and discusses the Marxist analysis of ideology as a mask for class interest, in particular, quoting Marx's well-known description of the belief of the bourgeoisie 'that the *special* conditions of its emancipation are the *general* conditions through which alone modern society can be saved and the class struggle avoided'. He then argues that the age of ideology is ended, supplanted, at least in the West, by a general agreement that each issue must be settled on its own individual terms, within the framework of a welfare state in which, presumably, experts in the conduct of public affairs will have a prominent role. Bell is quite careful, however, to characterize the precise sense of 'ideology' in which 'ideologies are exhausted'. He is referring only to ideology as 'the conversion of ideas into social levers', to ideology as 'a set of beliefs, infused with passion, . . . [which] . . . seeks to transform the whole of a way of life'. The crucial words are 'transform' and 'convert into social levers'. Intellectuals in the West, he argues, have lost interest in converting ideas into social levers for the radical transformation of society. Now that we have achieved the pluralistic society of the Welfare State, they see no further need for a radical transformation of society; we may tinker with our way of life here and there, but it would be wrong to try to modify it in any significant way. With this consensus of intellectuals, ideology is dead.

There are several striking facts about Bell's essay. First, he does not point out the extent to which this consensus of the intellectuals is self-serving. He does not relate his observation that, by and large, intellectuals have lost interest in 'transforming the whole of a way of life' to the fact that they play an increasingly prominent role in running the Welfare State; he does not relate their general satisfaction with the Welfare State to the fact that, as he observes elsewhere, 'America has become an affluent society, offering place . . . and prestige . . . to the onetime radicals'. Secondly, he offers no serious argument to show that intellectuals are somehow 'right' or 'objectively justified' in reaching the consensus to which he alludes, with its rejection of the notion that society should be transformed. Indeed, although Bell is fairly sharp about the empty rhetoric of the 'New Left', he seems to have a quite utopian faith that technical experts will be able to come to grips with the few problems that still remain; for example, the fact that labor is treated as a commodity, and the problems of 'alienation'.

It seems fairly obvious that the classical problems are very much with us; one might plausibly argue that they have even been enhanced in severity and scale. For example, the classical paradox of poverty in the midst of plenty is now an ever increasing problem on an international scale. Whereas one might conceive, at least in principle, of a solution within national boundaries, a sensible idea as to how to transform international society in such a way as to cope with the vast and perhaps increasing human misery is hardly likely to develop within the framework of the intellectual consensus that Bell describes.

Thus it would seem natural to describe the consensus of Bell's intellectuals in somewhat different terms than his. Using the terminology of the first part of his essay, we might say that the Welfare State technician finds justification for his special and prominent social status in his 'science', specifically, in the claim that social science can support a technology of social tinkering on a domestic or international scale. He then takes a further step, proceeding, in a familiar way, to claim universal validity for what is in fact a class interest: he argues that the special conditions on which his claims to power and authority are based are, in fact, the general conditions through which alone modern society can be saved; that social tinkering within a Welfare State framework must replace the commitment to the 'total ideologies' of the past, ideologies which were concerned with a transformation of society. Having found his position of power, having achieved security and affluence, he has no further need for ideologies that look to radical change. The scholar-expert replaces the 'free-floating intellectual' who 'felt that the wrong values were being honored, and rejected the society', and who has now lost his political role (now, that is, that the right values are being honored).

Conceivably, it is correct that the technical experts who will (or hope to) manage the 'postindustrial society' will be able to cope with the classical problems without a radical transformation of society. Just so, it is conceivably true that the bourgeoisie was right in regarding the special conditions of its emancipation as the general conditions through which alone modern society would be saved. In either case, an argument is in order, and skepticism is justified where none appears.

Within the same framework of general utopianism, Bell goes on to pose the issue between Welfare State scholar-experts and Third World ideologists in a rather curious way. He points out, quite correctly, that there is no issue of communism, the content of that doctrine having been 'long forgotten by friends and foes alike'. Rather, he says, 'the question is an older one: whether new societies can grow by building democratic institutions and allowing people to make choices — and sacrifices — voluntarily, or whether the new elites, heady with power, will impose totalitarian means to transform their countries'. The question is an interesting one; it is odd, however, to see it referred to as 'an older one'. Surely he cannot be suggesting that the West chose the democratic way — for example, that in England during the industrial revolution, the farmers voluntarily made the choice of leaving the land, giving up cottage industry, becoming an industrial proletariat, and voluntarily decided, within the framework of the existing democratic institutions, to make the sacrifices that are graphically described in the classic literature on nineteenth-century industrial society. One may debate the question whether authoritarian control is necessary to permit capital accumulation in the underdeveloped world, but the Western model of development is hardly one that we can point to with any pride. It is perhaps not surprising to find a Walt Rostow referring to 'the more humane processes [of industrialization] that Western values would suggest.[28] Those who have a serious concern for the problems that face backward countries and for the role that advanced industrial societies might, in principle, play in development and modernization, must use somewhat more care in interpreting the significance of the Western experience.

Returning to the quite appropriate question, whether 'new societies can grow by building democratic institutions' or only by totalitarian means, I think that honesty requires us to recognize that this question must be directed more to American intellectuals than to Third World ideologists. The backward countries have incredible, perhaps insurmountable problems, and few available options; the United States has a wide range of options, and has the economic and technological resources, though evidently neither the intellectual nor moral resources, to confront at least some of these problems. It is easy for an American intellectual to deliver homilies on the virtues of freedom and liberty, but if he is really concerned about, say, Chinese totalitarianism or the burdens imposed on the Chinese peasantry in forced industrialization, then he should face a task that is infinitely more significant and challenging – the task of creating, in the United States, the intellectual and moral climate, as well as the social and economic conditions, that would permit this country to participate in modernization and development in a way commensurate with its material wealth and technical capacity. Massive capital gifts to Cuba and China might not succeed in alleviating the authoritarianism and terror that tend to accompany early stages of capital accumulation, but they are far more likely to have this effect than lectures on democratic values. It is possible that even without 'capitalist encirclement' in its varying manifestations, the truly democratic elements in revolutionary movements – in some instances, soviets and collectives, for example – might be undermined by an 'elite' of bureaucrats and technical intelligentsia; but it is a near certainty that the fact of capitalist encirclement, which all revolutionary movements now have to face, will guarantee this result. The lesson, for those who are concerned to strengthen the democratic, spontaneous and popular elements in developing societies, is quite clear. Lectures on the two-party system, or even the really substantial democratic values that have been in part realized in Western society, are a monstrous irrelevance in the face of the effort that is required to raise the level of culture in Western society to the point where it can provide a 'social lever' for both economic development and the development of true democratic institutions in the Third World — and for that matter, at home as well.

A good case can be made for the conclusion that there is indeed something of a consensus among intellectuals who have already achieved power and affluence, or who sense that they can achieve them by 'accepting society' as it is and promoting the values that are 'being honored' in this society. And it is also true that this consensus is most noticeable among the scholar-experts who are replacing the free-floating intellectuals of the past. In the university, these scholar-experts construct a 'value-free technology' for the solution of technical problems that arise in contemporary society,[29] taking a 'responsible stance' towards these problems, in the sense noted earlier. This consensus among the responsible scholar-experts is the domestic analogue to that proposed, in the international arena, by those who justify the application of American power in Asia, whatever the human cost, on the grounds that it is necessary to contain the 'expansion of China' (an 'expansion' which is, to be sure, hypothetical for the time being)[30] — to translate from State Department Newspeak, on the grounds that it is essential to reverse the Asian nationalist revolutions, or at least to prevent them from spreading. The analogy becomes clear when we look carefully at the ways in which this proposal is formulated. With his usual lucidity, Churchill outlined the general position in a remark to his colleague of the moment, Joseph Stalin, at Teheran in 1943:

> ... the government of the world must be entrusted to satisfied nations, who wished nothing more for themselves than what they had. If the world-government were in the hands of hungry nations, there would always be danger. But none of us had any reason to seek for anything more. The peace would be kept by peoples who lived in their own way and were not ambitious. Our power placed us above the rest. We were like rich men dwelling at peace within their habitations.[31]

For a translation of Churchill's biblical rhetoric into the jargon of contemporary social science, one may turn to the testimony of Charles Wolf, Senior Economist of the Rand Corporation, at the congressional committee hearing cited earlier:

> I am dubious that China's fears of encirclement are going to be abated, eased, relaxed in the long-term future. But I would hope that

what we do in Southeast Asia would help to develop within the
Chinese body politic more of a realism and willingness to live with
this fear than to indulge it by support for liberation movements,
which admittedly depend on a great deal more than external
support ... the operational question for American foreign-policy is
not whether that fear can be eliminated or substantially alleviated,
but whether China can be faced with a structure of incentives, of
penalties and rewards, of inducements that will make it willing to live
with this fear.[32]

The point is further clarified by Thomas Schelling: 'There is growing
experience which the Chinese can profit from, that although the United
States may be interested in encircling them, may be interested in
defending nearby areas from them, it is, nevertheless, prepared to behave
peaceably if they are.'[33]

In short, we are prepared to live peaceably within our — to be sure,
rather extensive — habitations. And quite naturally, we are offended by
the undignified noises from the servants' quarters. If, let us say, a
peasant-based revolutionary movement tries to achieve independence from
foreign domination or to overthrow semifeudal structures supported by
foreign powers, or if the Chinese irrationally refuse to respond properly to
the schedule of reinforcement that we have prepared for them, if they
object to being encircled by the benign and peace-loving 'rich men' who
control the territories on their borders as a natural right, then, evidently,
we must respond to this belligerence with appropriate force.

It is this mentality that explains the frankness with which the United
States government and its academic apologists defend the American refusal
to permit a political settlement in Vietnam at a local level, a settlement
based on the actual distribution of political forces. Even government
experts freely admit that the NLF is the only 'truly mass-based political
party in South Vietnam',[34] that the NLF had 'made a conscious and
massive effort to extend political participation, even if it was manipulated,
on the local level so as to involve the people in a self-contained,
self-supporting revolution' (p. 374); and that this effort had been so
successful that no political groups, 'with the possible exception of the
Buddhists, thought themselves equal in size and power to risk entering into
a coalition, fearing that if they did the whale would swallow the minnow'
(p.362). Moreover, they concede that until the introduction of overwhelming American force, the NLF had insisted that the struggle 'should
be fought out at the political level and that the use of massed military

might was in itself illegitimate. . . . The battleground was to be the minds and loyalties of the rural Vietnamese, the weapons were to be ideas' (pp. 91-2; cf. also pp. 93, 99-108, 155f.): and correspondingly, that until mid 1964, aid from Hanoi 'was largely confined to two areas – doctrinal know-how and leadership personnel' (p. 321). Captured NLF documents contrast the enemy's 'military superiority' with their own 'political superiority' (p. 106), thus fully confirming the analysis of American military spokesmen who define our problem as how, 'with considerable armed force but little political power, [to] contain an adversary who has enormous political force but only modest military power'.[35]

Similarly, the most striking outcome of both the Honolulu conference in February and the Manila conference in October was the frank admission by high officials of the Saigon government that 'they could not survive a "peaceful settlement" that left the Vietcong *political* structure in place even if the Vietcong guerilla units were disbanded', that 'they are not able to compete *politically* with the Vietnamese communists'.[36] Thus, Mohr continues, the Vietnamese demand a 'pacification program' which will have as 'its core . . . the destruction of the clandestine Vietcong political structure and the creation of an iron-like system of government political control over the population'. And from Manila, the same correspondent, on 23 October, quotes a high South Vietnamese official as saying: 'Frankly, we are not strong enough now to compete with the communists on a purely political basis. They are organized and disciplined. The non-communist nationalists are not – we do not have any large, well-organized political parties and we do not yet have unity. We cannot leave the Vietcong in existence.' Officials in Washington understand the situation very well. Thus Secretary Rusk has pointed out that 'if the Vietcong come to the conference table as full partners they will, in a sense, have been victorious in the very aims that South Vietnam and the United States are pledged to prevent' (28 January 1966). Similarly, Max Frankel reported from Washington:

Compromise has had no appeal here because the Administration concluded long ago that the non-communist forces of South Vietnam could not long survive in a Saigon coalition with communists. It is for that reason – and not because of an excessively rigid sense of protocol – that Washington has steadfastly refused to deal with the Vietcong or recognize them as an independent political force.[37]

In short, we will – magnanimously – permit Vietcong representatives to attend negotiations only if they will agree to identify themselves as agents of a foreign power and thus forfeit the right to participate in a coalition government, a right which they have now been demanding for a half-dozen years. We know well that in any representative coalition, our chosen delegates could not last a day without the support of American arms. Therefore, we must increase American force and resist meaningful negotiations, until the day when a client government can exert both military and political control over its own population — a day which may never dawn, for as William Bundy has pointed out, we could never be sure of the security of a Southeast Asia 'from which the Western presence was effectively withdrawn'. Thus if we were to 'negotiate in the direction of solutions that are put under the label of neutralization', this would amount to capitulation to the communists.[38] According to this reasoning, then, South Vietnam must remain, permanently, an American military base.

All of this is of course reasonable, so long as we accept the fundamental political axiom that the United States, with its traditional concern for the rights of the weak and downtrodden, and with its unique insight into the proper mode of development for backward countries, must have the courage and the persistence to impose its will by force until such time as other nations are prepared to accept these truths — or simply to abandon hope.

If it is the responsibility of the intellectual to insist upon the truth, it is also his duty to see events in their historical perspective. Thus one must applaud the insistence of the Secretary of State on the importance of historical analogies, the Munich analogy, for example. As Munich showed, a powerful and aggressive nation with a fanatic belief in its manifest destiny will regard each victory, each extension of its power and authority, as a prelude to the next step. The matter was very well put by Adlai Stevenson, when he spoke of 'the old, old route whereby expansive powers push at more and more doors, believing they will open, until, at the ultimate door, resistance is unavoidable and major war breaks out'. Herein lies the danger of appeasement, as the Chinese tirelessly point out to the Soviet Union, which they claim is playing Chamberlain to our Hitler in Vietnam. Of course, the aggressiveness of liberal imperialism is not that of Nazi Germany, though the distinction may seem rather academic to a Vietnamese peasant who is being gassed or incinerated. We do not want to occupy Asia; we merely wish, to return to Mr. Wolf, 'to help the Asian countries progress toward economic modernization, as relatively "open" and stable societies, to which our access, as a country and as individual citizens, is free and comfortable'.[39] The formulation is appropriate. Recent history shows that it makes little difference to us what form of government a country has as long as it remains an 'open society', in our peculiar sense of this term – a society, that is, that remains open to American economic penetration or political control. If it is necessary to approach genocide in Vietnam to achieve this objective, then this is the price we must pay in defense of freedom and the rights of man.

It is, no doubt, superfluous to discuss at length the ways in which we assist other countries to progress towards open societies 'to which our access is free and comfortable'. One enlightening example is discussed in the recent congressional hearings from which I have now quoted several times, in the testimony of Willem Holst and Robert Meagher, representing the Standing Committee on India of the Business Council for International Understanding.[40] As Mr. Meagher points out: 'If it was possible, India would probably prefer to import technicians and know-how rather than foreign corporations. Such is not possible; therefore India accepts foreign capital as a necessary evil.' Of course, 'the question of private capital investment in India . . . would be no more than a theoretical exercise' had the groundwork for such investment not been laid by foreign aid, and were it not that 'necessity has forced a modification in India's approach to private foreign capital'. But now, 'India's attitude toward private foreign investment is undergoing a substantial change. From a position of resentment and ambivalence, it is evolving toward an acceptance of its necessity. As the necessity becomes more and more evident, the ambivalence will probably be replaced by a more accommodating attitude.' Mr. Holst contributes what is 'perhaps a typical case history', namely, 'the plan under which it was proposed that the Indian Government in partnership with a United States private consortium was to have increased fertilizer production by a million tons per year, which is just double presently installed capacity in all of India. The unfortunate demise of this ambitious plan may be attributed in large part to the failure of both Government and business to find a workable and mutually acceptable solution within the framework of the well-publicized 10 business incentives.' The difficulty here was in connexion with the percentage of equity ownership. Obviously, 'fertilizers are desperately needed in India'. Equally obviously, the consortium 'insisted that to get the proper kind of control majority ownership was in fact needed'. But 'the Indian Government officially insisted that they shall have majority ownership', and 'in something so complex it was felt that it would be a self-defeating thing'.

Fortunately, this particular story has a happy ending. The remarks just quoted were made in February 1966, and within a few weeks, the Indian government had seen the light, as we read in a series of reports in the *New York Times*. The criticism, inside India, that 'the American Government and the World Bank would like to arrogate to themselves the right to lay down the framework in which our economy must function', was stilled (24 April); and the Indian government accepted the conditions for resumed economic aid, namely, 'that India provide easier terms for foreign private investment in fertilizer plants' and that the American investors 'have substantial management rights' (14 May). The development is summarized in a dispatch datelined 28 April, from New Delhi, in these terms:

> There are signs of change. The Government has granted easy terms to private foreign investors in the fertilizer industry, is thinking about decontrolling several more industries and is ready to liberalize import policy if it gets sufficient foreign aid. . . . Much of what is happening now is a result of steady pressure from the United States and the International Bank for Reconstruction and Development, which for the last year have been urging a substantial freeing of the Indian economy and a greater scope for private enterprise. The United States pressure, in particular, has been highly effective here because the United States provides by far the largest part of the foreign exchange needed to finance India's development and keep the wheels of industry turning. Call them 'strings', call them 'conditions' or whatever one likes, India has little choice now but to agree to many of the terms that the United States, through the World Bank, is putting on its aid. For India simply has nowhere else to turn.

The heading of the article refers to this development as India's 'drift from socialism to pragmatism'.

Even this was not enough, however. Thus we read a few months later, in the *Christian Science Monitor* (5 December), that American entrepreneurs insist 'on importing all equipment and machinery when India has a tested capacity to meet some of their requirements. They have insisted on importing liquid ammonia, a basic raw material, rather than using indigenous naphtha which is abundantly available. They have laid down restrictions about pricing, distribution, profits, and management control.' The Indian reaction I have already cited (see p. 330).

In such ways as these, we help India develop towards an open society, one which, in Walt Rostow's words, has a proper understanding of 'the core of the American ideology', namely, 'the sanctity of the individual in relation to the state'. And in this way, too, we refute the simple-minded view of those Asians who, to continue with Rostow's phrasing, 'believe or half-believe that the West has been driven to create and then to cling to its imperial holdings by the inevitable workings of capitalist economics'.[41]

In fact, a major postwar scandal is developing in India as the United States, cynically capitalizing on India's current torture, applies its economic power to implement India's 'drift from socialism to pragmatism'.

In pursuing the aim of helping other countries to progress towards open societies, with no thought of territorial aggrandizement, we are breaking no new ground. Hans Morgenthau has aptly described our traditional policy towards China as one of favoring 'what you might call freedom of competition with regard to the exploitation of China'.[42] In fact, few imperialist powers have had explicit territorial ambitions. Thus in 1784, the British Parliament announced that: 'to pursue schemes of conquest and extension of dominion in India are measures repugnant to the wish, honor, and policy of this nation'. Shortly after, the conquest of India was in full swing. A century later, Britain announced its intentions in Egypt under the slogan 'intervention, reform, withdrawal'. It is unnecessary to comment on which parts of this promise were fulfilled, within the next half-century. In 1936, on the eve of hostilities in North China, the Japanese stated their Basic Principles of National Policy. These included the use of moderate and peaceful means to extend her strength, to promote social and economic development, to eradicate the menace of communism, to correct the aggressive policies of the great powers, and to secure her position as the stabilizing power in East Asia. Even in 1937, the Japanese government had 'no territorial designs upon China'. In short, we follow a well-trodden path.

It is useful to remember, incidentally, that the United States was apparently quite willing, as late as 1939, to negotiate a commercial treaty with Japan and arrive at a *modus vivendi* if Japan would 'change her attitude and practice towards our rights and interests in China', as Secretary Hull put it. The bombing of Chungking and the rape of Nanking were rather unpleasant, it is true, but what was really important was our rights and interests in China, as the responsible, unhysterical men of the day saw quite clearly. It was the closing of the open door by Japan that led inevitably to the Pacific war, just as it is the closing of the open door by 'communist' China itself that may very well lead to the next, and no doubt last, Pacific war.

Quite often, the statements of sincere and devoted technical experts give surprising insight into the intellectual attitudes that lie in the background of the latest savagery. Consider, for example, the following comment by economist Richard Lindholm, in 1959, expressing his frustration over the failure of economic development in 'free Vietnam':

> the use of American aid is determined by how the Vietnamese use their incomes and their savings. The fact that a large portion of the Vietnamese imports financed with American aid are either consumer goods or raw materials used rather directly to meet consumer demands is an indication that the Vietnamese people desire these goods, for they have shown their desire by their willingness to use their piasters to purchase them.[43]

In short, the Vietnamese *people* desire Buicks and air conditioners, rather than sugar-refining equipment or road-building machinery, as they have shown by their behavior in a free market. And however much we may deplore their free choice, we must allow the people to have their way. Of course, there are also those two-legged beasts of burden that one stumbles on in the countryside, but as any graduate student of political science can explain, they are not part of a responsible modernizing elite, and therefore have only a superficial biological resemblance to the human race.

In no small measure, it is attitudes like this that lie behind the butchery in Vietnam, and we had better face up to them with candor, or we will find our government leading us towards a 'final solution' in Vietnam, and in the many Vietnams that inevitably lie ahead.

Let me finally return to Macdonald and the responsibility of intellectuals. Macdonald quotes an interview with a death-camp paymaster who bursts into tears when told that the Russians would hang him. 'Why should they? What have I done?'' he asked. Macdonald concludes: 'Only those who are willing to resist authority themselves when it conflicts too intolerably with their personal moral code, only they have the right to condemn the death-camp paymaster.' The question 'What have I done?' is one that we may well ask ourselves, as we read, each day, of fresh atrocities in Vietnam — as we create, or mouth, or tolerate the deceptions that will be used to justify the next defense of freedom.

NOTES

1. This is a revised version of the talk given at Harvard and published in *Mosaic*, June 1966. It appeared in substantially this form in the *New York Review of Books*, 23 February 1967.

2. Such a research project has now been undertaken and published as a 'Citizens' White Paper': F. Schurmann, P.D. Scott, R. Zelnik, *The Politics of Escalation in Vietnam* (New York, Fawcett World Library, and Boston, Beacon Press, 1966). For further evidence of American rejection of UN initiatives for diplomatic settlement, just prior to the major escalation of February 1965, see Mario Rossi, 'The US Rebuff to U Thant', *New York Review of Books*, 17 November 1966. See also Theodore Draper, 'How Not To Negotiate', *New York Review of Books*, 4 May 1967. There is further documentary evidence of NLF attempts to establish a coalition government and to neutralize the area, all rejected by the United States and its Saigon ally, in Douglas Pike, *Viet Cong* (Cambridge, The MIT Press, 1966). In reading material of this latter sort one must be especially careful to distinguish between the evidence presented and the 'conclusions' that are asserted, for reasons noted briefly below (see note 34).

   It is interesting to see the first, somewhat oblique, published reactions to *The Politics of Escalation*, by those who defend our right to conquer South Vietnam and institute a government of our choice. For example, Robert Scalapino (*New York Times Magazine*, 11 December 1966) argues that the thesis of the book implies that our leaders are 'diabolical'. Since no right-thinking person can believe this, the thesis is refuted. To assume otherwise would betray 'irresponsibility', in a unique sense of this term – a sense that gives an ironic twist to the title of this chapter. He goes on to point out the alleged central weakness in the argument of the book, namely, the failure to perceive that a serious attempt on our part to pursue the possibilities for a diplomatic settlement would have been interpreted by our adversaries as a sign of weakness.

3. *New York Times*, 14 October 1965.

4. *New York Times*, 6 February 1966.

5. *Boston Globe*, 19 November 1965.

6. At other times, Schlesinger does indeed display admirable scholarly caution. For example, in his Introduction to *The Politics of Escalation* he admits that there may have been 'flickers of interest in negotiations' on the part of Hanoi. As to the administration's lies

about negotiations and its repeated actions undercutting tentative initiatives towards negotiations, he comments only that the authors may have underestimated military necessity and that future historians may prove them wrong. This caution and detachment must be compared with Schlesinger's attitude toward renewed study of the origins of the Cold War: in a letter to the *New York Review of Books,* 20 October 1966, he remarks that it is time to 'blow the whistle' on revisionist attempts to show that the cold war may have been the consequence of something more than mere communist belligerence. We are to believe, then, that the relatively straightforward matter of the origins of the cold war is settled beyond discussion, whereas the much more complex issue of why the United States shies away from a negotiated settlement in Vietnam must be left to future historians to ponder.

It is useful to bear in mind that the United States government itself is on occasion much less diffident in explaining why it refuses to contemplate a meaningful negotiated settlement. As is freely admitted, this solution would leave it without power to control the situation. See, for example, note 38.

7. Arthur M. Schlesinger, Jr., *A Thousand Days: John F. Kennedy in the White House* (Boston, Houghton Mifflin, 1965), p. 421. (André Deutsch, 1965.)

8. Walt W. Rostow, *The View from the Seventh Floor* (New York, Harper & Row, 1964), p. 149. See also his *United States in the World Arena* (New York, Harper & Row, 1960), p. 244: 'Stalin, exploiting the disruption and weakness of the postwar world, pressed out from the expanded base he had won during the Second World War in an effort to gain the balance of power in Eurasia . . . turning to the East, to back Mao and to enflame the North Korean and Indochinese Communists. . . .'

9. For example, the article by CIA analyst George Carver in *Foreign Affairs*, April 1966. See also note 34.

10. Cf. Jean Lacouture, *Vietnam: Between Two Truces* (New York, Random House, 1966), p. 21. (Seeker & Warburg, 1966.) Diem's analysis of the situation was shared by Western observers at the time. See, for example, the comments of William Henderson, Far Eastern specialist and executive, Council on Foreign Relations, in R.W. Lindholm, ed., *Vietnam: The First Five Years* (East Lansing, Michigan State University Press, 1959). He notes 'the growing alienation of the intelligentsia', 'the renewal of armed dissidence in

the South', the fact that 'security has noticeably deteriorated in the last two years', all as a result of Diem's 'grim dictatorship', and predicts 'a steady worsening of the political climate in free Vietnam, culminating in unforeseen disasters'.

11. See Bernard Fall, 'Vietnam in the Balance', *Foreign Affairs,* vol. 45 (October 1966), pp. 1-18.

12. Stalin was neither pleased by the Titoist tendencies inside the Greek Communist party, nor by the possibility that a Balkan federation might develop under Titoist leadership. It is nevertheless conceivable that Stalin supported the Greek guerrillas at some stage in the rebellion, in spite of the difficulty in obtaining firm documentary evidence. Needless to say, no elaborate study is necessary to document the British or American role in this civil conflict, from late 1944. See D.G. Kousoulas, *The Price of Freedom* (Syracuse, Syracuse University Press, 1953), *Revolution and Defeat* (New York, Oxford University Press, 1965), for serious study of these events from a strongly anti-communist point of view.

13. For a detailed account, see James Warburg, *Germany: Key to Peace* (Cambridge, Harvard University Press, 1953), pp. 189f. Warburg concludes that apparently 'the Kremlin was now prepared to accept the creation of an All-German democracy in the Western sense of that word', whereas the Western powers, in their response, 'frankly admitted their plan "to secure the participation of Germany in a purely defensive European community" ' (i.e., NATO).

14. *The United States in the World Arena,* pp. 344-5. Incidentally, those who quite rightly deplore the brutal suppression of the East German and Hungarian revolutions would do well to remember that these scandalous events might have been avoided had the United States been willing to consider proposals for neutralization of Central Europe. Some of George Kennan's recent statements provide interesting commentary on this matter, for example, his comments on the falsity, from the outset, of the assumption that the USSR intended to attack or intimidate by force the Western half of the continent and that it was deterred by American force, and his remarks on the sterility and general absurdity of the demand for unilateral Soviet withdrawal from Eastern Germany together with 'the inclusion of a united Germany as a major component in a Western defense system based primarily on nuclear weaponry' (Edward Reed, ed., *Peace on Earth* [New York, Pocket Books, 1965]).

It is worth noting that historical fantasy of the sort illustrated in Rostow's remarks has become a regular State Department specialty.

Thus we have Thomas Mann justifying our Dominican intervention as a response to actions of the 'Sino-Soviet military bloc'. Or, to take a more considered statement, we have William Bundy's analysis of stages of development of Communist ideology in his Pomona College address, 12 February 1966, in which he characterizes the Soviet Union in the 1920s and early 1930s as 'in a highly militant and aggressive phase'. What is frightening about fantasy, as distinct from outright falsification, is the possibility that it may be sincere and may actually serve as the basis for formation of policy.

15. *New York Times,* 6 February 1966.

16. *United States Policy Toward Asia,* Hearings before the Subcommittee on the Far East and the Pacific of the Committee on Foreign Affairs, House of Representatives (Washington, DC, US Government Printing Office, 1966), p. 89.

17. *New York Times Book Review,* 20 November 1966. Such comments call to mind the remarkable spectacle of President Kennedy counseling Cheddi Jagan on the dangers of entering into a trading relationship 'which brought a country into a condition of economic dependence'. The reference, of course, is to the dangers in commercial relations with the Soviet Union. See Schlesinger, *A Thousand Days,* p. 776.

18. *A Thousand Days,* p. 252.

19. *Ibid.,* p. 769.

20. Though this too is imprecise. One must recall the real character of the Trujillo regime to appreciate the full cynicism of Kennedy's 'realistic' analysis.

21. W.W. Rostow and R.W. Hatch, *An American Policy In Asia* (New York, Technology Press and John Wiley, 1955).

22. 'End of Either/Or', *Foreign Affairs,* vol. 45 (January 1967), pp. 189-201.

23. *Christian Science Monitor,* 26 November 1966.

24. *Ibid.,* 5 December 1966.

25. Although, to maintain perspective, we should recall that in his wildest moments, Alfred Rosenberg spoke of the elimination of thirty million Slavs, not the imposition of mass starvation on a quarter of the human race. Incidentally, the analogy drawn here is highly 'irresponsible', in the technical sense of this neologism discussed earlier. That is, it is based on the assumption that statements and

actions of Americans are subject to the same standards and open to the same interpretations as those of anyone else.

26. *New York Times*, 6 February 1966. What is more, Goldberg continues, the United States is not certain that all of these are voluntary adherents. This is not the first such demonstration of communist duplicity. Another example was seen in the year 1962, when according to United States government sources 15,000 guerillas suffered 30,000 casualties. See Arthur Schlesinger, *A Thousand Days*, p. 982.

27. Reprinted in a collection of essays with the title *The End of Ideology: On the Exhaustion of Political Ideas in the Fifties* (New York, The Free Press, 1960). I have no intention here of entering into the full range of issues that have been raised in the discussion of the 'end of ideology' for the past dozen years. It is difficult to see how a rational person could quarrel with many of the theses that have been put forth, e.g., that at a certain historical moment the 'politics of civility' is appropriate, and perhaps efficacious; that one who advocates action (or inaction – a matter less frequently noted) has a responsibility to assess its social cost; that dogmatic fanaticism and 'secular religions' should be combated (or if possible, ignored); that technical solutions to problems should be implemented, where possible; that *'le dogmatisme idéologique devait disparaître pour que les idées reprissent vie'* (Aron); and so on. Since this is sometimes taken to be an expression of an 'anti-Marxist' position, it is worth keeping in mind that such sentiments as these have no bearing on non-Bolshevik Marxism, as represented, for example, by such figures as Luxemburg, Pannekoek, Korsch, Arthur Rosenberg and many others.

28. Rostow and Hatch, *An American Policy in Asia*, p. 10.

29. The extent to which this 'technology' is value-free is hardly very important, given the clear commitments of those who apply it. The problems with which research is concerned are those posed by the Pentagon or the great corporations, not, say, by the revolutionaries of Northeast Brazil or by SNCC. Nor am I aware of a research project devoted to the problem of how poorly-armed guerillas might more effectively resist a brutal and devastating military technology – surely the kind of problem that would have interested the free-floating intellectual who is now hopelessly out of date.

30. In view of the unremitting propaganda barrage on 'Chinese expansionism', perhaps a word of comment is in order. Typical of American propaganda on this subject is Adlai Stevenson's assessment,

shortly before his death (cf. *New York Times Magazine*, 13 March 1966): 'So far, the new Communist "dynasty" has been very aggressive. Tibet was swallowed, India attacked, the Malays had to fight twelve years to resist a "national liberation" they could receive from the British by a more peaceful route. Today, the apparatus of infiltration and aggression is already at work in North Thailand.'

As to Malaya, Stevenson is probably confusing ethnic Chinese with the government of China. Those concerned with the actual events would agree with Harry Miller, in *Communist Menace in Malaya* (New York, Frederick A. Praeger, 1954), that 'Communist China continues to show little interest in the Malayan affair beyond its usual fulminations via Peking Radio.' There are various harsh things that one might say about Chinese behavior in what the Sino-Indian Treaty of 1954 refers to as 'the Tibet region of China', but it is no more proof of a tendency towards expansionism than is the behavior of the Indian government with regard to the Naga and Mizo tribesmen. As to North Thailand, 'the apparatus of infiltration' may well be at work, though there is little reason to suppose it to be Chinese – and it is surely not unrelated to the American use of Thailand as a base for its attack on Vietnam. This reference is the sheerest hypocrisy.

The 'attack on India' grew out of a border dispute that began several years after the Chinese had 'completed a road from Tibet to Sinkiang in an area so remote from Indian control that the Indians learned about this operation only from the Chinese press. According to American Air Force maps, the disputed area is in Chinese territory. Cf. Alastair Lamb, *China Quarterly*, July-September 1965. To this distinguished authority, 'it seems unlikely that the Chinese have been working out some master plan ... to take over the Indian sub-continent lock, stock and overpopulated barrel'. Rather, he thinks it likely that the Chinese were probably unaware that India even claimed the territory through which the road passed. After the Chinese military victory, Chinese troops were, in most areas, withdrawn beyond the McMahon Line, a border which the British had attempted to impose on China in 1914 but which has never been recognized by China (Nationalist or communist), the United States, or any other government.

It is remarkable that a person in a responsible position could describe all of this as Chinese expansionism. In fact, it is absurd to debate the hypothetical aggressiveness of a China surrounded by American missiles and a still expanding network of military bases backed by an enormous American expeditionary force in Southeast Asia. It is conceivable that at some future time a powerful China may be expansionist. We may speculate about such possibilities if we wish, but it is American aggressiveness that is the central fact of current politics.

31. W.S. Churchill, *Closing the Ring*, vol. 5 of *The Second World War*, (Boston, Houghton Mifflin, 1951), p. 382. (Cassell, 1952.)

32. *United States Policy Toward Asia*, p. 104. See note 16.

33. *Ibid.*, p. 105.

34. Douglas Pike, *op. cit.*, p. 110. This book, written by a foreign service officer working at the Center for International Studies, MIT, poses a contrast between our side, which sympathizes with 'the usual revolutionary stirrings ... around the world because they reflect inadequate living standards or oppressive and corrupt governments', and the backers of 'revolutionary guerilla warfare', which 'opposes the aspirations of people while apparently furthering them, manipulates the individual by persuading him to manipulate himself'. Revolutionary guerilla warfare is 'an imported product, revolution from the outside' (other examples, besides the Vietcong, are 'Stalin's exportation of armed revolution', the Haganah in Palestine, and the Irish Republican Army – see pp. 32-3). The Vietcong could not be an indigenous movement since it has 'a social construction program of such scope and ambition that of necessity it must have been created in Hanoi' (p. 76 – but on pp. 77-9 we read that 'organizational activity had gone on intensively and systematically for several years' before the Lao Dong party in Hanoi had made its decision· 'to begin building an organization'). On page 80 we find that 'such an effort had to be the child of the North', even though elsewhere we read of the prominent role of the Cao Dai (p. 74), 'the first major social group to begin actively opposing the Diem government' (p. 222), and of the Hoa Hao sect, 'another early and major participant in the NLF' (p. 69). He takes it as proof of communist duplicity that in the South, the party insisted it was 'Marxist-Leninist', thus 'indicating philosophic but not political allegiance', whereas in the North it described itself as a 'Marxist-Leninist organization' thus 'indicating that it was in the main-stream of the world-wide communist movement' (p. 150). And so on. Also revealing is the contempt for 'Cinderella and all the other fools [who] could still believe there was magic in the mature world if one mumbled the secret incantation: solidarity, union, concord'; for the 'gullible, misled people' who were 'turning the countryside into a bedlam, toppling one Saigon government after another, confounding the Americans'; for the 'mighty force of people' who in their mindless innocence thought

that 'the meek, at last, were to inherit the earth', that 'riches would be theirs and all in the name of justice and virtue'. One can appreciate the chagrin with which a sophisticated Western political scientist must view this 'sad and awesome spectacle'.

35. Lacouture, *op. cit.*, p. 188. The same military spokesman goes on, ominously, to say that this is the problem confronting us throughout Asia, Africa and Latin America, and that we must find the 'proper response' to it.

36. Charles Mohr, *New York Times*, 11 February 1966. Italics mine.

37. *New York Times*, 18 February 1966.

38. William Bundy, in A. Buchan, ed., *China and the Peace of Asia* (New York, Frederick A. Praeger, 1965).

39. *United States Policy Toward Asia*, p. 80.

40. *Ibid.*, pp. 191-201, passim.

41. *An American Policy in Asia*, p. 10.

42. *United States Policy Towards Asia*, p. 128.

43. Lindholm, *op. cit.*, p. 322.

NAME INDEX

SUBJECT INDEX

Absolute good vs. absolute bad, 163, 164
Abstractification: and cultural development, 209
  and money, 208, 210-212, 221-222
  origin of, 213, 214
  and specialization, 208
Abyssinian movement, 148-150, 151
Alienation: and bureaucratization, 219, 321
  definition of, 207, 214, 217
  and idolatry, 215-216
  and the manager, 218
  and ownership, 219-221
Allen, Bill Case, 263-269
America and conspicuous annihilation, 93
America as a colony, 94
American colonialism, 93, 113-134
American postwar economy, 99, 100-104, 106, 132, 133
Antiimperialist movement, 130, 131, 133
Authoritarianism and Third World development, 322-324, 326-328

Bank of America, the burning of, 270-272

Black movement in Santa Barbara, 259-260
Black Nationalism: and black-white relations, 160
  decline of, 150-153
  esoteric vs. exoteric, 157
  and religion, 154-157
Bourgeois policy and the status quo, 205, 206
British paternalism, 118, 119
Bureau of Indian Affairs, 79, 80, 82, 85, 86

Capital, definition of, 44
Capitalism, liberty, and war, 92, 104, 132
Capitalization of agriculture, 125
Centralization, 42, 46, 102-104, 126, 129
Change in social problems, 18, 19, 21, 41
Chartism, 244, 248, 249
Classless society, 37, 38
Cold War, functions of, 100-102, 106, 204
Cold War economy, 251, 255
Cold War policy and nuclear war, 94, 95
Colonial bourgeoisie, 97-99, 123, 124